MEMOIR OF A ROADIE

AXL SAID I MADE A GREAT CUP OF TEA... SCOTT WEILAND LIKED THE CARPENTERS... & OZZY DRINKS ROSÉ.

Joel Miller

Editor: Tim Goudie who helped me edit this mess of thoughts. I was told you are not finished with your book until you hate it. I think the truth is you are not finished until your editor hates it even more than you do.

Front Cover Art: Raymond Pettibon

Cover Design: Josh Geyer

California Legal Supervision: Ken Tennen, Esq. & Corey Boddie, Esq.

Certain names and identifying details have been changed. Whether or not so noted in the text. Copyright 2020 by Joel Miller.

Chapter 1
LSD & MOM

Usain Bolt ran the fastest recorded 100-meter dash in 9.58 seconds in 2009. A man by the name of Hicham El Guerrouj ran the fastest recorded mile in 1999 at 3:43.13. The fastest recorded marathon was 2:01:39 in 2014 by Eliud Kipchoge. All remarkable feats. For me it was 2001 and I was doing my personal best running the lights at the Grand Slam Summer Jam. If that doesn't sound like a remarkable feat, well, that's because it wasn't. If you run a google search, The Grand Slam Summer Jam is either a girls softball league or a 1980's themed concert tour. I was working for the latter.

It had been decided that Nigel, my boss, would not be allowed to run the lights for the band Warrant anymore. I'll explain why later. Both Nigel and I were working for the headliner of the tour, Poison. Just so we are clear, running the lights means what it sounds like: to run the light show during the band's performance. Running the lights for an opening band is an extra way for the headliner's LD, Lighting Designer, to make some extra money. In this particular case the headliner, Poison, didn't want Warrant using their LD. So, Nigel saw this as an opportunity for me.

That night one of the owners of LSD, the lighting company I had been working for before I got the Poison gig, Marvin Davies, flew out to check out the *Glam Slam Summer Jam*. I guess he wanted to make sure the client, Poison, was happy with his company's services.

According to Nigel my job was simple. I wasn't to operate any of the moving lights on the stage but only the par cans. The technical meaning of a par can is a parabolic aluminized reflector. I have no clue what that means and I'm quite certain no other roadie does either. So, we will all just call it a par can.

A par can is a highly directional beam. Often, we put sheets of colored plastic in front of them; That creates a rainbow of color on the stage. That just left the spotlights, and I'd tell the spotlight operator guys just to wing it. They ran the spotlights almost every night. It wasn't hard for them just to follow the singer and then light up each guy during solo performances. Most importantly, I wasn't to touch the button he had labeled MOM on the mixing console. I don't know what MOM meant, or what was supposed to mean, but Nigel was illiterate, so your guess is as good as mine. The good news was I could practice as much as I wanted during the day to get ready, he said. I had run the lights a few times for a band called From Earth to Andy while touring with Stone Temple Pilots. I hadn't done a good job and I knew it, but no one complained to me at the time either. Because of my LD stint with them I was acutely aware I was not cut out to be an LD. I was pretty sure this wasn't going to go well. However, I figured what did I have to lose? Nigel was an idiot and he ran the lights just fine.

His proudest moment was that while living in San Francisco, he drove a hearse. Why a hearse? It wasn't just because he thought it was cool, which he absolutely did, but it was also so that he could park the hearse in the hearse only parking spot next door to his house at the mortuary. If you were to ask Nigel about the hearse, his response was always the same, "I didn't have just any hearse. It was a 1963 Cadillac hearse. It was twice the size of any other puny hearse ever made. That was my hearse- I wish I'd never sold it." If you haven't been to San Francisco parking is a nightmare. Nigel was proud to be parking his nightmare next door at the morgue.

Maybe I'd figure it out. I practiced a bit during the day so that Nigel would think I was giving it my all. It was pretty boring pressing buttons with no one on the stage, so my practicing honestly didn't last very long.

That night Warrant hit the stage and I stood ready to push the console buttons at front of house. Front of house is basically a little roadie booth in the audience. From there the lighting designer and the front of house sound mixer push their buttons and do their best to look official. They both need to be able to see, or hear, the show from the audience's perspective respectively. Warrant started their set and I pushed buttons frantically. It was the beginning of what promised to be the most spastic light show in history. Nigel and Marvin watched on as I made Warrant's set look awful. Marvin had started in the industry as an LD. I wondered why one of them didn't come over to help me a bit. You know- ease me into it, but neither did. Changing things up, I stopped pushing the buttons rapidly and began to hold buttons down instead. When the guitar solos happened, the stage turned blue. When the slow parts of the songs came up, I pushed the buttons like a madman. When they played their hit song "Cherry Pie," the last song in their set, I tried to push the buttons even faster to bring congruity to my performance. I was pushing everything frantically when the stage went dark. I looked over at where Nigel had been standing but he was now gone. Marvin was still watching my performance in all its glory. He stood there like an Indian totem. Arms crossed, he showed no emotion whatsoever. I laughed out loud not knowing what to do. One of the guys on the spots spoke to me through the headset. "Hey, man, the stage is dark," he said. I ignored him and started pushing buttons again but nothing happened. I was hoping to turn the moving lights on just to piss off Nigel but I didn't know how. I did what any roadie in a bad spot would do. I pushed the MOM button that Nigel told me not to touch. BINGO! The lights all turned back on just as Warrant finished their set. They literally turned on as the last drum stick hit the drum. I couldn't have timed it better. Marvin laughed and walked backstage. I was never asked to do the lights again.

Roadie Ramble Moment
Push vs. Pull... The two words mean the opposite

thing and yet they both start with the same letter and have the same number of letters in the word. What genius pulled this off? They should have been pushed off a cliff.

Chapter 2
A Fistful of Dollars

It's important to know the making of a roadie, so let me tell you what I did before. A background if you will for the canvas of my life. Don't worry- there isn't too much senseless babble before we get to the Rock 'n' Roll stuff, so hang in there.

My father was a car mechanic and my mother a realtor. I hated high school and sat through it, although in retrospect it passed by quickly. I didn't like that I had to sit in class all day every day, regardless of whether it was time wasted or not. So, in the interest of saving my extra time, that I so clearly cherished, I agreed to leave the school. I wasn't the most courteous student, so the staff didn't want me to be there either. And so, my counselor suggested I leave. I agreed. I don't think anyone missed me.

That forced measure of being required to physically be somewhere all day every day never really left me. I think it explains why I've never had a 9 to 5 job. I enrolled myself at a community college and got a job at a local law firm. I loved Judge Wapner, on *The People's Court,* and thought that working at a law firm would be really interesting. I knew for certain I wanted to make a lot of money and build my own personal empire. Understanding the law was an integral part of that. I really wanted to live the American dream and become fucking rich. I just didn't know how. My choice wasn't quite as I had suspected. The law firm wasn't exciting at all. It was boring. My job was to fill the copy machines with paper, to photocopy documents, and to pass out the mail.

I was 17 years old and the guy who worked alongside me was a 35-year-old guy named Kurt. He was a strong dude, an ex-marine, a handsome man, but most significantly one of the laziest damn people I've ever meet. Kurt would spend much of his day doing pushups and squeezing a spring thing to improve his grip. "It's my way at releasing aggression. Because this world is so fucked up," he'd say. Why had the world stopped my friend Kurt in his tracks? He would often tell me how he would "switch shit up," if he was in charge of things. He wasn't in charge of things though. So instead, he drank a 40oz of beer at lunch every day and smoked weed in the afternoon before driving home. His car was the cleanest looking used Hyundai you'd ever seen, and I admired how proud of himself the guy was.

I learned a lot fast while working at the law firm and no longer being a high school student. The first thing I learned was jobs have fewer hot chicks than classrooms do. For a seventeen-year-old guy that was a bummer. The second thing I quickly learned was that I didn't want to be a lawyer. I didn't even want to work in a building. I'd look out the building windows and think about how I could escape my new bubble.

Like religion, I believed what dulled the masses was alcohol and drugs. I was determined not to become one of the masses but to instead give the masses what they wanted and in turn become rich. I couldn't sell alcohol. I wasn't even old enough to buy it. So, what was easier for me to get? Weed. So, I started selling weed to Kurt and kept an open ear to the guy's troubles. It's not just selling the weed but keeping a keen interest in hearing people's problems. That is the actual business. It's just listening. If you listen, they always come back for more smoke.

While working at the law firm a woman had a seizure in the office next to me. Having learned somewhere what to do I moved everything out of her way, and I managed to get a piece of cardboard in between her teeth. When the paramedics got to the office, they commended me on having done a good job. The woman never came back to the office, but I got a raise and pats on the back from everyone who worked there.

My favorite place to hang out while working there was with the ladies in the accounting department. When joking around with them I didn't feel like I was at work. While still receiving accolades and feeling high and mighty, I made sure to make my rounds to the accounting office to receive my due praise from the ladies. While down there my boss, the office manager, called me on the PA system. "Joel, please call extension 367." I picked up one of the phones. "What are you doing down there?" she asked me. "Well, Cynthia here says you look like the fat mouse in *Cinderella* but I say you look more like the fairy princess," was my response. I expected the women in the office to laugh aloud. No one laughed. Instead, they all stared at me aghast. "Can you come up here a minute? I need to talk to you," she told me and hung up the phone. "What the fuck was that?" Cynthia said to me. "Not funny?," I asked. "You better go up there and clear my name from this bullshit," she said. I enjoyed going to lunch with Cynthia and we were definitely friends, but I was absolutely afraid of her wrath. Running errands, she had once taken me to Victoria's Secret. I had been excited about going all day. Expecting to see women walking around in lingerie, it was a letdown to find you can't try on the lingerie.

When I got up to the office manager's office, I was given instructions before I was able to say anything. "I need for you to clean the dungeon," she told me. "The dungeon. What do we need to clean it for? No one goes down there," I said. She didn't reply. For the rest of the week, I had to empty and then deep clean this storage space in the parking garage we called the dungeon. It was home to mostly dust bunnies and dead rats. During the course of my cleaning I tried to apologize to her several times and thus escape my punishment, but to the accounting ladies' great pleasure, I was sent back every day.

Once done cleaning, things got back to normal. You would

think I bring the story up because I learned a good lesson in how to keep my smart mouth shut. But no, I bring it up because it's an example of how I learned nothing at all. It's a strong statement when you read something where the message is clear and yet the character, me in this case, was so dumb they learned nothing. Anyhow, in the spirit of further moronic, behavior let's continue on.

My next task to do out of what my ordinary job entailed would be to go drop something off at another law firm. That something ended up being a brown paper bag filled with money. Still in the office manager's office, I looked inside the bag. "How much is in the bag?" I asked. "It doesn't matter- just drop it off," she responded. I dumped the money on her desk. "Let's count it together," I said. She might have been my boss and was still getting over being mad at me, but I didn't want to have any trouble with something that was already seemingly shady. We counted the money together. It was $20,000.

I drove the money to the other attorney's office wondering what would happen if I just told them someone stole it from me. Maybe I'd pay someone on the street to punch me in the face. When I got to the firm, the secretary told me I could leave the money with her. I smiled politely at her, "I'd rather give it directly to whom I'm supposed to thank you," I told her. What was with these people? Don't lawyers deal with degenerates and criminals? Wouldn't you think dealing with those kinds of guys all day would knock common sense into people working in the legal profession? If a 17-year-old boy showed up at my door with what was supposed to be $20,000 in cash, I'd absolutely count it in front of them!

Deciding to be more firm on the matter, she said, "Well, young man, he's in a meeting so I don't think that is going to be possible." Now I felt like starting off by telling her, "Well, old lady...," but I didn't. "He can either meet with me now or I can leave with what I'm supposed to drop off," I said while sitting down to wait. I, of course, knew he'd meet with me. For whatever reason, I wondered what he looked like. I had visons of walking into an office where a guy looking like Magnum P.I. sat. The couple of people waiting in the seats next to me looked at me, then the bag, and then back at me. I knew they wondered what was in the bag. I waited patiently, enjoying the awkwardness of my situation.

I was soon thereafter escorted into a fancy office. To me, the lawyer in that office didn't look like he had been in a meeting. On the front of his desk was a gold desk name plate. I read his name aloud to myself- he was indeed the man I was supposed to give the money to. It wasn't a name that sounded anything like Magnum, P.I. though. Instead, his name sounded Polish. Introducing himself to me, he shook my hand. "You can leave the money with me, son. And thank you," he told me. He offered up a fake smile and leaned back in his big cushy leather chair. I was starting to learn about lawyers and this guy absolutely seemed like a lawyer. "Can I see your ID?" I asked him. He stopped smiling.

"Just kidding… I do want to count it together to make sure we are all set, though, sir. And if we can call my boss so he knows I dropped it off," I told him. Everything went fine from there and I'm sure behind closed doors they all had a good laugh. Lawyers were a lot more dubious than I had ever thought. Now that I had gained the trust of the lawyers in my office, maybe I'd do this more often with more money. That would be the time to fuck 'em!

While I worked full time, I also remained a full-time student at the local junior college. I wasn't sure what I was going to do with my life, but I certainly wanted to keep all options open and of course there were girls in school.

Chapter 3
When Jay Leno Tells You to Do Something, You Do it!

There was another deciding factor in how I was to plan my life direction. Allow me to further introduce my father. He ran a machine shop out of the garage of our house and specialized in rebuilding motors and gear boxes for Jaguar cars. When my parents bought the house we lived in, he had tripled the size of the garage so that he could work from home. The garage was any car buff's heaven. It could comfortably fit a dozen cars on the first floor while engines stacked three high were a permanent fixture lining the walls. Carburetors, starters, manifolds and other gizmos and gadgets that made cars work hung from the reinforced ceilings. In between the motors were lathes, milling machines, and his prized piece of machinery, a head surfacer. All this metal weighed heavy on an extra thick concrete slab.

My dad had grown up in a boarding school in England and must have been very sheltered as a child. His parents were very wealthy and the common thing to do was to send your kids off to school. He never really got to know them at all I don't think. He became a car mechanic because he befriended their chauffeur. Together with a few friends from school he purchased a car and they had all got it running. He must have got the bug from that experience because he was always wrenching on cars from then on. Later in his youth he raced cars and raised monkeys for a living. The race cars and monkeys mostly all came before my sisters and I did. I presume we three became the monkeys to raise.

While I was growing up, he worked for himself and therefore spent most of his time working by himself. While I think he was a bit crazy, I don't think being alone for most of his life helped his psyche. Luckily for him, people who own Jaguar cars are nuts too. Because of all the eccentricity in the garage, fantastic arguments and temper tantrums would often circulate in the kitchen of my household. Why the kitchen? Well, the garage was connected by a door to the kitchen and we'd hear it through that door all day.

He had done and still did work for the president of Mexico, countless celebrities, and a variety of well-known athletes too. While there are rules against running a business out of a residence, my dad was able to skirt around those issues by doing work for all the local political figureheads in Los Angeles who owned Jaguars too.

One of the local celebrities was the lead singer of the band Fishbone. Angelo grew up across the street from me. He would have awesome parties and would regularly practice in his garage. He was a pretty cool neighbor to have when you were a kid. He owned an XKE Jaguar, that he stored down the side of our house, and I looked forward to him coming by the garage with his buddies to "hang out," which he did for hours and hours when his band was not on tour. When he'd cruise over, it was usually with musician friends who were always super stoned, and as a group they'd listen to my dad talk about how the Volkswagen Beetle was the greatest car ever made. I think they just liked hearing his English accent and the random stuff he'd love to talk about. I'm pretty sure my father enjoyed the attention and I don't think he ever had any clue that they were stoned. Angelo and his friends all had funky hair, piercings, and made odd clothing decisions. My father would always make sure they knew it. They clearly found him entertaining.

He really did think the Volkswagen Beetle was the finest car ever made and he'd be happy to tell you all about why. For a short while I drove his 1973 Super Beetle to school. When I pulled down the sun visor the clip broke. A common occurrence and a very cheap fix, it shouldn't have been a big deal. However, he blew his lid. I never was allowed to drive the car again. I had to borrow an XJ12 Jaguar my mom was driving to get to school and back. While you would think that was a major upgrade, I didn't like the car. The interior leather smelled great and when you put the gas pedal down the lumbering tank moved quickly, but the gas mileage sucked.

One of the more well-known celebrities to regularly stop by was Jay Leno. It's well known that Jay has a lot of cars and one of those in particular is an old Rolls Royce that someone put an airplane engine in. He paid 3 million dollars for the car and it didn't run when he bought it. It had been made by some English Lord in the 1930's. I liked Jay, but I failed to understand how anyone could care about old cars as much as he did. I had grown up seeing so many expensive cars that they didn't mean anything to me. Most of the guys that came through the garage played around a bit fixing up an old sportscar, then got through their mid-life crises after having lost some money, and then got rid of the car.

Jay had never sold a car in his life and I'd bet still hasn't. When he walked you through his garage, he was like a five-year-old showing off their Matchbox toy car collection. He loved each and every one of them. I asked him one time if his wife collected anything.

"She does. She collects plates," he told me. "A lot easier to store than cars," I said. His reply was deadpan, "yes, a lot easier." I liked Jay. In his airplane hangar, filled with fancy cars and motorcycles, he had a pool table. I'd mess around on that while my dad discussed fixing motors and gearboxes with him. On one such occasion Jay told me he had something in his garage he knew would impress me. I had my doubts. He sat me down in some old American car and played me the song "Davy Crockett" on a record player. The cool part wasn't just the song: it was that he had pulled the record player out from the dashboard of the car to play the song. I had to admit to him that I thought that was pretty darn cool. "You know what's cooler though?" I asked him. I could tell he wondered if he had set a metal foundation for a burgeoning car enthusiast. "What?" he replied, genuinely intrigued. "The little car next to the Stanley Steamer," I said. We got out and walked back towards the front of the garage. Next to a Stanley Steamer was a beat up 1978 Toyota Corolla. A low blow, Jay laughed at me. I'm sure he fondly remembered his first attempt at humor and informed me, "it belongs to my old college roommate. I'm storing it for him right now."

Jay Leno and I in his 1934 Rolls Royce Phantom II.

Another time, Jay had driven over to the house in that Rolls Royce airplane engine car and sounded off all the house alarms as he had roared up our street. That had pissed my dad off. He had come over because he owed my dad money and he had come to say "hi" and pay him. As I grew older, our garage had increasingly become more of a hot spot for the high-end European car community. The odd hermit who lived amongst the hundreds of thousands of pounds of Jaguar parts in the Los Angeles suburb of Woodland Hills had become a sight to see for car guys. When Los Angeles had their big earthquake in 1994, calls came in from all around the world to hear what had happened to his metal cave. The answer was nothing had really moved. I learned my dad could have been a structural engineer with his piling abilities.

Back to the story... Jay had come over to say hello to my father and pissed my dad off because of the airplane car. I was upstairs in my room probably watching Baywatch. Like every other adolescent teenage boy, I was in love with Erika Eleniak. The introduction to that show may be the finest minute of television ever made. I really honestly believe that. Anyhow, I left Baywatch to come downstairs to say "hi" to Jay. I walked into the garage and my dad had just finished telling Jay that he'd have to go to the bank and get cash because, as the sign on his toolbox stated, he didn't accept checks.

Jay was worth hundreds of millions of dollars and my dad thought he was going to bounce a check on him? Though it embarrassed me, it didn't surprise me one bit. That was my dad. So, what did Jay do? He laughed and turned to me. "Come on Joel-let's go to the bank," he said. We both jumped into the Rolls Royce and headed off down the street. As we cruised down the street alarm after alarm went off. Jay smiled ear to ear. He loved this car. I could picture my dad in the garage getting angrier and angrier.

As we drove down the street, I hoped that every person I had ever met in my life would randomly be out walking their dog at that moment. This was the coolest thing that had ever happened to me. While we were waiting in line at the bank, I figured it was a good time to ask Jay for a job. He told me he'd hire me for sure as long as I went to college. I'd never really thought about college, but I figured if I did what Jay told me to do, he'd eventually hire me. I was a hard worker and I knew I'd climb the ladder quickly working for him. Maybe I'd even make those millions I had wanted to make. I started looking into how to apply to college the next day.

Chapter 4
The Wolf of Santa Barbara

Towards the tail end of working at the law firm I was involved in a car accident. This is how the accident went down. In addition to managing the copy machines it was my job to walk across the street every day and pull the files from storage that the lawyers needed. The files were all the old cases that had been settled. I guess stuff was always coming up with old cases and they needed to look at the old files often. I would push the hand dolly across the street and load up all the files I was told to go get. I liked going across the street because I could stop at the 7-11 and then lag a bit at the storage.

On my way walking back to the office one day a guy in a brand-new convertible Corvette took the corner, without looking, and hit me. Well, he hit the dolly mostly, but the dolly twisted away from me and ended up under his car. I scrambled around in the middle of the intersection grabbing all the paperwork that had gone everywhere. The guy didn't run from the scene or anything, in fact he immediately pulled to the side and asked me if I was OK. I was OK. My wrist was bothering me a bit, but I didn't think it was a big deal. He asked me what I was pushing, and I told him I worked at the law office next to the intersection. We both looked up at the big building. I was assuming that hearing I worked for a law firm would scare the hell out of him, but no.

"Man, that is awesome. Do you think they are hiring? I just finished law school and I'm looking for a job," he said to me. I was dumbfounded. I wasn't expecting that. He threw the dolly in the back seat of the Vette, drove me back to work, and together we walked into the law firm lobby. I was glad we were going there together because I didn't know quite what to do. A lot of the paperwork, in the boxes I had been pushing, was now creased and out of sequence, but the important part was I had picked it all up and had done my best putting it back in each file.

When we walked into the front desk area several of the attorneys were there to meet us. One of the partners had watched the whole incident out her office window. I watched on in amazement as he actually did ask them for a job.

I had always wanted to be an attorney. I had always thought that attorneys were the smartest of all the adults. My reasoning was that they knew the rules. They could either live by those rules or choose to live against them. The same as all of us, but because they had learned the laws, I figured they could skirt around them easier. You know, if they wanted to. That to me was very cool. However, this recent graduate quite definitely was changing my mind. There sure were some stupid lawyers out there. I decided while going to college, because Jay wanted me to, I'd study art history instead.

I applied to two colleges - a California state university that had to accept me because I was a transfer student, and UCSB because my friend's mom told me it was a nice place to go to school. Somehow, I got into UCSB. I was off to the University of Santa Barbara to study art history. By this point I had pretty much become a total alcoholic. So, I figured I could look at pretty pictures while fitting in to the college scene just fine.

Years earlier my parents had begun collecting Japanese prints. My father had enough Jaguar parts, and so he was looking for other things to do with his money. He loved art and thought buying Japanese prints was a good thing to invest in. As such, I had grown up going to auction houses on a regular basis. He was wrong about what to invest in, though: the Japanese economy took a nosedive that it still hasn't rebounded from.

The "somehow" part of getting into UCSB was actually, I think, because I had been able to get two strong letters of recommendation. A department head at the auction house Sotheby's wrote a great letter of recommendation for me, and the other came from a prominent Los Angeles art collector. I think it was those letters that got me in. I don't know what else it could have been. I was a jackass with mediocre grades.

I was paying for college myself, so it didn't take long for me to find a job. A friend of mine, Brendan, was working at an incoming call center where you could pay to get auction catalogs of government auctions mailed to you. The job seemed great. The basic scheme was people would call in from paid advertisements to get government issued auction catalogs for cars and/or houses. The inventory came from the government seizures of drug dealers and foreclosed properties, so we were told. Anyone can go to their local courthouse and get the same catalogs, but these guys were charging to send them to your house for you instead. The cost was either $69.99 -$99.99 or $89.99- $129.99 depending on who would answer the phone on our end. The product itself was the same. All the calls were incoming, meaning we never dialed out. Once we picked up the phone if we tried to close the deal for the higher amount, we'd get a better commission. The first number, $69.99 or $89.99, was if the person was a single sell and the second number was if they were a double sell.

A single sell, aka a single, meant they had called in for the car auction catalog and that is all we sold them by the end of the phone call. A double sell, aka a double, meant we sold them the auction catalogs for both the car and house government auctions. Everyone who called in pretty much was doubled. It was easy to sink that last hook in. Getting the higher amount of money, $129.99, was a bit harder though because the numbers just don't roll off your tongue as fast or as smooth. Try saying aloud $89.99 versus $129.99 and you will see what I mean. A lot more people pick up on what you are actually saying.

The guy who ran the show was a buffed-out dickhead named Tom. He was kind of like Ben Affleck from *Boiler Room* or the guy from *The Wolf of Wall Street*. This was way before either one of those movies came out, but he had the same I'm more awesome than you attitude going on. He drove up every day in his new Porsche and would tell us all what pieces of shit we were. I think his attitude was really just to scare off the applicants who weren't real salespeople, but I still didn't like the guy. However, I understood why they'd want to scare off people who intended to just sit around and collect a paycheck.

This dude had no clue that I was a phone sales powerhouse. I had started doing phone surveys at 16 years old and worked there for a couple years. I was a pain in the ass while working there, but they never fired me because I made them a lot of money. I would play games on the phone. Create my own sexually oriented random questions, use women's names and then talk in a deep male voice, but I would always complete the survey and get credit for it. So, they didn't fire me. My favorite was telling people on the phone my name was The Junkyard Dog. I learned that if you roll with it, you can say almost anything on the phone. All this stuff was hilarious to me. I was a little kid. I got very good at it, and though I didn't want to get fired, I was having a lot of fun doing it too.

Because of my previous job I already knew how phone sales went, how to get information out of people on the phone, and most importantly, keep people on the phone when I needed to. If this guy was as a great as he told us he was he would be on the phones and not "teaching" us and I knew it. Tom did spit out some good information though. He further finessed my "roll with it" style. If you are boring, people tune out. He taught us that all Visa cards begin with a 4, all Mastercards begin with a 5, all Discover with 6011, and all American Express with 37. Knowing this, if people were holding their card and we told them the first number(s) of the card they were holding they would read the rest of the number off. I couldn't believe it, but he was totally right. It worked every time.

Anyhow, after a week of listening to this pompous douche, the owners of the company put us out on the floor. The calls started coming in. One after another I bored the customer to death and took their money. This was way easier than calling people to do surveys while they were eating dinner. The people were calling me, and they had their wallets in their pockets. I finished my first day of work and I was ready to get my money. I'd listened to this guy spout off for a solid week and I had made no money doing it.

The owners of the company had set up an incentive program. They would give you cash bonuses if you reached certain goals. I not only reached their goals I had broken all company records. When I got to work the next day, and before I could sit down, Tom told me the owners wanted to speak with me. Tom and I walked into their office and before anyone could say anything I asked, "you are going to pay me my money, right?" I was waiting for some bullshit. They owed me close to $4000 dollars in just cash bonuses for one day's worth of work. The actual paycheck was going to be close to another $5000. One of the owners threw an envelope at me. I opened the envelope and sure enough it was filled with green back dollar bills.

"We can wait a few minutes and you can count it if you like," the guy said. "No, it's okay." I replied. Honestly surprised they had paid me, I put the money in my pocket. "I spent last night listening to a lot of phone calls," he said. "How come you spent a week with Tom here and didn't tell him you had experience on the phones, Joel?" I looked at the owners and then at Tom. "Tom never asked," I said. A little while later I was back on the phones. Instead of picking up the calls like I had the first day, they now had dozens of people listening to me on every one of the incoming calls. Overnight, I had become both a salesperson and a trainer. I would speak quietly, loudly, stutter, be aggressive, be passive, and it all depended on the first few words I heard from the customer on the line. I was good at hustling the phones and I liked that I was good.

Chapter 5
A Good Ol' College Try is but a Phone Call Away from Fancy Cars, Drugs, and Money

I was making a ton of money at this place. I bought myself a vintage 911 Porsche, that I thought was cooler than Tom's, and worked as many hours as I could outside of going to school. I worked so many hours I didn't even bother buying books for school because I wouldn't have time to read them anyhow. Michelangelo had been dead for hundreds of years. I figured what would your mandatory books tell me about him that some reference book that was free in the library couldn't? I'd go into the art library before an exam and cram for an hour. Using that strategy, I was actually getting really good grades. It was all working just fine.

Tom didn't like me, but I didn't care. I had figured out that while he was good at his job, he was also the cocaine and marijuana dealer in the office. He would sell to some of the hot chicks who worked there and a few of the guys on the phones, but the money was in that he was the hook up for the owners and their friends. These guys were making eight figures a year now, and Tom was a good guy for them to have around. One of the owners' dad was a superior court judge, and through him they knew how to get around any legal issues. I'm sure they had a lot of them.

I had seen Tom's weed a few times. It wasn't that good. The weed the people I knew in high school sold was way better than his stuff. It seemed logical for me to drive back down to Los Angeles and grab some better weed. I would then bring the weed into Isla Vista, the college town I lived in, and sell it in small amounts. I'd sell eighths and quarters mostly. No big deal. It was just for extra money. I met a lot of fun people, including some really good-looking girls! I paid for beer with my fake ID, and covered my rent. My job was easily covering my tuition.

I had been putting my pay checks in my bank account that I'd had since I was a kid. My parents had set it up for me. I had always put money into it to use for something for what I wasn't sure would be when I got older. The cash bonuses the job had been giving me became free money. My parents knew I was putting money in my bank account and covering the cost of college with no problem. They didn't know about the cash bonuses I was getting. That money I would have my own fun with. It's not like my parents would have told me what to do with any of the money, but I assumed it made them happy knowing I was paying for everything and yet still saving up some cash. They just didn't know how much cash.

I figured it was time to now open up a separate bank account with just my name on it and start packing away some weed money. I went to the bank with a big wad of $20 bills. It totaled something like $2500. As I waited in line at the bank the smell of weed was steadily becoming stronger and stronger. Everyone in line had been looking at me, but as I got closer to the window, even the people at the little tables trying to get loans looked at me; then the bankers looked at me, and the tellers *all* looked at me. The only one who didn't look at me was the security guard. I finally made it to a teller, "I'd like to open up a new account," I said to her. "OK, no problem." The lady ushered me to the desk at the farthest corner of the bank. I put the money on the desk, and she started to count it. The smell was unreal. "Been keeping your money under the mattress?" I quietly chuckled and replied, "yep, under the mattress."

Just then a bud fell out of the money. Talk about bad timing. I didn't know much about the laws back then, so I had been keeping my money with my weed. You should keep them in separate places always. Acting fast, I grabbed the bud and I ate it. The lady smiled and gave me the deposit receipt. She got her free movie tickets, or whatever they give the clerks for opening up new accounts, and I got my first "drug" money into circulation. It wasn't long before I was bringing up garbage bags of weed in the back seat of my old Porsche from Los Angeles. While I started out breaking up ounces, I was now selling dime bags to pounds at a time sometimes.

Keg bowling with other college degenerates.

College blurred along. A year went by. I studied, if you want to call it that, and more important to me at the time, I drank all day and night. It was nice to drink as much as I wanted, and not have to hide it from anyone. I had built up a hefty bank account for a young kid, but I didn't really like working at the call center anymore. I felt like I had done the best I could at it, and I was just burned out. I didn't know it at the time, but the FBI had started breathing down the owner's necks. Worried, the company had hired a new guy who was in charge of quality control. I think his real job was to get rid of some of their shadier guys. He was working for maybe two days when I got called into the office. I was definitely one of their shadier guys, so it wasn't a surprise. I was blamed for disconnecting my phone recording device so the quality control guy couldn't listen to my calls. It was all dumb because the phone recorder was actually inside the computer case. I told the guy to kiss my ass. I knew my days were numbered. They were going to keep finding reasons to write me up and then fire me.

There was another small problem, one that pissed a lot of us top sellers off. One of the lead sellers decided to write down all the sales he had made one day. I would usually work until I completed 100 sales and then I'd call it a day and go home. Now, not all the sales processed because people lied about credit card numbers or their credit card companies flagged the sale. So, if you got 100 sales you were probably going to get 40 completed sales, which was still great money.

Anyhow, this guy wrote down every sale one day and unlike us he decided to follow through and check each transaction. He wrote down the transaction id's per sale and the people's phone numbers. When we would get our paychecks, the company would list the transaction ID's for all the completed sales. He decided to call a few of the phone numbers, on his own time, that corresponded to the transaction id's that didn't process. What he found out was, the company was lying to us. They were processing more sales than they were telling us about.

I realized how dumb we all were. If they were going to rip off America, why would they be straight with any of us? That guy was fired immediately, but all of us knew something was up, and we weren't happy about it. The cat was out of the bag. Because of the heat from the Feds, key management positions kept shifting. Tom was no longer on the sales floor. In fact, he had nothing to do with the sales staff at all. His sole job now was training new recruits. However, it wasn't like our training had been. He now taught everyone how to conduct a *proper* sale.

The money that had just been rolling in was now coming to a halt. Of course, as one of the shadier guys, new recruits weren't listening in on my calls anymore either. These guys were being a lot more careful. They were going to get shut down soon, and most importantly they had made a lot of money already. I hated this place, but I was still making money too, so I stuck with it for the time being.

On one of my last days working there, they forced me to work on Christmas day. I knew I wouldn't make any money. Who would call in on Christmas day? The phones were dead quiet of course. On the chalk board each day the supervisor was meant to write a quote of inspiration. I got up, erased what was on the board, and instead wrote:

> And so this is Christmas
> For weak and for strong
> For rich and the poor ones
> The world is so wrong
> -John Lennon

I got a second write up for that one, but I didn't care.

Chapter 6
Not the Shittiest Writer in the Class

The guy who replaced Tom, and somehow the guy who was now my new boss, was this pimple faced overweight dork who probably served ice cream while his parents paid for his college education at Cornell or something. The heads of the company, including Tom, stayed away from me and the rest of the other big sellers in the office. We all ignored this new guy completely, and he seemed to know to ignore all of us. When you are a salesman you don't really feel anyone is your boss. You are the one who is making the cash register ring and they, the owners, are the ones all filling their pockets with the cash. It's not good to focus on their piece of the pie though. Focus on what you are getting and cruise forward.

Every now and then whoever was on the phone picked up on the fact that we were going to be charging their credit card. Once they gave you that credit card number it was incredibly hard to get out of the charges with a guy like me on the phone. The truth is all they had to say was, "I am not interested, and I am not authorizing you to charge my credit card." And then just hang up the phone. People didn't do that though. They kept talking and if you were savvy you could easily save almost any sale.

I was on the phone with a woman who didn't realize she was going to be billed for the service when she called. She started crying that her husband was going to beat her up when he found out. For me this was just too much. I was tired of working at the company. I couldn't avoid thinking about what was happening on the other end of the phone after I ripped people like her off all day.

I decided not to push on the phone. I told her I'd be cancelling the order. This was unusual for me. In fact, I'd never done it before. Through tears she kept asking me if I was sure there would be no charges. I told her that just to reassure her I would put my boss on the phone. I called the new pimple faced guy over and explained the situation to him. He told me he could save the sale for me. I told the guy that I didn't want to save the sale, and if I did, I could do it myself. I certainly didn't need his help. I told him I wanted him to tell her that we were cancelling it like I had asked him to do. The guy got on the phone and doubled her. The son of a bitch had just charged her double when I had just wanted him to cancel the call. Either he was a massive piece of shit, or he just hadn't been around this kind of thing long enough to understand what he had done.

He actually did a good job chilling her out and even told the lady her husband would be super happy when they saved all that money. As he was finishing up the call, the husband walked in and my new boss quickly got off the phone. It's what you are supposed to do to be honest. Husband and wife teams on the phone are bad news. You will never get the deal. It needs to be a one on one person to person transaction. While we are on the topic, the hardest sell is a college girl. They listen to everything you say. The easiest sell is a college guy. They don't pay attention to a thing. Anyhow, he hurriedly hung up the phone and smiled at me, "You see, Joel- that is how it's done." Whether the lady got beaten up that day or not I'll never know. Maybe she got beaten up for something else. Or maybe she was just lying all along. No matter what the case was I knew I had had enough. I left work that day and never went back. It took about six months, but the company did get closed down by the Feds in the end.

UC Santa Barbara is run on a quarter system. I had two full quarters left where I didn't need to work and I didn't really need any credits to graduate either. I decided to take a couple of screenwriting classes, I drank a lot, and I focused on selling as much weed as I could to keep making money. To get into the first screenwriting class we had to submit writing samples. If the professor liked what we had written he'd let us into the class. I wasn't chosen, but I kept going to the class anyhow. By the third class he gave up and let me in. To his surprise, and maybe mine too, I quickly became acknowledged as the best writer in the class. Being the best writer in the class was a far cry from winning an Oscar for screenwriting or anything but it was still cool.

I graduated in May of 1998. I had turned 21 years old two weeks before my graduation. I had a worthless diploma now, a bit of money in the bank, no debt, and a very cool car. I was ready to start making my mark on the world. I wanted to make my family proud.

Roadie Ramble Moment

A quick explanation as to why I think graduation ceremonies suck. The purpose is to have your name called out while walking across a stage. The diploma is often not actually given to you on the stage I might add. It is more often mailed to you later. So, a bunch of people who already know your name hear it being called and those that don't know your name... well they of course don't care. Is the purpose then to let your family know that what they've been paying for isn't all a lie? Do we as a society really need attention this bad? If the answer is yes, then understand the attention given to the graduate is from people who the graduate should know already care about him or her. How does the graduate know they care? Well, because they showed up. They've sat in the sun for hours hearing random names and listening to dull speeches from kids who have a better understanding of how to tell people they are going to conquer the world than any idea of how to actually do it. Talk about a lot of bullshit and a bunch of wasted time.

Chapter 7
BJ & JJ (Brian, Joel & the Two Joe's)

I decided to backpack around Europe next. My parents pushed the idea. "Before getting bogged down by life go travel and see the world," my mom told me. So, I did. I left for three months. When I left the U.S. I weighed 170 pounds, and when I came back, I weighed 140 pounds. I ate healthy and walked a lot every day.

One of my roommates in college, Brian, decided to go with me. We would land in London, hang out for a bit, and then breakoff from one another to do our own thing. He was going to meet a friend of his in Spain, and I was going to keep heading east to see as much of Europe as I could. I had just got a degree in art history. Nothing beats seeing all the great art you just studied for a year and a half right off the bat. It really was a wonderful way to bookend my college studies. Once we landed in London, Brian and I went to go see my family.

I was born in England and had a lot of family there. Brian and I could save some money on hotels, and I could get to know my family better. My cousin Simone's father had been one of my dad's best friends growing up. He told me stories that really intrigued me. He told me how my father had run his car into the back of a police car when he first got his license to drive. I had never heard that before but certainly enjoyed picturing my dad shitting his pants. My father had a really bad temper and was strong as an ox. It was a bad combination. I never saw him drink but he often would get angry out of nowhere and become very violent. Because he was so strong it was scary. Arthur, my dad's cousin and Simone's father, then continued to tell me how they would go out, get drunk, and my father would get into fights at the bar. He once followed this guy when he left the pub, rammed him off the road, and beat the crap out of him. I couldn't picture my father drunk, but I could picture him chasing some guy down who pissed him off. I had a great time hearing these stories and Brian fucked my cousin Simone that night. All in all, we were off to a great trip.

After Brian slept with my cousin, we decided we should stay in a youth hostel instead, just in case her dad found out. Brian and I made our way to the center of London. My paternal grandmother was very wealthy but didn't want us staying with her. She certainly had the room for us. She lived in the center of London so it would have been ideal. Maybe she was why my father was so nuts? We did go visit her, but Brian didn't try to sleep with her. So at least things didn't get awkward again. We hit up museums and a lot of pubs, and then the two of us headed off to Amsterdam. In Amsterdam I met a pretty English girl named Wendy. She ditched her boyfriend, I ditched my friend Brian, and she and I travelled around Europe together for a while.

Wendy and I eventually pushed on together to Greece. While in Greece I met two guys named Joe. So, if you are following along, the travelling troupe became Joe, Joe, Joel, and Wendy. The two Joe's were professors who taught Greek architecture at some University in England. It was awesome travelling through Greece with these two. Some of the places we went to weren't exactly tourist destinations. It kicked ass going to important historical landmarks without any tourists and on top of it getting university level guided tours.

After not bathing for three days, we all woke up in a fruit field, looking at a farmer holding one of our empty bottles of wine in one hand and a shotgun in the other. After that Wendy bailed. The travelling troupe of Joe, Joe, and Joel had a better ring to it anyhow, and the three of us travelled on. When I found out we were in the Mount Olympus area, I left the Joe's and stayed with a girl I had met in Austria for a couple days. The girl had been in tears because they wouldn't let her dog on a train. I smuggled the dog in my luggage for her, and she gave me her address before we both went our own way that day.

From Greece I headed down to Israel, Jordan, and Egypt by myself and then after that flew back to Germany. When I got to Germany, I was a mess. My beard was matted with mud and I looked and smelled homeless. I walked into a youth hostel, and the man at the front desk told me the hostel was full. My heart just sunk. I was too tired to figure out where I could stay. I was contemplated going outside to sleep on the street, when two gorgeous girls approached me. "You can stay with us if you like," one of them said. I was shocked. I mumbled "okay," and followed them. They took me to another youth hostel, but before checking me in the man at the desk, made me go take a shower and change my clothes. I took the girls out to dinner that night and found out that one of them had grown up on the same street as I in Woodland Hills, California. It's a small world.

From Germany I headed into the Czech Republic. While on that train I met Stefanie. She was a bubbly, pretty, dirty blonde-haired girl. She talked a lot while I mostly stayed quiet that day. I had learned from my travels that when you get off a train while backpacking, you have to rush to the local youth hostel to get a spot. They fill up fast, and I wanted to make sure I got one of the beds. I was tired. I had been travelling hard for months. I jumped out of the train and rushed off to the youth hostel without saying anything to her. Sure enough, I walked right into her shortly thereafter. Smiling at me, she stopped in her tracks. "We may both find a place together to stay if you want to try," she said. We did find a place, and we ended up hanging out for a week in Prague together. It was magical. I adored her. It was refreshing to be open and honest with someone. I told her my deepest, darkest secrets, and she told me hers. What did we care? We'd never be seeing one another again. What were those secrets? In hindsight they weren't deep, dark, or secret. They were the jumbled thoughts of what kids think about. Our time together was the encapsulation of what I now know to be the beauty of adolescent attraction. At the end of a perfect week, she turned and asked me, "So, when are we going to see one another again?" I stuttered for a moment. That hadn't been our plan. That hadn't been what we talked about. In what was a minutia of time, a fraction of less than a second, I realized; I was going to miss her. We'd have to see one another again! And I for one hoped it would be soon. When we said our goodbyes, I flew back to Los Angeles and she travelled on to Russia. I vowed to never not stay in touch with her. I hoped with all my heart that she thought the same thing.

Once back in the United States, I knew I had to figure out a career. Even though I was still new to screenwriting, I liked it a lot. I figured something in the entertainment industry may be a fun thing to do. I found a "job" (if you want to call it that) in the art department, working on feature films.

Chapter 8
Bottom Feeding Grunt

Working in the movie industry really wasn't all that exciting. It would have been a lot more fun if they were paying me, but I had only managed to land a gig working as an art department PA on a film called *All the Rage*. The abbreviation PA stands for production assistant. In the film industry they should really call PA's BFG's, bottom feeding grunts. Whether I worked as a BFG or PA, my pay was "experience" they told me. The "experience" was running around town doing errands. When on set, I would stand outside so that people could grab me if they needed help with anything.

The film had some great names in it. Joan Allen, Jeff Daniels, Gary Sinise, and David Schwimmer, to name a few. I had met a number of celebrities through my dad and found them all to be cool but working on a movie set was different. I found that stress levels were high working on films. Some of the actors didn't seem to be affected by the stress of memorizing lines, or making a movie, or whatever it is that actors trip out about, but others were just straight out dicks, overly odd, or heavily focused on what?... I'm not sure. Joan Allen and Gary Sinise were really nice to me. Josh Brolin and I had long conversations about travelling; both of us had recently been to Egypt. However, Andre Braugher was the most interesting to me. He would walk around singing all the time. In the regular world that might be weird but in the film world it was A OK. I wondered if the real reason he became an actor was so that he could walk around singing comfortably all the time. He was a good singer. I did try to make small talk with him but quickly learned that he was not the dude who played Punky Brewster's teacher in the TV show. "Do people make that mistake a lot, "I asked him? "No," he told me.

The downer of the movie was Jeff Daniels. He was a massive dickhead. He was such a prick that at the end of the movie he asked for everyone on the set to get together so he could address us as a group. He then apologized to all of us collectively for what he described as, "being difficult." He told us that he had just done back to back movies and he was ready to go home for a much-needed break. In addition to being homesick, he wanted us to know that his attitude had a lot to do with him becoming the character he played in the movie. I wanted to ask him if he practiced taking a shit with his legs in the air while getting into character to do the movie *Dumb and Dumber.* Anything else that he might have told us that day I'm honestly a bit unsure about. While he spoke to us with other words all I heard was, "I'm sorry I'm a dick. Yep BFG even you, you minion little fuck. I sure am sorry. I really mean it too."

Hollywood schwag movie candle!

At the end of the production everyone got a sweatshirt but me. I didn't mind though. I got a really amazing candle. I mean, it wasn't just any kind of candle. It was taller than usual candles, and that meant something special. I guess the crew gift theme for the film was "ways to keep warm." Unfortunately, my candle has since runneth over. I guess I'll never be using it.

If there was a real upside to doing the film, it was that I had the opportunity to see Giovanni Ribisi act. It was exciting to see a truly gifted actor work. Because of him, I was inspired to keep working on my creative endeavor - writing screenplays.

I was the only man in the art department who wasn't gay. It certainly made me feel like the odd man out. So, I stayed a little more quiet than usual and kept my head down. I felt fine working with all the other guys, but I just had a hard time finding anything in common to talk about with them. After *All the Rage* was done the production designer, my boss, pulled me on to the next movie and made me a paid set dresser.

That film was called *Things You Can Tell Just by Looking at Her.* What's a set dresser you ask? Well, the title set dresser basically means furniture mover. Set dressing is all the stuff in the background when you watch a movie. Your job is to physically set up the location, so it looks like how your boss, the lead man, wants it. Then when his boss comes, the art director, you move it all around to how they like it. Then the production designer comes, and you move it all around again to how they like it. Then the director comes, and you move it all around one more time, unless the actor wants it moved then you got to do it again... to how they like it. The job was thankless and boring, but it was nice to be getting paid.

There were some big names on this movie too. Glenn Close, Cameron Diaz, Calista Flockhart, Holly Hunter, and Carmel Wynne Smith to name a few. Who's Carmel Wynne Smith you ask? Carmel Wynne Smith might not be a name you know but I mention her because her mom might have been the only person who went to see the movie. It tanked at the box office.

Working on *Things You Can Tell Just by Looking at Her* was much the same as working on *All the Rage.* A lot of odd but focused people. I had a lot more to do on this film. They kept me working. On one busy production day I was outside by myself loading a cart with furniture. It was hot and it was hard work. While loading stuff up I noticed this skinny dude watching me. The guy just stared at me. As I continued to bust my ass, I wondered what the hell the guy was looking at and why he didn't come over to give me a hand. I thought any reasonable guy would have offered help at that point. Finally fed up with being stared at, I decided to walk over to the guy. I was going to ask him what the hell he was so fond of staring at but as I approached, I realized it wasn't a dude. It was Calista Flockhart. Seeing me walking towards her she rushed into her trailer. I turned back around awkwardly and kept loading the cart. I should really look into getting contact lenses I thought to myself.

The best thing that could ever happen to a crew on a non-union film is for the film to go union and that was precisely what happened. What that would mean was that all non-union crew could now be in the union if they paid their fee. Getting in the unions in the film industry is tough so I had really lucked out. Maybe if I joined the union, I could climb the ladder a bit and the job would be a bit more interesting.

The day after the crew found out the film was turning union everyone was obviously in a great mood. This was a huge career step for a lot of the crew. I spent most of my morning hanging clothes in a closet with another set dresser. Maybe ten minutes into hanging clothes my walkie went off. "Joel, where are you?" the production designer, my boss, asked. I wasn't used to getting called but pushed the button and responded quickly. "I'm in the closet." After a few quick moments, my boss asked the same question again. I responded once again. "I'm in the closet." I asked William, the set dresser working with me, if I was using the walkie correctly. He smiled away. I looked down at the walkie and once again heard the production designer ask where I was. Holding the walkie up to my face I spoke directly into the speaker. "I'm in the closet with

William." This time, William quickly pushed the button on his own walkie talkie. "Oh, honey I've been out of the closet for years." The walkie lit up with laughter from the crew.

I didn't really like working with this crew but figured as my career expanded so would my contacts. I knew I should stick with the job. However, if I was on the fence my decision was soon made for me. The next day I learned that my boss had flown out his partner from New York and hired him as a set dresser for the production. I was immediately demoted back down to the illustrious position of art department PA. Yep, I was back to being a BFG. I never actually quit, but they stopped calling me for anything, and I in turn just stopped going in to work. I didn't think what they had done was a very nice thing to do. But hey, it's a tough world!

Soon after my mom found out that one of her friends' son was directing a film called *Lucky 13*. He was happy to bring me onto the production as a non-paid art department PA. I took the opportunity. The first few days they had me working in the production office, and it didn't seem like I was going to see the set.

There wasn't really anything interesting to do in the production office. The coolest thing was a miniature cityscape the production designer, who I hadn't met yet, had set up on a big table. It had nothing to do with the movie we were working on but was pretty neat. The production designer had worked on the film *What Dreams May Come* and I was looking forward to meeting the guy. The production office was on Hollywood Blvd and even though I was raised in Los Angeles, it was exciting to be working both in the heart of Hollywood and in the film industry. On the third day Marcus, the production designer, showed up at the production office. He was a skinny guy who looked a lot like the father in the TV show *Alf*. He didn't say anything to me but handed me two handheld mirrors. For the remainder of the day I held the small mirrors at different angles while Marcus pretended to shoot the miniature city through his hands. He'd hold his hands up to look like a square in front of his face, then look through the fingered square intently on the streets and cityscape that surrounding them. After a few hours of this, he walked away from the table and went to look out the window. Clearly in deep thought, he didn't move from the window for about fifteen minutes. "Take those home with you," Marcus said to me. I put the two mirrors I'd been holding all day in my pocket. "No, no leave them on the table and meet me here in the morning," he said changing his mind. I put the mirrors back on the table and went home for the day. I wondered if I had done a good job. Was this what all production designers did all day? Well, that and have furniture moved around the set before shooting of course.

The next morning, I showed up at the production office as instructed. The lady in the office was once again having me sort through production paperwork when, roughly an hour into the day, Marcus showed up. He talked to the lady a bit and then asked me to leave with him. We climbed into Marcus's Jeep Wrangler and headed down to the production. I was happy to finally get out of the office. I was hanging out with the production designer. The head art department guy. I had blown him away with my mirror holding skills and maybe we'd get along and he'd even hire me in the future. Maybe he had sobered up and maybe, just maybe I'd be able to do something production related. While driving through the city, all this was going through my head when Marcus's phone rang. The guy was already driving fast and erratically. I was hoping he wouldn't add a cell phone call to the equation. This was before it was illegal to talk on the phone while driving, not that I think Marcus would have cared. Marcus looked at the phone and handed it to me. "It's my daughter. Talk to her," he said. "Hello," I said. "Well, hello there. Who would this be?" she asked me. "Um, my name is Joel," I said into the phone. "Well, hello, um, my name is Joel," she said. "Your name would be?" I asked her.

"You already know who I am. You are with my father. Just tell him to call me. Oh, tell him I want to meet you," she said and hung up. Marcus cut a corner hard and pulled into a dirt parking lot fast. He didn't ask me why she called or if he could even have his phone back. We got out of the Jeep and I handed it back to him anyhow. The parking lot was in the middle of a bunch of sound stages. This place was very cool. I was eager to get inside and check it all out. Before I could, Marcus stopped in his tracks in the middle of the parking lot. Reaching down on the ground he grabbed a handful of dirt. Picking it up in front of his face he dropped it back on the ground. "Isn't it beautiful Joel?" I didn't know what to say. He had absolutely not sobered up though. This guy was out of his mind. "Yeah, Marcus, it's nice," I said. "No, no look at it!" Marcus picked up more of the dirt and we once again watched it together as it dropped back down to the ground. After the dust had settled, he looked sternly at me. I was expecting to hear something else he thought was profound. "Can you get me shrooms?" he asked.

The next film I worked on was called *Second to Die*. I was getting paid on this one. I had worked on a short film previously but hadn't made too many friends on the film after sleeping with the director's girlfriend. However, one of the producers on the short film had hired me to work on *Second to Die*. The production designer was a guy named Alex Tavoularis. He was a heavy hitting veteran in the film business. He had been the art director on many of Francis Ford Coppola's films. Alex and I got along well. I didn't learn much from him in the way of how movies are made but enjoyed his company. Alex would sit and doodle all day. More interesting than the film was Alex's doodling. Doodling had done him well. He had doodled his way at one point into being a conceptual storyboard artist on *Star Wars: Episode IV A New Hope*. I think what I took from meeting Alex was that if things become dull... doodle. If at work... doodle... If in class ...doodle. When on a boring call...

definitely doodle. When on a boring date... doodle. When getting lectured by your wife by all means... doodle. But maybe when driving, having sex, or talking to your mother... don't doodle. Even the greatest of doodlers have some rules.

The person who funded the film had won the lottery and thought it would be fun to make a movie. The only thing worse than the script was that the female lead, who had been my favorite Baywatch babe growing up, had lost her sex appeal. Well, to me at least. She chain smoked and was frighteningly skinny. One of the wardrobe people had accidentally left a book of continuity polaroid's out on a table. They were photos of her in lingerie. I didn't even think about keeping them. Handing them back, it felt like I was handing over the secret truths behind Hollywood's glamour. That book wasn't just evidence of what had happened to her. To me it was a book of washed up bombshells. She only being an example. I wanted my adolescent years, that perfect image of her-of all of them- to always remain in my head. It shouldn't be like this... This wasn't the Baywatch babe I had watched the show to see. For fear of finding out any more truths that could, no that would, leave a dirty stain on years of mouth open infatuation, I decided it was time for me to leave the movie business. Or it may have been I wasn't making any money or climbing any ladders. Either way, I was done with the movie business!

Chapter 9
We're Going to Need Tacos... Lots of Tacos

Humble Gods T-shirt, late 1990's.

Not wanting to work on any more films, I had to find something else to do. I hit up a buddy of mine, Doug Carrion. Doug had played in a band called Humble Gods. With all my buddies I had gone to many a concert. Still in high school, we would post their fliers, sell their T-shirts, and help with whatever. In return we got into the shows for free, got booze, and met girls. What else could a rebellious high school student want? Doug had been in the punk bands The Descendents and Dag Nasty. If, like me, you grew up listening to punk music these guys were Gods. Doug agreed to sit me down and explain to me anything I could want to know about how the music industry works. Together we could find something within the industry that sounded cool. We spent hours going through every aspect and hiring position of the industry. I thought working in a recording studio or rehearsal studio might be a good gig for me. So, when I got home I went back to what I knew, the telephone. I got my hands on a yellow pages, opened it up to the music section and started calling anything music related to try and get a job. I thought music may be more rewarding than the film industry. I landed a non-paid job working for a little recording studio. They were just opening their doors and were having a hard time assembling a kitchen they had bought at Ikea. I helped them put the kitchen cabinets together and they hired me as their non-paid runner. I got lunch every day and they covered my gas during working hours. It was a step up from my nonpaid film industry jobs. To fit in, I bought myself a Martin guitar. I didn't know how to play, but when at the store, I strummed guitars, and I bought the one that sounded the best.

Now this is where you'd think lots of drugs would come back into the picture, but no. These guys were all rehab people. In the 1980's they had partied hard. The engineer had recorded and/or mixed albums for U2, Billy Idol, Lionel Richie, Joe Cocker, and Bob Seger to name just a few. I loved music and I thought it was really cool to be hanging out with these guys. The first gig I remember doing for them was for a band called Dogstar. Keanu Reeves was in the band. I quickly learned to like Keanu. He was a real nice guy. He'd hang out in the studio lounge watching hockey games. Never a hockey fan, I didn't understand what was going on in the game. Keanu tried hard to explain to me what offsides was, but I couldn't understand the concept. I think if I remember correctly, eventually Keanu just gave up. I'm quite confident Keanu came to the decision I wasn't very bright.

For lunch he asked for and received Taco Bell. When I got back to the studio, the change for the order was something around five dollars. He told me to keep it and I refused. After a bit of back and forth "take it, no I don't want it," talk he pocketed the money. I felt like I had won a small victory. I knew the couple dollars wouldn't change my life, and I wanted him to think I was a standup guy.

I decided to make an effort to connect on a mental plane with him. "I have a story about the movie *Speed* if you want to hear it," I said to him. I was sure that was exactly what he wanted to hear about. Keanu didn't say anything but kept eating the Taco Bell I had just bought for him. I assumed it was hard for him to focus on anything other than eating when indulging in Taco Bell because that was certainly the case for me when I ate Taco Bell, and so I continued on. "It's a really good story, man. I wouldn't lie to you." Keanu kept eating. "I was backpacking through Europe but then found myself in the middle east," I started. Keanu now looked at me blankly and took a bite of his soft taco. "Would you like some more hot sauce?" Still staring at me blankly, he shook his head - "no."

"Ok, so I'm in Egypt on a bus. Next to me, in front of me, behind me, everyone has a machine gun in hand, and we are all on the same bus. Both in front and behind the bus are armored vehicles. When you get to the border of Israel and Egypt you get out of the bus and walk into another bus. It's the same scenario, it's just Israeli guys with machine guns instead of Egyptian guys. But I was in the Egyptian bus, and they were playing the movie... *Speed*. I couldn't control myself. There was just so much irony in the situation and nobody was picking up on it. I started laughing. I began to explain to the people around me why it was so funny that *Speed* was playing, but instead I got dirty looks from guys with machine guns who were trying to watch the movie."

Keanu wrapped up the paper from his taco. He wiped his mouth and put both the napkin and the wrapper in the Taco Bell bag. "That is actually a pretty good story," he said. I got very excited. "I told you it was a good story, dude." On that last note he actually cracked a smile.

The next day Keanu pulled into the driveway of the studio in his black Porsche. "Looking good brother," I said to him. Keanu nodded but didn't say anything. He was a quiet guy. Together, we walked into the studio. "I just got the suspension all done," he said to me. "Drive good? I used to have a 911. It was awesome," I said to him. He looked hard at me. I'm not sure if he was doubtful or just trying to figure me out. It could also have been he just wanted me to stop talking to him. "Yeah, it drives good. Real expensive though," he said. "Well, yeah, man. It's a Porsche, and you are kind of the most famous guy in the world right now." It was true. *The Matrix* had been recently released. I didn't know anyone who hadn't seen it. "They probably charged you double. You should have sent your assistant," I continued on. It was an odd way of trying to get him to hire me to be his assistant. Keanu nodded thoughtfully but didn't reply. Not that I know what he could have said. Maybe I was expecting "Yes, young Joel. I will pay you to make sure I don't get ripped off on my Porsche next time."

Soon after Dogstar, Billy Idol came into record. To me this was very cool. He recorded a couple songs including the song titled "Bitter Pill." Billy didn't hang out much at all. He didn't want anyone in the studio when he sang. He was a super nice dude, but I didn't get much time to talk to the guy. Steve Stevens, his guitar player and a co-writer on some songs, on the other hand hung out quite a lot and was fun to talk to. Steve gave me a few guitar picks. The first schwag I had ever been given, I thought they were awesome.

Steve Steven's guitar pics.

It was while working at the studio I first heard crazy Rock 'n' Roll stories. Going to narcotics anonymous meetings and picking up the chicks there to go do a bunch of blow with Billy Idol. Or a certain 1970's mega rock star hanging out with a harem of gay dudes. It wasn't the harem of gay dudes that was a big deal but it's what they all did. These guys would regularly blow cocaine up her ass with a straw because her nasal cavity was gone from snorting so much blow. The music industry tag line to the story, "don't blow on the wrong end of Sally Hix's straw." Another story was about a contest on an 80's hairband tour. The band would get blowjobs in the bus bathroom and then see who could cum higher on the bathroom wall. What's worse- blowing the 80's hairband guy in the bus bathroom or being the one holding the measuring tape? I learned these and other fine stories worth sharing around the dinner table. Though gross and/or bad all these stories captivated me. I wasn't sure how it was going to happen but I wanted to spend my life working in the music industry.

Various record producers came and went from the studio. Some of them were cool and some of them were dicks. What I liked about all of them was that each of them were a little bit different. They were all people going against the grain. None of them were interested in suit and tie desk jobs. These guys were successful being individuals. I wanted to be one of them.

One thing lacking at recording studios are groupies. Women are always trying to get backstage at concerts to meet the band. If they only went to recording studios to hang out, they'd meet lots of bored rock stars. Ladies, it's all about the time and place!

One of the producers that came through was a guy named Joey Carbone. An Italian- American from Brooklyn, Joey had been the musical director on the TV show Star Search and had toured with Bette Midler as her piano player. I wasn't feeling well one day, and he asked me if he could get me anything. I think he meant a cup of tea or an Advil. It was cool of him to ask me because I was only the runner. The lowest guy on the totem pole. Just him asking me made me feel better. "Would you mind playing me 'The Rose' on the piano?" I asked him. Slightly reluctantly, Joey sat down. He played the song for me that he had played so many times before. I loved it. I thought my job was amazing.

I soon found out a band had blocked the studio out for a couple weeks. Because there would be not just continuous work but also continuous paychecks, the owners of the studio agreed to pay me $20 a day for my services. The band, I quickly found out, was the aforementioned Poison. I was excited to hang out with real rock stars. This job was way better than the film industry. I'd go out with my friends at night, meet girls and get drunk, and come into work the next day hungover. I'd sleep on the couch until they needed me. When not sleeping, I was practicing my guitar and getting lessons from some of the greatest guitar players in the world. Watching Steve Stevens and Carl Verheyen (Supertramp) play my guitar was mind blowing. C.C. Deville gave me lessons daily. He liked the sound of my guitar so much he used it on a track they recorded at the studio.

It was a perfect adolescent life when not running dumb errands. On the Poison gig the producer made me drive back to a T Mobile location to get another warranty card. He had filled one section out wrong and didn't want to cross it out. That kind of stuff sucked. The cool stuff was days like when C.C. Deville hung out a lot at the studio and we spent the day talking. We quickly become friends. One day when the studio was quiet, we watched a National Geographic special called *Raising the Mammoth.* He watched the whole thing on the edge of his seat while continuously eating bagels. By the end of the show, I witnessed him eat four whole bagels. When the credits started to roll, I grabbed another bagel off the plate. "You want another bagel man?" I was really hoping he'd eat another one. It was starting to become an impressive feat to me. "No, I'm good," he replied. "You know you ate four of them?" I asked. "Yeah, I grew up in a Jewish neighborhood."

Though this job was fun, I still wasn't making any money and I absolutely didn't want to become a recording engineer. So,

I decided to leave the studio and work as a headhunter for a few months. When I left, the owners cried. Unfortunately, I can't say it was tears of sorrow, but instead they were tears of excitement. One of the partners, Kevin Anderson, deemed me to be "the first and worst 2nd engineer" they'd ever had. Years later, I still proudly hold the title, as it's still how he chooses to introduce me to anyone. The other partner has the good intuition, Kevin says, not to return any of my phone calls. Years later, though years ago, I found a little over fifty grand on a government unclaimed money website belonging to a couple of the producers I met while working at the studio. Though I'm sure they were pleased, the extent of their gratitude was nothing more than a cordial "thanks." Not mentioning any names, but it is rather funny one of the producers co-wrote a song called "Don't You Forget About Me." I'm Just sayin'.... Kevin loves to bring up that they didn't even buy me a beer every time we hang out and then he inevitably makes me pay the bar tab for still being the, you guessed it, first and worst 2nd engineer he has *still* ever had. The other producer wrote a song called... Ah, fuck that guy- I don't know what he wrote. Now, I want it to be known, I'm being sure to add this anecdote to the book, though irrelevant to *my* story, because Kevin made a big deal about ensuring it was placed here "for the world to see." As he found me the audio engineer to do the audiobook for this memoir, I don't really have a choice, so says he. I make note that he wants anyone and everyone to fully comprehend his position on my personal work ethic. Oh, and lest I forget I promised to be sure I make mention that I was a fine couch tester, and furthermore, that he was pleased I did not snore on that studio couch while recording was in session.

Chapter 10
If Shit Doesn't Stick to the Wall, Keep Throwing Shit at That Wall. Throw it like You've Never Thrown Shit Before

Going back to work in the real world- the IT, internet technology, game was taking off and headhunting was a good way to make some cash. Headhunting, by the way, is the art of snatching people from companies to go work for other companies. I was back doing what I knew I was good at. I was back on the phones. The owners put me on a three-month test run to see how things would go. The one thing that was constant in the office was foul language. The owners were a husband and wife team who would argue all day long while I worked. "Who the fuck does this asshole think he's talking to?" I'd hear the wife scream out of one office. The husband would then throw something down at the floor and yell from his office. "Who the hell are you talking about?" he'd ask. Yelling would continue back and forth until things would escalate into one of them stomping into the others' office so that they could yell directly at one another. It was hard to repeatedly tell my bosses they needed to shut the fuck up so I could close deals.

The mediator in the office was a Great Dane puppy whose favorite past time was to slobber all over me. My one argument with my bosses was that they wanted me to wear a suit every day to work. With the dog slobbering all over me all day I refused to do it. When the job got boring, I got my best friend hired on and working there became fun again. It was good to have a bud to go to lunch with. My friend may have been the worst recruiter in history, but I certainly made up for it. I made the company over $250k in two months. I was back! I was their only employee, other than my friend who had effectively made them no money in two months, and of course a cute receptionist.

> ### Roadie Ramble Moment
> *Why do dogs beg for food from fat people? You would think they would be smart enough to know to beg for food from the skinny people at the table. Skinny people are going to eat less and are therefore more likely to have more food to hand over. Is man's best friend becoming less evolved? This is the only part of the book that I've thought about through the lengthy editing process. I think I figured it out, though. Dogs beg from fat people because fat people are usually nice. Dogs know they might actually get a scrap or two of some food. Skinny people are just angry assholes.*

It wasn't long before it was time to tell these guys they needed to figure out my pay. I had suitably proven to them that I was a good employee. I marched into their office and told them. A few days later we had a meeting. They offered me 5k a month plus health benefits. I looked at them in astonishment. I realized right then and there that if I was going to get anywhere in this world, it would be by climbing my own ladder. I wouldn't work for anyone again. Out of respect I gave them my two-week resignation and did as little as possible. They let me go after one week. The problem I now had was what was I going to do? My friend got laid off immediately. He also wondered what he was going to do.

Over the Christmas months I went to work selling porcelain dolls in a mall kiosk, but I couldn't handle the Christmas music and I left that job too. The song *Wonderful Christmastime* by Paul McCartney is quite certainly the worst song ever written. I then tried working for a chimney sweep. That lasted one day. I tried selling cars on a car lot for a weekend. But the car salesmen were such big scum bags even I couldn't work there.

And then something came my way. This skinny, bald, English guy named Nigel kept coming over to my parent's house to kiss my dad's ass. He wanted his Jaguar fixed. My father had been raised in England but one of his many odd rules was that he wouldn't do any work for anyone who hailed from England. He was fond of telling anyone who would listen that he didn't like English people.

What didn't make sense was that he was raised in England and that he fixed English cars almost exclusively. Par for the course-it was hard to make any sense of most of my dad's actions. He was incredibly difficult to deal with, but because he specialized in cars where it was hard to find someone with both the knowledge to do the work and the parts to fix the car, he got away with it.

Everyone in the Jaguar industry knew my father. Nigel was English but lived in Los Angeles now. Nigel, so he says, showed up at my house with cash in hand. He needed a gearbox rebuilt for an E Type Jaguar and agreed to pay not just in full but also up front. He had figured out how to make my dad work with an English native. It was to give him money.

More interesting than either Nigel or his car was what he did for a living. Nigel was the lighting designer for Stone Temple Pilots. To me, it was one of the coolest jobs in the world. He had fled England because of speeding tickets he always said. After racking up too many of them he'd have to either pay the tickets or go to jail. Instead of doing either, he moved to the United States. This was typical of Nigel. There was always a plan "C."

I was always slightly standoffish to people who befriended my father. Maybe it was my age, or maybe it was his judgement of character. Neither of my parents did much socializing outside of the family. So, his friends were always his recent customers and those customers were as crazy as he. Nigel fit that character. Here's an example of what I'm talking about, years earlier my father had befriended Harvey Rader, a man who ultimately was extradited back to England. He was extradited for illegal crap he did back there but before he was extradited, and while they weren't able to prove it, he was accused of killing an entire family and burying them in the desert somewhere.

I didn't know the band Stone Temple Pilots, or STP, well but I did have one of their CD's. I had hardly ever listened to it because I listened to Guns N' Roses almost all the time. Nigel needed a kid to help set up the lights and stage for the next STP tour. He told me that being a roadie was hard work, really hard work, and asked me if I wanted to take the job. I said yes without thinking about it at all. I didn't think anything would actually come from the conversation. I didn't even tell any of my friends about it. However, I was wrong- a couple days later I was on an airplane to my first gig.

Chapter 11
C.C. Told Me There Are Always Hot Chicks at Airports

Stone Temple Pilots crew T-shirt, 2000.

C.C. had told me, during one of our deep talks at the recording studio, that hot chicks were always hanging out in airports. "No one wants to see ugly people. But good-looking women are always flying all over the place," he said. I had made a mental note at the time. Any information that involved hot chicks was good to know. C.C. was full of profound wisdom.

Nigel, living in the same city as me, and I got on a morning flight. I had a middle seat and was stuck beside a man who had trouble breathing. The poor guy literally had to squeeze into the chair he was sitting in. I was wondering if I was going to have to listen to this guy wheeze all the way to Las Vegas. I put on my headset; I'd have to deal with it. Luckily it wasn't a long flight. I wasn't paying attention, but a flight attendant started talking to my neighbor. After a quick conversation he squeezed out of his chair and left down the aisle. As he tottered away, he reminded me of the Rock Biter from *The Neverending Story*.

Up the aisle came an absolutely, stunning blonde lady. She

hurriedly sat down next to me. In the seat for maybe half a minute, she tapped my arm wanting to speak to me. I removed my earphones and wondered if Nigel had somehow put her up to this. This was too good to be true. She began by telling me she was a stripper on her way to Las Vegas for the weekend. Or maybe I should say a peeler. Nigel called strippers peelers or shoe models and honestly, they both did sound cooler than stripper. Anyhow, her girlfriend lived in Texas and she was flying there to see her after the weekend was over. This all sounded amazing to me. To make things even better she told me she was afraid of flying and asked if she could hold on to my arm while we took off.

I glanced over at Nigel. What was the catch here? Nigel shrugged his shoulders and went to sleep. Then it all quickly ended. Before the flight could take off, the lady jumped up out of the seat, and the Rock Biter guy from *The Neverending Story* came back. Saying nothing to me, he took his time and squeezed back into the chair. They closed the doors of the plane and the flight attendant came over to us. "Pardon me, sir. Your wife is going to have to calm down or we aren't going to be able to take off with her in the plane," she said to me. Clearly not asleep, Nigel found this hilarious and did a poor job trying to hide his laughter. Obviously, this was way too good to miss.

"I don't have a wife," I pleaded with the flight attendant. The stripper came rushing back down the aisle and apologized to me. She asked me if she could buy me a drink. "Are you old enough to drink?" she asked. "I am, but it is 6 o'clock in the morning." She walked away. Nigel and the Rock Biter went to sleep. The flight attendant went back to work. I never saw the lady again nor did I ever find out if she stayed on the flight or not. I had bought my ticket to the theme park and had just boarded the roller coaster. Was this how crazy my life was going to be now? If so, this was going to be awesome!

Chapter 12
"I Dub Thee... a Roadie"

STP all access pass, 2000.

They hadn't announced it to the public yet but STP was going to be co-headlining with the Red Hot Chili Peppers (RHCP). Before we met up with RHCP we did a few radio shows. RHCP was still on the road with the Foo Fighters. On May 20th, 2000 I worked my first show in Las Vegas at the Sam Boyd Stadium. I had just turned 23 years old four days earlier. The line-up for the show was STP, Godsmack, and System of a Down. I don't remember the night very well. It was all exciting, but how long was this all going to last I wondered. I didn't know what I was doing. Surely someone would figure that out and get rid of me. During the first couple shows I was a lost soul. Everyone was telling me what to do, I was rushing to do it all as fast as I could, and I didn't know if any of what I was doing was actually good.

This is how my day went. The first thing for me to do in the morning was to set up the grid to put the lights in. The grid is made with metal square beams called truss. The truss bolts together and is then pulled up in the air by span sets. The span sets are attached to shackles which in turn are attached to motors. It was all kind of like the Construx Fisher Price set my parents bought me when I was a kid. Once the truss is off the ground, you have your grid. Then you throw the lights in it. Once the lights are all mounted in the grid the motors pull the whole thing up into the sky, or what we call trim. Trim is where the grid lives, or stays, for the remainder of the show. Now, once the grid is out of the way everyone else on the crew can start to position the backline and sound equipment. I never had much to do with the backline. The backline are the amps, synthesizers, and whatever station the backline guy fixes up for themselves. Their stations are just areas where they can work on the instruments throughout the day. Sometimes they are on stage and sometimes they are not.

Eager not to lose my job, I sucked as much information in as I could and worked my ass off. Other people on the crew soon realized if they told me what to do, I would do their job as well. Nigel was only right about one thing ever… being a roadie was tough. My whole body hurt at night. We'd start working at 6-7 or so in the morning and the bus would move on to the next destination around 2AM. I felt like I was working on a chain gang. The main thing that kept me going was knowing that if they sent me home it would be both embarrassing and I'd be left not knowing what I was going to do with my life again. This was way cooler than being a phone salesman, working in the studio, or even working at that doll kiosk in the mall. I was also making decent money. I couldn't even imagine when I got home what people would say when I told them what my job was. Who could have a better job than I?

Chapter 13
You can't teach a Young Dog Old Tricks

STP tour itinerary - First Leg.

What made the shows hard was that no one was spending any time teaching me anything. I was just being thrown out there to figure it out every day. Nigel was not a teacher. He hadn't even told me to bring black shirts on the tour. I was wearing a white T-shirt, my personal clothing attire at the time, on stage. Ever seen a roadie work in a white shirt? I think I may have been the only one ever. However, I learned to rely on one thing. The show would both start and end every night no matter what. That kept me going. It's important to realize when you are just a cog in the wheel that the train is going to keep moving, with or without you on it. I'd work as hard as I could all day knowing that soon enough, I'd be eating pizza on the bus again, going to sleep, and waking up to do it all over again.

Much like a Bigfoot sighting, the white shirted roadie.

Like the law firm and the film jobs before, everyone on this crew was way older than I. They were all in their mid to late 30's. They had all toured for a long time and unlike me they really did know their jobs. My new gig meant for the first time I was not only going to have to learn what I was doing but eventually master my job. There weren't enough people working on the tour to be able to fly under the radar. Not perfecting your job or not doing it at all was, well, obvious.

Chapter 14
Concerts are Better on Drugs

Before touring, I had only ever even been to one concert in my life. In college I had eaten mushrooms with some friends and had gone to see The Steve Miller Band play. I was so messed up that for all I knew flying monkey's jumping through trees appeared at every concert. I had eaten a different batch of shrooms than my friends and found out that my batch was much stronger than theirs was. Sitting in the nosebleed section of the Santa Barbara bowl my friend's girlfriend asked me to watch her purse while the two of them went to grab a drink.

Shortly after they left, I noticed I was sitting next to someone's purse. But who's purse was it? I sat on a bench staring at the purse while hippies danced all around me. One of the dancing hippies approached me. Through the loud music she spoke to me, "Hey, man. Just wondering what you are on, man?" Absorbed by her flowing dress and the flowers in her hair, I answered her. "Oh, I'm a first time shroomer." "Excellent, man," she said with a big smile. "Can I give you a hug?" she asked me. "Yeah, sure, if you want." But before she was able to hug me, I asked her what was at the time the most important question in my life. "Do you know who this purse belongs to?" She answered with a constant smile that hadn't left her face. "Yes, it belongs to your friend. She asked you to watch it." Through literal tears of joy, I yelled, "What a relief! I've been wondering for a while." The truth I'd come to find out later was my friends hadn't gone very far. Instead, they sat watching me from one row away to see what I'd do without them. They hadn't been gone for more than a few minutes but to me it had seemed like ages. While I didn't realize how out of my mind I was, they sure did.

I pulled the purse in closer to me with one hand and held her hand with the other. Helping me stand up, I danced with her and her friends. Enjoying both dancing myself and watching the monkeys dance to the same beat in the trees, my train of thought was broken upon hearing someone rap Steve Miller's song "Fly Like an Eagle." "When did Steve Miller start rapping?" I asked no one in particular. I turned back to my new hippie friend. "Is that Steve Miller?" I asked. "No, Steve Miller is white and that is a very good looking young black man, hunny," she told me while throwing her arms up in the air and applauding. I focused on the stage, and it was true. It was not Steve Miller. Maybe I was at the wrong concert? I decided to part ways and go find my friends. Not holding her hand, and standing by myself, I realized I was not sober at all. I walked to the edge of the bench and looked down upon a step. Not wanting to fall or drop the purse, I decided I needed to get down on my hands and knees and crawl backwards down the few stairs. I did that, and at the bottom of the stairs, I found both the venue security and my friends watching on. I gave my friend's girlfriend back her purse and arm in arm she walked me back up the same few stairs. The hippies cheered on as I walked the few feet back to them. I was proud to introduce my friends to everyone. Altogether, the hippies, the monkeys, my friends, and I, danced through the rest of the concert.

Chapter 15
Tending the Rabbits

93X Fest 2000 T-shirt.

OK, back to touring. The third show on the tour was in Somerset, Wisconsin. I had been on the road for four days and this was the first show where we got schwag. There would be plenty more to come, but getting schwag this day meant that I was able to wear a black T-shirt on stage. That was a big deal. STP toured with a skeleton crew for the first couple weeks of the tour and we all fit on one bus. Because it was such a small crew, and a well-known band, the local stagehands expected me to be a veteran. I learned that if I kept quiet, I could pretend that I knew what I was doing. Looking the part now, with my black T-shirt, also didn't hurt. Each city did have locals that knew what they were doing. I'd let those guys do the work while I'd pretend that I was sorting out other things, which a veteran for sure would need to be doing. I'd then watch them at the same time. It wasn't that I didn't want to do the work, I was just green, and no one was teaching me. So, I watched everyone and began to teach myself as I went along. If I asked a dumb question that I should have known the answer to, what did I care? I'd be in a different city the next day. I'd probably never see the guy again anyway. Using this strategy, I was learning quickly. Each day I could do more of what my job entailed confidently.

Somerset, Wisconsin may not seem like an exciting place to venture, but for me it ended up being just that. Having a couple shows under my belt I felt like I knew what was in store each day now. The first two shows had been in New York and Las Vegas. If you had to pick a place in the United States for being the most unlike NYC or Las Vegas, it might be Somerset, Wisconsin. There really is nothing there; it's a farming community.

Nigel and I began to set up the stage in the morning and split the local stagehands into groups. The guys working the show were drinking beers at 7:00 a.m. during load in. Load in is where we unload all the trucks and start to get the stage set up. Load out is where we break down the stage and load up all the trucks to leave. The stagehands at the venue all looked like they hadn't bathed in weeks. The beers were to nurse the hangover-from the night before-of course, a little hair of the dog. What had surprised me, and what I had recently learned, was roadies didn't drink during work hours. At least the ones I had met so far didn't. After work, or when you are not required to be on call, we could do whatever we wanted. I really mean whatever you wanted. No one cared.

I was assigned these two guys to help me get all the lighting set up. They were both hard workers and were excited STP was playing there that night. One of the guys couldn't be more like Lennie Small from John Steinbeck's *Of Mice and Men*. He was even introduced as being, "strong as fuck but not all that bright." This dude was indeed incredibly strong and sure enough, he absolutely wasn't very bright. I had already started establishing how I would be as a roadie, a quiet person who mostly kept to himself. I had no clue what I was doing and found that if I kept quiet and worked hard, I may just keep my job. Someone had to bark out orders though and that guy was

Nigel. Nigel had a heavy English accent. While I was born in England, I kept quiet enough to where it was hard to pinpoint if I was from the United States, England, or anywhere else for that matter.

93X Fest 2000 all access pass.

The brighter of the two men, we will call him George, was trying to make up conversation. "Where you guys from?", asked George. Nigel had been asked this many times and knew in places like Somerset, Wisconsin there wasn't much point in getting into too many details. In the heaviest American accent, he could muster up he said, "I'm from Iowa."

"Oh, I have some family in Iowa," replied George. "He's not from Iowa, George. He's from England," I interrupted. George swung around to look at me. "Oh, yeah-that's not around here, huh. I never heard of it," he said to me. "No, it's not around here, George," I said bluntly. I thought at this point the conversation would be over. But Nigel felt compelled to spurt out "oh, you know Joel here is a Jew." Both of them stopped working and in unison with another couple locals stared at me. Nigel was giggling hysterically.

What were they going to do to me? They just kept staring. George finally said something after what seemed like twenty minutes. "Where's his horns?" he asked Nigel. They had never seen a Jew before. That day, all day, I was a celebrity. The local stagehands couldn't believe they had met a Jew. It was a big day for everybody.

From then on when we were with any backwoods type characters, Nigel would take great pleasure in asking me, "are we speaking in code names today?" This was Nigel's personal homage to the movie *Raising Arizona* and he greatly enjoyed the reference.

The show that night was awesome. The band kicked ass and the audience loved it. When we were done loading out, we were invited to go to the local BBQ. They had set up a huge fire that we could see in the distance and they were presumably going to party all night. I apologized to them that we were off to the next venue and couldn't stop by. I was starting to get the hang of things. It was a good thing too. Over the next 36 days we would do a total of 24 shows. That may seem like a regular routine for some, but it was to be the hardest I've ever worked in my life.

Chapter 16
Fuck You Nigel

So much was going through my head, all while just trying to keep up with everyone. I hoped I wouldn't get fired from this great experience. Would anyone hire me after STP finished touring? Would the band fire me when they figured out, that I didn't know how to fix anything? They had labeled me as the tour carpenter. I had never hammered anything in my life. Would I get to witness road debauchery firsthand? Would my friends now be a bunch of rock stars? I didn't know the answer to any of the questions.

WBCN 104.1 FM River Rave 2000 artist pass.

The fourth show I worked was in Massachusetts. The line-up was Cypress Hill, Everclear, Filter, Godsmack, and STP. We would do a lot of shows with all these bands. Nigel had worked for Everclear in the past and knew the band well. Always eager to share stories about what an asshole he was, he told me a story where years earlier he and another roadie, Tootsie, who was also on tour with us, had taken a limo meant for the band. The limo pulled up to the gig and the driver asked if they were Everclear. Nigel thought about it and replied, "yes." They hopped in the limo and drove back to the hotel. The actual band had to take the crew van. In the music industry when you mess with someone like this, it's called a "wind up." Roadies love wind up's. It's what gets us up in the morning. Or the afternoon if it's a day off and we are hungover.

Nigel didn't watch Everclear play that day because he was a fan. He watched them in hopes that they would note him standing there and think of him when they needed to hire a lighting designer again. He watched on trying to look cool as Everclear performed. As their set ended each member of the band walked off the stage, and each one looked at Nigel as he had hoped they would. Each said the same thing: "fuck you, Nigel." Musicians are such a friendly sort. When they had all left the stage I turned to Nigel. "I think that went well. Think they will hire you?" Nigel rolled his eyes at me and left the stage. I pulled the stagehands together and we all started the set change. A set change is where one band leaves the stage and the next one comes on.

Chapter 17
The Case of The Missing Case

HFStival 2000 FedExField artist pass and gig shirts.

The fifth show was a bit different- STP was co-headlining with Rage Against the Machine at the HFStival. I love Rage. Their self-titled first album was released in 1992. I was a freshman in high school. By my junior year I was listening to them all the time. I too was tired of the system. Required to sit in the classroom for hours every day, I felt like a prisoner. I hated it. Counting out the days of my prison sentence Zack's words struck me. He was spitting out poetry and all of it was what I felt too. When I was 19-20 years old, I'd go to Lake Havasu regularly and party with all my friends. I remember seeing a bunch of white guys covered with swastika tattoos on a boat listening to Rage Against the Machine with a confederate flag overhead. The message of Rage struck a nerve with me once again. People filled with hate are always so ignorant. While I don't deny they were feeling misplaced energy behind the music, they clearly weren't paying attention to the message itself. That event placed a whole new resurgence of Rage in my life. The band's music had really made an impact on my youth.

The show that night was in Maryland; I knew it was going to be awesome. After seeing STP perform a few times now I realized they were good, really good. Scott was not just a singer from a band but a true rock star. Scott could control thousands of people with every movement of his body. The stage was his home. He would literally jump onto the stage, bullhorn in hand, and we would witness magic. I saw a man filled with energy, anger, emotion, and brilliant fluidity as he moved from one side of the stage to the other. I wondered, who were these guys I was working for and how did they get to be this good? I was mesmerized by all of it. I was constantly tired, yet living in a dream. Third Eye Blind played, Staind, Filter, Godsmack, Slipknot, The Deftones, Cypress Hill… The bands came on and off the stage one by one. Last up was the Blue Man Group. I wasn't quite sure how these guys would fit in. I didn't think it was quite their audience but what did I know. I was new at this.

Unfortunately, the Blue Man Group was not what the audience had been waiting for. They were pelted over and over again with soda cans and anything else the audience could get their hands on to throw. Yet their show continued. The Blue Man Group guys completed their entire set and walked off the stage, all bleeding. They left the stage looking more like the red man group. The clean up on the stage began immediately, and apart from a few more things landing on the stage here and there nothing else was thrown. The audience had spoken, and I felt bad for those blue fellas.

I stood by and waited to do what I was told. STP was up next. I knew how to get my gear set up now and I was starting to be able to ignore the audience to get my job done. It's a bit of a mind fuck when you are 23 years old and people are getting hammered and showing their tits all around you. Boobs vs. set up the stage so it looks good? It's a hard decision for a young guy, trust me.

Finally, STP went on. By now it was now dark, and the crowd was amped from having seen Godsmack and the other bands perform. Scott ran out on stage, screaming through his bullhorn, and the party began. This was the first show that was really huge. The shows I had worked before had thousands of people in attendance, but this show had upwards of 90 thousand.

All the bands lined the stage to watch STP perform. I didn't need to ask why all the other performers stood by and watched STP. It was because I now knew it was a privilege to watch them perform; they were that good. The show ended and I jumped to my job. I now knew to clear the stage as fast as possible and get all the gear in the road cases. I filled the road cases and sent them off to the trucks with the local stagehands. Nigel stayed in the truck and accepted the cases as they came. He was fast at loading the truck, he had done it for years. If I sent the cases off to the trucks fast enough maybe Cesar Reivax, the production manager of the tour, would let me watch Rage a bit before leaving for the next gig. It all sounded good, but I soon found myself in a predicament. When loading a truck, you write down and memorize a pack. Three cases fit across the back, then you load five on top of those three, etc. Well one of the cases never made it back to the STP truck. In between

Nigel and I, it had disappeared somewhere. I was bummed I wasn't going to get to see Rage perform. I was going to have to find out what the stagehand had done with the road case.

I looked and looked but couldn't find it anywhere. What if someone stole it? While I knew I had a major problem on my hands, I was irresponsibly focusing on other things. The stage was massive. I could sense Rage commanded a real crew presence. Their crew was a step above what I had been seeing all week from the roadies who worked for other acts. The security for Rage had locked down the stage for real. I knew the box wasn't going to be on the stage because I had seen the stagehand roll it towards the trucks. However, if they were going to fire me, I wasn't going to say I had got fired and had never seen Rage perform.

The problem I faced was the stage manager for Rage wouldn't let me on the stage. So, I resorted to what any new roadie would do. I begged the guy. "Look, man, I can't find a whole road case. The trucks are ready to leave, and I really have to check to see if it was left up here. I'm probably going to get fired over this," I whined. The stage manager reluctantly let me up. I walked to the back of the stage where the cases were lined up. There were dozens upon dozens of them. It was clear that they were all road cases for Rage and none of them were mine. A black scrim hung at the back of the stage but in front of me. In front of it was a massive audience waiting for the final performance of the night. And, more notably the culmination of one of the best band lineups they would ever see at any music festival.

The stage in front of the scrim was black and empty. I sat down on a random road case to take a brief moment to myself. Not knowing what would happen if I didn't find the lost road case, it might be my last opportunity to be a part of something like this. As I sat down, strobe lights criss crossed and through the scrim I saw Zack. Well, to be specific I saw his profile. I watched on as he cocked his head back. His dreads falling behind him, he picked the mic up high. And as he did so, he screamed the opening line to the song, "Bulls on Parade."

I saw spit, but I felt the words, "Come with it now" resonate through me. Life's fury and angsts were heard through the almost one hundred thousand people all screaming the same thing as I was. But out of all those people only one person saw Zack as I did that night. That poetic glimpse of what makes music magic will forever be engrained in my head. The mental snapshot should one day be an album cover. It was beautiful. I sat for but a few more seconds relishing the personal moment I had just had with rock royalty. But I knew I was overstaying my welcome. I had to find that road case or I would never be seeing another show again. I rushed off the stage and thanked the stage manager for letting me look. I was happy.

Roadie Ramble Moment

It's hard not to think of bull riding when hearing the song "Bulls on Parade." Let's discuss the origins of bull fighting. In Spain bull fighting has been a tradition since 711 A.D. Between the fighting of the bulls and the running of the bulls, Spain loves messing with bulls. While traditional bull riding found its origins in Mexico, it is important to note that informal rodeos began as competitions between neighboring ranches in the American old west. I can only assume that when the Spaniards found out the Americas were riding the bulls and not just running and spearing them, they must have shaken their heads and said in disbelief "Los Americanos es pinche loco." America's response I'm sure was, "Well, Yee Haw, Los Espanoles!"

I walked up the concrete driveway back to the trucks hiding a grin. My life was awesome. What was happening was unreal. My dad was crazy as hell but how he managed to hook me up with this gig made it all OK. Nigel was waiting at the top of the ramp. He wasn't happy. "Cesar is on the bus and wants to talk to you." I hung my head low knowing this wasn't going to be good. Cesar was not just my boss but everyone's boss. He was big in all senses of the word. Big personality, big guy, and for me the head honcho. He weighed close to, if not over, four hundred and fifty pounds, was at least six foot eight inches tall, and hailed from both New York City and Brazil. He was scary as fuck. He had toured with Queen to Def Leppard. He was the best a band could hire, the top of the food chain. He was a roadie God. He knew everything about the industry. He had grown up in it. He both commanded, and deserved, the respect of every guy out there. Fortunately, or unfortunately, he was the guy I had to answer to on my first tour and he took no shit. As I got on the bus, I could still hear Rage Against the Machine performing in the background and I was bummed I was missing it. I should have instead been bummed I couldn't find the road case and I knew it.

As I walked up the steps to the front lounge, the crew all walked out of the bus past me. I wondered if everyone got off so there would be no witnesses to Cesar killing me. Cesar sat in the front lounge waiting for me. "Sit the fuck down," he said. I did. I could see the guys outside the bus chatting and joking around. They knew I was going to get reamed. I was wondering if they were laughing because they all knew I was going to get fired too. I had been on the road for only eight days, but I had already learned no one fights for you. You must be independent and resourceful. A lot of these guys don't care about themselves. Why would they care about you?

"Where's my case?" Cesar asked. I looked firmly at him. "I told the stagehand guy to roll it to the far truck on the left where Nigel was," I said. "Oh, yeah? Who's that guy?" Cesar said now, leaning forward. "I think his name was Robert. I know what he looks like," I replied hopefully. "What state are we in?" asked Cesar. I had to think about it. I understood. I didn't know who any of these people were. I honestly wasn't totally sure what state we were in either. "Look out the window. All these guys, this is what we fucking do for a living. This is our career." I said nothing. "I'm never giving you a second chance. Get out of my fucking sight!" I got up and walked to the door of the bus. I stopped and looked at Cesar. "I won't make a mistake again, sir," He didn't reply. I meant it. Everybody got back on the bus. No one looked at me or said anything and I realized they were all indifferent as to whether I stayed or left.

Chapter 18
De Niro's Poop Chute

The bus we had was an older bus. It was probably from the early 1990's. The driver was a little Texan guy named Hobo. Most of the bus drivers on the road don't talk a lot. They keep to themselves, focus on keeping the bus clean, and drive through the night to get us to the next gig in the morning. It's really a lonely job. Hobo was a bit different. He talked a lot, loved rodeo, was super homophobic, and always wore cowboy boots.

I think if I was to take a poll, most people would think that a tour bus is a full-on party zone. While I've been on buses where we did indeed party pretty hard, it's usually not that way. More often you will find there are drugs everywhere, random girls from who knows what city, a wide variety of the shittiest alcohol, various farm animals, and of course no bus is complete without an improvised disco ball. So, for the most part it is actually a pretty quiet place.

Before anyone enters a tour bus, they should know the tour bus rules. When on the road the only place you have to call your own space is your bunk. The only places you have to store your stuff is in your suitcase, which goes under the bus, or your bunk. It is a major no, no for anyone to ever go into anyone else's bunk. Everyone needs a little space to call their own. A bunk truly is that little space.

Next rule: there is no pooping on the bus. If you have to crap you tell the driver and they find a stop. The driver does not want to have to clean the bus lines. With all that being said Robert De Niro came to one of our shows and used the bathroom on the bus. Every roadie knows to tell anyone coming on the bus the bus rules. But who is going to tell De Niro he can't crap on the bus? Long story short, Robert De Niro is the only person that I am aware of who has pooped on a tour bus. I'm sure there are others out there, but no one else has made it out alive.

By the time I would get on the bus after the show, I was wiped out. Every night we'd have pizza as after show food. I mentioned that earlier. I'm still not a fan of pizza. Because of being a roadie, I've eaten more pizza than anyone should have to in their life. I'd heat up a slice or two, eat it, wash my hands and face, and go to sleep, all in no particular order.

I was always the last to finish working. By the time I got on the bus the rest of the crew were either sleeping or watching The Crocodile Hunter in either the front or back lounge or sometimes both. The Crocodile Hunter was a pretty big hit on the STP crew bus. They had all showered and eaten by the time I got on the bus. We'd all have to shower at the venue, but I often didn't have time to do so. By the time I was done working most of the venue was quiet, many had gone home for the day, the trucks were gone, and the bus was ready to leave. As soon as my foot hit the steps to get on the bus, the driver would start driving. Roughly six hours later, I'd be up to do it all over again.

What I liked about this older bus was that we each had little windows in our bunks. The newer buses didn't have any windows in the bunks for some reason. Sometimes the next gig would be a long drive and I would fade in and out of self-inflicted consciousness, i.e. sleep, looking out my little window while watching America pass by. I slept great in my little cubby hole. The bunks had a power jack, and I would listen to whatever CD I had purchased on our last day off through earphones. We travelled all over the United States and I saw a lot. I loved seeing the wildlife, the thousands of miles of prairie, the desert cactus, or the deep woods. On America's highways there is often a bit of space between the highway and the woods. Just enough space to park a car and walk into the woods. My mind would wander, and I'd wonder how many dead bodies were deep in those woods sometimes, or what treasures were buried in those deserts. Less reflective times, I'd write poems and just relax. I was always tired. It's easy to relax when you are exhausted.

On the night of the Rage Against the Machine show, I had a lot to think about. I looked out my little portal to the world and knew I wasn't ready to go home yet. I would not get a second chance. Cesar had made that clear. I had made a mistake and Cesar was either going to end my story now for me or I'd have to pull my shit together. I had been thinking quite a bit about my friends back home and how cool it would be if any of them could have been out there with me experiencing even a part of all of this. I wanted my friends to see just how amazing touring the country was. I knew I'd have to stop that and focus 100% on my job to make this work. I went to sleep with a new personal goal that I would not screw up again. I did, a lot, but never again was it because of any lack of focus on my job.

Chapter 19
Case of the Missing Case, Solved at a Church Gig. Praise the Lord!

X-Fest 2000 Star Lake all access pass.

The next day we arrived at the Post-Gazette Pavilion in Pennsylvania. I found out before the show they had found the lost road case. It was going to cost the band $1500 to get it to the next gig in Atlanta. STP played Pennsylvania a few lights short that night. I felt awful not only because the band had to pay a bunch of money to get the case back, but because their stage show wasn't complete because of me. Still, no one ever brought it up to me again.

On May 31st STP played at the Tabernacle in Atlanta, Georgia. The Tabernacle had been a Baptist church for almost 100 years. In 1994 a group of investors purchased the building in hopes of making it an entertainment venue for the 1996 Atlanta Olympic Games. That never happened and they turned it into a House of Blues. It's changed hands a few times now, but it has been a concert venue ever since. It's a great place to see a show. It only sits 2600 people and it was the smallest venue I had worked to date. Cesar lived in Atlanta and I think he was happy to be home. I would find that night, in a mid-sized venue, STP was even better. The audience was just as loud, but in an intimate room you could feel the music through the marrow of your very bones. I got goosebumps!

It made me feel good to look at audiences from around the country and to see people happy. I loved the smiles and all the people loving life. It was a lot better feeling than ripping people off on a telephone. I was now part of something special. I wasn't in the band, but I was absolutely part of the ensemble. The stage setup and my new found attention to detail were undoubtedly making for great and memorable performances. The shows weren't great for just the audiences, but also for me. I honestly felt like the music was helping us all grow collectively as one. It was like listening in on a Churchill fireside chat, dissecting a Martin Luther King speech, or watching the Rolling Stones on one of their first tours.

Scott Weiland had a well-publicized drug problem. I had been told that in the past he would always go off on a bender and the tour would be over. With that in mind, I knew each performance was something to savor. I wasn't sure if it would be their last. I think the audience had the same feelings as I. At the Tabernacle that night 2,601 people bowed down to Scott Weiland and STP. If you didn't catch on to that, I was that one extra person.

All access Oklahoma City All Sports Stadium pass, 2000.

The next shows were in Oklahoma, Iowa, and Kansas. 311 joined the lineup somewhere in the jumble. I can't quite remember which show. What I do remember is I now had my feet wet. I felt a lot more comfortable with what my job encompassed. I had worked a total of ten shows, but it felt like I had been at it for months. It was all a mixture of hard work and excitement. At this point in the tour, Cesar was acting as the stage manager. I stood by him most of the time and tried continuously to take mental notes. I learned that first and foremost it was important to keep the flow going- to keep the bands coming on, and going off, the stage on time and to keep the set changes quick and methodical.

While in Iowa one of the bands had left all their cases on the loading dock. I went over to the roadie responsible and told him that all the cases had to be moved off the stage. He nodded at me. I went back and stood next to Cesar. A song later, the guy still hadn't moved a single road case. I walked back over to the guy. "Hey, man. I told you- you need to clear the stage," he nodded acknowledgment again. I turned around to make sure Cesar was there and saw that Nigel was now standing next to Cesar as well. The moment was right to make a statement.

"Maybe I didn't make myself clear. Clean the fucking stage, or I'm going to start pushing your cases off of it." The guy threw his arms up in the air but didn't say anything to me. He started clearing his cases off the stage. Neither Nigel nor Cesar said anything, but I knew very well I had made a good move. I think stepping up that day was the defining moment Cesar decided to start grooming me to climb the roadie ladder. When I walked into the bus later, Nigel was telling the crew what I had done. Everyone was impressed with my newfound tough guy act.

Rock Fest 2000 The Rock! 98.9 FM all access pass.

Now a tough guy, the next night, while in Kansas, one of the bands kept playing when it was time for them to get off the stage. Calmly, and not aggressively, I walked over to the singer and swiped the mic out of his hand. The band did nothing about it. They walked off the stage, and we started the set change. I was getting the hang of all this. Soon enough I could help Cesar more. I walked over to talk to him. "You know, Cesar, I think I'm the kind of guy who works better with his head than with his hands," I said to him. My intention was to make it clear I wanted to be a hands-off guy as soon as possible and run the show like he did. Cesar laughed loudly in my face. "Get your fuckin' ass back to work." Our conversation about my immediate advancement was over in less than two seconds. Still smiling, I went back to working with my hands.

K-ROCK 93.3 K-Rockfest 2000 artist pass.

After the above three festivals, we played at the State Palace Theatre in New Orleans. The venue was constructed in 1926 for the Loew's theatre circuit. The building was hypnotic. I say that because when packed at capacity, the floors above would literally bend as people jumped up and down. The building itself was like watching a crowd do the wave at a baseball game. I couldn't imagine seeing a show so good the building itself partook. Now that's Rock 'n' Roll! I spent the whole show wondering if I was going to be buried alive with the band in the place. I've been told the building was destroyed in Hurricane Katrina. There are plans to renovate it, and I really hope they do. It's one of America's greatest venues.

Roadie Ramble Moment

Why can't we be buried in the same grave? There is no need to be selfish about space once dead. Instead of digging the hole six feet deep what about digging it ten feet so you chuck a couple people in there? You can then put one person in the hole and when the next one pops off use the same plot. I figure that is romantic and would save a bunch of space and money. Just something to think about while home eating Cheetos.

Chapter 20
Who's the Best Looking 12-year-old in Sacramento?

Show poster for June 8th Aerial Theater.

From Louisiana we headed into the state of Texas. I was excited about Texas. I was looking forward to some Texas BBQ. STP played first in Dallas and then in Houston. While in Dallas, I got my first fan club member. Maybe because she was the only fan club member, she'd actually be more like the fan club president. The doors had just opened and sure enough towards the front row was a young lady with a cardboard sign that read, "I love Rifken." She wasn't the best-looking girl, I'd ever seen but if her intent was to start a trend, this could be good. I laughed and went backstage to tell everyone. Who was Rifken? Well, that was me and I'll tell you how I got the nickname a bit later.

While waiting for food, all the guys on the crew were telling the personnel they were vegetarian. I knew these guys weren't vegetarian, so I was wondering what was going on. Texas is famous for their BBQ. When I got up to the food lady, I figured it out. All the meat was out on the table. There were flies everywhere. I smiled and told the lady I too was a vegetarian.

Throughout the show the girl with the sign popped up and down in the audience. Everyone, including the band, took note. Sure enough, when we got to Houston just before the band went on, I saw the girl again with the same sign. I looked out to see if she had a friend with her this time, but she didn't, and so I focused on my work. It didn't seem like I would be having that fan club after all.

From Texas we cruised to my state, California, and played in Sacramento. When we pulled up to the hotel, the lobby was a madhouse. A beauty pageant was being held there. Now this may sound like the perfect ingredients for a debaucherously good time, but it was one of those beauty pageants for little girls. I walked through lots of little girls wearing way too much makeup and made my way into an elevator. Crammed into the back, I was the only guy amongst overweight women and made up little doll figures. I was happy when I got to my room. Once there, the phone rang. The woman on the other end informed me she was the woman holding up the sign in Texas. I didn't waste any time *informing* her that though I was charmed, I was married. "Well, I'm already here and I look very forward to seeing you," she said. Unhappy about it now, I mumbled something and hung up.

I took a shower, wrote my room number on my hand with a Sharpie, and went back down to the lobby to meet up with everyone and get some food. I had gotten into the habit of writing my room number on my hand. With all the hotels we stayed at, it was easier for me than trying to remember my room number each time. If I went out and got too drunk, I could find my way back home. Everyone else found this practice amusing. I found it useful. When I got to the lobby it was still a madhouse, but now it was filled with 17-year-old girls.

A circle of roadies sat in the lobby with big grins. We all left quickly, before any of us would get arrested.

From Sacramento we drove on to Mesa, Arizona. While in Mesa, I went out with the sound guy and the guitar tech. Other than a few nice dinners, this was the first time I'd gone out with the "guys." They had me pay for the taxi. I think that's why I got to go. I didn't mind, I was just glad to be invited out. We went by some guy's house and then the three of us went out to the bars. The sound guy had a girl he knew meet up with us with some of her girlfriends. With our new friends in tow, we all started drinking. They were all doing blow and I didn't know it. On STP there really weren't any drugs around. I honestly think a big reason they kept me around was because I didn't do any drugs. I sure knew it wasn't because I was good at the job. So, that's what made the most sense to me. The sound guy knew people all around the country who could get cocaine, Xanax, OxyContin, and Vicodin. Because of Scott's drug problems, if anyone wanted to smoke weed or do any blow, you had to keep it on the down low. For the most part the crew really didn't do any drugs. Because of the nature of the situation, these two didn't let me know that we stopped at the guy's house to buy an 8 ball of cocaine. I couldn't understand how they kept drinking as much as they did, and yet no one dropped. 2 am, 3 am, 4 am, 5 am.... Finally, at 5 am I called it a night. I got a taxi back to the hotel and crashed out. We had the next day off, and I slept most of the day. I didn't talk to anyone much. The following morning, we all met at the bus to go to the gig. Everyone but the sound guy was in the bus when I got on. He climbed aboard just as we were about to leave, which wasn't all that unusual. The unusual part was he had blood caked all over his chin. He looked like Alice Cooper. No one said a word to him. He sat down and started talking and talking. He had met this girl and had a great time. She would be around later. He had known her for years. He loved Arizona. Finally, the drum tech, Mugs, who was one of the more outgoing guys on the bus, said "Hey, what's that on your chin, Tampax?" Pax walked into the bathroom on the bus. "That fuckin' bitch. What the fuck?" were the next things we all heard out of the bathroom. Now, Tampax doesn't exactly roll off one's tongue, and so the nickname was soon abbreviated to being "Pax."

We all had our laugh at Pax's expense and then Mugs turned his attention to me. "Your lover call you again, Rif?" Not too happy about it, I replied. "Yeah, man." "What she say to you?" he said in a slow Bostonian drawl. "She asked me if I saw her. I told her I was busy working and didn't." Suzi piped up. "Maybe you should talk to her, Hot Lips. Maybe she's a nice girl."

Suzette, aka Suzi, handled the band's wardrobe. She was feisty, pretty, and I liked hanging out with her. If ranking her on the Gilligan's Island scale, I would say she leaned heavily towards being a Mary Ann. Even though everyone picks Mary Ann over Ginger, it's important to make note that Ginger was a hot babe. I think it's wrong to hate on Ginger. Anyhow, whether you like Ginger or Mary Ann, Suzi was most certainly a Mary Ann over a Ginger. She was a short brunette but stood tall when her fists were in the air. She worked hard at her job and was very good at it. She would make me do a bunch of stuff that I was finding really wasn't part of my job, but I ended up doing it anyhow because she was very persuasive. I felt her friendship comforting in a world filled with tough, we will say, misfits instead of assholes.

Mugs started laughing uncontrollably. "Hot Lips?" he asked me. "I'm gonna go lie down in my bunk," I said. I felt like screaming out to everyone like a little kid would. "Why can't my family just be normal?" and then stomp off to bed. Though it would have been funny, I knew that would result in more crap for me, so I just crawled into my bunk until we got to the venue. As I crawled into my bunk the front lounge erupted. "Hot Lips, Suzi?" asked Cesar laughing.

Chapter 21
Is a Place Called the "Weenie Roast" a Good Spot to Meet a Groupie?

After Arizona we headed back into California. On June 14th I was back in Santa Barbara. The Santa Barbara bowl is a gorgeous venue. It was awesome to be back in my college town. It's where I had been to the only concert I had attended while not a roadie. My little sister, who was still in high school, drove up with Nigel's wife. I perched her up on the stage and she got to watch the whole show from the sides. It was awesome because she was literally, other than the crew, the only person up on the stage. At the end of the night, I got a call in my hotel room from the girl with the sign. "Did you see me tonight?" she asked. "No, and I really can't talk to you. I'm sorry," I said, hanging up the phone. How was this girl getting all my information?

Live 105 BFD Shoreline Amphitheatre artist pass, 2000.

We would do four total dates in California before heading back to the east coast. At Shoreline Amphitheatre, in Mountain View, a few more bands were added to the bill. Along with Everclear, Godsmack, Incubus, and Third Eye Blind, we played with Limp Bizkit, Moby, Slipknot, and the Offspring. It was a good show for sure.

KROQ 106.7 Weenie Roast 2000 performer pass.

At the KROQ Weenie Roast they added Creed, Korn, Ozzy Osbourne, and Black Sabbath to the bill. I loved Korn and Ozzy so I knew the show would be a good one. At the Weenie Roast I wasn't allowed to hang any backdrops. The bands stood on a 360-degree revolving stage. It was designed so that we could set up our gear on the back of the revolving stage while the band scheduled to play before did just that on the front of it. Just before the band went on, I took part of our Mylar backdrop and threw it over the stage divider. It was the best I could do. No Doubt went on just before STP and I got to meet Suzi's husband Adrian, the drummer of No Doubt. The two had been married just a few months earlier. Suzi didn't really need to work for STP. She did what she did because she wanted to. She was very good at it though. Everyone in the band watched over her, including me. If anyone ever messed with Suzi, and I don't think anyone ever did, you'd have to deal with all of us. She was everyone's sister and my road mom.

Every band has at least a couple wardrobe cases where they keep their show crap. Scott wore a lot of women's clothes on stage. He had two road cases of outfits for the shows. Suzi would wait on the side of the stage and grab Scott's clothes as he would strip down during the show. After losing the road case I was determined to make sure nothing belonging to the band was lost again. I started grabbing Scott's clothes so Suzi wouldn't have to worry about doing it. I was also responsible for getting Suzi's wardrobe cases to and from her before and after the gigs. A lot of times the wardrobe people have to get their cases out to the trucks themselves. She of course didn't do that.

In addition, during the band's acoustic part of the show I would hang hundreds of strands of Christmas lights. They looked great, but it was time consuming, and I hated it. Christmas lights are not made to be put up and taken down every single day. I devised tactics to make them last longer, like rolling them on big sticks. This kept them from tangling up, but they still broke. Try getting new strands of Christmas lights during June. I would trade tickets to store employees all over the country if they could find me Christmas lights in the store's storage. Suzi used to hang sarongs from the roofs of the dressing rooms. It made for a harem vibe. She did it because she said the band liked it. To compliment the sarongs, she had also taken a liking to me hanging Christmas lights in the dressing room. I already had a lot of work but found myself doing as she told me. I was known by everyone as the Christmas light tech. By the end of working with STP, the only thing more than pizza I was sick of was Christmas lights. I never wanted to see a Christmas light again.

Suzi always called me "Hot Lips." It was my first roadie nickname and it didn't make me sound very masculine. It didn't stick, as no one in the world calls me that but her. I still have no idea why she started calling me Hot Lips, but she still does. At one of the shows I was having a rough day and had cut my finger open. When she hit me up, over the walkie talkie, that she needed the Christmas lights hung, I had full intention of going down to the dressing room and telling her that she would have to hang the damn lights in the dressing room herself if she wanted them up. I saw her at the door of the dressing room and told her that I just didn't have time to hang Christmas lights anymore.

"Oh my God, Hot Lips. What did you do to your finger?" she asked. "I cut It." Suzi bandaged up my finger with Neosporin in front of the band. When it was all wrapped up, she looked at me and said, "OK, all done. Now go get my fucking Christmas lights and hang them." The band loved it. After that day I solidified myself in their eyes as a giant weenie. I didn't care. I had a fixed finger and a kickass road mommy. "Now how's your girlfriend?" she asked me. "She doesn't call anymore." Suzi changed her voice to sound like the sign holder girl on the phone. My whole demeanor changed. I really had no idea it had been her the whole time. I didn't know Suzi had it in her to be so cunning. "Oh my God. It was you?" I asked in shock. Suzi smiled widely. "I was wondering how she knew where I stayed, dude. Very tricky, Suzi. Very tricky…" I laughed. "Women are much better at wind up's, Hot Lips," she said. I now believed her.

Chapter 22
Chalong and the Weenie Roast

The security at the Weenie Roast was intense. They kicked everyone off the stage. They didn't care who you were. They even kicked off Dennis Rodman and Carmen Elektra. Trying to keep them around, I told the security that they could both stay on the stage if they wanted to, but the security guy gave me a dirty look and told them that they had to get off the stage. Rodman told the security dude, "hey, man- listen to the little white boy," I smiled and nodded. He was talking about me! I thought what he said was hilarious. Isn't everyone little to Rodman? I was excited to be acknowledged by him. However, it didn't work. They kicked them off the stage. I can't think of another gig I've ever done, where I couldn't keep whomever I wanted around. However, they were gung-ho about booting everyone. The show itself was awesome. The testosterone at the event was unparalleled. STP, Korn, Ozzy Osbourne, Black Sabbath, Slipknot, Godsmack... Come on, beat that line up!

After the Weenie Roast, we played at Del Mar and I got the first couple days off at home since the beginning of the tour. It was nice to have finished the first leg so close to Los Angeles. The band had a rider, a wish list the band asked the promotors for at each show, but no one had updated it since their last tour. On the rider were cases of Yoo-hoo and beer that no one drank. The bottom of the bus was loaded with all this stuff. I had taken quite the liking to Yoo-hoo and was drinking a heck of a lot of it. After Del Mar I loaded up Nigel's truck with schwag. I took 20 cases of beer, three cases of Yoo-hoo, and dozens of T-shirts. No one on the crew cared about the show shirts. They already had lots from previous tours. I couldn't get enough of them. I hadn't done a previous tour.

While at home Nigel came by every day to see my dad. So

much for a break from the guy. My father was glad to see me back. When I got home, on my bed was a CD and a press kit of a young Asian girl. I brought the stuff downstairs to the garage. "Hey, Dad, what's this all about?" I asked. "It's Chalong's daughter. I told him you'd get her a job singing with the band you're working for- the Rock Pilots." I knew better than to even engage in a conversation with him regarding any of what he was talking about. "Ask Nigel, Dad. They don't care about me. Nigel can help you."

Chalong was a local mechanic who would come over to use my dad's prized head surfacing machine. He was from Thailand and his English was terrible. He would buy lots of cars with blown motors. He'd then rebuild the motors and sell the cars.

We had three nights off and during that time I went through a lot of cases of beer with my friends. It was nice to be home, but I was ready to get back out on the road as soon as I stepped onto my parent's front doorstep. I was thinking that I may just be fit to be a roadie lifer. I liked what I was doing.

Everyone I knew got an STP shirt when I got home. My little sister decided to cut up a bunch of them to make tight fitting girl shirts and started selling them at school. The band didn't know it, but they had a steadily increasing fan club in the San Fernando Valley.

Chapter 23
The Princess of Darkness

K-Rock Dysfunctional Family Picnic crew pass.

The next show was June 23rd and we were back on the East Coast in New Jersey. STP was playing the Dysfunctional Family Picnic. I had gotten into the habit of practicing on one of Dean's guitars every day. If either Dean or the guitar tech were around, they would give me a quick guitar lesson. It was a fun way to break up the day a bit when things were slow. It had also got me to stop biting my fingernails. It was easier to try and play with them. Not to mention, it was gross to be biting them with all the grime underneath from working on the stage anyhow. On this day Cesar walked by me while I was trying to play a Neil Young song. "How are things going?" he asked me. "OK, man. Need anything?" I replied. "Guitar playing going well?" he continued on. I could sense something was wrong. I put the guitar back on the stand. "No, no take your time. Wouldn't want to bother you." The message was clear. No one wanted to see me with nothing better to do than practicing playing a guitar. If I was on the road, I should be working. If I wasn't working, I should not be in plain sight for everyone else to see. That was it. I never did learn how to play.

That night, Black Sabbath again graced the stage and of course kicked ass, but before that a lot happened earlier in the day. In between acts there was a midget wedding, which was kind of fun. Seeing Pauly Shore again, I figured he must be hanging out and touring with Limp Bizkit. I had seen him at a few of their shows now. I liked his movies and found him to be a chill guy. He basically spent all day picking up women. Not a bad way to spend a summer. For lunch I sat with Howard Stern and his two daughters. I would come to learn that both Stern and Ozzy Osbourne were big fans of STP. At many of these radio shows the people on stage would watch the bands from bleachers that had been set up by the venue. There would be many times where I saw both Howard and Ozzy watch the band from the side of the stage. It never got old to see very cool people as the band's fan base. When I'd see Ozzy sitting on the bleachers, he would always sit front row and not move. He sat so still, I wondered if he was asleep sitting up. I was certain that under those black sunglasses, the guy never blinked.

Watching Ozzy perform always amused me. He's blind as a bat. We would tape a square on the stage at every show with about a foot of neon tape at each side. Ozzy knew that as long as he stayed in that space, he was safe. So, he would just walk back and forth in the square. Before every performance Sharon would have to drag him out to the stage. "Do it for the children Ozzy," she'd say. "I don't give a fuck about the children," he'd bark back, and then he'd go out and perform. It was always the same. My favorite Ozzy fun fact was that we were told not to leave out any type of pills, because regardless of what they were, Ozzy would eat them. I loved the guy. It was all just too good to make up.

When Limp Bizkit was scheduled to be on the stage Fred Durst was nowhere to be seen. He had called in and said his limo was stuck in traffic. Standing next to Sharon Osbourne, I overheard someone tell her that Fred was actually waiting just outside the venue. He didn't want to go on stage until it got dark. While it's true a show is much better at night, if Fred didn't go on as scheduled, the other acts would lose performance time. The venue's had curfews. So, I watched on wondering what was going to happen. It took about fifteen minutes, but as he wanted, Fred did go on stage just as it was getting dark. It seemed like his plan had worked. I figured the next couple of acts would just play one less song to get back on track time-wise. That isn't what happened though. Sharon stood by the power racks and watched the show from the side of the stage with us. Towards the end of Limp Bizkit's performance, she looked at her watch and then over to me. "Which one of these turns off the lights?" she asked. I pointed for her to ask our new lighting guy Aso. Aso immediately took her over to the power distro rack. "Great, turn it all off," she said. Aso didn't say a word and did as he was told. The stage soon went dark. Sharon smiled. "OK- time for set change. Don't plug that back in until they clear the stage. Thank you," she told us. Aso nodded in response and she walked away. Fred Durst stood in the middle of the stage wondering what had just happened. I think he figured it out pretty quick.

The Dysfunctional Family Picnic show was Aso's first show working with STP. He had previously toured with both the bands Garbage and the Cranberries. He was certainly a very good lighting technician. If asked to describe him, I would say I would consider it a compliment if I had overheard someone calling him a fat tub of shit. If you were to bear a child with down syndrome, you'd wonder what the rest of the sperm must have been like who didn't quite make it to the egg. Those underachieving sperm make me think of Aso. He was from upstate New York. He was scruffy and incredibly crass. I don't know if he was named Aso after the mountain in Japan, if the nickname was short for him just being an asshole, or if it was because he liked to show his asshole to everyone. However, his favorite thing in the world was to be naked when it was inappropriate. As ugly as he was, it was always inappropriate. He had brought with him an oversized shower brush and he'd try and take showers with it at every show. We all knew when he was showering because he'd love to sing loudly in the locker room.

Often there would be fans wandering around the venues, looking for the band after the show. We'd always direct them into the locker room where they would find Aso taking a shower. I think he enjoyed it as much as we all did.

It was nice not to have to work so hard at the lighting anymore. It wasn't just because I didn't know what I was doing, but also because Nigel had added on a lot more lights to the stage when Aso and our new rigger, Steve, came aboard. Important to me, one of the good things about Aso was he would go get drinks with me on our days off. We had nothing in common and usually didn't like one another much, but it sure was nice to grab a beer with someone on a day off.

Aso fit in immediately. His favorite pastimes included starting up trouble with Mugs and giving Hobo, our homophobic driver, a hard time, no pun intended. To wind Hobo up, he took great joy in bringing up the topic of being gay on a regular basis. For a time, Aso had also toured with a musical theater group as a roadie. He would intentionally provoke Hobo by continuously bringing it up. He made mention of it so often you'd think he was bragging about having toured with Led Zeppelin.

"Back when I was on that musical theater tour, I would hear all kinds of crazy stuff, Hobo. This one time we all got real drunk at a bar..." "I don't care, I don't want to hear it," Hobo interjected. Aso continued on "... and this one guy turned to the other guy, cause this cute fella was walking by, and he said 'I'd suck the shit outta that guys cock.' "Jesus Fucking Christ," Hobo barked out. Aso continued on, "Please don't take the Lord's name in vain. Anyhow, as I was saying, I've always wondered if he really meant he'd suck shit out of the guys cock, or if he was just saying it as slang. I've always regretted not asking him." I'll spare you the rest of the dialogue, but Hobo would then would rant about why gay people are not loved by God or whatever crap he believed. Hobo never missed STP perform but would undoubtedly always shake his head when Scott was dressed in full drag at the end of the show.

Mugs hailed from Boston. A big dude, he was the biggest guy on tour other than Cesar. You could count on him to throw a wise crack at you any time of the day. He had a dry way of telling a joke and he was consistently hilarious. My favorite stories were when he would bring up his one legged, hooker, neighbor. He had gotten mad at her and took a shit on the hood of her car one time. After that incident they somehow sorted out their problems and now got along well. I wondered if he had crushed the hood of her car. He weighed at least three hundred and fifty pounds. Mugs had also given me my nickname, Rifken. This is how that happened. It's not the most interesting story, but he was watching Seinfeld one day and an episode came on where Elaine's boyfriend's name was Joel Rifkin. Mugs started calling me Rifkin and the name stuck.

Joel Rifkin himself is a serial killer out of New York. I didn't like the name and I think that is why it spread like wildfire. I spelled it differently in defiance, but the nickname itself stuck. Maybe it's because roadies don't read and write, so they didn't care how I spelled it. My name would be Rifken forevermore. I would tell people, when asked, that the name was because I was quiet and wrote all the time. The guys would joke that I was like the Unabomber because I was a quiet, smart, asshole, plotting to destroy the world. But really it was just because of Elaine's boyfriend on the show. Everyone liked Mugs. If he couldn't get a laugh out of you, no one could. Most of the laughs were at my expense but they were funny, and I laughed along with everyone else. If he was the Skipper, I was absolutely his little buddy Gilligan.

Rigger Steve was the other new addition to the tour. It would be an injustice to not take a whole section to properly introduce him. So, we'll do that a bit later.

Chapter 24
Donald's Carpet Matched the Drapes

The next show up was at the Trump Marina. My job had changed quite a bit now. Having Aso around meant that I didn't have to worry about making sure the lights worked, a great relief. However, I still did the focus every day. I had been doing the focus myself for all the shows. When the rig goes up in the sky, all the par cans need to be later focused to points on the stage. This is what we call the "focus." The set up for our rig was simple. It was a stick at the front of the stage and a stick at the back. What that meant is we had just a few pieces of truss bolted together parallel on the front of the stage, and we had just a few pieces of truss bolted together parallel on the back of the stage. It was all simple. Off the back truss I would hang the backdrop. Just in front of that, I would hang the big white star. Throughout the show a video projected on the star.

STP backdrop color test swatch, 2000.

Nigel was very focused on speed. I think it was timing how fast we could put the show both up and take it down that kept the roadie part of the job fun. After a while all jobs become monotonous. Our goal was to finish as fast as possible so that we could go do whatever else we wanted to do with our days. For Nigel it was so he could go play *Starcraft*, a video game, on his computer. On occasion we'd be able to get a runner to take us out of the venue. Usually, we would just to go to shops and buy stuff. It was nice to get away from the venues. Once the stage was set up, I could often skip away for hours. I would either take a nap or go wander around. However, before the show started, I always made sure everything was safe and ready to go.

During load in we'd usually joke back and forth. That day Nigel used this time to remind me of what an asshole he was and how clueless my dad was. "Hey, Rifken, did you hear what your Dad told Chalong?" Nigel asked me. "I don't know if I want to know," I replied. "Your dad gave the CD back to him and told him his daughter was too fat," Nigel told me through tears of laughter. "Isn't the girl something like fourteen years old?" I asked. "Yeah," Nigel laughed even harder. "What the fuck?" I said. "I told him she was too fat, but I didn't think he was going to go and tell him that," he said. "Not cool man," I shook my head in disgust. "He now has her on a diet," Nigel replied while continuing to laugh away. He was having a hard time controlling himself. I think he peed a little.

The Trump Marina show was a good one. They left us a lot of schwag, T-shirts and hats, so I was a happy roadie. The band was to perform on a small stage inside the smallest room they had played at to date. This show was going to be loud. It didn't take long to set up, and then we went out to go have some fun. Nigel, Aso, and I had quickly become the three musketeers. None of us gambled, but we had a lot of fun cruising around Atlantic City. The band played to a very full room that night. I wondered how bad the carpet was going to look at the end of the show. At the end of the evening, my ears rang. They did after most shows, but that night they -rang loud. And the carpet... well, the carpet still looked the same. What I learned from the evening was that Trump makes quality carpet.

Chapter 25
Dudley Do-Right Meets a Fist Full of Felons

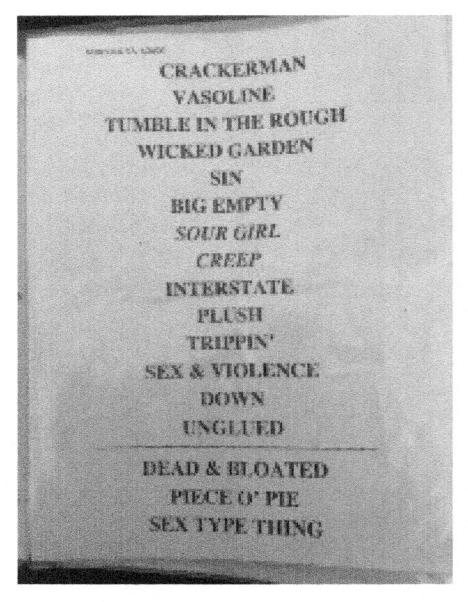

CRACKERMAN
VASOLINE
TUMBLE IN THE ROUGH
WICKED GARDEN
SIN
BIG EMPTY
SOUR GIRL
CREEP
INTERSTATE
PLUSH
TRIPPIN'
SEX & VIOLENCE
DOWN
UNGLUED

DEAD & BLOATED
PIECE O' PIE
SEX TYPE THING

Norfolk Virginia 6-26-00 STP setlist.

In Virginia I was able to get away from everybody. I had to go buy some things I needed for the upkeep of the goods on stage. Taking the stage up and down every day causes huge wear and tear on the fabrics and other stage dressings. The PA for the day was a gorgeous girl named Andrea. She had short cropped brown hair and amazing hazel eyes. I was going to get to leave all these assholes for the day with this lovely princess. I knew I had to look my best. I cruised back to the bus to get ready. In the bus bathroom I brushed my teeth, washed my balls, put on a clean shirt from the Trump casino, and was ready for my date. Andrea and I had a nice time chatting for the few hours we spent together. I smiled wide, I made jokes, I was going to tell her about even bathing myself for the outing; when she revealed to me that she liked women as much I did. "Joel, you are super sweet, but I'm a lesbian," she said to me. "Well, mother fucker," I replied aloud. My intensions were to say that in only my head but somehow it didn't happen that way.

"Don't get me wrong, though. I do appreciate you bathing," she said. "You could tell, or did I say that out loud, too?" I asked. "Oh, yeah," she said. I beamed with pride again. The date had quickly gone back to being a good one. I didn't often receive compliments.

Show poster Star Pavillion June 27, 2000.

Y100 Fez 2000 all access pass.

On June 27th we played at Hershey Park. They put lots of Hershey's chocolate in your hotel room there. I was a very happy roadie. On June 28th we played the FEZtival in Camden, NJ. 3 Door down and No Doubt played the show. I spent a lot of the day with Adrian and we talked about Fishbone. Adrian is a huge Fishbone fan. The highlight of the show for me was the Violent Femmes were on the bill. The bass player hung out at the festival all day and we chatted about music. At the end of their performance, they all clambered together like clowns into a 1970's station wagon and drove off. Was the wagon their tour bus? Did they live locally? Either way it was very fitting, and the randomness of it made me even a bigger fan of the band.

On our next day off in Cleveland, a bunch of us went to the Rock & Roll Hall of Fame. We got in for free by showing our laminates. I'm not going to lie. It made me feel special. It was fun going through the museum with all the roadies. Amelia pointed out clothes in the David Bowie exhibit. She had made several of the items and had done repairs on most of them at one time or another. I wondered how many museums you could go through and point out pieces you had actually held. Forget about made.

After our quick stop in Cleveland we made our way up to Canada. STP was now paying for me to travel outside the country. I had wanted to see the world, and little by little it was happening. As we approached the border, Cesar prepared for issues. Half the roadies, if not more, on our bus had felonies. Recently, Cesar had brought Clif onto the tour to be our production manager. Clif and Cesar were close.

Clif and I got along well, but he had a bad temper. However, Clif and Nigel absolutely did not get along. Clif had two or three DUI's. His last DUI experience ended when he woke up in someone else's living room. A bit of a problem. However, there was a bigger issue- he was still in his car when he woke up. I remember a couple of the crew were left in the US for the few shows we did in Canada. I can't remember who they were. I do remember when they called me up to the window to talk to me. The band and crew were all sitting behind me on a long bench, waiting their turn. "Have you ever been arrested, Mr. Miller?" the Canadian customs person asked me while looking at my passport. "Yes, sir," I said. Everyone on the bench looked up at me. I knew they were all thinking what kind of trouble I could have ever gotten myself into. In college I had been arrested for public intoxication and fueling a fire. I had been in front of my own house trying to put out a fire someone else started. I was arrested for starting it. It was bullshit and I'm still pissed off about it. On my record it is just listed as public intoxication. I told the man behind the desk I was drunk in college and got arrested. He stamped my passport and I made it through. I know the band had to pay for Scott Weiland and Clif to get into the country. I didn't know how much, but I knew it wasn't cheap. Scott had been sorted out before we got there. Without him there would obviously have been no reason for the rest of us to go. Mugs was very upset because they gave him a real hard time over a DUI he had got many years earlier. It did seem a bit ridiculous. I don't know why he cared so much about possibly being denied entry to Canada, but he did.

Chapter 26
Undressing the Set Dressing

The first show was at a venue called The Warehouse in Toronto. It's a small venue and so it was yet another great place to see STP perform. From Toronto we'd all head home for a 10-day break. I ached everywhere and I needed the time to recuperate. I was excited to go and see my friends. It's an odd feeling to travel home in between being a man and needing to still grow up. I came home feeling I had direction for the first time in my life, but I was still living at my parent's house. I wasn't sure if I'd make a career out of this new job, but I did know that for now I was going to focus and see what experiences I could chalk up.

For the stage dressings on the next leg we were going to keep with the same easy setup we had been using. Smoke machines, red Mylar flowing all over the fucking place, a big white star, and a solid red shimmering backdrop. At the front of the stage an ego riser where Scott could reign over all. An ego riser is what it sounds like - a step the singer can stand up on to rise above everyone, including the rest of the guys on the stage. And that was our whole stage set up.

I had started saving the Mylar as the pieces fell off the backdrop every day. We had three sticks, pieces of truss, that sat on the stage upright. Strobe lights were fitted inside each stick. I had been waiting to tape the Mylar together, creating very tall hula skirts. When complete, I could tape the top of that skirt around the front of the sticks on the stage. I knew it would look great.

While in Canada, at The Warehouse, I noticed all the left over Mylar was bunched up on the bottom of the stage. I looked up and saw that the backdrop was at trim. Seeing that we didn't need it, I cut a lot of it off and was able to finally make my hula skirts to go around the sticks on stage. The stage now looked way better.

After the show Nigel came to talk to me as I was loading out. "Hey, Rifken, can I ask you a question?" he said. "Sure man, what's up?" I expected this conversation to start who knows where but to quickly be about how great the stage looked. "Where did you find the extra Mylar to put around the sticks on stage?" he inquired. I was happy to tell him. "Well, as pieces have been falling off of the backdrop, I have been saving them. I was taping them back to the top of the backdrop, but they were just getting bundled up and it looked worse. So, I've been keeping them to put around the sticks. I realized that a bunch of the Mylar was just sitting on the stage, and so I cut some of that to finish them off. Looks pretty damn good. Right, asshole?" Nigel shook his head. "Yeah, Rifken - looks great," he said and left the stage. I wondered what he was so bothered about. Did his character die in *Starcraft?*

That night when I boarded the bus, most of the crew was still crying with laughter. But nobody would tell me what they were all laughing about. What I hadn't thought about at the time was the venue we were playing at. It was a small and not a mid-sized venue. We call the mid-sized venues sheds. Of course, in a smaller building some of the backdrop would have to lay on the stage as trim would be at a lower height. All I had done was neuter our backdrop. Luckily, we were heading home for a break, and Nigel could have more Mylar made.

Chapter 27
Death Proof

While back home I went out and got drunk with my friends. However, for the first time I felt like I did not fit in with any of them. The short time period I had been away had changed me dramatically. I had just jumped off a train, which every morning I gassed up, spent the day gaining maximum speed, and sure enough at the end of each night, the damn thing blew up. Every day was a steady, gradual build that climaxed in an explosion of awesomeness every night. The shows were always a new experience and each a test to see how much my body could physically take before breaking. While everything hurt, it hurt good!

My friends on the other hand hadn't changed nor was anything exciting going on at home. I had only been gone for one and a half months, but at no other time in my life had so much happened. What made it all even better was I knew things were still revving up. While I spent nights drinking with buddies, I spent my days preparing for the tour that was quickly approaching with the RHCP. Quite a bit of time was spent with Nigel at the lighting warehouse called Light and Sound Design, or LSD. I was still on the STP payroll and so they had me running around while we were all on break. A couple different days I went down to the band's storage to see if there was anything we could pilfer for the tour. Anything I could use would save the band money. The STP warehouse was a neat spot for a fan. There was a room filled with Dean's guitars, and the massive lava lamps were stored there from the tour before. As neat as it was, there was nothing there I would be able to use, so I stopped driving down there.

I drove home on one of these days, and when I got there, my dad was waiting for me. He was going to go buy an E Type Jaguar and needed a ride to the man's house so that he could drive the car back. We had a nice drive over. I felt good about starting what I thought might be a career and I was appreciative of my father getting the ball rolling for me. He had really done me well on this one.

When we got to the man's house, I walked, with my dad, up to the front door. If he didn't end up buying the car, he'd need a ride home, so I knew I'd be hanging out for a while to see how it all went. A nurse opened the door and escorted us in. A man was sitting in a chair hooked up to oxygen. He looked like he may die any minute. I'd been in these situations with my father before and I wasn't all that surprised to see the dying man. He'd buy Jaguars regularly from people who were in failing health. This guy's health wasn't really failing though I'd say it had failed. With the help of the nurse, the man stood up to walk us out to the car. There wasn't much to go over. It was a nice car and my dad had rebuilt the motor himself a few years earlier. "I'd love to take it for one last drive," said the man. "Why don't you. You can take Joel with you." What the fuck? I don't think my disapproving face was very discreet. Not that the dying guy or my dad noticed. Maybe the nurse noticed?

I didn't want to drive with this old dude. He could barely move. How was he going to drive the car? The man disconnected his oxygen tank. "I'll drive the car out of the garage for you," my father told him. My dad pulled the car out into the driveway, and it was easier for the man to get into the car. Once in the car, the man turned to me. "Come on, let's go." I got in and drove with the guy down the street. I didn't want to make much conversation with him, because I wanted him to concentrate on driving. Fortunately, we didn't drive very far. I was very relieved to get back to the house in one piece. The man was wiped out. I was waiting for him to pass gas and fall asleep.

"How did the drive go?" my dad asked both of us. "I have to go lie down," he said. We walked with him back into the house and though completely exhausted he was beaming. It was truthfully a nice moment. Us guys love our toys. He passed away a week or so later. If my memory serves me correctly, I think my dad had already re-sold the car before he died.

When I got home my mom had something urgent to talk to me about. "Joel, who's Alicia?" I honestly had no clue. "Well, can you please ask her to not call after 9PM. We go to sleep at that time," my mom told me. The hamster in my head began reading through my little black book... Alicia... calling after 9PM... Dammit! It didn't take me long to remember who Alicia was. She was a stunning blonde who was on the skids with her husband. I had run into her at a concert and we had hit it off. After my mom had talked to her, I never heard from her again. I had never got her number.

It was time for me to purchase a laptop and a cell phone. I was excited to get both. The computer meant I could watch movies and listen to music in hotel rooms. The cell phone meant I could call home, or my friends, during the day without everyone in the production office listening in on my phone calls. It wasn't that they were private, it was more that they were boring. More importantly, the phone meant that when hot girls like Alicia called, my mom wouldn't ruin it. And when hot girls like Alicia wanted to party in my hotel room, I had a computer that could play music, you know, to rock out to.

On a larger level, it wasn't just all about experiencing the learning curves of being a roadie. I was experiencing America. I was meeting new people and seeing new places. I kept finding that I was seeing and telling myself, "I never thought I'd make it here." As we travelled on, I began to love the country itself. The elements were a big factor.

Growing up in Los Angeles, I had been sheltered from the harsher elements. One night we were all drinking in a bar next to the hotel somewhere in the Midwest. Because we were so close to the hotel, I decided to go back to my room to use the bathroom. When I got to the hotel, the rain started out of nowhere. Entering the hotel lobby, I turned around, glad I had not got soaking wet. Once up in my room, the wind picked up, and the rain came down even harder. I watched mesmerized as It continued to keep picking up. I thought the windows of my hotel room were going to blow out. A few drinks deep, it was awesome to watch. I didn't make it back to the bar but watched the show through the windows. It was moments like these that were the endcaps to this great story I felt I was living. It's a wonderful feeling when you don't know what tomorrow is going to bring, but you know it is going to be exciting.

Chapter 28
I Went to Alaska and all I got was this Bucket of Chicken Wings

STP tour itinerary- second leg.

Next up was Anchorage, Alaska. I was glad to get away from home and to be back touring. In 1996 Scott didn't make a New Year's Eve show in Anchorage. This concert was to be a long overdue make up for STP not performing that night. The lights weren't working, the sound guys had major issues in the beginning of the show, we had no Mylar on stage, and the STP white star was never shipped with the backdrop. Nigel had ordered a new one because the old one was dirty, and they hadn't shipped it back yet. In a nutshell the evening was riddled with problems. But the crowd loved it. How many bands play in Alaska?

I was very excited about making it to Alaska. The band, the

tour manager, and Scott's drug counselor took a plane flight and got to see many of the things I had wanted to see. I imagined they saw avalanches, moose stampeding, bears fighting mountain men, eagles soaring, and buffalo roaming. I imagined that with a private plane and an unlimited budget the band may as well have shot a National Geographic video while up there.

In other words, I was jealous. I don't know what they did see, but I'm sure it wasn't quite to the level of majestic splendor I created in my head. We, the crew, did no such thing. We went out in Anchorage and ate pizza and chicken wings at Chilkoot Charlie's. Not quite the same level of entertainment.

Anchorage was a nice enough place. The air certainly felt clean. Knowing I may never make it back to Alaska, I felt like I was missing out. While I knew I was there because I was being paid to work, I couldn't help but hope for something more. I never wanted to be limited in what I could do. However, I was also acutely aware that for now this was a good gig. Maybe being a roadie was a temporary career for me.

Cesar had left us temporarily to go out on a different tour. He had left Clif in charge. While there had been a bit of friction at first because Nigel brought me in and the two still hated one another, Clif and I now got along well.

Nigel's nickname when he toured with Pantera was Dr. Death. He was a morbid guy. He was a ghostly pale skinny guy with a full body alien tattoo who always moped around with a hood over his head. Clif was a hardened stocky dude covered in lots of tribal tattoos, and it wasn't that he didn't like to take shit. It was more that he wouldn't take any shit. His parents had named him Clif, not Clifford, and not Cliff. He said they had dropped the second "f" because they couldn't spell properly. He fidgeted constantly from having done too many hard drugs years earlier. Though sober now, he had had his fair share of ups and downs stemming from drugs and alcohol. Nigel complained all the time how he hated the job. Clif loved his job. Nothing would have made Clif happier than to see Nigel get fired, but that wasn't going to happen. Once it became apparent to Clif that though I may have been hired by Nigel, that was about the only thing that related me to Dr. Death. He had no issues with me. I never complained, and I did all I could to help anyone with anything. Clif yelled at me here and there but it was because, like Cesar, he was trying to teach me rather than scold me. It's hard to be genuinely mad at a guy who is working his ass off.

Part of my job was to make sure the band was safe while on stage. Every day I would take neon green, or pink, or both, gaffers' tape and tape down arrows that all directed towards the stage from the dressing room. I would then tape off the edge of the stage, so it could be clearly seen. If the rock star falls off the stage and gets hurt, we all lose our jobs and go home. I always felt like the guys didn't need the tape because I never saw them even come close to falling off the stage but maybe that was because of my great taping abilities. I don't know.

Clif had reprimanded me earlier. He wanted me to tape off the stage first thing in the morning from now on. I liked to do it later in the day so the tape would be vibrant and easy to see. People walked on it all day and of course it was dirty by nightfall. I also didn't think it was at all necessary when the lights were on, or it was still daylight out. Who would blame lack of neon tape for falling off the stage when it was light out? So, I would do it at my leisure. Still, he was the boss now that Cesar wasn't there, so I taped off the stage as soon as I was done with setting up everything in the mornings. It was important for me to get the rig up in the air as soon as possible so the backline guys could start setting up their instruments and amps. So, setting up the rig was always first on the list.

I also learned that as soon as the show was over, I needed to take down all the soft goods immediately. During the last song of the night, I assembled all the stagehands so that we could rush the stage as soon as the musicians walked off. I waited on the side of the stage like a rabid dog ready to attack during the encore performances. Backdrops don't look good after being trampled on. I would have the backdrops all off the stage within a few quick minutes after the show. The faster I packed my stuff, the quicker I too could be done, the less damage to my materials, and the less I'd have to fix later. If I couldn't get to the back truss, because of the venue, I'd raise the back truss high in the air so that my backdrop was safely out of everyone's way and avoid damage while they worked.

Just an STP bitch taping off the stage.

I waited a few days, after Clif took over, and then spread the word that I had run out of neon tape. I told people to tell Clif that I had then taped off the remaining stage edge with black gaff tape. I was so green still that this was totally a possibility. After all, I was the guy who neutered the backdrop in Canada. Clif's face when he walked out on the stage was magnificent. He looked down at the stage edge and saw the neon tape. "I knew even you wouldn't be that dumb," he said to me. Clif walked back to the bus while I smiled from ear to ear. I knew that had been a good wind up.

Chapter 29
Rifken Records: A Sound So Unique...

Molson Canadian Rocks Simul Bash artist pass.

From Alaska we flew into Vancouver for a quick show. In Vancouver the new Mylar pieces arrived and so did a brand new shiny white star. To keep the white star white, I began hanging it towards the end of the day instead. Doing so, didn't bother anyone, not like taping the stage. When the truss went up in the morning, I would just throw a rope over the truss with a loose knot at the bottom. When I was ready to hang the star, I would assemble it in the air with some stagehands and pull the rope to hoist it up as we went. When at trim, I held it in place with sandbags on the ground. It wasn't a perfect system by any means, but it did keep it exponentially cleaner and it was super-fast to get it both up and down.

My pulley system for hanging the STP star.

We had also changed out our backdrops. The Mylar was no longer very long strands attached at the top of the backdrop by Velcro. Instead, there were smaller rows of Mylar throughout the backdrop. Making it easier to replace the damaged/lost pieces.

While it might seem like these changes are rather unimportant, and arguably not even worth mentioning, I have good reason for not leaving the details out. That reason is because the improvements in the set design not only benefited the way the show looked, but they provide a good timeline if you explore the development of my learning curve. In other words, I was getting better at all this stuff.

While in Vancouver, Scott got into a bar fight and beat the crap out of the guy. The concern was if the guy pressed charges Scott might be held in Canada. If that happened, we'd have to cancel shows. It didn't help that Scott was on probation either. I came up with a plan. I told Nigel, "hey, if anyone says anything, I'll just say it was me who hit the guy in the bar. We could just say Scott was never there." Nigel looked at me and rolled his eyes. "What? It's not a bad idea," I said. "No one is ever going to believe you could fight anyone and win, Rifken." It was true. Well, maybe not true but it was unlikely. No, no it was true.

From Vancouver we headed down to Portland, Oregon. When

the Vancouver show ended, we all went outside to find that management had booked the crew a passenger van for our all-night drive down to Portland. The band had booked themselves a private plane for the flight. I slept on the floor in between two bench seats. It was a rough night, but I'd had worse. When we got to Portland the crew was pissed off. Suzi bitched at the band hardcore. "Are you fucking assholes fucking kidding me? What the fuck were you thinking. A fucking van on an overnight. How was your fucking plane flight? How am I? Ohhh, FUCKING tired from sleeping in a van - that's how I am," she yelled at them in the dressing room. That was pretty much the gist of it all. I'm sure the crew thought she summed it up very well.

To settle things, the band told us they were going to give us $100 each for the inconvenience. I was stoked. I was ready to take the passenger van every night. The rest of the crew was not impressed with the extra few bucks. Our buses were waiting for us in Portland and everyone began to quiet down when we saw them again. I was glad to see that a roadie uprising was avoided.

101 KUFO RockFest Tattoo the Earth artist pass.

In addition to the van ride, the Portland show, at the KUFO rock fest, sucked. It was hot, it was dry, and all kidding around aside we were all tired from a rough night in a van. Each of the bigger name bands on the bill had a production office in a honeywagon, which is a trailer behind the stage. The bands performing at the rock fest were Slayer, Hatebreed, Mudvayne, Sepultura, Nashville Pussy, Cold, Sevendust, (Hed) P.E., some smaller bands, oh- and Slipknot. It was to be a testosterone party in the dirt. There was to be lots of big trucks and cheap beer. We had played shows like this before, but I always wondered how the crowd was going to react to a cross dressing drug addict who liked to talk shit at shows.

Determined to make the most out of this shitty show, Nigel, Aso, and I focused on other things. The first order of our business was to give the STP crew our own production office. We took down the sign that said Slayer, ripped it up, and made our own that read, "Rifken Records – A sound so unique you'd swear you'd never heard it before." We proudly hung the sign. Next, we went through the other dressing rooms and grabbed what we could find. We started with a couple great gift baskets with candy and fruit in them. They looked nice on our table. Aso and Nigel walked into the office with a big bloody animal head that had been meant as a present for Sepultura. Kind of like when your cat brings dead mice to your door. The promotors must have been trying to be like big lions. I wondered if they had even hung it in the honey wagon in lion suits? Were they then the same lion suits the promotors used at furries parties? Anyhow, we hung that bloody animal-furry lion-found thing proudly on our wall. Next, we needed some beverages. We grabbed sodas and waters and the three of us sat down and admired how resourceful we could be.

Relaxing on our lazy boy, I couldn't help but notice that all the beverages we had found were Pepsi products. It was only then that I realized the show was a Pepsi endorsed event. I marched out of the office, with a Pepsi in hand, and found one of the venue staff. I poured the Pepsi out onto the dirt in front of the kid. I had learned how to pour properly from Marcus back when I worked on Hollywood movies. I say kid, but he was probably the same age as me. We both waited and watched as the Pepsi can emptied. It made a little bubbly lake and then expanded to a little bubbly river before it sank into the dry earth.

"Scott won't drink this shit, man. Someone has to run out and get him some Coca-Cola," I told the guy. "We can't bring Coca-Cola into the venue man it's a Pepsi...." I cut the young man off and threw the can on the floor. "Well, that's fine, but someone has to tell Scott that, and I'm not going to be the one to do it. I'll tell the guys in the Rifken Records production office that you said you would ask Scott. How does that sound?" I looked firmly at the guy and said nothing else. "All right - I'll check," he said and began to walk away to sort it all out. "Hey, man. You going to pick up that can?" I asked him. He turned back around and headed towards where the can was on the floor. "Na, just fucking with you but seriously go get some fucking Coke. Rock stars love Coke," I said to him while waiving my finger. Aso and Nigel watched on. "Hey Aso, can you grab that can, you little bitch," I said to him. "Rifken, I don't work here. I'll kick your fuckin' ass." I picked up the can. "I suggest you wait till you have a cold Coca-Cola in your hand my friend. You guys like that last bit about how rock stars like Coke? Get it Nigel... Get it?" I said. "Yes, Rifken we get it," he replied. "Man, this running a business thing is hard. What else do we need to do to get Rifken Records off the ground, guys?" Within the hour we had twenty-four Coca-Cola's delivered to the Rifken Records production office. We took turns in the lazy boy and drank them one after another.

What weren't allowed were Red Bulls. I hate the smell of them. Or maybe It's just because I'm bitter. Let's discuss the Red Bull Girls being fixtures at all the concerts. The girls never had tickets to the show. Instead, they would cruise into the venue in the Red Bull car, looking hot as hell, and offer up Red Bull's to everyone out of a Red Bull backpack. Though the girls would give us cases of Red Bull, no problem. I had come to the conclusion that you could get a Red Bull car if you tried hard enough, but there was no fucking way you'd get a Red Bull backpack. Nigel, Aso, and I had made it our mission to get one. We failed at every show; it was impossible. I started to kick the girls off the stage, telling them the only way they could stay is if they gave me one. There was no question it annoyed me that I couldn't get one. They would offer to make out with each other, show me their tits, go backstage, whatever. But I made it clear I didn't care about any of that. I wanted a fucking Red Bull backpack. Aso and Nigel were married and must have been embarrassed to see tits other than their wives or relatives, and I was well in hindsight just dumb. Truth is, there were lots of girls making sexual advances, but none of them had a Red Bull backpack and I was determined to get one before Aso and Nigel did. We were all tired of striking out. But should have got used to it. No one ever managed to get one.

While I was busy putting neon tape on the steps to the Rifken Records trailer, because I hadn't had time to set up liability insurance, I noticed a telephone cable in the dirt. We absolutely needed a landline. I immediately started pulling the telephone line. With a good pull I was able to get to the end of the line. We quickly found a phone and, bobs your uncle, now had a landline. Rifken Records was officially in business. If I wanted, I could call and get us liability insurance now.

Roadie Ramble Moment
Where did the idiom "Bob's your uncle" come from? Not to let the cat out of the bag, but no one has been able to hit the nail on the head. However, if you want to burn the midnight oil, you will find it is of United Kingdom origin and most people believe it was implemented first by coded Cockney content. The full saying, straight from the horse's mouth I might add, is actually "Bob's your uncle, Fanny's

your aunt." Here's what I have to say about it... let's not just use the saying "once in a blue moon." To cut to the chase we should not let odd idioms which beat the odds to become part of popular vernacular just slip away. To sum it all up, that's right if you want to know the whole nine yards here; it's to jump up on the bandwagon to make forgotten idioms relevant again. We can call the movement the IRA (Idioms Relevant Again.) Who wouldn't like an organization called the IRA?

It didn't take long for us to get a knock on our door. It was Clif and two of the worker guys from the event. "Sorry to bother you guys, but it seems you took the telephone line to the ATM machine," said Clif. "Our apologies, we just figured they must have forgotten to install a phone in here this morning," replied Nigel. Clif rolled his eyes at the five of us, who were now lounging in the Rifken Records office drinking ice cold Coca-Cola's and playing video games. The couple other guys in the office were part of the STP crew who had now made themselves comfortable on our two new couches I had pulled out of the Sepultura and Slayer honeywagons. My dictatorship was working. Rifken Records had a presence that was expanding rapidly. "I'll handle this," Clif told the two worker guys and came into the office by himself. "Coca-Cola?" Nigel asked as he handed Clif a cold one.

The show in Portland was one of the few times I saw Clif and Nigel get along. Nigel, Clif, and I turned back around and stepped outside to discuss with the staff the phone line issue. Outside the honeywagon was a good place for the discussion, because we had by now "borrowed" everything from every dressing room at the venue. It was a quick chat and went something like this...

As mentioned, we walked down the Rifken Records staircase, the two steps from the trailer door to the dirt, and Nigel handed the guys the end of the telephone line. "Here ya go," he said. And then the three of us went back inside again.

Clif couldn't help but laugh once back inside. "What the fuck guys," he asked? "Sir, can I offer you a seat? Another Coca-Cola perhaps? If you care to wait, I believe the runner is bringing back ice cream," I said to him. Clif sat down. "You know what? Fuck it. Yeah give me one of those minute maid things," he said and sat back in the second lazy boy chair we had "borrowed" from the promotor's office.

We would later find out that we had permanently damaged the phone line, and the machine itself now had to be reset, or something like that. But because of us, there was no ATM at the show. Someone was probably a little pissed off about that.

Some time passed and Just before the show, Clif, Aso, Nigel, and I were outside joking around, when a passenger van pulled up. A man got out of the van and approached all of us. Clif and Aso were smoking cigarettes, and Clif was telling us to not start anymore trouble. The man approached us hurriedly. He was a fidgety little dude. "Excuse me guys, would you mind going in the trailer for just a minute. Slipknot is in the van and the band doesn't want anyone to see them without their masks on," he said to us. We were definitely the wrong people to say that too. I was expecting Clif to tell the guy to go fuck himself, but he actually surprised me. "Sure, no problem," Clif said in the most matter of fact tone he could muster up. "OK, thanks," the guy replied happily. He ran off and got back into the van.

We all stood there waiting. Nigel started laughing before the van even parked. He knew we weren't going anywhere. Once parked, the van waited... and so did we. After a few minutes the band got out of the van. We cheered them on enthusiastically. Aso took his shirt off, spun it around high in the air, and then threw it at them. This was turning into a great day.

"Excuse me, but do you know what happened to this head on a plaque that was in the Sepultura dressing room?" one of the venue guys abruptly asked us. Now standing next to us, he had approached us without any of us even noticing. We all looked around. Where the hell had this guy come from? "The promotor is looking for it," he said. Clif looked at us and quickly walked the other way without saying a word. Copying him, hands in pockets, Aso, Nigel, and I walked in the other direction. Nigel and Aso jumped into a golf cart, and I followed suit by hopping onto the backseat. The venue guy was left standing alone.

"How did you know the key was in it?" I asked. "Shut the fuck up Rifken we are on the run," said Aso. "All right. Well, at least put your shirt back on so the paparazzi don't get any ideas when we get stopped on this thing," I replied. As we drove past the promoter's office, a very pissed off man barreled out of the front door. It didn't take long for us to find out it was the promotor and we had just taken his personal golf cart. I don't know how he could have blamed us for taking it though. It was after all the nicest one and you know... the key was in it.

Chapter 30
A Bunch of Assholes and Some Nazis

Eventually, we had to start working. During set change the sun set. Mother nature was doing a set change of her own I guess you could say. On top of being exhausted, we were all covered head to toe in dirt. It really had been a long couple of days. The crowd was rowdy as hell. There had been a non-stop mosh pit since doors opened hours and hours earlier. The barricade had blood smeared all over it from bloody noses, vomit, and whatever else expelled from people. The crowd kept getting louder and louder. Dean turned to me and said, "If I make 10 grand tonight it's not worth it. It's not worth the humility." I looked back at him and faintly smiled not sure how to reply. Nigel looked at me and his expression was quite clear. "I'll take it if you don't want it," was what he was thinking. Nigel left us and made his way out to front of house to get ready for the show.

No matter how rowdy a crowd, roadie intuition had taught us how to maneuver through the verm quickly. We were like sperm trying to get to the Cervix. Verm is short for vermin btw. It's what people in the music industry refer to the audiences as. Nice to know what the industry calls the guys who at the end of the day pay their bills, right? Anyhow, as Nigel made his way through the audience, I saw that a small section of the front row had morphed into neo Nazis. Maybe Dean was right. They can keep the 10 grand.

When STP hit the stage, the crowd went crazy. They had been waiting all day for this. Well, this, Sepultura, and maybe to watch the Slipknot guy jump up and down on a trampoline.

The Nazi guys immediately threw up Nazi salutes and I waited for Scott to go berserk. I wondered if the guys came to enjoy the show or just piss people off in the crowd. I couldn't understand what the appeal to STP could have been for them. The singer of the band likes to wear women's clothes. These guys were OK with that? Wait, no they weren't? No, maybe they were? I didn't know what they were going to say or do.

During the first song I didn't hear Scott say anything about or to them. I don't think he saw that they were throwing syringes on the stage. I didn't know what to do. I didn't want to run out there and get stuck with a needle. Getting Aids by flying needle- what a great obituary that would be. It didn't take long for Scott to stop the show. He stared right into their blackened souls. If Scott thought the audience was a bunch of assholes, he had no issues telling them that.

Dean, Robert, and Scott all had no problem getting into fist fights. There were several times during the tour Scott and/or Dean jumped into the audience and started swinging punches with the verm. Both I and Rigger Steve, if he was around, would jump in after them, and after it was over, I'd always get yelled at by one of the guys in the band. "Man, when you follow us, we have to both handle our business and watch you. Just stay on the damn stage," they'd yell at me. I ignored them though; jumping in with the verm was fun!

Back to Scott and the Nazis... "Hey, anyone who brings me a full handful of these guys hair right here can come backstage and hang out with us after the show," he said into the microphone. The Nazi guys and security mutually agreed it was time for them to leave immediately. They were escorted out of the venue. I carefully picked up as many needles as I could. I was relieved to find they were all new with the caps on them. I wondered if that had been a Nazi conversation earlier that day. Leave the caps on or take them off? "Oh, Adolf. [I'm sure he had a fake Nazi name] leave the cap on. Don't be a dick!" is probably what Nazi Hermann said to Nazi Adolf.

After the show I packed the backdrop in a big bag and brought it back with me to the hotel. We were going to send it back to Los Angeles and add two additional Velcro rows to it. The shorter pieces of Mylar affixed to a solid piece of fabric had been working better. I had been throwing the backdrops into separate hampers before, but it was hard to keep the Mylar from getting damaged and untangled with all the handling. The plan now was to roll the backdrop with the Mylar left attached on it in smaller sections. We hoped for less damage and less creasing of the Mylar pieces. The truth was at night with all the lights going, it didn't matter if the pieces were creased or not. You couldn't tell. I was proud that it all definitely looked good.

Chapter 31
Nothing Beats Fucking a Stripper

The runner who gave us a ride back to the hotel that night was both a gorgeous stripper and a massage therapist named Heather. She made sure to tell us that her boyfriend was a roadie for Phish, and we all believed her, because she certainly had that hippie vibe going. She had strands of fabric in her hair, wore a flowing tie dye dress, and sported a permanent smile.

You could count on the van drivers to always do two things. The first was to be playing Stone Temple Pilots in the van when they picked us up, and the second to tell us how much they loved the band. Most often they were let down when they realized they were picking up the crew and not the band. What the van drivers didn't understand was we were a bunch of bitter assholes. We didn't want to hear their cassette tape of STP. We heard it every damn night! While playing STP, one thing never failed. The driver would try to engage in a conversation about what kind of music they did or did not like; I think you'll guess our collective roadie thoughts on this one... that's right, we didn't give a shit. You're getting the hang of this.

Heather was different, though. In my words I'd say, "she was hot." Nigel would say "She was fucking hot, baby." Aso would say, "she looks like a dirty whore... yeah." And though Mugs would say, "I prefer the slasians." I think we'd all agree Heather wasn't just hot nor was she a slasian or even a baby whore. She was a gorgeous American made angel. Oh, if you don't speak Mugs, a slasian was a slutty Asian, btw.

She drove us all back to a super nice hotel. We got back to the hotel sometime around midnight. The band had put us up in a really nice place because of our awful drive in the passenger van the night before. Everyone was happy to get to their room, but I had other plans.

Nigel grabbed the bag with the backdrop in it, out of the back of the van. He was going to send it off to get fixed for the next show in three days. It was incredibly rare we would have a hotel room after the show. Usually, the band would want to get us to the next city. We would then have a day off, and then the following day do the next show. I didn't know anyone in any of the cities we played at and so I had no one to call on those days off. I would either hang out with people from the crew or just catch up on sleep.

We weren't leaving Portland until the morning and I wasn't going to miss this opportunity. Everyone got out of the van, but I took my time. I didn't invite Heather up to my room because I am of course both a gentleman and she was dating that fish/fishy person. Or Phish, or however you spell that hippy band name. So, knowing that ungentlemanly crap wouldn't work, once everyone was out of the van, I smiled my roadie best at Heather. "Drinks? You fly, I'll buy?" I asked her. "I do have a boyfriend," she said.

"I don't care. You can't leave me with these assholes. Come on, know of a good jazz club?" I asked. "I actually do." I watched the key turn in the ignition and off the two of us drove. It was hard to turn down my roadie smile and I knew it.

The jazz club was everything a good jazz club should be. It was relaxing, dark, and a lot of fun. Heather and I hung out all night and she did, of course, make it back to my room with me in the end. In the morning the band and crew watched her get into the passenger van and drive away. She made a point of saying goodbye by holding my hand and giving me a big kiss in front of everyone. It was awesome.

"Did you fuck Heather?" asked Nigel. That was none of Nigel's business, because as I said before, I was a damn gentleman. So,

I Immediately lashed back at him, "I did, but when your wife called me to wish me good night, as she usually does, I told her that you fucked her, Nigel." I was starting to get the hang of being an asshole roadie. It had certainly taken long enough.

Spending the night with Heather was the talk of roadietown. Well, there is no roadietown, so it was really the talk of the bus. What mattered was that I had had a nice evening. I was genuinely pleased to get away from everyone, and everything. Oh, and it didn't hurt that I did it with a gorgeous woman. The only embarrassing part was when Suzi gave me a hard time. I respected Suzi and didn't want her to think I was a man whore. Not that she would have cared. But when she cornered me and asked me all kinds of embarrassing questions, I turned red and squirmed. She loved it. I couldn't be a smartass to her either because she was ... Suzi!

Chapter 32
Musicians are Vampires

We all headed off to the airport. Once we arrived in Houston, I got some much-needed rest and had a normal day off. I bought some CD's, a DVD of the movie *Arthur*, and a couple tools for work. Aso and I ate lunch and dinner out together, I watched my movie, and went to sleep.

The following day STP played the Aerial Theatre at Bayou Place. Early, around 11AM, the band bus pulled up. The band usually did radio interviews or maybe they just hung out in their hotel rooms all day. I'm not sure. I do know they weren't ever at the gig during the day if they didn't have to be. When bands have been playing the same songs for years, they don't need to do a sound check. In fact, I only saw STP do a sound check a few times and I think that was because they were being recorded. It was more for publicity rather than necessity.

The driver opened the band bus door, but no one came out. I watched the bus for a few minutes and decided to wander over. I walked up the front steps, into the bus, and saw the whole band in the front lounge. "Hey, guys. I just wanted to thank you for the extra hundred bucks."

I remember them all looking at me not sure how to reply. Should they say, "you're welcome?" They knew everyone was super pissed about the situation. Finally, Robert said, "Well, it's good to have you around Joel." No one had called me Joel in a while. I wasn't sure if the band was privy to all the shenanigans of roadies. At the time I figured they'd want to be, because, well… I was having fun. Looking back on it all, I just hope they too were having a lot of fun. I'd like to think they all were, but sometimes I wonder. I walked back onstage to work.

I did have a few ulterior motives when I went in the bus to say thank you to the guys. The guys are what I always called the band members by the way. I thought this was a good opportunity to say something to them without bothering any of them. I wanted the guys to know who I was. I wanted to make sure that if the discussion came up to fire me one of them would pipe up and say, "no ,don't fire him I like that guy." I wanted them to know I really did appreciate this job as the opportunity it was. I hoped that they would remember that if a crappy situation would arise again, one guy, me, would always still have the foresight to appreciate working for them. I knew taking the time to quickly thank them was a good move. It wouldn't take me long to find out I was right.

Chapter 33
Hallelujah! It's Raining Phlegm

The next show was back in Houston. It was a radio show, but we were the only band performing. We lit hundreds of candles on the stage for a two-song acoustic set. It was a nightmare to keep them all lit but it sure looked awesome.

After Houston we drove on to Memphis, Tennessee. The home of the king, Elvis Presley. Portland had been hot, then Houston had been like working in a fire pit. And if we can all agree Houston had been a fire pit, then Memphis was like working in a fire pit in the depths of hell. STP played at a venue called Mud Island. I knew it as the place where Jeff Buckley drowned, a sad day in music.

Having done it for a while now, I had become cocky at how fast I could focus the par cans in the rig. In the major cities the stagehands belong to unions. In a union city, most of the time, the locals want to have their own guys up in the air to focus the lights. This was the case in Memphis. The guy in Mud Island doing the focus was working incredibly slow. Nigel was cussing away, "this fucking guy. How slow can you get?" At first mumbling under his breathe, his ranting was becoming louder and louder. "I need to get you up there Rifken or we are going to be here all day," he said to me. As the words crept out of Nigel's mouth puke fell behind him, like brown snow, covering the stage. The guy had puked out of the truss. Puke spewing twenty-five to thirty feet is gross. It spreads everywhere. There was at least six of us who shook our heads and said the same thing, "fuck man." The other five guys I'm sure wondered which one of them were going to have to clean it up. I was relieved it wasn't going to be me. The guy climbed down from the rig and went into the stagehand break area. He ended up being taken to the hospital. The dude had had heatstroke up there.

I geared up and climbed up into the rig. It was my turn. I realized very quickly I had no room to make fun of the guy. It was unbearable. The interior of a shed is black and there is no air circulation up top. There are no fans or anything up there either. The average adult human is 50-65% water. I think I sweat out 20% up there. After I was done, I had to go sit down. I drank lots of water and sweet tea. Sweet tea was new to me and I loved it. My shirt had an outline of salt on it from all the sweating. I think that hour up in the rig in Memphis is the hardest hour I have ever worked in my life. It was no joke.

The heat isn't all bad though. A great time to see a rock show is in extreme heat. When the sun went down it was still scorching, and so topless girls were everywhere. Everyone was drunk. It was a Rock 'n' Roll party. To top it all off our after-show food was awesome fried chicken. It is to date the best fried chicken I have ever eaten. When I got on the bus to go to the next city, I was exhausted. From the looks I got from the crew, I knew I was working as hard as I possibly could. It was at this show I showed Clif I could hold my own and get the job done. As the bus rolled on, I tried to watch the Crocodile Hunter but didn't make it through much. I peeled off my shirt and collapsed into my bunk. RIP Jeff Buckley.

Chapter 34
Scott's Coke Problem

I woke up in Maryland Heights, Missouri. I hurt everywhere but I was ready to do it again, though less ready than I had ever been before. The venue was the Riverport Amphitheatre. Like many venues, it's gone through various names, but it is now called the Hollywood Casino Amphitheatre. It can fit 20,000 people, if including the grass sitting areas. In 1991 Axl Rose was charged with inciting a riot there. An audience member was taking photographs and Axl got pissed. When no one did anything about the guy continuing to take photographs, Axl slammed down the microphone and left the stage. The rest of the band soon followed. An angry audience began to riot, and so dozens of people were injured. GNR didn't play in St. Louis again until 2017. Axl was arrested almost a year after the riot, but a judge ruled he did not incite the riot.

After we were all set up at the Riverport Amphitheatre, Nigel pulled me aside and walked me out to front of house. He wanted me to have a good look at the stage every day from out in the audience. Together, we leaned back on one of the walkway rails and looked at the stage. "What do you see Rifken?" Nigel asked me.

"I see an overweight woman showing Mugs her tits," I said. "I think that is Aso," Nigel replied. It was true, Aso was chasing Mugs across the stage, holding his shirt up. His belly jiggling with every step. "That's true. What else do you see though?" he continued on. Mugs turned back around, he heaved his chest out, and Aso stopped in his tracks. Standing tall, Mugs looked like a Silverback Gorilla. Aso turned around to run but wasn't quite fast enough. Mugs grabbed Aso's arm and slapped his ass real hard. Aso tried getting away, but Rigger Steve entered the pursuit and pulled him down onto the stage. I turned to Nigel, "Well, Nigel, in America we call this game grab ass. At least that is what I think is going on."

Nigel was trying to make a serious point and while I was joking around, I honestly did take what he was trying to show me to heart. At the end of the day the whole show is for the verm to see, and this is where they see it from. It was a great talk. In all aspects of life, it is good to take a step back and look at the big picture. I was beginning to take pride in my job now that I wasn't as nervous about not knowing what I was doing.

While I think Nigel also thought things were going well, he wanted to make sure I was going to be prepared for the next step. The next step was we were going to be going on tour with the Red Hot Chili Peppers. Steadily approaching, we were now only eight days away.

I had got into the habit of jumping into the sea of people to find a kid or two in the audience and bring them up on stage, with one of their parents, to watch a couple songs. I enjoyed doing it immensely and hoped that for some little kid I was providing them with an unforgettable memory. Maybe one of them became a musician. I can only hope.

It is a powerful thing to visualize a sea of people. As a mass, I'd say it is like watching a rolling wave. Various haircuts, heights, movements, men, women, food, drinks, all that stuff... just a collection of differences going on that make up the beautiful blend of what I'd call us, the music fan. However, if you separate those masses into individuals, it's fun to see how very different we all truly are. I think each of our differences become our strength. I loved being a spectator to all of this. I think I miss watching the audiences more than watching any of the bands that I worked for. Nightly, as I watched the crowd surge with excitement, that big rolling wave of both individuals and a mass, I too was full of renewed excitement. For this reason, I always looked forward to the next show. Like all of them, I too was just another one of the verm.

While in Missouri someone, who no doubt had a tiny penis- I mean a really teeny little fucker- broke away from the verm ocean and threw a can of Coca-Cola at Scott. I know what you are thinking. At least it wasn't Pepsi. But no, no, throwing Coca-Cola is still a bad thing. Scott slipped on the Coke and fell on his ass. Like a pro, he got up and kept performing, but he was understandably pissed off. As soon as he could, he made his way over to the bass tech Parker and yelled at him. Parker handled the situation poorly to say the least. He threw his hands up in the air and turned his back on Scott.

Parker might have been best described as being a good ol' boy. He wasn't dirty, but he wasn't clean. He wasn't a genius, but he wasn't dumb. He never combed his hair, but he was sure to clean his teeth. He wasn't big nor, was he little. He wasn't loud but wasn't quiet, and he wasn't fast or slow. He was one of those guys who just fit in anywhere. Not the kind of guy you'd invite first to a party but glad when he showed up to one. While not a sport, but an activity that didn't require one to be very active. He spent his free time flying a kite during down time in either the middle of the venue or the parking lot. At both the beginning and the end of the day he was a decent dude and treated me well.

So, who's fault was the situation really? The guy who threw the can obviously, but I mean who on the road crew is responsible to make sure this kind of thing doesn't happen. Each tech is responsible for their performer including the little area their performer rocks out in. However, we all try and help each other out. So, while it wasn't really Parker's job to be cleaning the deck, Scott needed someone to yell at, and Parker was the closest person at the time. I'm not sure if that is a rock star thing. It may just be a people thing. But because Parker handled the situation badly, I figured he was now going to be fired. I liked Parker and I didn't want that to happen. When the show was over, I thought a lot about the incident. I thought that while I was having a lot of fun, I was still just a kid, and this job was Parker's career. As Cesar had told me in the bus, these guys were pros. I had maybe had my fun and so I made a decision.

I walked into the band's bus and told the guys I needed to have a word with them. I had only addressed the band once before and that was to say thank you, for the hundred bucks, a few days earlier. The band all came to the front of the bus while I waited just inside the door at the bottom of the steps.

I addressed all of them. "Guys, I'm sorry, but I told Parker I'd watch the stage tonight. It's not his fault you fell, Scott. It's mine. I'm sorry, man. I fucked up." The band looked at me stone faced. "Why did you tell him you'd watch the stage when it's not your job?" Scott asked me. "Well, he was doing stuff," I told him. I didn't know what to say.

"I want you to watch the stage from now on," Scott said to me. "Okay. Sorry again, guys," I quickly responded. I hurriedly left amongst dumbfounded looks. I hoped what I had done would keep Parker from getting canned. But it didn't sound like they were going to fire me either. Maybe it was a win, win.

We had a day off the next day and a lot of the crew went out. Bunkie and Pax went to see Poison play. I wanted to go because I had worked with them at the recording studio and I thought maybe they'd remember me. I knew It would be fun to talk to C.C. again. However, I didn't go. I was just too wiped out.

Bunkie was the guitar tech. He wasn't that friendly, but he wasn't a dick either. Like the rest of the crew he'd been around awhile, but I don't think he had much patience for new guys like me. He was yet another big stocky fella on the crew. A partier, he always seemed like he was coming off of a bender. A grumpy fella, there was no question he really didn't care about me in anyway whatsoever. His favorite thing was to refuse giving guitar picks to stagehands. He had found out people were selling them online and so wouldn't give any to anyone. At least that was what he said. As a result, picks floating around for sale during the tour were really rare.

STP No. 4 tour guitar pics.

So Instead that night I hung out with some of the other crew. Blake the accountant was leaving us to go work with the Counting Crows. One of my favorite bands, I wondered if I would get to work for them one day. As I was thinking about working for them, Parker, the bass tech, approached me. He was a bit drunk but wanted to tell me I was doing a really good job. It meant a lot to me. No one had told me that yet. It was nice to hear. I wondered if they were going to fire him. I wondered if they were going to fire me.

Chapter 35
Out of the Trailer Park and into Kid Rock's Winnebago

Chicago Motor Speedway gig T-shirt.

The next night we performed at the Chicago Motor Speedway. STP was playing with Korn, Kid Rock, and Metallica. I had been super excited about this show. I had seen Korn play already but was amped to see them again. I couldn't wait to see how good Metallica would be. It was a kickass bill, and I knew the show would not, no could not, suck. Kid Rock was the icing on the Rock 'n' Roll layer cake.

When we got to the speedway, Kid Rock had just pulled up in his Winnebago. As I got out of the bus, people were already setting up the AstroTurf by the Winnebago door. I watched on, and more and more people just kept coming out of the RV. A midget, obese women dressed like strippers, Joe C. who I thought was a kid, and an eclectic group of other Kid Rock Entourage emerged. In a few minutes' lawn chairs had been set up and beers were in hand. I think I was more pleased than surprised. This was totally how I pictured Kid Rock to tour. While I was intrigued to see more, I had to get to work.

Bands were playing all day. Veruca Salt was on the bill, and it was cool to see a kickass female fronted rock band. Third Eye Blind played again as well. Through them I learned how hard it is to hear the music every night of a band you think sucks. When they performed, I would hide in the bus and make some calls on my new cell phone. On this day I called Stefanie in New York. I hadn't talked to her much since we had spent time together while in Europe. Though we had stayed in touch regularly through email, it was always nice to hear her voice again. She had a Jersey girl accent that I adored. The conversation finished up with her asking me if I could get her into the show the next time STP played in NYC. "You bet I can," I told her.

Because there were a lot of bands on the bill, and too much entourage, the back-stage area was crowded. I had parked my ass in a small office, that you had to walk through, to get to Cesar's office. Kid Rock's strippers also found it a perfect place to hang out and apply their 187 layers of make-up. The smell of cheap perfume that filled the office was nauseating. The girls took great pleasure in my disapproving looks. After some back and forth banter regarding how I looked like a "cute kid," and I in turn informing them that they looked like "overweight trailer trash hookers," an argument ensued.

The next scene was a mixture of boobs, rolls of fat, and me lying on the floor. I'm not sure what happened, nor in what order, but at some point, I heard Cesar's voice. "Rifken, what are you doing with these hookers?" The girls all laughed uproariously and left the office. The smell of them I'm sure didn't leave the room 'till weeks later.

"Come here," said Cesar. I walked into his office. "Sit down," he said. "I'm all good," I told him still standing. Cesar glared at me. "Or I could sit down," I said and sat down. "Wipe that makeup off your face. You look like a clown." I licked the back of my hand and started cleaning my face like a cat would.

"What the fuck did you tell the band last night?" Cesar asked. He was a get to the point type of guy. "I didn't want Parker to get fired." I decided to be matter of fact.

"So, you tell them shit that has nothing to do with you is your fault? That's fucking stupid," he said to me. It was then that I realized I was being scolded. "Are they going to fire him?" I asked. "No, they aren't, and it looks like you're now the stage manager," he told me. "Shit, what's a stage manager?" I asked.

"This fucking guy," Cesar said to no one in particular. "What's a stage manager? Get the fuck out of here," Cesar laughed. And that was all he said. He went back to work, and I sat there feeling uncomfortable for a moment. "I kind of know and I'll figure out the rest fast," I said to him. I left the office wondering what else I'd have to do now.

The truth was it was true I kind of knew what a stage manager did, but I wasn't totally sure. I was certain I wouldn't know how to do everything a stage manager's job entailed. Whatever those things were. Leaving the office, my brain ran with how the show that night was going to go.

One thing I knew for sure was that the stage managers I had seen always had a good wristwatch. I scrounged up a Rugrats watch I had got from Burger King on our last day off. I put it on and wondered if I now looked like a real Rock 'n' Roll stage manager.

The conversation in the office was the last I ever had about Parker and the Coca-Cola incident. I don't think Parker ever found out what went down. We never talked about it again. He stayed on working with STP for many years.

Though I knew the guys were great on stage I was eager to see how they would compare to bands like Metallica. Would they get nervous and not play as well? Would they change the show at all? I wondered if STP and Metallica would collaborate on any songs together. Man, that would be cool.

Kid Rock's show was good. I found out the overweight trailer trash girls were his go-go dancers and Joe C. was part of his band. I don't know who the rest of the people were, but I did know they all drank a lot of beer. If anyone has thought of burglarizing a trailer park, I would recommend doing it on a night Kid Rock is playing in their town.

As STP got ready to play it was the same as usual. A heavy anticipation hung over the verm. It's always the same, a quiet rustle. Imagine a forest when an earthquake is about to hit. There's still noise out there, but all the animals know something big is coming. Per the usual, the sides of the stage were filled with performers from earlier in the day. They all wanted to see Scott. Also, per the usual I felt good knowing that I got to see STP play almost every night. Kirk Hammett and Lars Ulrich stood next to me and watched on. I was surrounded by rock royalty.

STP started the show kicking ass and kept that same energy throughout the night. A couple songs into the set I got that feeling we all get when we know there is something hovering right behind us. I wonder if that is a human primal thing? I turned around and there was James Hetfield watching the guys behind me flanked by his security. "Sorry, brother, am I in your way?" he asked me. Ha! James Hetfield was asking me if I was in his way. I smiled and stepped out of *his* way to make sure he could see the show better. It was a cool moment. I wondered if that was the mark of a good stage manager?

Unfortunately, I wasn't going to get to see Metallica play because I had to load up the trucks. I had gone as fast as I possibly could and was ready to rush back to the stage when Nigel kicked himself. "Rifken, would you mind jumping up to the front of the truck to grab my wooly jumper. I left it on a road case right in the fucking front," he said. His wooly jumper meant his sweatshirt, it's an English term. I jumped into the truck and climbed over the truss to the front of the truck. Once there, I heard the back door of the truck close and then lock. I wasn't really surprised. I laid down on a road case and closed my eyes. The truck then started up and began to move. I laughed. They weren't going to bother me on this wind up I told myself. The truck drove for a little while and then stopped. After about 10 minutes, and me ignoring any calls on my radio, the truck door opened. I jumped out of the truck and rushed back to the backstage area. Nigel and Aso laughed away but I acted as if nothing had happened as I ran by them. I got to the stage just as Metallica were walking out to play their encore. Life was perfect.

Zetafest 2000 artist pass and concert T-shirt.

Hard Rock Café Rockfest artist pass, 2000.

Crew Shirt STP No 4, 2000.

Chapter 36
Naked lion chicks... Are you kidding me?

In Miami, Florida we played with The Deftones, Nickelback, Local H, and again with the gorgeous ladies of Veruca Salt at Zetafest. After Zetafest, we made our way to Orlando to play at the Hard Rock Live. The best part about Orlando was that we got to go into the John Lennon white room and hang out. In there, they have the couch where Lennon wrote most of his music and a white piano where if you look, you'll see that each key is signed by a famous musician. It's a magical place for any Lennon fan. Reading through the signed keys I recognized some names but was clueless to others. I wanted to write down the names I didn't know to research them. Hearing new music is a passion. Each and every person who signed a key on this piano must be a treasure that I hadn't found yet.

John Lennon's piano.

"I personally liked John Lennon's earlier stuff better," said Steve. "You mean like the Beatles?" I couldn't help but be condescending. "Yeah, those guys," Steve replied. "I know what you mean Steve. I wonder if back in the day the audience left

Mozart concertos and talked about his early stuff being better as they got into their chariots," I said. "You mean carriages, not chariots," Steve said. "It's my story, Steve, and I meant chariots." I then changed my voice into my best Austrian accent. "You know, I do believe that Wolfgang's first symphony was much better than this ninth symphony, Arnold," I said to Steve. "Arnold?" Steve asked. "Yeah, Arnold Schwarzenegger is the only other Austrian I know," I said. "What about Strauss?" Steve said. "Well, fuckin' a Steve. We should sign you up for composer Jeopardy."

Myrtle Beach House of Blues T-shirt.

From there we headed to the House of Blues in Myrtle Beach. Next door to the gig in Myrtle Beach was an alligator farm. It looked way cool. Kretz, STP's drummer, and I walked over to check it out. We ended up getting a private tour from Jerry, the tour guide and resident expert on reptiles. The guy was an awesome tour guide and fascinating.

Snap... snap says the baby alligator.

Kretz and I learned lots of cool stuff. We started the day by each holding a 3-year-old alligator and then checking out a congregation of albino alligators. Jerry told us the alligators we were looking at had not evolved at all in over 80 million years. When we had got our fill of the gators, we moved on to check out the cats. With a small chain around its neck, they had a liger sit down, like the sphinx, and we each took turns next to the most massive cat you could ever see. What was the purpose of the chain? "Stay away from the animal's head," one of the gorgeous lion tamer girls told me. "Did you think I was going to hug this thing?" I replied. Next, we held a couple baby tigers. One of them being amongst the rarest cats in the world with only twenty-three known to exist. They were so cute, but their paws were huge. You could tell they were going to turn into something a few hundred times bigger than a house cat soon.

Hanging out with some household kitty cats.

We walked on to the Galapagos tortoises. While walking along the path, Jerry was feeding us with information. No Galapagos tortoise has died of natural causes. The longest living one died in a fire at one hundred and eighty or so years old. So, no one knows just how long they can actually live for. No tissues have been found to deteriorate and their eyes have not been found to have problems either. "Evolution at its finest," Jerry told us with a confirming smile.

Everyone likes a little scratch.

When we got to the tortoises he said, "go ahead and feed one." The three of us stepped into the tortoise area itself. They quickly retracted into their shells. Jerry gave me some lettuce. "Go ahead, feed him," Jerry told me. He then handed some lettuce to Kretz. The two of us looked on at this giant tortoise wondering how we could get him to pop back out of his shell. I put the lettuce on the floor right in front of him and nothing. I knocked on his shell and nothing. Kretz and I gave up. There were now a fair number of onlookers. Jerry bent over and gently scratched the tortoise's shell where his head had been a few minutes earlier. His head slowly popped out again, and his giant neck began to extend. Jerry scratched his neck, and he seemed to be much more comfortable once again. He ate the lettuce, and we laughed away. Kretz and I were having a wonderful time.

Lastly, we went into the snake exhibit. I do not like snakes. I took a picture of a snake that had enough venom in it that it could kill up to forty men with just one bite. I learned that with that one bite, the recipient would be dead in under eight minutes. The aquarium was dark, and I looked on at him through neon light. "It puts a shot glass worth of venom into your system and you bleed to death out of every orifice," he told us. "OK, I get it, I get it," I said. I didn't want to hear anymore. It didn't sound like a pleasant way to go. "How thick is this glass?" I asked him.

Big scary snake... phooey.

Not missing a beat Jerry continued on. He was like an out of control Gatling gun. However, instead of bullets he was spitting out information on fucking crazy animals. He told us that Cleopatra died from a King Cobra and not an asp. Though death is painless from a King Cobra it takes an hour or so to die. They call it a King Cobra, because it will eat other snakes including venomous ones.

Then came scary frogs. While looking at the frogs, I thought we were getting a break from all the death talk. Jerry put his head next to mine and looked into the glass tank alongside me. "It's a frog that you can lick and get high on, but if you overdose on it, it will leave you paralyzed," he told me. Death or paralysis? Probably not worth the high. At the end of the day Kretz and I held an albino boa. I couldn't wait to get the thing off of me.

Jerry was a wealth of knowledge. He continued on to tell us alligators only eat once every 2-3 weeks and a Gallapagos tortoise can last a year with no food. All this food talk made me hungry. Kretz and I had taken all this new-found knowledge in, and with it we headed back to the venue to get dinner.

While all this stuff was interesting, I'm holding out on what was the most interesting factoid of all. Jerry told us that the girls who took care of the lions walked around naked. Why? Not like I needed to know a reason, but it was because the program they were in kept them working and living with the lions. Because they had very few hours off, they didn't have time to do their laundry. I dreamt about stinky lion tamer girls for the rest of the day.

After dinner Jerry and all the lion girls came over to watch the show from the side of the stage. It was a kickass rock show that had now come after a fantastic day. I couldn't get over how gorgeous the lion girls were. Jerry had a good life. At the end of the night, he gave me his business card and told me, "next time you come back, we can go swim in the river with an elephant. I just have to set it up. If the elephant likes you, she will pick you up and put you on her back." "And if she doesn't like you?" I asked. "She'll just throw you," he replied. I made a sour face. "You're in water- she's not going to hurt you." My facial expression didn't change. "The only way the elephant can hurt you is by stepping on you, but we'll go into deep water." I had to say it was actually quite convincing. Going swimming with an elephant would be pretty cool...

The next day was a driving day. I opted to hop on the band bus to get some sleep. On that bus, rode Kretz, Suzi, Tootsie, and Nigel. Tootsie had been with the band forever. We didn't call him Tootsie because of the movie "Tootsie," nor was it because he had flatulence issues. When he spoke, his voice would inflect to make a little toot when he was done saying what he had to say. He was their front of house sound guy and a laid back, good dude.

I slept till 3PM on that bus and when I awoke, I heard Kretz playing guitar in the back lounge. He was hanging out with Suzi, while Nigel and Tootsie were watching a film in the front lounge. I had recently started watching a lot of films in hotel rooms. I was thinking maybe I'd make a movie of my own one day. I hadn't liked working in the art department but maybe I'd like being a director?

Getting out of my bunk, I opted to hangout in the back lounge as Nigel and Tootsie were already well into the movie they were watching. I listened to Kretz play guitar for a while. When he put the guitar down, I put on a CD of African drum music. I had recently bought a box set of it in Florida. I thought Kretz would be into it. After all he was a professional drummer. After a few minutes Suzi said in her sweetest of voices, "Hot Lips, what the fuck is this?"

"It's an "African drum CD set," I replied. "How long is it?" Kretz asked. "Oh, I have 5 CD's worth," I told him. Not saying anything both Suzi and Kretz glared at me. I got the point. Laughing, I took the CD out of the player. Back in my bunk, I continued to listen to the African drums on my Walkman and began to write.

Chapter 37
Touring with Bands Named After Food

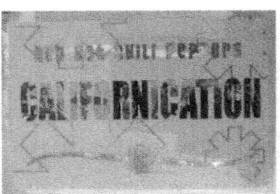

Red Hot Chili Peppers Californication tour passes.

Boston was to be the last show before the Red Hot Chili Peppers jumped on the tour. The show was recorded by VH1. I found out while in Boston that Fishbone would be the opening band for the STP/RHCP tour. I was excited to see Angelo's face when he saw me at the first show. He had no clue I was a roadie now. What were the chances that the only decent sized band I knew in the world would be the opening act on my first tour? I was now even more excited to get to the next leg of the tour. I couldn't wait to see RHCP, and I was especially eager to see Flea perform.

The first show with RHCP was at the Saratoga Performing Arts Center or SPAC. The venue is owned by the state of New York and holds roughly 25,000 people if including the lawn seating.

New to the tour, were a couple lighting guys Nigel had added to the crew. Everything looked the same as it did for the radio shows, but more lights were now on stage. Other changes were, I had to roll out this dance floor material called Marley every day before the show. We put it down because Anthony Kiedis had knee issues. It would roll out onto the stage and then we'd put our gear on top and around it. In addition, we got a heavy-duty barricade for in front of the stage. Having to put up our own barricade was good for me, because I got paid extra for putting it together. Like everything else, I got to be quick at setting it up. It's not hard to get quick at things when you do it every day. It was nice to get paid a bit extra to do something I would have done if Cesar told me to do it anyhow.

The two people hired were Corey and Tabitha. Corey clearly had a drug problem. He was always in a rush to do a million things at once. Tabitha was nice enough but had an authority issue. She wasn't graceful about anything. Aso didn't really care who else had been hired as he was perfectly happy to do all the lighting work himself. Tabitha and Corey marked the beginning of a lot of people getting both hired and fired. I was constantly reminded of how the touring industry is unforgiving and relentless.

Red Hot Chili Peppers Californication tour crew T-shirt.

Cesar had come back on board now, and I was nervous about it. I wanted to make sure he knew I had been doing a good job in his absence and that I was continuing to learn stuff. The Chili Peppers crew kept to themselves. I had really thought I'd make some new friends. I had been excited about some new blood to hang out with, and different people to get to know. What I found was not what I had hoped for. Everyone was cold. Not just to me but to each other. I further retreated into my shell. Much like that tortoise had done a few days earlier.

I pretended I wasn't excited about anything. That I got from

Nigel. I watched my back at every turn. That I got from everybody. I watched Aso and Nigel and how they handled themselves on the stage, and they too were acting differently now. Everyone just had a certain seriousness about their jobs and what needed to be done. I hoped that once we all got to know each other, we'd all have fun, but for the meantime I just kept to myself. I would do my job and then I'd either go wander around the stadiums or hide in the bus.

Red Hot Chili Peppers Californication tour T-shirt.

Because we played before RHCP each night it meant we finished work earlier. I could now shower after I was done working. I could even relax a bit because I didn't have to deal with the lights at all anymore. I'd say I was happy about it, but I wasn't. I wanted a lot of work to do because then I wouldn't worry about getting fired. If I was constantly working, I was needed. While I thought maybe Cesar and Nigel would protect me from the ax, I sometimes had my doubts.

While I was excited to see Fishbone, Angelo was dismissive of me. He was bitter that I was getting paid the same as he was, and I was on my first tour. I shouldn't have let him know that. There were only two people in the Fishbone crew. I found myself picking up after both of them every night. They would leave instruments and their drum rug at almost every venue and leave. Since I had made it a point to always do an "idiot check," and grab anything and everything that I thought may be ours, I began to grab stuff that was theirs as well. I didn't understand how a musician could leave their sax repeatedly. I also got into the habit of taking the pizzas from our bus and bringing them to the Fishbone bus. After a couple weeks of it, Cesar told me to stop. It wasn't my job to pick up after them or feed them he told me. I kept doing it, but I kept quiet about it. I'm sure Cesar knew. He knew everything, but he didn't say anything to me again about it. If it wasn't helping Angelo, I am not sure if I would have kept doing it. One of the nice things about having Fishbone around was that Angelo's father followed them to every show and hung out. I always liked his dad growing up, and it was nice having him around too.

Because Fishbone played before us, I watched every one of their shows. I loved the song "Aids and Armageddon" and I made it no secret. They began to play it every night. It certainly made me feel good to think that I was increasingly having an impact on everything.

Chapter 38
Come on Down to the Price is STP

I was retreating into myself, and I don't think I necessarily minded doing so. I was spending more and more time by myself and writing. I wrote a long letter to my parents thanking them for the opportunity to be on the road. I was also finding that I was missing my friends back at home less than I had been earlier on in the tour. In the beginning I had wished they were all with me, sharing in my experience. I had been finding myself wishing I could still go to parties with them and hang out with everyone on my days off. I didn't like not being around them all. I was now coming to terms that we were all growing up. I wasn't missing out on anything, but neither were they. We were all driving down our own roads.

A major change for me was that I was now certainly becoming tougher. I was mimicking the people I was now surrounded by. Maybe I was on the road to becoming a man, or maybe I was just on the road to becoming a roadie. What was next for me? Drugs and then go to rehab? That was a real question. I honestly wasn't sure. I was learning that being a roadie is a lonely existence, and though I was uncertain of where I was going, I was determined to plow on. Whereas, my friends were worried about where their lives were leading them, I was excited where mine was taking me. I was in a good place.

As the shows continued, I spent more time talking to both Angelo and the guys in STP. Suzi had made a rule on this leg of the tour. Her rule was that only the band, and me, were allowed in the dressing room. The only reason I was allowed, was because I helped her do her work. Because of Suzi's rule, I now spoke to everyone in the band a lot.

I learned a lot about my employers. Dean had worked in construction and had been successful at it. It was his brother, Robert the bass player of STP, who had to talk him into leaving his construction business to focus on the band. I know the cliché thing to say is follow your dreams, but it's a scary thing to take that plunge. I had more respect for Dean knowing he had done this.

STP was called Mighty Joe Young when they first formed. They had to change their name when they got signed because of some copyright issues with the movie I was told, and so they chose STP. Initially, the motor oil company had no issues with it. They even sent the band schwag. However, when Scott got arrested the first time after being signed to the label, the company pushed for STP to change their name. I learned that Stone Temple Pilots meant absolutely nothing. It was the moniker the band came up with - having no choice but to change their name yet again.

When you have a band that has a name with no meaning, you have a wonderful opportunity. You can make nothing mean something. It was unintentional, but the fact they were able to do that made them all the much better to me. They were leaders and not followers in every sense.

I found Kretz to be a genuinely nice guy. The Fishbone guys had told me that when the band first hit the scene, Kretz wasn't much of a drummer. Through the years he had become really good. I wondered if that was really true. Could you really get a record deal and not be very good? There were plenty of musicians I thought sucked but definitely not these guys. I had never thought about it. Did guys in major bands get better in time? It was an interesting thought. With most bands their first album is the best. So, I naturally assumed the whole band had to be great and that it took true genius to write the songs on that first album. After that first album most bands are tapped out and they fizzle away. How many acts have great songs on multiple albums? So, the question sat with me. Do great musicians continue to perform better?

The DeLeo brothers were similar in attitude. Neither was afraid of a fight. They were both big guys and took no crap. They were moody and had bad tempers. But most importantly, both shred on their instruments. Every night Robert's fingers would be bloody because he hit the strings so hard. They were both proud of the band they had created.

Dean was a huge Led Zeppelin fan. Upon request, he would happily play you any Zeppelin song. If in a good mood he would show you, on the guitar, how every STP song was influenced by a Zeppelin song. It's a neat thing to watch. Robert's first concert was Rush. I wondered if he had brought the sound of Rush into STP with the same enthusiasm Dean brought Zeppelin. I never did get a chance to ask him.

Scott Weiland was much more complicated than anyone else in the band. I saw him as a spoiled little kid who was incredibly talented. Although he was a well-known drug addict, I never saw him do any drugs. I had heard many horror stories about what a dick he could be, but he was always good to me.

I once looked through his CD collection and the case was filled with the Carpenters and the Doors. When something would happen at a show, and the band had to improvise for a bit, Scott would often go into a Carpenters song. To me that was magic. I never heard him finish one of these tangent songs, he'd always go back to the show before finishing it, but I hope one day they release some live performances of Scott singing the Carpenters.

Many singers had issues with asthma, and when playing at higher altitudes, Scott would have to run backstage, on occasion, to suck off the oxygen tank. When that happened, the rest of the band would always play Zeppelin. STP was a hell of a jam band.

I felt Scott improved as a front man every night. I looked forward to watching him perform every day. I had never known a heroin addict before. I wondered what gratification he got from all the drugs. Scott tore the stage up without them. So, I figured doing drugs had nothing to do with him being a rock star. I had visions that he was like this giant drug succubus. He would suck drugs in before the shows and spit all the good feelings associated with them back at the audience throughout the night. Once empty, the show would be over. That was all bullshit though. He was just talented at everything. It was that simple. It never crossed my mind that he did drugs for other reasons. Listening to his lyrics, I figured he thought he needed them to create the persona and talent he had created for himself. After watching him day in and day out, he absolutely did not.

Maybe some of all this talent would rub off on me? I was a mix of thoughts and emotions. Maybe every guy at twenty-three is? Or if not, they should be. I was rapidly changing my life completely. While everything was exciting, I was keenly aware that I was starting to get lonely, the daily grind was starting to be hard on me both physically and mentally, and while I was proud of myself for getting through show after show, I still related to no one. I kept on though. There was no question about backing off. I was going to get through this tour.

Chapter 39
The Underwear Commercial Guy

On July 31st we played the PNC arts center again. On August 2nd we played Tinley Park, Illinois. On August 3rd Cincinnati, Ohio at The Riverbend Music Center on the banks of the Ohio River. All tired, on August 4th the bus rolled into Columbus, Ohio. It was at this show the band fired Steve Stewart, their longtime manager. Steve hung out with us, the crew, on the bus after being told to fuck off. He didn't seem to be a train wreck, so I figured he must have known it was coming. In actuality it was very clear, the band was not happy about having to let him go. When we all went on the stage no one was in a good mood. Energy feeds off of itself. We were all out of it. Some guy in the audience pissed off Dean, so Dean spit on the guy. I ran out to the front of the stage in front of 15,000 people ready to kick the guy's ass.

Who's tough? That's right... I'm tough.

I didn't even think about it. I didn't know how to fight. If judging me on appearances I was a hardened, quiet, asshole who was using the name of a serial killer. I was finally feeling comfortable in my tough surroundings. If I were to jump into the crowd with Dean and get my ass kicked, it would make for a good story. At least that was my rationale.

While in Ohio, I met both Scott's parents and his brother Michael. I made sure they were comfortable and did my best to get them whatever they wanted while at the venue. While Scott's mom enjoyed herself and was an absolute delight, his father was rigid and not an easy guy to win over. Scott had told me his dad had been a Notre Dame football player. To break the ice, I told Scott's parents how I had met Joe Montana earlier in the tour. I explained to them that it was my job to clear the stage before the show each evening and how Montana had followed everyone else off stage when I asked them all to leave. "I didn't recognize who he was," I told them. When I circulated back around, he was back on the stage again. I walked back over to kick him off again. "Sir, you are going to have to leave the stage. I try to keep it clear during the shows," I said to him. I continued telling Scott's parents the rest of the story.

Aso had come over to Montana and me the second time I was kicking him off the stage. "Rifken, what the fuck? He's Joe Montana," Aso said in front of him. "Oh, you're the guy from the underwear commercials," I said aloud. Aso put his head in his hands. "Are you fucking kidding me, Rifken?" Montana laughed and shook my hand. "It's OK. Really, I get that all the time," Montana said. "I doubt that's true. Rifken, here is just an idiot," Aso said to him. "I'd rather be an idiot than a fat asshole, which is what you are," I retorted. We both walked off continuing to argue and left Montana standing on the side of the stage by himself.

When telling Scott's parents, the story, I left out the arguing between Aso and me. Scott's dad thought the story was amusing anyhow. "Yeah, that is pretty bad," he said to me. "You know what's even worse? I met him at another show later and I still didn't recognize him. He had to remind me he was the underwear commercial guy," I told them. "He said the underwear commercial guy?" Scott's dad asked. "He actually did, yeah." Scott's mom and dad both laughed this time. "And my son hires you?" his dad asked. "Reluctantly, I promise," I told them smiling.

During the show I made sure to check up on them again. "We all good?" I asked. "Look at him. Dressed up as a woman parading in front of all these people, and that's my son," his father said to me. I wasn't prepared for this. I didn't know what to say. His mother gave me that awkward smile only a mother can offer. "I see thousands of people enjoying themselves, sir. I think you should be proud of your son," I said to him. I said it as polite and humble as I knew how. Scott's dad didn't reply to me. Scott's brother was thoroughly enjoying himself. He was having no problem meeting lots of girls and fit in well with the group. He was a quiet, nice guy. He ended up travelling with us for weeks. I don't know if that was planned or not, but he was easy going and fun to have around.

Chapter 40
The Detroit Sasquatch

The next two shows on August 7th and 8th were at Pine Knob, now the DTE Energy Music Center, just outside of Detroit. It was our first double header. A double header is where you play at the same venue two nights in a row. All musicians love to play at Pine Knob.

There was a stagehand who had hair down to his ankles. It was all matted together and he looked like he had a beaver tail growing out of his head. I called him the Detroit sasquatch. I was convinced he lived outside the venue in a cave amongst the local pine trees. I loved to be in Detroit to see this guy.

However, the bands liked playing Detroit more because of the verm there than the cleanliness of the stagehands. Detroit loves music. A band could be awful, and the verm would scream and clap like they were watching the Rolling Stones open up for the Beatles. Historically, STP's crew opened up for the band themselves when playing in Detroit. Our roadie band was called Irish Cock. For the last couple weeks, the roadies in Irish Cock had been practicing during sound check. They had put together a great version of STP's song "Sour Girl" with alternate lyrics. Irish Cock had changed the chorus words to "Rifken's a Jew" instead of "what would you do." The world was of course a better place for it!

For whatever reason, I was asked to help with the soundcheck early on in the day. Pax asked me to kick the bass drum. I kicked it. "Hit it harder, Rifken," Pax yelled out. I was kicking the pedal pretty damn hard. "Rifken, what the fuck. Kick the fucking drum!" Pax yelled back out. I pulled the beaver guy over to one side. I'd bet he could kick a drum damn hard. Sure enough, he was a kicking machine. I went back to working on my own stuff.

Because I didn't have to break down the gear that night, after the show it meant I could relax a little. After STP, I watched RHCP for the first time. I had seen parts of their show but wasn't able to watch the whole of it before. Flea was amazing. He had a ton of stage presence. Anthony Kiedis didn't move around much because of his knees but I liked his vibe. John Frusciante was an awesome guitar player. The guy played a flying V guitar and it was a magnificent instrument to see. The veins in his arms bulged. They looked like they were ready to burst at any moment. During the set he handed his guitar to his tech who I was standing next to. The guitar was covered in blood. The tech was totally bummed out. It was part of his job to clean the guitar. Who would want to clean the blood off of a junkie's guitar? Not me, thanks! Later I'd find that Frusciante was a decent dude. He was a super quiet guy and kept to himself. Chad the drummer hit the drums like he was trying to break through them. I loved watching him play. If you are going to play the drums hit 'em hard! Not like me.

I was excited to finally watch the whole Chili Peppers set, but I think more excited to know I was working for the better band. STP was a kickass rock show. RHCP felt like just another performance. I thought, and still think, that the issue with concerts is that more often than not bands sounds much better on their CD's. STP was unquestionably much better live, and that was the difference for me.

Chapter 41
Irish Cock

I knew the night of the second show was going to be a fun one. Many of the roadies had met girls the night before and had their new prizes hanging out. We really didn't have much to do all day, so we made our way into Detroit and hit up the stores. I left most of the crew hanging out in the city and headed back to the venue a bit early.

I had begun to write a script about a struggling artist and wanted to work on it. I was modeling my character after Scott Weiland. I called the script An Artist's Art. It was about a guy who paints a picture and destroys it in a fit of drunken rage. The next day an art critic comes over and together they create a new art movement called Destructionism. The guys life spins out of control as he is forced to put his creativity into his product knowing that he must destroy it to find critical acclaim. I thought if I could finish the screenplay, maybe I could get STP to be in my movie or at the very least do some of the music for it. Maybe they'd even pay for the movie to be made? I started spending a lot of time on my writing project. I was looking for opportunity and I saw this as one.

With most of the crew out and about the bus was quiet, I sat down in the front lounge to speak to Cesar. He was too big of a guy to sleep in any of the bunks, so he'd sleep in the front lounge of the bus after everyone else had called it a night. Today he was doing some paperwork. He was a funny sight with his tiny reading glasses on his big head.

"Hey, Cesar, why didn't you fire me when I lost the road case that day?" I asked him. This was a big unanswered question for me. I had seen so many other people get fired. I had come a long way, and I wondered what separated me from the rest of the people that had come and gone. "You were a kid looking for a career in music and I wanted to give you the chance to make it happen," he replied. "Thanks, Cesar. I mean it, too, thanks." Cesar smiled at me. He didn't smile often. I could feel like he was proud of me. When any of the crew wanted to know where Cesar was, they'd got into the practice of asking me where my dad was. He really had become a second father to me in a lot of ways.

On the 8th Nigel and I filled the stage with smoke. You couldn't see a single thing on it. The song Crackerman started up and the audience went crazy. Out from the smoke came Irish Cock. On walked Mugs, megaphone in hand, wearing all leather and a big afro wig. He looked like an overweight Rob Halford, from Judas Priest, with a circa 1980's Tina Turner hairdo. He turned around to face Aso, who was the drum player, and revealed to everyone he was wearing assless chaps. I pranced out on the stage in small shorts and rolled up sleeves to hand Mugs a face towel. Parker played bass and Pablo, our guitar tech, played guitar. Mugs handed me Scott's megaphone and I handed him the mic. Not wasting any time, I grabbed cable from the deck, aka the stage, and hurriedly moved it… nowhere. I kept running back and forth on the stage to fix nothing. They played half the song and then walked off the stage. I looked around the stage to see where everyone had gone and then followed them off. We filled the stage with smoke again, and STP came on to finish the song. It was all a lot of fun.

That night, during the show, Scott yelled out to the audience to, "come on down." The crowd all rushed the stage. Watching 12,000 plus people rush towards you is frightening. But everyone was cool, for the rest of the night everyone, and I mean everyone, in the audience sang every word to every song. Detroit's fans were not ready to disappoint.

A little over half way through the song "Plush" from the album *Core*, at three minutes and thirty-seven seconds to be exact,

Scott would always jump. I don't know who started it, but if I had to guess I'd say Suzi. Anyhow, everyone on the crew used to do a little hop at the same moment. If you were seated, you'd raise your feet. It was a feet off the floor moment, no excuses! It always amused me while explaining to the stagehands how our load out was going to go, I'd hop out of nowhere. They'd always look at me like I was a nutcase. I would of course never explain the STP hop to anyone, so it made it for all the more fun. I'll bet everyone on the crew still does the hop at 3:37 when that song comes on. I know I still do.

That night just after the STP hop, Kretz stood up and left the drum set. We all looked back at the drums to see what was going on. Moments later Chad Smith sat down on the kit and finished out the song. It was killer.

Chapter 42
Ballin' in the Front Lounge

STP basketball jersey, 2000.

We had all been touring roughly three and a half months now, and we had become a family. A dysfunctional family but nonetheless still a family. I was beginning to associate the smell of the fog from the fog machines to being home, much like the smell of oil in my dad's garage had made me feel comfortable throughout my youth. Certain rock stars were doing too much blow, while other rock stars were rumored to be back on heroin. It seemed to me Kretz was playing the drums a bit slow, out of time, and was pissing off the rest of the band. Robert was stressed out trying to hold everything together, and Scott was spending more and more time with his drug counselor when not running on his treadmill or watching the Lakers game. We were collectively living Rock 'n' Roll.

Every day I'd have to find a place where I could set up Scott's treadmill. Most often the venue and Suzi had figured it out, and I'd have to just put the machine in place and plug it in for him. Scott would run hours every day on it. If you left the guy in a room with a treadmill and a TV to watch the Laker game, he was easy to deal with. Take them away and he'd blow up.

On the crew side we had a new driver I hadn't really spoken to. A few of the guys had messed with Hobo a bit too much and he had left the tour. Hobo had passed out on the couch in front of the bus. You never want to do that. If you make it to your bunk you are pretty much safe. If you pass out in one of the lounges, especially the front lounge, you are asking for trouble. One of the sound guys had taken photos of Aso dangling his balls over Hobo's open mouth. Not wanting to be part of the incident, I had gone to the back lounge when it had all gone down. I knew when Hobo saw those photo's he was going to kill someone. Though no one died, Hobo did leave us after we left Detroit.

After a day off, we played the Charleston Civic Center. During load in my dad called me. "Dad, a bit busy right now, anything important?" I asked. My dad wasted no time getting into what he wanted to talk to me about. "No, you are going to listen to me. I have a man on the phone who is going to hire you." A third person chimed in with a faint, "hello." Oh man, the guy was actually on the phone. I couldn't help but laugh a little. When did my dad learn how to make three-way phone calls? "I have to answer this other call. You two chat." My dad left us. "Hello," I asked into the phone. The man was still on the line. "Hey," he said back. I could hear he was slightly distressed. "Don't worry, man, just tell my dad you are going to hire me. You don't really have to," I told him. "Oh, OK, I just want to get my car running again," he told me. "Yeah, yeah no worries," I replied. My dad clicked back on the line. "Did you two speak to one another? He started his company out of his garage. He's done very well," he said. "Yeah, we talked, Dad. We had a good conversation. All good here," I said. "All set then, Steve?" my dad asked. I found out later the man on the phone was Steve Wozniak. The co-founder of Apple. I should have shut up and made him hire me.

After Charleston we headed out to New York City for another

day off, and then another double header at Jones Beach Amphitheatre. I was excited to get to NYC. I had a couple friends I could have hung out with on my day off, but I opted to head up to Oyster Bay and hang out with an old college friend, Brenden, for the day.

In New York City, it wasn't hard to hail a cab. The drive up to Oyster Bay is an hour and a half or so long and so I figured I'd strike up conversation with the cabbie. "How things going, man?" I asked. "Pretty good, I just got out of jail this morning for beating the shit out of my wife. I'll be off my shift in a few hours and when I get home, I'm gonna put her in the fucking hospital," he told me. "Well, fuck man. So, what's the pretty good part?" I asked him. The remaining hour and fifteen minutes I didn't say anything and neither did he. It was a very uncomfortable cab ride.

Oyster bay was a bit more relaxing. Brendan took me to Teddy Roosevelt's house and then we hung out with a couple gorgeous girlfriends of his. I had to leave the fun at midnight, to head back into the city. The next day I'd have to be in the hotel lobby at 7:30AM. I thanked everyone and headed back to the city in a taxi. The taxi cab ride back was a good one this time. The man who picked me up was a struggling writer. I told him I had been working on a film script and he wished me luck. How many writers are taxi cab drivers? Actors are waiters and writers, I think, drive taxis. That's how I figure it. Hanging out with Brendan showed me I needed to keep my nose to the grindstone. Being a roadie was a lot of fun, but if I wanted to rub shoulders with Oyster Bay type people one day, I'd have to figure out how to make more money than I was going to make by being a roadie. It was all very humbling.

Venue crew meal pass.

Jones Beach is truly a marvel. The stage literally sits in the water. We played there two nights. It's a magical place. In the morning of the first day, I was the first one out of the bus to go get some breakfast. When I got into the designated breakfast area, they had a whole omelet bar laid out. This was not the norm and I was happy about it. I told the lady what I wanted in my omelet. She gave me a dirty look and told me, "you can make it yourself and put whatever you want in it." I shrugged my shoulders and started filling the frying pan with eggs and whatever else was there. Nigel walked in first. "You are letting him cook?" he asked. Nigel thought this was hilarious and the lady didn't respond. Next was Jerry Bowker, our video guy. "Wow, Rifken, who let you close to fire?" he said with a big smile. The lady now paid a bit more attention. Tootsie walked in next and saw me holding the frying pan. He just laughed. "Would you like me to help you with that?" she asked. "Sure," I said casually and sat down. She made me a kickass omelet. The next day she didn't even ask. She just made me an omelet. Years later I see it as another example of how roadies, or maybe just me, can be inept at real life.

Roadie Ramble Moment

One device in the kitchen I do know how to use well is the microwave. The only part of operating this piece of high end kitchenry that I'm puzzled about is the "microwave on high" function that I presume mine has. I've never owned a microwave with a high or low button selection that I am aware of. I do have a power button though. So, is it this power button that is hiding the high and low heat level to set my Top Ramen to? In addition, I ask if you've ever had something to cook that asked for the temperature to be set to low in the microwave? I haven't. Still, my Top Ramen tastes just fine not selecting a heat level, and so I don't think it's a big concern. However, with all the technological breakthroughs we still haven't figured out how to make microwaves that you can put metal into? Guangdong Galanz Group Co.,Ltd., say that five times fast, in China is the largest microwave manufacturer in the world. They make roughly 50% of the microwaves sold today. If they don't figure out this metal thing soon, I'll let the high setting issue slide; I say we find another manufacturer to hand the microwave making torch to.

While at Jones Beach, I had a more important reminder than how to make an omelet. Remember, the rig is pulled up to trim by motors. You control the climbing and descending of the motor with a remote, we call it a pickle. If you are not careful, you can get the cable attached to the pickle or the whip (the whip is the cable coming from the motor) caught up in the chain. That morning I had done just that, I got the whip caught in the motor, but luckily realized it quickly. I ran the motor chain back and the problem was solved. Seeing me run the chain back, Nigel scolded me. He told me a motor is 180v, and this mistake could have been a big deal. He informed me it takes 30v to kill someone. I was worried Cesar, not the motor, was going to kill me if he found out. I'm not sure what would have been worse, getting fried on a stage surrounded by the water of Jones Beach or having Cesar crush me like a bug. Aso and Nigel never told Cesar, and so I survived on.

Since then I've learned that I would have survived anyhow, it is amps that kill you and not volts. A motor is actually 208v and it would blow a breaker if there was a short probably before even shocking you. It certainly would not kill you. It was important for me to watch what I was doing either way, but it became yet another instance of the crew messing with me.

That night Adrian Young hung out with all of us again. He took the bus back, and we all hung out after the show, as we didn't have to do a load in in the morning. We had some good laughs. I was really learning to like him. He was a good dude.

Chapter 43
Hi! My name is (what?)

The new STP management, a big company called Q Prime, showed up on the second night. One of the management guys struck up a conversation with Kretz. While Kretz is a great guy to talk to, the management guy thought he was speaking to Scott Weiland. We all thought it was hilarious. The band's new management company couldn't even look at a photograph to see who each guy in the band was. We immediately sent a runner out to get name tags. The crew all wore name tags that night that said *Hi! My Name is Scott*.

At the end of the show, Scott took his pants off and danced around naked. I guess you could say he was really feeling the moment. It was raining, so maybe he liked to dance naked in the rain. Or maybe being close to the ocean he wanted to Free Willy. If I had to bet, I'd say the new management questioned what they had gotten themselves into.

On August 14th, 2000 a reporter for the New York Post basically wrote in a published review that STP blew RHCP off the stage the first night at Jones Beach. He noted Scott was mad at the audience because they weren't appreciating the band as much as he thought they should, at the end of the show Scott pulled his pants off and cupped his junk. He had only done that so that he wouldn't get arrested for indecent exposure. The Post felt the entire audience had come to see RHCP. I don't know why Scott took his clothes off, but I don't think he was mad at the audience at all. I think he just liked doing nutty rock star kind of stuff. I also think he knew that after his performance RHCP were going to have a tough time competing. He was right. RHCP had been completely outperformed.

On the second day of Jones Beach, I overheard part of the

RHCP crew talking about how the band knew they were getting blown off the stage. They weren't happy about it. I rushed off to the STP dressing room. The first person I saw was Robert, and I told him the cool news. He rounded up the rest of the band. "OK, Rifken, tell us again," Robert said to me. "The RHCP guys are pissed that you guys are blowing them off the stage. I overheard them all talking about it." Everyone in the band looked on at me very seriously. Dean stood up, and then rushed me. He grabbed onto me, and Robert started giving me a noogie. "Is this some shit you guys would do to each other when you were kids?" I said. Next time I looked up, it was Scott giving me a noogie. "What the fuck?" Scott moved his arms to try and give me a wedgie, but I was able to stop him in time. I yelled "I was a high school wrestler, bitches," as I broke away from them and made my way to the other side of the room where Kretz was trying to read. Triumphant, I held my hands in the air. "Last time I tell you guys good news," I said. At this point we were all laughing. Suzi walked into the room wondering what we were all so happy about? "Hot Lips, are you going to put up my Xmas lights?" she asked.

This was great news. It's a great feeling to find out that all your hard work is being noticed. The energy on stage that night was intense. The next show was at Darien Center by Buffalo, NY. The night before one of the buses hit a deer. The front driver's side of the bus was bashed in and the windshield looked like a spider's web. I didn't know we had such a great artist on the crew, but Bully, one of the two pyro guys, spent much of his day drawing a deer carcass on the parking lot asphalt in front of the bus. I, like most of the crew, stopped by periodically to see how it was coming along. At the end of the day the asphalt was covered with entrails, a decapitated head, and all sorts of other deer parts I wouldn't have known existed. All done in great detail with chalk, it was clear Bully had forged his way ahead pursuing the wrong career.

The rest of the day I remember well. I had smashed my right thumb when a road case slammed shut on it, not once, but twice in the same day. It went from black to bright red. The pain was excruciating. I drowned my agony with a gorgeous blonde gymnast who was working at the show. She took me to the bars on Chippewa street that night. We found some of the guys from the crew at a spot and we all got wasted together. The crew was determined to all get me a hooker. I'm not sure why because I was there with a girl. The rest of the night was a bit of a blur, but I did wake up in my bunk on the bus. Remember, your bunk is a safe zone. Unless you are in NYC, you can almost always find the bus parked in the hotel parking lot. If the night gets too crazy, it's a good idea to sleep in the bus. That way, worst case scenario, you won't miss call in the morning. No matter how bad things are you must report to work in the morning.

On August 16th we headed back into Canada. We were set to play only four more shows with Fishbone. After that we'd have a 10-day break and play at the smallest show we'd do on the tour, the Whiskey on the Sunset Strip in Los Angeles.

I was going to miss touring with Fishbone. I had spent time connecting with the guys in the band, especially Angelo. Even though he was a bit grumpy at the beginning of the tour, he warmed up quickly. He liked talking about being a kid on Hatteras, where we both grew up. Angelo's father didn't go with us up into Canada and to me it felt like one of the troops had left. It made me comfortable knowing I had people around me I'd known my whole life on my first tour. I was lucky, it was like setting a new ship off to sea. Except I was a dinghy, and it was a big ocean not a sea.

Chapter 44
The Go Get the Coffee Guy

We flew up into Canada on a small plane. Mugs was deathly afraid of flying and especially did not like small aircraft. He was seated next to an old lady and as we were about to take off, he grabbed her arm. Frail, I wasn't sure if he was going to break it. On the other side of the aisle was where I sat. I saw an opportunity for a good wind up and began humming the song "La Bamba" to myself. Mugs gave me a very dirty look. "What, it's a good song," I said to him. Pretending I was unaware of anything odd about my song selection or the timing of it, I changed the hum to Buddy Holly's "Donna." "When we get out of this plane, I'm going to kick the shit out of you. What do you think about that Rifken?" Mugs asked me. "I guess that depends on if we make it there or not," I smugly replied. No one on the crew really found me funny. Unexpectedly, the old lady leaned forward. "You need to keep quiet young man," she said to me. "Man, tough crowd," I said to no one in particular and went to sleep.

Homemade STP mix tape!

We landed in Toronto and all loaded up into yet another white passenger van. The driver was a young guy who sure enough had a STP tape cassette playing when we climbed in. We all loaded into the van and he took off immediately. Hearing the music, Nigel rolled his eyes.

"I thought I was going to pick up the band. None of you guys are in the band, huh?" he asked. I couldn't help to laugh. Jerry answered the kid. I liked Jerry because he would sometimes give me a hand but more importantly, he had never been a dick to me. The counter opposite of Cesar Reivax, Jerry Bowker was a skinny dorky guy. He was easy going but very particular and was absolutely proud of his job. Jerry answered the guy. "No, man, you are out of luck."

"So, you the go get the coffee guy?" the driver asked Jerry. While I liked Jerry, he absolutely had an inflated ego. This kid asking him one of the dumbest questions I've ever heard anyone ask another human being was especially funny. We all laughed our asses off. Jerry didn't find it at all funny. Through an uneasy laugh, he said, "No, I'm not." Nigel and I were now crying with laughter. "What do you do then if you don't get them coffee?" the driver asked. "Don't worry about it. Just get us to the hotel. And can you turn the tape off please?" He had evidently quickly become tired of the driver. From then on Jerry was known as the "go get the coffee guy." He didn't really get mad when anyone called him that other than when I chose to. I think it was because if there was a "go get the coffee guy" in reality that guy would have been me.

The Molson Amphitheatre, Toronto gig sweatshirt.

The next morning the same kid picked us up in the van. He

again wasn't very happy that no one in the band was with us. He didn't play any music this time or talk to any of us. As we pulled up to the Molson Amphitheatre there were police barricades and policemen everywhere. The driver drove the van right up to one of the barricades and the cop motioned him to move on down the street.

Instead, the driver rolled his window down and the cop walked over. "International rock superstars- move the barricade," he said in an official tone. I watched on in astonishment as the cops scurried to move the barricades to let us through. Again, everyone in the van was crying with laughter. Well, everyone but Jerry. "I love this guy. Do you realize dude if you tried to pull that crap in LA the cops would have beat the shit out of you? And what the fuck is an international rock superstar?" I asked the guy. The driver didn't reply to me, but I think he was very proud of himself.

The show had sold out in 24 hours. To clarify, sold out meant 16,000 seats were sold in one day. I expected it to be a raucous event. It wasn't. The audience was quiet. Scott was trying hard to get them going and to wake up, but he wasn't getting anywhere. He yelled at the audience "This isn't a Celine Dion concert," and "This isn't a motherfucking dinner theatre," but he still didn't get anywhere. The Canadians weren't having it. As with a lot of concerts, festivals excluded, the people sitting in the front were quiet and still. So, Scott yelled at the people in the back, "to come on down to the stage," and they did in heaps. Scott kept yelling, "Come on - I'm not afraid. Come on down." I wondered if we were going to get crushed, but other than there not being a lot of arm room in the audience the Canadians stayed civil.

From Toronto we headed into Quebec. I loved the European feel of the place. I spent my day off walking around the old city. The city is surrounded by walls, and I felt like I was walking through a mini Jerusalem. I ended up at a store that sold medieval clothing, and I spent a good amount of money on some corsets for my two sisters. I thought they were cool looking. Immediately when I got back, Mugs told everyone that I had spent the day buying lingerie for my sisters. The word spread like wildfire. Everyone was immediately making fun of me about it. I had gotten better at this point about blowing stuff off. It seemed like every day I did something these guys would give me a hard time about. So, I didn't really care that much.

From Quebec we went into Montreal where the show was going to be taped. I put time into making sure everything looked as good as it could. This was also going to be the last show with Fishbone. I knew I was going to miss them. I felt a bit like my crutch was going to be pulled out from under me. It was nice that I could go to their bus whenever I needed a break from STP and the crew. There, no one would give me a hard time.

Angelo had been playing sax on Plush and that had been a treat. I spent some time with Fishbone that day, just hanging out in the bus, knowing it was our farewell. Angelo was telling me how when STP first started out they played a lot of punk. I loved punk music. That soon transitioned into him telling me stories about all the dumb stuff I did when I was a little kid. The rest of the band thought those stories were funny. We grew up on a steep hill and I had ridden my skateboard into Angelo's ivy and hit a tree. His mom had come out and had cleaned me up. That story seemed to be the crowd pleaser. Why do people like stories about kids getting beat up?

Most days I'd wander around the venue to generally see what everyone was up to. RHCP had a yoga instructor that travelled with them named Michael Jackson. He was a tall, skinny, white, guy with a bunch of pimples. I know… exactly how anyone would envision a guy named Michael Jackson to look like! I loved bugging the guy mostly because he wanted nothing to do with me. Whenever I saw him, I'd loudly say his full name,

Michael Jackson, in a high-pitched voice and then try and do some toe tapping and finish it off with a "hee hee."

Michael Jackson would spend most of his day setting up a room backstage. The dude made great efforts to make his daily square room both comfortable and yoga friendly. While I was backstage bothering Michael Jackson with yoga questions, I saw Anthony Kiedis hanging out with a young kid and his father. The kid was there through the Make A Wish Foundation. I overheard Anthony telling him, "Man, you look good. Your skin has good color." That made the kid smile. It's very powerful when a kid is running a conversation with an adult and not vice versa. They discussed music and life in general. I was humbled with the way Anthony handled the situation. It has to be very hard when a dying kid asks to meet you as their final wish. You could tell the kid was excited to be talking to Anthony, yet he kept himself reserved. I'll never forget his face nor his strength. I'll also always admire Kiedis for how I saw him handle the difficult situation.

Chapter 45
Buttered Rain

The Fishbone guys were trying to come up with something to do for their last show. I told them that they should all come out wearing nothing but socks like RHCP had been famous for doing back in the day. But I told them to instead all wear socks that would drag across the floor. "You know 'cause black guys are famous for being well endowed," I said. I think a couple of the guys pissed themselves when I said, "well endowed." The whole bus lit up with laughter. "It was just an idea, shit guys," I said. "He said well endowed," Angelo laughed on. Leaving the bus, I thought one of them may actually roll down the bus steps after me uncontrollably laughing.

After leaving them I hit up the dressing room to see Suzi. The guys and I all chatted, and for the first time Scott called me by my name. They had clearly been talking to him about me. I profoundly respected him and I was pleased that I was really on his radar now.

As the show started, everyone in Fishbone came out wearing nothing but socks dragging on the floor. They had listened to me. I loved it! At the end of the show, Angelo threw his sock into the audience and ran off the stage. As he ran by me, he waved. "Aw, Jesus Angelo. I didn't need to see that," I yelled at his back. I could hear him laughing all the way down the hallway.

By this point I was working as the stage manager for STP. I knew what being a stage manager really meant now. I was even getting good at it. I would split up all the stagehands in the morning and try and make sure everything went smoothly throughout the day. I'd make sure the set looked good and spoke to the security daily about how to handle the audience.

While STP was performing, I'd grab anything off the stage that had been thrown up there. I would clean up any liquid so Scott or any of the other guys wouldn't slip. I'd grab Scott's clothes as he threw them on the stage. Basically, I was there for anything and everything.

While I was working as a stage manager and cleaning up some beer on the stage, Dean jumped on my back and started riding me across the stage like a horse. At that same moment hundreds of garbage bags of buttered popcorn fell from above. The popcorn kept falling until the stage and everything on it was covered. The popcorn rain was RHCP having their own fun. I didn't quite get the joke, but I did eat some of the popcorn as it fell, it was good. When RHCP came on, we did nothing to retaliate, Cesar forbade it.

After STP left the stage, Bobby Leigh, the Chili Pepper's tour manager came out to have a "relaxed chat" with me. The point of it was to further wind me up. Set change is go time, and on top of everything else, I now had a lot to clean up. Bobby was trying to waste my precious set change time. Bobby was an easy-going guy who looked more like a rock star than any of the band members themselves did. He watched on with a big grin, eating popcorn, and watching us all clean the stage like frantic squirrels. I don't think Cesar found it very funny.

Earlier in the tour I had spent my day hitting on one of the security girls at a venue. Bobby had noticed her too; we had discussed how cute she was. This is how males' bond. As the day progressed, and I got busier with work, he too began to chat her up. Years later I ran into Bobby at a film convention, and over a couple of drinks, reminded him of the cute girl. More had happened with the girl than I had ever known. He had flown back and spent the weekend with the girl after the tour. Months after that she had called him and told him she was pregnant. Bobby at the time was maybe 35 years old. Bobby flew back to see her. When he got there, he was invited over to her father's house for dinner. While eating, she confessed that she had lied to him and was only 16 years old. The father spent the rest of the evening telling Bobby what it's like to be a man. He was dying of cancer and his wife had died a few years earlier. He wanted Bobby to marry his daughter immediately. I'm sure the dinner was very awkward. He did say they had very good fried chicken though. In the end the girl had a miscarriage and Bobby Leigh saved himself lots of money in child support.

I wished Fishbone on their way and we ended out the tour. The next night we were to do a performance for Music Plus TV, Canada's version of MTV, and then head home for ten days. The guys had one more gig doing the Late Show with David Letterman, but I'd be skipping that. The gig at Music Plus TV went very well. It was fun to see all the people outside peering through the windows to watch the performance.

That night the band put us up in suites in Canada. I had never stayed in such a nice hotel before. I felt like royalty for the whole three hours I spent in my rooms. I had just enough time to shower and take a catnap. I headed down to the lobby and took the van to the airport. I was looking forward to going home and getting a break. I was tired, but still full of adrenaline from the ride I was on. The most important part was I knew I'd be coming back on the next leg. I was determined to spend my time at home not just catching up with my friends, but working on my movie script. I now knew what I wanted to do with my life next.

Chapter 46
Alpha Dog

When I got home, I found out that just after the Pine Knob double header on August 9th a few people I had grown up with had killed a 15-year-old kid named Nick Markowitz. Years later they would make a movie about the murder called *Alpha Dog*. While I was growing up and enjoying myself on the road, some of the people I had known since elementary school had grown up to murder a kid execution style over a drug deal. I had bought weed, to sell, from Jesse James Hollywood and used to see him regularly before going on the road. He had a Honda that he had put a ton of money into. He had it tricked out through my friend's car stereo shop. He was now all over the news as the man who ordered the murder. All the people involved in the murder used to hang out at the shop almost every day. I had not heard about what happened because I was away and busy working. It was an odd feeling to see people I knew on the front page of the Los Angeles Times. If I had kept selling weed, would this kind of thing have been something I would have potentially been involved in? I didn't know, but I was glad I was doing something else with my life. Once home, I met with friends. It was common knowledge around the valley that Jesse's dad had sent him down to South America. Yet I saw his dad on TV, pleading that Jesse turn himself in. How could we all know this, and the police didn't?

A friend of mine's father was a police investigator and had told his son that the police had compiled a list of small marijuana dealers, and I was on that list. I didn't know if it was true or not, but I was very ready to get back on the road and get away from all of this.

To get away from it all, I took a couple of my girlfriends to see a concert. Steve Stewart, STP's previous manager, managed a band called Palo Alto and I thought it may be fun to go see them play. The three of us got drunk and had a good time. On the way home Cherilyn, who was driving, got a DUI. The other girl, Megan, and I crashed at Cherilyn's parent's house. The two of these women would play big parts in my life as a young man. Megan Ryan was one of my closest friends. She was a tall, gorgeous blonde, with a loud hearty laugh. It wasn't a sexy laugh but it was an incredibly distinctive one, and we all loved to hear it. She was a dating machine and wasn't secretive about her fast-paced relationship status. When she was on her period, she'd spend the week changing her hair style. I think whether a lover or a friend, she was a firecracker who was fun to be around. Cherilyn Gamal was a tall Egyptian brunette, who worshipped Courtney Love, and wanted to be a musician. However, she had no musical talent. Autotune can only do so much. If you typed "long legged vixen" into google, I'd hope she'd show up. We'd regularly get into arguments over who would kick whose ass. Truth is, she'd probably win, but remaining truthful I damn well would have enjoyed it. She and Megan had met in an all-girls high school. Most of the circle of girls I hung out with had gone to the same high school with them, and I had met them through either one or the other. Megan and Cherilyn knew each other well. They had dated the same guys, hooked up with each other once or twice, and, most importantly to me, always went to same breakfast place to catch up. Having gone there with them a few times, I knew why. I loved the place.

In the morning I picked Cherilyn up from jail. After the DUI Cherilyn didn't seem too concerned about the situation. She said her parents would get her out of it all. I told her I thought she was being irresponsible and should reflect on the current situation a bit more. She didn't talk to anyone for years. Megan and the rest of the girls wondered what the hell I had told her. I wasn't sure. Years later when I ran back into her at a pub on St. Patty's Day, ...I moved in with her.

When I got home from picking Cherilyn up at jail, I wasn't able to park in the driveway. My dad was busy mopping the driveway with kerosene. Years earlier, he had begun surrounding the house with kerosene to keep the bugs out. Now he just coated everything that was concrete with it. I parked in the street. "Hello, Joe Ellie" he said to me with a big smile. I don't know why he liked to make my name sound like a girl's name when he had given me a boy's name, but nonetheless he did it all the time. "Jesus, Dad, the smell of that stuff is no joke," I said. "It burns off quickly," he replied. I went inside and went to sleep.

Now, I'm a light sleeper but that day I was tired. While I was fast asleep, my father came into my room. When I didn't wake up, with his thumb and forefinger he pinched my nose closed. If you have never been awakened by someone pinching your nose, consider yourself lucky. For some reason, it was the way my dad liked to wake me when I was a little kid and didn't get out of bed. Not a little kid now, I think he just did it because he thought it was funny.

"You can park your car in the driveway now if you like," he informed me. I knew I had to get up to park my truck in the driveway now or he'd keep bugging me. He didn't like leaving cars in the street. I wondered if I'd pull into a wet driveway one day and find out the wet wasn't water but kerosene and then my truck would blow up. I could picture my dad in court. "It is rather unfortunate Joe Ellie's truck blew up with him in it, but I had to keep the driveway clean, your honor," he'd say.

Now awake, I decided to logon to this new thing called the internet. I loved signing into AOL and writing to people. I figured I'd write to Megan. I knew she was mad at me still. She hadn't called me in a couple days.

I was concerned about her because she was drinking and doing a lot of blow with the other girls. Pre-partying with us before a date she had, I watched as she drank a whole box of wine. Why drink a box of wine before going out? Wasn't the point to get drunk together on a date?

Ready to leave, she threw on a big heavy coat. It looked like a pimp coat but she was wearing it. So, it would have made her... well, not a pimp. For some reason I was focusing on a bit of peach fuzz on her upper lip. She had a girl mustache. Both of us drunk, I figured I'd tell her about the fuzz. It would be better to get rid of it before going on her date, right? "All I'm saying is I'd be more on top of shaving the peach fuzz above your lip than drinking a whole fucking box of wine, Megan," was something along the lines of what I said. "Excuse me, motherfucker," was something along the lines of how she replied. While I was kind of joking around when I told her about her hairy lip, she was absolutely not joking around when responding. "You know what, JOEL. If I have a fucking beard, I don't want to hear about it from you," she told me. Trying to retrace my steps, I was ready to tell her anything, "OK, OK, no worries. I was just trying to be helpful." She opened the front door to leave. "You fucking asshole. You mother fucking piece of shit. Why the fuck do I talk to you?" she spewed. There may have been more that came out of her mouth, but all those expletives were certainly amongst the wrath of angry woman I heard that day. She slammed the door of my friend's house and left. Our friend Samantha spoke up. "That went well. Good job, Joel." The rest of the girls there greatly enjoyed my foot in the mouth moment.

I was realizing more and more that while I was missing home, there wasn't much at home for me to miss. I was finding I had less and less in common with any of the people I considered friends.

Chapter 47
Fucking Idiot

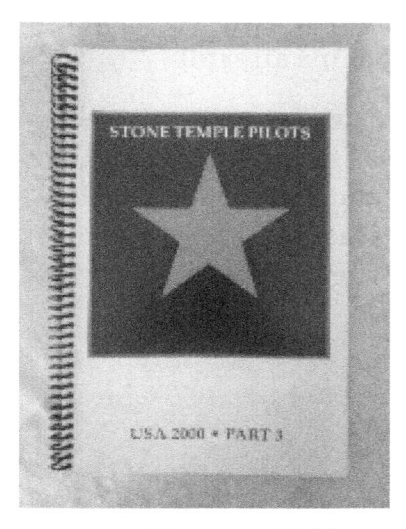

STP tour itinerary- third leg.

On August 31ˢᵗ STP played a show at the Whiskey in Hollywood. Nigel was determined to get as much of the show rig as we could on the tiny stage. When we were done setting up, I wondered how the guys were going to fit up there. STP played five songs and the Chili Peppers played six. The event was hosted by Mark and Brian, radio DJ's on KLOS, I think. The show was a lot of work for the short performances. It was neat to see how Scott was able to completely change his stage presence to accommodate a really small venue where there wasn't much room to move around. At the Whiskey he was able to successfully draw in every person in the audience. The guy was a master.

Juliette Lewis was interviewed by the radio hosts and throughout she kept staring at me and smiling. It's no wonder I don't remember the DJ's on stage. She was gorgeous. When she was done with the interview, she walked off the stage but didn't make any further note of me. As soon as I got on the bus, I told the crew guys that she had been staring at me. Mugs wasted no time bursting my bubble. "She's dating Brad Pitt you fucking idiot." Everyone loved when Mugs called me a *fucking idiot* in that heavy Bostonian accent. But he did have a point, maybe she wasn't staring at me after all.

The next two shows were at Irvine Meadows in California. My little sister, who was still in high school, Megan, and Samantha cruised down for the second show. They got there very late and only saw STP's last few songs. It was fun to have them all there but a shame they missed most of the show.

Show poster Coors Amphitheatre, 2000.

After Irvine we headed down to the Coors Amphitheatre in Chula Vista, near San Diego. As we headed away from Los Angeles, things starting to ramp up again. The farther I was away from home, the more I felt like the roadie I had now become. And what I had now become was a pretty hardened asshole. To survive out on the road I felt I had to be.

STP had finished their show at the Coors Amphitheatre, and I was loading the gear into the truck with the local stagehands. Loadout was the worst time to talk to me. It was my busiest and most rushed part of the day. As we were about to start loading the truck, this pretty girl approached me and said "hi." I replied, "Hey, this isn't really the best place for you to be right now." "No, I know you," she responded. "I'm sure you do, but I have to do a lot of work right now and you are in the way," I told her. "Your name is Joel. I'm Erin. I grew up with you." She was right. I was so busy I hadn't even recognized her. I had been a total dick. While she was in the way and it wasn't a good time, I did realize that I was going to have to work on my people skills. I got her phone number to catch up later but kicked myself for being so rude. There were elements in who I was becoming that I didn't think were good. For whatever reason, being rude to Erin was the humbling experience I needed at that moment. It made me realize I should make a conscious effort not to become a bitter prick like many of the roadies I worked with. I was sure gorgeous women like Juliette Lewis didn't like bitter pricks.

Chapter 48
The Ultimate Roadie

Gig bowling shirt made for band members only at the Shoreline Amphitheatre. Given to me by Scott.

Show poster September 13, 2000.

Austin, Mountain View, Sacramento, Fresno, & Las Vegas all came and went. In Fresno the guys played the song "No Way Out." They had only played it a couple times before. The show was really good, one of their best thus far. I had now become immersed in the internet and I wanted to try and live stream the shows. I didn't know if the technology was there yet, but I figured it would be a great way to transition my job into something that could make me real money. No one in the crew really cared about the idea, and I was failing at changing anyone's mind.

I had now honestly become tired of everyone. The bigger problem may have been that perhaps all of us were tired of each other. It's hard to live in close quarters with so many people. It doesn't help when you also have the addition of a physically demanding and stressful job. We all did. I was glad Nigel and Cesar liked me, so I wasn't worried about getting fired as much anymore, but I was burning out. No one ever helped me with my work and the massive workload was wearing me down.

Show poster for Wyoming, Idaho, & Washington.

From Vegas we drove to Casper, Wyoming in our brand-new tour bus. It had only done one tour. That tour was with Ozzy Osbourne and the drawers in the front lounge were filled with candy. I liked this bus full of candy. The only thing I didn't like was it didn't have the little windows in the bunks. So, I began spending quite a bit of my time in the front of the bus sitting in the captain's chair. The captain's chair is a chair that you can pull down and sit on next to the bus driver. I'd look out the big windows and unwind. From the front of the bus I experienced wonderful things. I saw a sign with a population of three. How many people did it take to make the sign I wondered? Once again, I enjoyed America as I watched it pass by. You know, dead bodies in the forests and deserts and stuff. I worked on my film script, listened to my Walkman, but mostly I zoned out. The new driver kept to himself, and I enjoyed sitting up front where no one would bug me.

While on the bus a week or so earlier, I had seen a new band called Disturbed on MTV. While the crew was watching the music video, I spouted off on a tirade. I wanted everyone to know that what we were watching wasn't music. It was just a bunch of guys yelling. I had become a diehard STP fan and really felt the bar across the board needed to be elevated to their level. Cesar told me, "to be careful who I talked shit about." Earlier on in the tour I had seen Eminem perform at a radio show. He sang the song "So You Can Suck My Dick." I shook my head and walked off the stage. I couldn't believe the crap I was listening to.

I'm now a fan of Eminem. He's a brilliant lyricist and wrote some great stuff, but that day I left wondering what had become of music. After seeing me walk off the stage shaking my head, Cesar pulled me aside and yelled at me. He told me I should never again let anyone know if I do or don't like a performer. I may have to work with them one day, and I wouldn't want anyone remembering my attitude. It was during this bus ride I found out the next leg of the tour's lineup. It would be STP, Godsmack, and none other than Disturbed. What were the odds that the one act I had opened my mouth about on MTV would be the next band I'd be working with? Cesar had been right yet again; I was going to have to keep my mouth shut.

From Wyoming we did five more shows in seven days. I was ready to leave RHCP behind and experience headlining a tour. My job would be harder yet again, as STP would now be finishing the night instead of RHCP. That, of course, meant more work hours for me. But I still felt STP's performances were getting better and better, and I was ready for it.

The overall feel of the crew was genuine excitement. We all wanted to be on our own tour. We were informed a new guy would be joining us. Nigel told me he was a badass, the ultimate roadie. I couldn't wait to meet the guy. His name was Rigger Steve. What would an ultimate roadie be so good at? I looked forward to finding out.

Chapter 49
Cinderella Lost Her Shoe

On September 28th the crew all got hotel rooms in Hollywood. I had been staying at my parent's house and commuting to storage, or to our rehearsal facilities, as we all were getting ready for the next leg of the tour. It was rare that I had both a hotel room and an easy gig at home in Los Angeles. So, I decided to have a bit of fun. I called up Megan, Tracy, and Samantha, and they came down to Hollywood to party a bit in my hotel room.

As discussed earlier, you can't really use the bathroom on a tour bus to take a crap. So, I had come into the practice of getting to the hotel, taking off my clothes, using the toilet, and then taking a long shower. My muscles were always sore so the long shower felt great. Even though I was coming from home I was still in this practice. When I got to the hotel room, I had to use the toilet bad. I quickly stripped down but as I was sitting down on the toilet, I hit my head on the doorknob. I had sat with a lot of downward momentum and I hit myself hard, really hard. I found myself on all fours, naked, staring at the tile, and seeing stars. I managed to crawl up on the toilet to empty out, but I had a massive bump on my head from the incident.

> ### Roadie Ramble Moment
> *Why do the toilet seats we buy for our homes have a lid but yet the ones in public places don't? Why do the toilet seats themselves in public places have the front of the seat missing, and the ones at home are a complete round circle? Is it expected that in public, us guys will piss all over the front area of the toilet seat? Well, of course it is. However,*

is the reason also so that our junk doesn't touch the toilet seat while sitting to take a crap? If both examples are the answers to the questions initially probed, then why is the toilet seat swap OK at home? Does deductive reasoning suggest that guest bathrooms need to have public style toilet seating as well? Is the public toilet seat design a discreet way for manufactures to clue us guys in on something? Is it an awareness campaign that we are all dirty bastards in public, but yet at home we are expected to clean up our own piss?

Let's dissect this issue more to further understand the root of the problem. Why don't men clean the tip of their dick off with toilet paper after taking a piss? There is always a dribble. Maybe a little man maintenance is in order? This dribble is most often the culprit of the piss on the seat problem. The answer to this question is actually quite simple. It is because we are fucking men! That is why. A last posed possible problem since we are on the topic of urine coming out of wiener problems: When alcohol is involved why do we piss everywhere? The answer to that question has a simple answer, too. The answer is because it is damn fun.

When the girls got to the room, we all began to drink. I decided I was going to stay good, because it was "a school night." As the night continued on, I gave the girls keys to the room and went to sleep. I'd let them all get really drunk without me. Megan and Tracy met some guys in the lobby and went to the spa on the roof to party with them. I got a call during the night that Megan was absolutely blitzed at the Saddle Ranch on Sunset. I rolled over and went back to sleep. I was glad they were having fun.

The next morning there were drunk people sleeping everywhere. I quickly suited up to get to the lobby. As the crew all loaded into the tour bus, I watched on as my drunk friends stumbled out of my hotel room. Megan only had one shoe on. They all looked worse for wear, and good-looking girls of course got everyone's attention. I slumped down in the bus and figured I would pretend I didn't know any of them. That became hard when they all came up to the bus looking for me. At that moment I just wanted the bus to start moving. Cesar stared at me sternly and didn't turn away for a very uncomfortable amount of time, but I think all in all everyone thought it was pretty darn amusing. I found out later that Megan had got so drunk she had peed in the hotel lobby after getting back from the Saddle Ranch. "What happened to your head?" Cesar asked as the bus finally started up. "I don't want to talk about it," I replied.

Chapter 50
No Way Out

"No way out" music video crew pass.

That night on September 24th the band shot the music video for the song "No Way Out." It was a small show of 100 or so people at the El Rey Theatre in Los Angeles. The idea was to have the actual audience shoot the music video. It was a quick and easy gig. After they performed the song a few times, the cameras that had been given to the audience were all collected, and the band played a few more songs for either fun or for the crowd. Maybe both.

After the El Rey we got another break. I don't know if the band was excited that we were about to embark on a full-fledged STP tour or they were just excited about the video, but they rocked at the El Rey show. It was an awesome display of musicianship. I also got to meet the famed Rigger Steve. Living in Los Angeles, he had come down to the gig to hang out.

Sizing him up, he seemed like a pretty tough dude. Most importantly, he seemed like a guy who could help me with my workload a bit, and I knew I could really use the help. The venue was very loud, but Steve was determined to introduce himself. "Rifken, I'm Steve. Nigel tells me you were born in England." I nodded at him. "Yeah, that's true." I kept it short. I didn't really want to yell over the music. "That's good. I'm going to get you drunk and tattoo a US Flag on your back," he told me. "I'd appreciate that," I said. He continued on, that he had heard a lot about me and he was "determined to make me a man." I wasn't sure I wanted to know what that meant. When Scott got mad at some dude in the audience, he would stop the show and stare right at the guy. "Have you ever been to prison little boy? I have; I'll make you a man," is what he'd always say. I thought of that when Steve told me he wanted to make me a man and hoped it wasn't under those terms. After the show I went home for five days off. We were officially done with the RHCP leg of the tour.

Over the next few days, I hung out with friends and counted hours to when I'd be back out on the road. I was to fly out on the 29th. However, on the day of the 29th I missed my plane. Even though we could turn our taxi cab receipts in, and get refunded by production, I opted to save the band a few bucks and always took the bus to the airport. It was a dumb mistake. I waited in the terminal and was able to jump on the next plane. It meant that though I would miss load in, I would make it to the venue for the concert that night. I hoped I wouldn't get into too much trouble.

X Fest 2000 artist pass.

When I arrived in Indiana, I ran out of the airport and hailed a taxi. The taxi I got wasn't the most normal of taxi cabs but I didn't complain- I was in a rush. The taxi was a 1980's Cadillac and the driver had to weigh at least 500 pounds. I sat down in the back seat of the car, and the driver got in. When he did so, the entire car dropped at least two feet. I sat forward and watched the tassels across the top of the windshield knock back and forth. I needed him to take me from the Indianapolis International airport to the venue. It was an hour-long drive. I told him where I had to go and reclined back on the gold couch, which formed the backseat of the car. Lastly, I fastened my purple seatbelt. "You know where you got to go is far, right?" When the man spoke, it was hard to understand him- he had no teeth. "Wherever it is, I gotta go there," I said to him. "You got da money?" He tried to turn around to look at me but had trouble because he was such a huge guy. "Yes, sir," I showed him a few hundred dollars. Seeing the money, he seemed happy and we began to drive. I was relieved to be one step closer to getting to the venue. As the car putted away, I found myself unwillingly reclining more and more. I wasn't able to sit upright in my seat, because the front of the car now sat so high. It was clear the shocks in the car were all blown out.

Quickly I learned my new friend was a talker. Not wanting to make the situation uncomfortable I agreed to everything he said with casual grunts of approval. At roughly the half way point from the airport to the venue, I pissed the guy off. It was of course the worst time to piss him off, because it was right in the middle of our long trip. He had been telling me a story, and all I had understood was David Lee Roth. At the appropriate time I said, "oh cool… yeah, great band." He immediately went into a crazy tirade, and I held on to the door arm as the whole car shook. Over the next few minutes, I tried to awkwardly step back from my predicament. I was stuck in the car with this guy!

I soon learned that he had been backstage at a show and saw David Lee Roth. He had wanted to meet David Lee Roth but when he approached him, the guy had been jumped by a few of his bodyguards. I assumed because he was such a huge dude, they panicked as he approached David.

"Oh, yeah, sorry. I thought you meant someone else. Yeah, I hate that band. Real shitty songs, man," I threw them all under the bus. Fuckin' David Lee Roth was gonna get my ass kicked and I never had even met the guy. When we got to the venue, I paid the driver. As I counted the notes off, they disappeared into his massive hands. I thanked him and ran into the venue. Normally I'd be amped to tell everyone about my crazy trip, but I knew I was going to get a lot of heat. I walked up the steps of the bus, and the first person I saw was Mugs. I knew he'd have something smart to say: "Well, if it isn't Runway Rifken."

Roadie Ramble Moment

I've had lots of things break on my cars. Why is it that no matter how messed up a car gets, the last thing to go wrong is the irritating warning sound that your seatbelt isn't on? In addition, why is it only the people in the front seats get the warning? Beep... Beep... Beep... Are people sitting in the backseats not as important? Food for thought- next time your "friend" asks you to sit in the backseat of the car but takes the front seat, AKA calling shotgun, question whether the phrase is a metaphoric one for putting a shotgun in your backseat friend's mouth 'cause you don't give a shit about them dying in a fiery unseatbelted death while you watch on wondering how you broke your fingernail in the accident.

Chapter 51
Ultimate Roadie Stuff

That night I found out more about our newest roadie, Rigger Steve. Let me take a step back and explain what a rigger does. A rigger is a guy who marks the points on the stage. The points are where a motor is set to hang that day. The rigger then hangs the motor and attaches the chain coming from the motor to the truss. We then pull the whole rig, bolted truss, up into the air. Nigel had been doing the rigging, but I think he wanted to take a step back and not have to work as hard. Arguably, I think the reason was he'd have more time to play the game *Starcraft* on the bus.

Family Values Tour VIP pass, 2001.

Rigger Steve was an absolute veteran. He had toured with Kiss, hung the bell for AC/DC, and had been the show rigger for both Ozzfest and the Family Values Tour for years. You wanted something hung. Rigger Steve would figure out how to make it happen. He was larger than life and fearless. A testimony to his fearlessness, he had taught me the "leap of faith." A leap of faith is where you jump from one truss to another truss while in the air. We do it, so that we don't have to climb up and down separate ladders. The leap of faith is not in the "things to learn" section of the OSHA handbook. My guess was Steve could probably pull off a leap of faith while doing a pirouette if he had wanted to. When he wanted to be, he was the ballerina of the roadie skies. It should be noted that when on the ground, he made his mark as well. Every night Scott would climb up on his shoulders, and then Steve would run a lap through the audience with him on his back while Scott sung. The audience loved it, and Steve must have got a hell of a workout.

Steve had served time as a kid for stealing cars but didn't like to talk about it. He lived and breathed roadie oxygen. He was always filled with, you guessed it, roadie energy. I never saw him without a cigarette and cup of coffee in hand. He'd have them even while climbing. Like many roadies, he didn't drink alcohol or do drugs anymore. That is if you don't consider a cigarette a drug.

If you looked him up from top to bottom, he had a chiseled physique, bright blue eyes, and strong workers hands. If you looked at those hands closely, he was missing the top of one finger. Most of the time his story was it happened while saving a damsel in distress. I would find out later, from his mom, that one version of Steve's story was actually true. A snake bit him on a beach and they had to remove the top of his finger.

It was nice to have Steve around, but when you were tired, he was tiring. Steve pick up talks were aggressive, serious, and most often too long. They were always well thought out. He would tell me that his neighbors in Venice, California thought he worked for the FBI. He always left dressed in black, with ropes over his shoulder, and he'd be gone for months. It did make sense. He did have both the build and the psychotic necessities to make for a great Navy Seal. If someone asked for a photo of what you could expect a roadie to look and act like. I think nine out of ten of us would have picked Rigger Steve as our poster boy. His claim to fame was he had had sex in the back of a bus with a woman who was deaf and mute, and he had made her scream with pleasure. If you didn't believe him, he had the video to prove it. I had checked it out. While I wasn't sure if it was a scream I heard in the video, there was definitely quite a bit of noise going on. My personal definition of a roadie, when asked, is that we are the athlete's foot of Rock 'n' Roll. The proper definition of a roadie is "anyone on the road who is working for a touring band." The second part of that definition should be "… and is also not able to live and work in a normal society." Years later, Steve took his life. Though, as I said earlier, he could hang anything. He didn't hang himself. He sat in his Jaguar in the garage one night and let the motor run. You could say he drove off into the roadie sky that evening. I would come to find out he had met the wrong girl and had started doing drugs again after many years of sobriety. I still miss the guy very much.

Chapter 52
A Long Day with Green Day

STP tour itinerary- fourth leg.

Green day was set to play with us in Indianapolis. I was excited to see them. We hadn't played with them yet, and I was a fan. During the day I found out the Kottonmouth Kings were also on the bill. This was kind of cool, because other than Fishbone, they were the only band I actually knew personally. Most of the guys in the band had been in another band called the Humble Gods. I used to sell Humble Gods T-shirts at their shows. They were the house band at a club on Sunset, and I had spent many nights both going to their shows and hanging out with them afterwards. It was great to see them all. I was able to use my pull to make sure they had enough stagehands for an easy set change and to make sure there was room on the stage for them to see STP perform. They had been good to me, and so it made me feel good to help them out. Even if it wasn't a big deal, it was me doing something for them.

Fuel was also on the bill. I didn't know their music, but they only had a couple guys on their crew, and so I did what I could to help them out as much as possible. The crew guys were incredibly appreciative. When Fuel played, I really liked their music. It's always a good feeling to be useful to a band whose music you think kicks ass. Next came Papa Roach and then Disturbed. I knew I'd be seeing Disturbed quite a bit, so I made a point to be helpful and try and get to know their crew guys. The band and all the crew guys were super cool. I was happy. This was going to be a fun leg.

Green Day came on. I watched their show, and it was mediocre at best. At the end of their act they set the drum set on fire, and Tre, the drummer, ran around the stage like a fucking idiot. He then started tugging on their backdrop. It's not a good idea to tug on anything attached to a truss. No one should ever rely on the truss having been bolted together well. Even if bolted together properly, someone could have still left something on top of it. If something heavy enough falls from above, it can kill you.

So, the drummer was pulling on the backdrop, and Cesar told him to chill out. Tre ran to the other side of the stage and started tugging on the backdrop again. I looked at Cesar, and since I was the stage manager, I decided to put a stop to that shit. I walked over to Tre and told him, "Stop pulling on the fucking backdrop." Meanwhile, the show was still going on. He turned to me and told me to fuck off. Quickly, three of his crew guys start pushing me, and one of them took a swing at me. Luckily for me, I dodged it and he missed. Defending myself, I cocked back to take a punch at the guy, but their security, a huge Samoan dude, grabbed my arm. As he did that, Mugs stepped up to the security guy. Mugs was pushed out of the way by the three other guys. In other words, everything escalated fast! Before anything escalated any more than that, though, Cesar stepped in. He pushed Mugs out of the way and literally picked me up and put me behind him. Tre, the one who had started this mess, had already run away.

The Samoan and the roadies stood their ground and looked on at Cesar. "We have a problem here?" Cesar asked them. Nobody replied- they each turned and walked away. Mugs was not happy about the situation. He had bruises all over him. I kept quiet the rest of the night. It was awkward, unprofessional, and a bit embarrassing. We were all fighting in front of twenty-four thousand people. The awkward part was we were playing with Green Day again the next day in Atlanta.

99X Big Day Out all access pass – main stage, 2000.

On October 1st we played in Atlanta. Green Day pulled into the gig late. The Kottonmouth Kings were on the bill again. I said "hi," but it wasn't the same throwback as the day before. They were all stoned. Incubus was also on the bill. I didn't know them, but they all grew up in my neighborhood, and we had a lot of mutual friends. One of the guys in the band had a gorgeous sister who had dated my buddy. I was trying to figure out what to say to the guy to get his sister's phone number, when Green Day's drum tech approached me with the roadie who had taken a swing at me the day before. I looked around, hoping to find someone I knew, but I was not on the stage and none of the STP crew were around. Where was Rigger Steve when I needed him?

I had been in Atlanta back in May. The stagehands working that day were mostly the same guys as the ones who I had worked with at that show. One of the stagehands and I had got along well and had been chatting while we worked all morning. Unfortunately, he had a broken arm. He was the only guy I knew, and I didn't know if he would, or could, help me here. I knew one thing. If I was going to get my ass kicked, I wasn't going to be a bitch about it.

"What's your name?" asked the drum tech. "Why do you give a shit?" I replied. He stood up to me and was immediately surrounded by the local stagehands. I guess more than just the broken arm guy remembered me. "Step off, man," said the guy with the busted arm. The drum tech stood still for a moment to maintain his self-respect, but turned and walked away.

"Thanks, guys," I said. I was humbled. I was certain I was going to get my ass kicked, and I was super relieved I hadn't. I explained to the stagehands what had gone down the night before. "Why are you guys getting involved in this shit? I don't want you guys getting in any trouble because of me," I said to them.

I'll save you the conversation, but it was because I was told I was a good dude. Well, maybe they didn't use the word "dude," but you get my point. Most roadies were assholes to them, but I hadn't been. I had remembered them. I came in the morning and asked about their families and how this guy had broken his arm. They all appreciated it. I understood where roadies were coming from. We were all always tired and weren't very nice. These guys knew that and appreciated even more that I was a bit different. I treated them all with appreciation and respect. I probably sound like a bit of a pussy. I don't know- maybe they thought that too.

To clarify, it wasn't that we didn't care about the stagehands.

We didn't care about the stagehands, the cities they lived in, or anything about their lives for that matter. I guess I was somewhat different than everyone else. I evidently did. Most of our locals were pretty decent guys. I wondered what the Atlanta stagehands thought of everyone else on the STP crew, but I didn't ask. I got back to keeping quiet and hoped to finish the day without any other problems. Papa Roach played, Everclear, Eve 6, Incubus, and then the Kottonmouth Kings.

Linkin Park was also on the bill that day. I sort of knew the drummer. They were another band that had all grown up by me. The drummer had given me their demo only a year earlier. It was a demo for an album called *Hybrid Theory*. I didn't think much of it. I was clearly never meant to be in A&R. He had been interested in my friend Tim's sister. He was an odd dude. He lived in an apartment and I had brought beer into his place. It wasn't that he didn't want one; he didn't even want the beer in the apartment. Maybe that is why I didn't like his demo tape. So, Brad, the drummer, walked by me with another guy from the band. I stopped him to say "hi." He said "hi" but excused himself to go to the restroom, which was right next to where we were standing. I hung out waiting for him while talking to a stagehand, and when he left the restroom, he walked right by me without saying a word. What an asshole. It was then I realized I was never meant to get along with drummers. There seemed to be a trend going on here. I had just been told I was a decent dude, and then this guy disses me. From that moment on, it was clear to me that stagehands were much more decent than rock stars.

Green Day went on the stage and finished their set the same way - drum set on fire and the guy running around like a fucking idiot. Tre went right back to pulling on the backdrop. I couldn't believe this guy. This time instead of running out to the stage, I just grabbed the remote control for the motors. I raised them into the sky as high as I could take them. Tre isn't very tall, so it took no time at all for the backdrop to be over his head. He stood their trying to grab onto it but he had trouble reaching. It was hilarious. The drum tech walked over to Mugs, who was standing off stage, to ask what was going on. He mustn't have been on too many tours in his life because it was pretty damn obvious what was going on. All he needed to do was look at the guy on the stage laughing. That guy was me by the way. Either way Mugs spelled it out for him and he charged over to me. I had now put down the remote and was ready for a fight. He put his stuff down and asked me, "What's your fucking name, and what city are you from?" He was ready to start brawling.

I ignored him and ventured to where Cesar was sitting. It wasn't very far from where I was standing. I wanted to make sure that if we started fighting, Cesar would hear I was still trying to be professional. Cesar was hanging out with Gus. Gus was the production manager for Ozzfest. He's another serious guy in the business. Cesar and Gus weren't just colleagues, they were good buds. Cesar wasn't worried about the situation. In fact, he was amused by it. The drum tech walked away.

Cesar, Gus, and I walked to the back of the stage and started pushing the empty road cases all into place for load out later. The key to a quick and easy loadout is to have the cases all together like a herd of goats. Keep them as a pack and all goes smoothly. Not that I've ever herded goats before.

As I was pushing the road cases into the corner, Green Day's tour manager walked up to me and leaned on one of my cases so I couldn't roll it anymore. "What's your name, bro, and what city are you from?" asked the tour manager. I didn't understand why all these guys wanted to know what city I was from. Were they going to egg my parent's house? I told the guy to ask Cesar. He walked the few feet to where Cesar and Gus were and asked the same question's I had now heard a bunch of times. Cesar nonchalantly told him, "His name is Rifken and he's from L.A." I wondered. Now what? Cesar sat there looking at the guy maybe wondering the same thing. After a few moments Cesar told the guy "I heard a local lighting guy was messing with your guy. Sorry about that." I think Cesar was giving him a way out. Throwing him a bone.

The tour manager answered quickly, "We don't want him on our stage again?" The "him" meant me, not this fictitious local lighting guy. "He's the stage manager," said Cesar. "I don't want him on our stage," the guy said again. "Not a problem," said Cesar firmly but still nonchalantly. I questioned what point this guy was making. STP only had two shows with Green Day and we had just done them both. What was he trying to achieve? Why would I ever be on the stage with them again? While I was contemplating this, the guy spoke again, "and you know what? I don't want you on the stage either." If I was holding anything, I would have certainly dropped it.

What was this guy thinking? Stepping up to Cesar? And in front of Gus? This guy was just dumb. I was relieved. I now had nothing to worry about. This guy had just dug his own grave. Cesar laughed a light laugh, almost a giggle. There was no question he was enjoying all of this more and more. During load out none of the local stagehands helped Green Day.

Cesar lived in Atlanta. This was not the right town to pick a fight with him. Doing it in front of Gus meant he had to save face, even if he normally would have let it go. I'm not sure if he would have done what he did or not if Gus hadn't been there. He was a hard read.

When STP came on the stage the usual happened. All the opening bands lined the stage. The first thing I did was kick Linkin Park off of it. I told everyone I wanted a clear stage. I booted them all. I didn't have much power, but I ran the stage, and if Brad wanted to be a dick, I could be one too.

It's rather amusing in hindsight. Linkin Park would shortly thereafter tour with STP, and Chester would replace Scott for a while years later. So, I suppose they got to see the band often enough from the best seat in the house. I wasn't on those tours, though. I was on this one, and here I could kick their asses off the stage, and so I did.

STP doing killer rock star shit!

Chapter 53
"De Plane! De Plane!"

After the show we had to hurry. Some of the guys on the crew, including me, were flying out on a redeye to the next gig in Philadelphia. Cesar wanted a select few of us there first thing in the morning. The gear would be arriving early, and if we were there, we could start working before the rest of the crew showed up.

During the day I had been hanging out with Suzi in the dressing room and while trying to do something with Scott's glasses, I can't remember what it was, I broke them. Suzi looked at me coldly and told me Scott was going to kill me. On top of worrying about Green Day, I was now worried Scott was going to get rid of me over breaking the arm off his Ray Ban sunglasses. Parker, the bass tech, put some tubing on the arm of the glasses and heated it up. The rubber held the arm of the glasses in place, sort of. I gave them back to Suzi and she said, "OK, let's see how this goes, Rifken." She usually called me "Hot Lips." She was clearly not happy with me. It felt like when my mom was mad and called me by full name. That's never a good thing.

While I was grabbing my things from the bus to leave to Philadelphia, I was told the band wanted to have a talk with me. Was it about the glasses or Green Day, or both, I wondered? I walked into the dressing room and found out quickly they wanted to talk to me about Green Day. They cut right to the chase. The Green Day guys had watched them play from the side of the stage. I figured things couldn't be that bad? They asked me what had happened, and I told them everything. They all looked on at me seriously throughout. Not knowing where this inquiry was going, I apologized. I told them it was important to me that I represented the band well.

And furthermore, I was really sorry about the whole situation. Everyone sat quietly. I don't remember who laughed out loud first, but they all grabbed me and rough housed me a bit like they had before. I was beginning to feel like I had a few older brothers. No one cared at all. I was relieved. I hurried off to the van that would take the small group of us to the plane and off to the next place. I was just glad to be away from Green Day.

My Billy Preston phase. RHCP tour laminate verso, 2000.

We got to the airport and while I was waiting in line, I realized I had done something dumb. Actually, not something dumb but something really dumb. In my haste I had left my driver's license on the bus. I didn't carry my wallet around with me during gigs. I didn't need money, so why would I have it on me? None of us had any luggage to check in, and so we were all to check in at the gate. Luckily, I had made it through security with my Gerber knife, which I had forgotten to leave on the bus. A Gerber knife is similar to a Leatherman multi-knife if you've never seen one before. As I approached the gate, I decided to show the two African American guys working for the airline my RHCP laminate. It was the only form of ID I had on me.

Because people start to copy the laminates as a tour is underway, we change them up throughout the tour. We add stickers to them and sometimes even laminate photos of the crew on them. My tour laminate had a photo of me with a huge afro wig wearing oversized sunglasses. Underneath the photo was my name. Luckily it wasn't my roadie name, but my real name. I figured it was worth a shot. The two guys at the desk heard me out. I told them how I worked for the band and had forgotten my driver's license on the bus. The rest of the crew had already checked in and were now waiting for the plane.

The two guys clearly wondered if this was all a joke. "It's not a joke," I said to try and hurry things along. They called their boss on the phone, and I took a seat with the rest of the crew. Nigel and Aso had already pissed themselves laughing at the situation by this time. Mugs looked on at me. Laughing too hard, he wanted to say more but all he managed to get out was, "You gotta be fuckin' kidding me?" Rigger Steve beamed proudly. "Go into war with conviction, Rifken," he told me and then winked. Who goes into war with a wink?

I fully intended to get on that plane. The school of Steve was making steadfast progress. Cesar then got real serious. "Everyone shut the fuck up," he said. Everyone, of course, did. The boss finally came. He too was African American. Great I thought, I'm sure the afro wig in the photo was really helping this situation. I explained to the boss what I had done and apologized. He handed me my ticket and walked off without saying anything.

I walked back to the seats in the airport where everyone sat. I was now very eager to board the plane. The rest of the crew sat in disbelief. Fighting on-going laughter because Cesar would no doubt still yell at everyone, we all quietly boarded the plane. The crew, including me, sat in their seats. "I think he's going to pull this shit off," Cesar said. That opened the keg again and the laughter all started up, but this time Cesar could be heard over everyone. Through tears he said, "OK, everyone seriously shut the fuck up 'till we are in the air." When the plane took off, I let out a huge sigh of relief. I didn't know how the guys were physically able to still be laughing but they all were. Cesar had been saving up and he kept laughing occasionally throughout the whole plane ride. "Kid, don't do that ever again," he told me. I haven't. I've never left my ID anywhere by accident again in my life.

Chapter 54
New York City! Get a Rope!

While I was done with dealing with Green Day, Cesar was not. I soon found out that when Green Day's buses and truck were ready to drive on to New York, their next show date, they were all stopped by the Atlanta Police just outside the venue. Upon suspicion of narcotics, both the Green Day bus and truck were completely ransacked. The band and crew had to wait hours until the search was done.

New York was also Cesar's home town. The New York stagehands were his family. While he had been born in Brazil, he had been raised in New York City. Green Day were to do appearances for David Letterman, Howard Stern, and then perform at the Roseland. While at the Roseland the locals didn't help the crew with anything. They had to do the load in and load out by themselves. I'm sure it was a good lesson to be careful who you mouth off to.

I'd love to say these were the real repercussions to Green Day's tour manager mouthing off to Cesar. But there is some uncertainty as to the events that happened following the argument. Maybe it was all part of the Twilight Zone, or it's possible that after decades stories change. Cesar is adamant the bus, and truck were never pulled over by the police and the stagehands in New York did not refuse to help the band. When asked, "I would never be that petty," is his official response to the matter. However, if Cesar had arranged for either of these things to happen, he would certainly be smart enough not to tell any of us. I was petty, if I could have made these things come true, I damn well would have, but I certainly can't rejoice in the responsibility of having made it all happen. What really happened, is perhaps inconsequential. Both Cesar and I can say with certainty that if any of us who got involved in the arguments saw one another again, none of us would recognize one another.

The first time I went to the Roseland, I was warned to be careful with the union guys. I was told to be very respectful and to let them do what they want. The union in NYC is strong and you don't want to be on their bad side. I started off the day by bringing in two twenty-four packs of beer and putting them on the stage. Once all the stagehands working that day were all together, I said my piece. "Hey, guys. I'm new at all this, but I was told you are the best in the country. I brought these beers for you, as a token. I'm open ears to anything you would want to teach me. I work hard, and I don't bitch. The beers are a small price for an education, but the one thing I have learned is that some beer is better than no beer." I instantly made friends. Cesar was impressed when he heard what I had done.

The Philadelphia show went fine. The rest of the crew and the band were highly amused to hear about the difficulties of getting on the plane. Scott ended up not wanting the glasses anymore. Or maybe, they all lied to me. It's even possible Scott never knew I broke them. I had questioned if he would be so vain as to care as much as Suzi said he would. I knew he was into the clothes he wore on stage. I just couldn't believe he would be that mad over a pair of glasses. Either way, it was good for me to never find out.

Steve had new found vigor. He was excited that his master plan of making me "a man" was going well. While it could be argued the progress was slow, things were coming along. As he was drinking his morning 12th cup of coffee, he yelled across the stage at me. Nigel was on the stage and made a point to be in earshot. He loved Steve talks. Steve was clearly preparing for one. "I'm proud of you for getting on that plane Rifken," he told me. "Well, thanks, Steve," I said and kept on with my work.

Thumbs forward or thumbs back?

"I have a question, Rifken? Do you talk to people with your thumbs forward or thumbs back?" he asked. "I don't know what you are talking about Steve. I'm trying to work." I intentionally replied back a little whiny. Rigger Steve put his coffee down. He put his hands on his hips and started lecturing me. "Rifken, we are going to make a man out of you. You are going to be a hardened machine, a war mongering achiever, a man amongst just men, a pit bull amongst chihuahua's...." With full intentions to keep going I stopped him, "I get it Steve." The stagehands had begun giggling a bit. That was good. It was good for morale. He was standing in front of me tall and proud with his hands on his hips. "Face me and tell me who you work for like a man," he said. "Are you going to punch me Steve?" I asked, pretending to be quite ready to be done with this scene, so we could move on. I was of course enjoying it. Steve stood firm. "Like a man." I turned to Steve and sullenly mumbled, "I work for STP right now at the current time. I mean as we stand here today. I'm kind of like their bitch," Nigel began to laugh. I really couldn't help myself. I loved to fire Steve up. He grabbed me by the shoulders, shook me hard, and straightened me up. "Hands on hips and with pride," he said with the authority of a drill sergeant. I put my hands on my hips, cocked my head back, and cried out, "I work for STP, sir! I am their bitch!" Steve yelled back, "That's right you are!" Before I could pull my hands away from my hips, he grabbed my arms. "Said, with your thumbs back," he pointed out proudly. Steve had noted that when I put my hands on my hips, I had placed my thumbs facing backwards, facing my ass. He lowered his voice to make the next couple comments more personal. I was ready to listen, to find out what the actual point of all this was. "Thumbs backwards, people listen. Thumbs forward, well that's kind of gay." Steve was done. He picked up his coffee and walked off stage. My morning lesson was over. I put my hands on my hips with my thumbs facing forward and yelled, "Everyone back to fucking work!"

After a Steve talk that was in front of the local stagehands, I'd have to be firm for a while. I didn't want them to continue to take the piss out of me. I enjoyed the talks, usually, but it was important the locals knew I was their boss for the day, and they needed to listen to me. I had become proud I could make the day fun for everyone, but I was also proud that I ran my crews like a well-oiled machine.

To accomplish this feat, I made up various tricks to keep things in motion. My favorite of these was the red, white, and blue broom. The first time I implemented the broom wind up was when at the end of the night, Mugs and I watched on while a stage hand pulled the drum riser skirt out of the hamper and was putting it back on the riser. I approached him and asked, "Why you putting the skirt back on, bud?"

Incredibly meth'd out, he had a hard time coherently answering me. "I'm sorry, boss. I'm sorry, boss. I just saw it was supposed to go here. So, I was putting it up on here." Mugs threw his hands up in the air. "Jesus fucking Christ," he said, flustered. "I got this, Mugs," I turned back to the guy who was still kneeling on the floor, "You are good, bro. I got a big job for you." The guy jumped up, happy to help. "The band has a broom that is important to them." I said to him. "A broom?" he asked in awe. "Yeah, but it's not just any broom. The broom is painted red, white, and blue. That's why it is a big deal," I whispered. "Oh, OK- I get it. I get it. It's an American Broom," he replied. "That's right, it's an American broom. I can't find it, but It could be anywhere in this place. I got so much shit to do. Can you find it for me?" I asked him. "Oh, yes, sir. I'll find it. I'll find it for sure." In no time at all he ran off. "All right, Mugs, put the skirt back in the basket," I said. "Fuck you, Rifken," he said, now frustrated with the whole situation. Mugs went to break down the rest of the drum kit... and well I put the skirt back in the basket. "You know come to think of it, maybe it is a French or even an English broom, Mugs," I said to him enjoying all this. "I don't give a fuck, Rifken. Go play with your crackheads."

At the end of the night, as we were closing the door of the last truck, the stage hand returned with honest to God tears in his eyes. "Sir, I've looked everywhere. I can't find the band's broom." I kind of had to stop for a moment. I didn't think I'd see the guy again. "Bro, I have been looking for you. The broom's been in the truck the whole time. The driver had it up front with him in the cab. I sent a guy to try and find you and tell you the super good news." Still overemotional, the guy beamed happily. "I'm so glad," he said, wiping the tears from his eyes. "Me too, man, me too," I replied.

Chapter 55
Who's the Go Get the Coffee Guy?

On the 4th we headed to Wilkes-Barre and played with Disturbed for the first time. Because there was going to be a huge amount of testosterone on this tour, Cesar had made the tour laminates for Disturbed the perfect color – pink, complemented by just a hint of puke green. Ours were a cool silver with a red star. Red is the color of sex, birth, death, and all that other great shit.

Pink tour pass made for Disturbed & all access pass made for STP. The sticker was added to the STP pass after we found counterfeit pass holders backstage.

Rigger Steve set to designing his tour roadie shirts. Asking me for my input, we decided to design them together. On every tour Steve liked to make shirts for the crew. Everyone got a short sleeve and a long sleeve shirt. It was his fun little side project. When I met him, he gave me one for Ricky Martin. He had worked his last tour. The shirt said "I do the work of ten men." I wore the shirt the next day on stage but put white gaff tape over the word *men* and replaced it with *boys*. I was showing my defiance. If he was going to make a man out of me, I was going to make it hard for him. Steve faked disgust with what I had done but knew it was damn funny. I had poked the bear and I knew it would come to haunt me. But it was funny, so it was worth it. He would get me back and I'm sure I wouldn't like it. Before any tough guy wind up stuff, though, Steve handed me a "Rig Hard" bumper sticker. Every real roadie needed to own one. Looking down at it, I was honored to now have one.

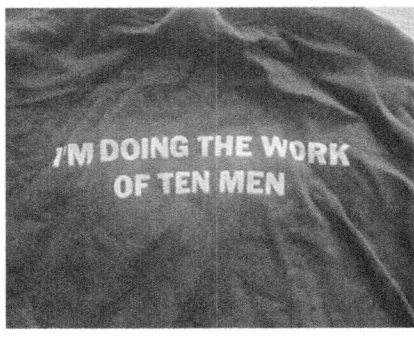

Rigger steve Ricky Martin tour T-shirt.

Walking back through the parking lot, Scott grabbed me at the bus. Walking up the steps he asked, "Hey, Joel, can you help me out?" It was clear he wanted me to follow him, and so I did. "Man, no one is here. Do you know how to make coffee?" he asked me. "I don't know how to make coffee, man," I told him. It was true, I didn't. We both stared at the machine.

"You really don't know how?" he asked me. "No, man, you actually drink it, and you don't know how. I don't even drink coffee. I guess we can figure it out, though." I picked up the coffee grinder. "What are you supposed to be doing right now?" Scott asked me. "Well, setting up the stage so you can play tonight," I told him. "No, go do that," he replied. "You sure? You do pay me to be here," I said. "It's all good," Scott replied. I really did have things I needed to be doing. I left

Scott in the bus smelling the coffee grinds and then smelling the coffee grinder.

Walking into the venue, in front of the stage I found Robert speaking to David Draiman, the lead singer of Disturbed. Disturbed had just got their first private plane to use between gigs. I listened on to hear Robert reminiscing about how cool it was when STP got their first private plane. Now, I'm not talking shit here. Neither Robert nor David were gloating. They were doing what anyone of us would do. To me, the conversation was two guys talking about how very cool the ride to becoming a rock star is. Who wouldn't geek out if they just got a private plane? Overhearing their conversation, I hoped too I would be able to reminisce on the same topic one day. I was young, eager, and working damn hard. I bet I could make stuff like this happen in my life.

Later in the day, Steve and I set to designing the STP tour shirts. We pre-sold them, collected the money, and then began to get them made up. Disturbed left, pink laminates in hand, and we wouldn't see them again until the 20th with Godsmack, when the proper tour started.

That night, on the bus, I crashed out hard. I had stayed up the night before drinking a lot. Because you never know who's going to be on the bus, it's proper protocol to put your pants back on while in your bunk. You can zip up, button up, or whatever you got to do while in the aisle, but there is no reason for your little buddy to be flapping in the wind in front of the other roadie folk. Aso, of course, ignored the rule, but everyone else was pretty good about it.

I put my jeans on to go take a leak. The bathrooms on the bus are in the front. When I stepped into the front lounge some of the guys from the other bus were hanging out. I didn't wonder why they were on our bus because I didn't care. I came out of the bathroom to head back to bed. When I walked back into the lounge, I noticed there was a young couple there that I didn't know. "Rifken, would you like to meet our new friends," asked Steve. "Nope," I replied. I headed back down the hall. "Show us your tits again," said Cesar. I heard a cheer from the front lounge. I guess she did. "Why do you call him Rifken?" I heard the girl ask as I jumped back in my bunk. "Because he has an attitude problem," Aso told her. It was true I did have an attitude problem. I overheard Aso yelling as I fell back to sleep, "Jiggle those titties!"

I would have unquestionably forgotten about the whole incident if I wasn't reminded the next day at the gig. I guess the young people had gotten into a car accident with the other roadie bus. While the cops were en route to the scene, or whatever had gone on, they all hung out on our bus. Steve spent the entire time hitting on the young lady and ended up having sex with her in the back lounge, while her boyfriend drank beers with the guys in the front lounge. The beers were on the house, so I guess both of them got a bang for their buck that night.

The next day's gig was in Buffalo, New York. Steve had a twinkle in his eye and an extra spring to his step as he chain smoked his cigarettes and drank his 5th cup of coffee. Getting laid, our most carnal of instincts, can make a super roadie feel great.

Roadie Ramble Moment

I don't mind that the English language is a mess. English was my first language so I didn't have to deal with all the problems associated with understanding it as a second language. However, it totally ticks me off when two great words come together to form a compound word and then create something bad.

Case in point, "laid off." Getting laid is good! Off makes me think of beating off. Which is good! And yet, being laid off is totally bad. It's total bullshit. I think someone else in a higher position than me felt the same way. At some point that guy created severance pay. In a noble effort, they tried to make these two great words not be all bad. I tip my hat to the severance pay creator guy.

My usual load in was interrupted by my father calling in the morning to ask me to help him. He had been arguing for a while now, months on and off, with the actor Caroll O' Connor over a Jaguar car radio. At first, they had got on well, my dad was a fan of *All in the Family.* Now they yelled at each other regularly over the phone. I wasn't sure if it was that he didn't want to sell it to him, or he just wanted more for it. Used to these odd arguments between customers and my father, I had learned to turn a deaf ear. My dad called to tell me that he had informed O'Connor that I was an attorney and I'd be suing him for bothering him.

"Dad, I worked at a law firm filling the copy machines with paper. I was seventeen years old. I'm not a lawyer," I said to him. "Well, you know what to do," he replied wholeheartedly believing I understood all about the legal profession. "No, I don't. I know how to fix a jammed photo copier. That is what I learned, Dad. You don't think he has enough money to get a lawyer too? Look, Dad, just work it out with him. You used to like the guy." I excused myself and told him I'd have to call him back. I was trying to finish up the front truss and get it in the air.

Off the phone, I was now able to complete and bring the front truss off the ground, so we could start hanging lights. As it raised up into the sky, Steve leapt up on top of it. Like Gene Kelly swinging around the light pole in *Singin' in the Rain,* Steve swung around the chain. He called for me to stop the motors. I knew this was going to be yet another entertaining way to begin the day. I stopped the motors and, along with everyone else, looked on at Steve.

"Ladies and gentleman, gentleman and ladies, let me introduce to you young Rifken here," he said. "Oh God," I said to no one in particular. Where was he going to go with this? The blonde gymnast girl I had spent the night with the last time I was in Buffalo wasn't there, so I already knew this show wasn't going to be as much fun as the last time I was in Buffalo. I was certain Steve's speech wasn't going to make it any better either.

The next few minutes were like a stage play. Steve threw his hands in my direction. The stagehands all looked at me and smiled, and I in turn played the tired, worn out, roadie kid.

Steve swept his hand across his growing audience, "We are all the crew members of a Viking ship in the heat of battle. Our job is to row, and we are all rowing and rowing." Steve jumped back down onto the stage and further spoke to the stagehands. "I'm fighting, being the swashbuckler that I am, and I've lost my sabre in the heat of battle. But all is ok. I turn to Rifken and I cry out, 'Rifken, throw me your sabre.' But where are you young Rifken?" he said while turning around to look at me. Steve scoffed at me and then abruptly turned his head away. "He is eating a ham and cheese sandwich while you are all rowing and I have no sabre left to fight with. Isn't that right, Rifken?" Steve continued on.

"I don't eat ham and cheese sandwiches, Steve. I'm a Jew," I replied. I began to raise the truss again with the pickle. Steve raised his voice, "As I was saying. We are in the depths of battle and we are rowing and rowing…" "One of the dorkier stagehands turned to me, "What Vikings use sabres?"

The truss was now at head height and in the right position for us to start hanging the intelligent lights. Each Icon, intelligent light, we hung weighed roughly 75 pounds. The Icon was relatively new to the intelligent moving light market. It was a cool light. What made it cool to me was that it was powerful enough to light a cigarette. Heavy, it took two people to hang. However, if you swung it just the right way you could take it off by yourself and swing it right into the road case. It's the reason why my wrists are both pretty jacked up now, but it saved a lot of time during loadout.

Nigel had been listening to Steve's speech and of course thoroughly enjoying it. Nigel, a Tarzan fan, had come to the conclusion that Tarzan spoke to all the animals in the forest using only one word, ungawa. Part of our daily routine would be crying out ungawa as we did "manly" work. Loading the Icons singlehandedly was quite definitely a manly enough activity for a roadie to cry out ungawa. We soon fittingly coined this term our "war cry."

Nigel jumped out into the jungle, our stage, and with the assistance of a very skinny pimple faced stagehand was ready to hang the first Icon light of the day. He cried out to the young man in his thick English accent, "Let me hear your war cry." The young man stared blankly at him. The two hung the Icon light off the truss and Nigel belted out a loud war cry. "Ungawa," he said with both deep tone and strong conviction. They moved the road case to the second position and Nigel said, "OK, young man, now your turn." The kid pulled his end of the Icon light up out of the case and let out a wheeze. I think the Icon light weighed more than he did. The wheeze was meant to be a scream but it was more the sound of well… a dying guinea pig. We were all silenced. "What the hell was that?" Nigel asked. Trying to divert attention, Steve turned to me and yelled out, "I wasn't done here. Rifken, are you ready to row or what?" I certainly was. I couldn't help but laugh. That was the worst war cry any of us had ever heard. It was time to get this show on the road. While the young man never knew it, he changed our war cry forever. From that moment on, instead of a deep ungawa, we would all let out a wheezing cry, when lifting anything heavy.

In the spirit of messing with Steve, after this incident, I would search out ham and cheese sandwiches and eat them in front of him as often as I could. On one such occasion I was searching through our after-show food sandwiches when I saw a sandwich that said "regula." Tired, I didn't think before I spoke. "What the fuck is a regula sandwich?" I asked no one in particular. Mugs answered back in his usual monotone Bostonian accent, "it's regular you fucking asshole." While monotone, he was still able to say things with a clear disdain that only a Bostonian could pull off. Again, everyone laughed. People just loved it when Mugs called me either a moron, an idiot, or an asshole. For the rest of the tour, when I'd get on the bus at the end of the night Mugs would announce my arrival, "Well, if it isn't the regooola"

Chapter 56
Out Toying with the Runner

Once we were done with the load in in Buffalo, Aso, Steve, Nigel, and I, headed out to have a bit of fun. We grabbed the runner to head into town and find a toy store. Nigel collected toys. He'd say, "they aren't *just* toys. They are *Star Wars* memorabilia." But I'd always reply, "that is just a longer way of saying toys, Nigel." Whether toys or memorabilia, he was always buying, boxing, and sending "boxed figures" he found back home. However, when we got to the runner's van, plans shifted gears quickly. The side of the van read "school security officer" across the side of it. Steve and Aso's brains raced. They decided they first wanted to cruise the van around the campus and pick up on girls. It didn't take too much to convince the runner that that was a good idea. And it wasn't much longer after that I found myself in a sorority house. Steve was in heaven. Books were put away and tops came off quickly. They happened to be our tops, and not the girls, but hey who was taking note of this stuff anyway. When we got back to the gig, we could still tell everyone we got naked in a sorority house with the girls and we wouldn't be lying. After a "safety" inspection of the sorority house which involved Steve introducing himself to every girl in the house and getting reassurances that they felt safe, we finally headed off to the toy store.

Nigel and Steve had taken a liking to the runner, I think because he was easily influenced, and had made it their mission of the day to help this young man find direction in life. The runner informed them that what he really wanted to do with his life was to teach kids how to sail. To further complicate his life, the runner was also having women problems. Feeling the need to spill his guts, he told us how his parents forbade him from dating the girl he "wanted to spend the rest of his life with, forever." "Well, let's go pick her up," Nigel said. "Should we?" he asked. "Not if you like her man. I can promise you this won't go well," I told him. "We can trade her off for Rifken here," Aso said, jumping into our conversation. We drove by and picked up the runner's girlfriend. We learned from her that she was raised Jewish and he was Catholic. Both sets of parents didn't want them dating one another. "Well, there ya go. Tallied up, that is two against four. I'd say you two lose." I figured I'd lean against the grain of what the common consensus was saying, as I really didn't like any of these people. "Well, what are you in college for then?" asked Steve. "My parents are making me. But the good news is I'm almost done," he replied. The next half hour or so of conversation was filled with Nigel, Steve, and Aso, trying to talk the two into dropping out of college tomorrow and running off together.

The runner was genuinely listening to them. I asked the runner, "what makes you think listening to a felon and two illiterates is a good idea?" Nigel interrupted before the runner could say anything. "Money, Rifken, and we three make a lot more of it than you." I realized I was going to lose this war. I was outnumbered. Furthermore, I didn't care what the kid chose to do with his life. We headed off to the toy store where Nigel traded STP tickets for mass produced memorabilia dolls. A usual occurrence.

The next day was a driving day. We drove on to Milwaukee, Wisconsin and I spent the drive pondering the worth of education. I had been reckless during my schooling years. I liked telling people that I had graduated college in three years, I hadn't bought a single book, and that I could have triple majored if I had spent just 6 months more in college. I was twenty-one by a few days when I graduated, and on paper it read great, but what did it really do for me? As time was passing and my career path was developing, Nigel, Steve, and Aso, were right- college hadn't helped me with anything.

Maybe because I had put nothing into it, that is what I got out of it. I had rushed through and missed out on what could have been a lot of fun. In college, though the education is important, I think so is the fun. Maybe I should have bought all those books and hung out longer at those sorority houses. I laughed at myself. In the biblical sense I would have been more of "the man" Steve was determined to make me, if I had been more serious about my education. My education would have been hanging out at those sorority houses, of course.

On the other side of things, I had paid for college myself. If I had stayed longer, I would have just spent more money. When I graduated, I was ready to conquer the world. I think that is where you should be when finishing college. So, maybe that was how it was all meant to go.

Living life in the moment, here I was now, having the experience of a lifetime. If it was just college women, I had missed out on, I was certainly meeting lots of them now. If I wanted to learn more, well I could always read more. I began to mentally rest easy again. Towards the end of the day, I came to the conclusion that all was good.

We found out later the roadie pep talk had worked. The runner in Buffalo did drop out of college on the advice of Nigel and Steve. We were informed he had begun teaching canoeing at a summer camp. The girl stayed in school but was planning on going to stay with him on her next school break. Nigel and Steve were incredibly proud of themselves. "Isn't that romantic, Rifken?" Steve asked. When I heard the news all I could say was, "ungawa to the guy."

Chapter 57
The Creation of a Cinematic Masterpiece

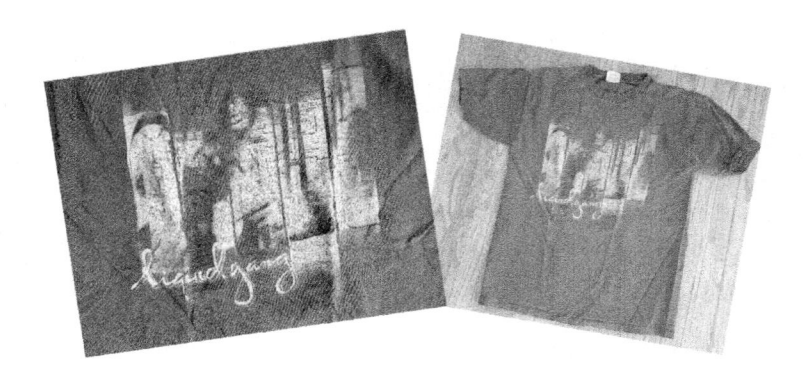

Liquid Gang tour T-shirt.

In Saint Paul we played with Disturbed and a band called Liquid Gang. The plan was to do shows with Liquid Gang until Godsmack jumped on the tour. We had also started doing shows with the band Static X. I took pride in being the stage manager now. I would do what I could to help the opening acts. Mostly by making sure the stagehands were ready to help as much as possible. Because of this, I began to get to know some of the other crews.

One of the roadies for Static X seemed to be a really good dude. Because of this, and also because alliances on the stage with other roadies is a good thing, I made an effort to talk to him more and more. If the later part of that last sentence sounds odd, it is because I really did feel like I was building alliances with people rather than making friends. It was necessary to have people watch your back. I found out my new friend had become a roadie for Static X because his sponsor was the singer of the band, Wayne. He worked incredibly hard but he had had a tough life. His childhood had been filled with sexual abuse and heavy drug use. As I learned more about the people, I was surrounding myself by, I appreciated my family unit and my current life that much more. I was taking notice that these guys were all still struggling. I had got lucky and I was sleeping in nice hotels. They were all crammed into one tour bus and sharing rooms at Motel 6. I was taking a lot in every day and valuing my opportunity.

Backstage shenanigans STP tour, 2000.

When Disturbed came on board, I joined part of the stage talent by playing a grim reaper. I would select a stagehand to be a second grim reaper each morning. Disturbed opened their show with David in an electric chair. He would get electrocuted with grim reapers standing on either side. Over the PA a pre-recorded tape would list the reasons why David should die. Strobe lights would hit the stage and then David would fry. Once declared dead, he would stand up on a blacked-out stage and the two grim reapers would remove the electric chair from the stage. While it was important for me to watch the shows to make sure everything was going smoothly, I decided to have a bit of fun and always be one of the reapers. From the show on October 10th till the end of the tour I was one of the two grim reapers at every performance.

Anyhow, I was selecting who would play our other grim reaper from the stagehands when I heard a thump. I turned to look at the stage and saw Rigger Steve lying down at center stage.

Everyone looked for a moment, and then we all went back to work. Steve stood up, and through theater antics, made a big commotion to tell everyone he was OK. We all just kind of ignored him and kept working.

A few hours later I climbed up into the rig to throw my rope back over the truss. Someone had pulled it down. After I had completed my mission, I climbed back down the ladder and found Rigger Steve standing at the bottom of it drinking his coffee. "You didn't tie the rope off," he said. "I know- it's a pulley system I have set up," I replied. "Earlier I fell out of the rig, because you didn't tie your rope off," he said. "I didn't tell you to hang off of it, Steve." I went back to work. Steve looked fine. I didn't know what he was so upset about.

What I, or we, didn't realize, was that he was genuinely bummed out that no one seemed to care that he fell out of the sky. He hadn't fallen far because he seemed fine, so we didn't understand what he was going on about. We just let him talk about it and no one replied. It was one of the few times I ever saw Steve serious. He was really ticked off.

That night some kid threw a beer at Scott on stage not once, but twice. Scott erupted at the guy; I understand rebellion but why be a douchebag? I immediately jumped into the pit looking for the beer thrower. When I grabbed him, he tried to get away and I pulled him down to the ground hard. Somehow, I hurt my hand when I manhandled him. Security quickly grabbed the guy, so it was uneventful, but the rest of the night I found it hard to work with one good hand.

The next show on the 11th was in Madison, Wisconsin. I was tired and my knuckles still hurt from the night before. While in Wisconsin I found Scott and told him I was sorry about the beer being on the stage. I told him I'd have a towel with me from now on during the show and I would clean up any liquid immediately. He didn't say anything to me. There were more important things going on that day.

Verso close-up of Sex and Violence tour T-shirt, 2000.

The guys had started shooting the music video for the song, "Sex and Violence." I found it cool that Dean was shooting the video himself. Not having much to do, I walked into the production office to hang out with Cesar. I did this regularly now. I had started spending a lot of time with Cesar and, because of that, everyone called him my dad. It did make sense that he would be my "road dad." He was nurturing me to be a production manager one day at this point.

Sitting down in the office, I began to call my friends back at home to say "hi." After a quick call Cesar told me to get off the phone, so I did. He picked up the phone and in a monotone voice said to whomever was on the other end, "I need two lesbians, a miniature pony, and a midget. Yeah, this afternoon." That was all he said; he hung up and went back to work on paperwork stuff. What that all meant to me was this was going to be one hell of a fun afternoon. I wondered who he called? Whoever it was didn't ask any questions. How could anyone not ask any questions during that call?

Sure enough, a couple hours later there were two strippers, a drunk dwarf, and a miniature pony in the hallway by the production office. This was all for the music video. The rest of the casting process was just as fast. Because Dean was behind the camera, shooting the video, the band decided I would play Dean. I was to dress up as a sheep. Next, it was decided that Suzi would dress up in bondage clothes and Steve would be a guy chasing her with no shirt on. The rest of the band were to all wear other animal masks.

Behind the scenes of STP's Sex and Violence music video.

Right out of the gates, we had issues. The miniature horse was scared and kept pooping in the hallway, the dwarf was drunk and kept puking, and the strippers didn't want to make out with each other. We would have done better just picking out two girls from the audience. What was happening was all real movie magic and I was part of it. Thinking on his feet, Cesar sent someone out to get booze for the dwarf. "We'll get him drunk again and all will be good," Cesar said. No one cared if the girls made out and, just like that, the script changed. It was only after the script changed the girls started making out. Working with talent can be tough!

After a while, the girls got more comfortable and while in the shower, they decided they only had one rule. That rule was that the drunk dwarf couldn't throw up on them. After we got the dwarf drunk again, Cesar was right, all was good. He stopped puking. The girls took turns giving him piggyback rides for the camera, and it was like it was all meant to be. I know what you are thinking. What about the livestock? Well, to answer that question the pony calmed down and stopped pissing and shitting everywhere.

Everything came together around the same time. It was like the stars were aligned that day... we were able to finish the video and we all learned creating movie magic isn't easy. Dean did a fine job. That night Scott told the audience the band had a kick ass crew. That was nice to hear. A crazy day; I again felt like I had a new, albeit odd, family. The video never made it to wide circulation. I'm not sure if it was because I played a bad sheep or not. If dying to check it out, you can find it on the STP greatest hits collection, titled *Thank You.*

Chapter 58
Who's Tyson? My...ke Tyson

The next day was a much-needed day off. I was truly wiped out. I learned Robert De Leo had bought a nice home in upstate New York. Looking at photographs, I wondered if I kept working if I'd be able to buy myself a house one day too. It didn't matter what kind of house. Any house would do. I just wanted a place to hang my hat. My head filled with what I would do. What kind of art would I fill my house with? What cars would I put in the garage? Would I want to throw parties in my own house or is that better to do in other people's houses? It was all fun for me to think about.

Because I'd been away from all my friends for some time now, I was beginning to become distanced from them. Not physically of course, that was obvious, but mentally. I had no real reason to keep calling people to find out what they were up to. It was never anything very interesting. So, I wondered would my new friends be roadies and musicians? I wasn't sure I'd want that either. I thought I had a lot to think about. I didn't really though. I now think your life develops as it's meant to, and the friends that come and go are part of the fun of it all.

The next few shows were in Alabama, South Carolina, and Florida. I really enjoyed watching Disturbed now. They kicked ass. I had been dead wrong about these guys. They had great stage presence, the music kicked ass, and they were all really good dudes. The crew was small, tight knit, and I liked hanging out with them.

The Alabama show was on the 13th. That night elsewhere in the world, Mike Tyson fought a boxer named Brian Nielson. I watched the fight in the bus while it was recording for the other crew to see after the show. At the end of the night I got on the bus and the backline guys were just starting the fight. I saw opportunity. "Oh, this is good. Mike Tyson wins in the 6th round. You guys are going to dig it." I got angry stares before I got jumped and smacked around. It was worth every second of it.

Before the show in South Carolina, I thought I'd take a stroll through the parking lot. I had gotten into the habit, before the shows, to go looking for guys selling unlicensed T-shirts with our merch guy. Our merch guy was an old Mongols biker with long gray hair. He was always stoned, and like almost everyone else, I enjoyed his company. Merch guys travel separately from the band and crew. It was good to have someone to talk to who was out of the group but still part of the group. If that makes any sense. With him I'd "confiscate" T-shirts under the pretense that they shouldn't be selling them. I'd tell them that if I saw them again, I'd take all their shirts and call the police. They would then go to the other side of the parking lot and sell them there. My reward for doing this was I'd then wear the T-shirt. I got a kick out of the band looking at my new schwag, wondering if they were now selling shirts that looked like the ones I was wearing. They'd look at each other wondering who approved the designs. It was great fun.

Bootleg STP shirt taken in parking lot, 2000.

As I was wandering back by myself through the parking lot that day, I saw a small crowd, and I decided to head over to see what was going on. I found a few people looking down a minor embankment, watching Scott Weiland himself fish in a "stream." I had definitely found myself in the right place at the right time.

I'm not saying there is anything wrong with fishing, but I can guarantee you Scott hadn't been taking notes while watching the fishing channel. The stream itself was maybe a foot wide, and Scott was fishing with a pink plastic toy fishing pole purchased from Toys R Us with no bait. It was clear to me I should get him out of there as fast as I could. The crowd was increasing quickly. I sat down next to him. "Quiet here, huh?" I asked Scott. He looked over to me.

"You ever go fishing, Joel?" he asked me. For whatever reason he never called me Rifken even though everyone else did. "Honestly, no, I haven't," I said to him. After a quiet moment I asked, "maybe on our next day off we can go fishing? It would be cool." I smiled. "I'd like that, man," Scott replied. "Let's go inside, huh?" I asked, hoping he'd be OK with that. "Yeah. OK, I guess we should." Scott handed me the pink fishing pole and we walked through the crowd into the venue. I was glad to get him back inside with no issues. I questioned, and still question, what was going through his head at the time. The one common thread that always goes through my mind is that the situation was sad.

Chapter 59
Drivers Get the Scoop

As things were winding up to start the tour with Godsmack and Disturbed, things were winding down with the radio show circuit. We did what I think was our last show with 3 Doors Down that night. On a very cool note, I had also started to get an extra fifty dollars a day to work as the acting stage manager. After Florida we would have a few days off, including a long driving day.

STP VIP guest pass, 2000.

While driving to Pittsburgh, which would be our first show with Godsmack, Robert told me the house next door to the one he bought was for sale. They were asking $200,000, and it was on forty-acres. I wondered what it would be like to be Robert's neighbor. Would they hire me for their next tour? That would have been the neighborly thing to do, right? My brain ran with all the ideas.

It was going to be a twenty-hour drive to Pittsburgh, so I had a lot of time to write, and relax. The new driver I mentioned earlier was a guy named Skip, short for Skipper. If you recall, Skip was a quiet guy. How quiet? Well, he was the kind of guy who could go for weeks without talking to anyone. That's how quiet. It's good to be a quiet guy in the music industry.

I spent our driving day talking to Skip. I like getting the silent types to open up. I found out fast that Skip had been the driver for Axl Rose on the Guns N' Roses Use Your Illusion's tour. It was no secret to anyone that Guns N' Roses was my favorite band. This little bit of new information certainly piqued my interest. I put my computer away and instead concentrated on conversating with Skip. I was in heaven learning all the fantastically worthless information about my favorite band.

It was a nice change to be an interested music fan again. To again be one of the verm. I learned that Axl would watch *Apocalypse Now* before every performance. I wondered if he watched the whole movie? I mean, it is a long movie. I didn't ask. I learned that "Don't Cry" was the first song the band wrote. I am a Blind Melon fan, and I learned that Shannon Hoon had grown up with Axl and sang backup on "Don't Cry" for the album. All this was very cool to me!

Skip had also toured with Courtney Love. He told me she had been a dancer at Jumbo's Clown Room back in the day. Jumbo's was, and still is, a Los Angeles bikini dancing bar. While touring, they had stopped to get gas at a truck stop. Courtney had wandered out of the bus and fell in a big puddle of oil. A trucker picked her up and had carried her back to the bus. Skip remembered the trucker asking him, "Hey, is this thing yours?" He, himself had taken her back from the trucker. Drivers always have great stories. They are like a waiter. People will talk about anything in front of them. They are part of the background of a place. A fly on the wall that people don't pay any attention to. Or in our case a cockroach in a zoo. Would you make mention of a cockroach if you saw one in a zoo? No, probably not. The Lions are cooler to talk about.

Interrupting my chat with Skip, Steve rushed up to the front of the bus with great urgency, Nigel in tow. "Rifken, serious question. If you are backing your car out of a parking spot, we'll say it's my new Jaguar, and there is a big muscular man in the passenger seat, we will call that man me, and you put your arm over the back of my headrest while you are backing out of the parking spot, is that kind of gay? Or don't you feel at least gay a bit?" Nigel Jumped in, "I mean it's almost like giving him a hug." Steve continued on. "Yeah, you know not just any hug, kind of a sexual hug." I had to clear my head. I wanted to make sure I gave them a good answer. "Has this really been what you fucking morons have been thinking about all day?" I asked. They both shrugged their shoulders. "Well, yeah," Nigel said. Steve nodded in agreement.

Chapter 60
Straight Pimpin'

While on the same drive, I gave a script I had written before touring, to Dean. It was a screenplay called *Part of the Machine*. It was about a musician whose inspiration came from his disabled brother. His brother spoke throughout the screenplay only using song lyrics. Sort of like the character Harry Noble in the movie *Batteries Not Included* who repeated commercials as dialogue. Dean never brought the script up to me again. Not to pat my own back, but I'm pretty sure it was because the script sucked.

In Pittsburgh I spoke to Stefanie, and she confirmed she would be able to hang out while I was in New York next. I decided to go down to the hotel bar and get a celebratory drink. Sitting down, I ordered a vodka on the rocks. Just as I started to get really cozy with my drink, a gorgeous girl sat down next to me and began to chat me up. It's rare in a man's life, unless he's famous, a pretty girl instigates such a scenario. She asked me what I was doing in town and I happily told her. I, in turn asked her what her story was. She worked for her friends' company I learned. This was going great.

Her job was to hang out with men when they needed a female partner. That sounded interesting to me. And so, to continue the conversation, I probed, "so when a guy is in town and doesn't want to go to a business meeting alone, or something, he can call you?" I asked. "Exactly," she said and took a sip off of her cocktail. "What an interesting job," I replied. Imagine all the people you would meet and all the different scenarios. I was enjoying this young lady. She finally laughed and whispered to me, "I sleep with men for money." I laughed at myself this time. How did I not catch on? Now in the know, I whispered back to her. "Oh, like a hooker?" What I received was an uncomfortable smile back, "actually, I'm an escort." "Oh, I had a friend back in college who was an escort. I bailed her out of jail once and she paid me back right away," I said. After that our conversation quickly hit a lull. "Well, If I were you, I'd be talking to that fella." I pointed to one of the guys on the crew. She wasted no time and rushed over to him. After a quick phone call on the pay phone in the lobby, they went upstairs together. Man, he was going to be happy I sent her over to him I thought to myself. I drank my cocktail. The two were back downstairs in no time. She wiped her face and bought me a drink from the other side of the bar. That was good enough for me. I pointed out another guy on the crew, and in no time at all she went upstairs with that guy, again after a quick phone call on the pay phone in the lobby. This happened three times total, and I got three free drinks. Thinking how lucky I was to meet my new friend, I called it a night.

The next day I went up to the first guy I sent her off to. "How did your night go?" I said with a big ol' grin. "It was OK. Why do you give a shit?" said the roadie. "I'm the one who sent her over to you," I whispered to him. "Keep that to yourself, Rifken. I'm serious. OK." I didn't say anything to the other roadies, but instead put the evening in my memory bank arsenal to maybe use later, just in case I needed some ammo to use on these assholes. I now knew fucking whores could be a touchy subject.

Chapter 61
Breathe That Roadie Air

We had three days of total downtime in Pittsburgh, and I used that time to completely relax. I needed to recharge my batteries for the remaining part of the tour. The first day off I realized I was falling under the weather. Mike who had toured with the Chili Peppers was now on a tour that was a rave party. He would set up the lights, the DJ's would perform, and they would rave all night. A few of the guys on the crew were going to go to the rave, but I opted to stay in to try and get better. I was certain I was getting sick, and I was pretty sure it was from all the cigarette smoking on the bus. When a bus sits still, you can't leave the windows open and have the AC on at the same time. So, everyone leaves the AC on and the windows up. If you smoke on a bus, it circulates through the air system and you breathe all that crap in.

After a full day of sleep, I did feel a lot better. A few of us headed out to go see Frank Lloyd Wright's Falling Water house. It wasn't often I got to do anything cultural while touring. While I had now crisscrossed the country, I had mostly just seen the venues.

Roadie modeling session at Frank Lloyd Wright's Falling Water house.

The whole outing was just what I needed. While I was very well aware of the house itself, I wasn't aware of the art collection in it. There were a lot of Japanese prints, a Tiffany lamp, a Diego Rivera, and even a Velasco hung in the guest house. Amongst other things I learned, Albert Einstein had stayed in the house. To me this was all cool stuff.

The cultural excursion, and the time to rest up, gave me the break I needed. I knew the last leg of the tour was going to be an ass kicker, and I hoped these last few days of relaxation would be enough to make it through. I was ready to get going again and excited to see Godsmack perform. Call for our first day on the Godsmack and Disturbed tour was 4AM. I went to sleep early the night before, not just because of the early call, or that I was still a bit under the weather, but also because I didn't want to be tired when I saw Stefanie in New York. I'd be seeing her in four days and counting.

Chapter 62
Groupies Are a Drag

Before the show many of us sat around a large table in the cafeteria to eat. I always looked forward to dinner. The food was always good. The band had hired on a personal chef named Jamie. Jamie had been taken from the Chili Peppers. A lot of the crew gave Jamie a hard time. The overall consensus was that it was lame the band now had a private chef. I think the crew was jealous that they weren't getting the special treatment too. I loved the food in the cafeteria's and didn't mind one bit. In Canada we had been served caramelized Brussels sprouts. I had grown up hating Brussel sprouts. As a little kid I, like probably most of you, had a standoff with my parents and sat at the dinner table for hours because I refused to finish my dinner and eat 'em. However, these Canadian caramelized Brussel sprouts were amazing. I had so many full plates of them they cut me off. I started bribing other people on the crew to go get me more plates. I even, through a lot of persuasion, got Scott to try some. After trying one, he too ate an entire plate of them. I pooped green for two days. I wondered if the band's, "special Jamie food" made them poop green. I bet not!

On this day the crew had all sat at the same table following Steve's lead. It was clear Steve had chosen to sit where he did, because of a gorgeous blonde girl who had sat down before any of us had. She was Sully, the singer of Godsmack's, "friend." The table filled up with horny roadies who loved staring at this babe.

Enjoying an audience, she explained to everyone how she would fly out and stay with Sully a week or so here and there. I had seen her before. She had been at a show with Tommy Lee earlier in the tour. I, as usual, quietly ate and listened. She was upset to be leaving tomorrow because she was pretty sure Sully was going to have another girl fly in the next day. It was both interesting and amusing to watch Steve try and *console* her. After a half hour or so she turned to me, "Why are you so quiet?" she asked. Everyone at the table looked at me to see what I'd say.

I replied, "I don't have much to add to the conversation." Tootsie, the sound guy, felt like turning the knife. "Don't be like that, Rifken." A skinny little fella with a long nose and long hair, he had been STP's sound guy since the early days. "Let her know your thoughts," Tootsie tooted. I continued to ignore them and finish my kickass dinner. "I would like to hear you say something," the girl said. I wondered why she had poked the bear. Whatever the reason may have been, it worked. I spoke, "fair enough." I put down my fork and knife. "I think you are a dumb bitch. You are sitting at a table with a bunch of roadies who have been undressing you with their eyes for the last half hour while feigning to listen to your pathetic problems. Half of us may as well have our dicks in our hands right now. If you want to date a rock star, this bullshit you are whining about goes with the territory. If you want a white picket fence then get the fuck out of here and go date a guy with a real job who wears a suit and tie to work every day. Now, I think I'll zip my pants back up to go get seconds of the chicken." As I got up, Tootsie turned to her, "See, it's always worth asking Rifken his take." Steve smiled widely, "Who's up for dessert?" When I returned, we all ate the rest of our meals in silence. Steve kept looking up at the table with an extra wide smile. For the rest of supper, the girl did everything to avoid eye contact with me. I didn't wonder why.

Shortly thereafter, the show began and went well. The highlight for me was watching while Sully played an extended version of his song "Voodoo." He went around the stage and played a bit on each instrument. I'd learn this was a nightly routine and I loved it. I was glad, too, because I knew I'd be seeing it a lot of times.

Various Return of the Rock tour passes, 2000.

Chapter 63
But Steve… My Pussy Hurts

The next day while in Dayton Ohio I hit a wall. I couldn't kick the flu I got while in Pittsburgh, and it was now getting worse. I had started vomiting the night before. I couldn't think of another time I had been so sick. To make matters worse Steve felt particularly gung-ho that morning. Two huge curtains were to be hung parallel from behind the stage up to the top of the arena. The idea was to visually block off the seating area behind the stage. While Steve could have easily had a group of stagehands help him do this, he wanted to do it with me. "Steve- look man, I can't do this. I feel like shit. Get some stagehands to help you out," I said to him. "'Can't' lives on 'Won't' street', Rifken," he replied. Figuring it was easier to help him, I gave up arguing. "All right, Steve, let's give it a go."

We started hanging the curtains, after taking a quick break to throw up again, Steve gave up and told me to go to the bus and get some sleep. I didn't argue, and slept most of the day. A couple of the other people on the crew weren't feeling so good either. We all blamed Nigel because he had been sick before any of us. The crew flu became known as the Nigel disease. That night I got a visit from a Rock Doc. A Rock Doc is a doctor who comes to the venue, when called, to fix us up. I didn't have health insurance so I didn't go to a doctor for much of anything. The doctor visit at the venue was easy. He just asked me questions about the band and prescribed me some pills called a Z Pack. Taking the opportunity, I asked him for some steroid cream to kill the eczema on my phalanges, aka fingers. Amelia, the tour PA, refused to listen to why I needed the cream. Her awkwardness regarding the situation was a treat to me. "It's not as bad as you think Amelia. I just have a slight irritation on my…" Amelia cut me off. "Rifken, I don't care. I don't want to hear it. I'll give the prescription to the runner," she said. "OK, but I don't want you to think I have any..." I was cut off again. "Rifken, quick fucking with Amelia and go work," Cesar said. I figured I'd go bug Suzi next.

Whatever is in a Z pack fixed me right up. Being sick and trying to be a roadie was really tough. Cesar and Nigel let me know that they were working on locking in our next gig. It would be for Rock in Rio in Brazil. I was glad to hear if they got this gig, I would be one of the people going. I didn't know who it would be for, but I didn't really care. I would be bummed to leave STP, but happy I would have more work. If I kept it up, maybe I could buy that house next to Robert one day.

Now, I know what you are thinking. You know what I care about more than Rock in Rio? I care more about what happened to the hot blonde groupie chick at the dinner table. Well, sure enough, that day the blonde groupie left, and a new blonde came in her place. She wasn't just any blonde though. She was Jenna Jameson, the most famous porn star on the planet. Jenna had flown in with a brunette girl, and Sully spent all day with these two in his personal tour bus. For the rest of the tour, that was where he was most of the time. Jenna and her friend, would show up at some of the shows, and when there, spend a lot of "time" with Sully. There was no question he was a lucky guy.

Chapter 64
Who knew? Rock in Rio ... Is in Rio!

On the 23rd we had a day off in New York. It was the day I had been looking forward to. I was happy to see Stefanie. She showed me many of the sites. Though I was still fighting the Nigel disease, seeing her certainly made me feel a lot better. We walked through central park, went to the Guggenheim, Rockefeller center, the world trade center, we ate lunch, we ate dinner, we went out to coffee. We went out to everything. It was a nice day.

STP Roseland artist pass, 2000.

The Roseland show was on the 24th. I was looking forward to seeing the local stagehands. I hadn't seen them since the Green Day debacle had gone down. When we got there, I was welcomed by wall to wall smiles. One of the older stagehands walked up to me before I could say anything to anyone and spoke. "No one fucks with our family," he said to me and gave me a dude hug. I smiled. "What beer do you guys want today?" I asked.

Stefanie came to the show early, and I beamed while proudly

introducing her to everyone. Throughout the day, I showed her how everything worked on the stage. She feigned interest, and I ate it up. While showing her the lighting setup, Nigel and Steve walked over to us. I had intentionally not introduced them to her. It was a safe assumption that because of that, they now wanted to meet her.

"Hey, Rifken, who's your lady friend?" asked Nigel. "Yeah, who's this gorgeous young lady, Joel," Steve chimed in. "What do you want?" I replied. "We are doing glitzy loadout again today. Are you in?" Nigel asked me. "That's going to be a bit hard in New York," I replied. Stefanie held her hand out. "I'm Stefanie," she said. "Ew, you don't touch them," I told her. "Now that the pleasantries are out of the way, Steve and I have an important question for you," Nigel said. He of course continued on, "If you are walking down the sidewalk and you see a big strong looking man, like Steve here for example. If you assume that he has a very good-looking girlfriend, does that make you kind of gay?" "You know because your first thought was how good-looking he was," Steve clarified. "And strong," Nigel butted in. "Yeah, and strong," agreed Steve. "I got this," I told Stefanie. "Do you two constantly explore your own sexuality all day?" I asked them. "I don't know what that means, but Steve and I have a serious question here, Rifken. We came to you because you are the college educated one." "Fine, are you asking me if we are doing glitzy loadout? I asked. "Yeah, that and..." Nigel interrupted Steve, "...and the big man looking at your girlfriend thing." I didn't answer them, but escorted Stefanie on for the rest of my roadie tour. At the end of the evening, I wished Stefanie off and loaded out the show. The moment she left, I knew I was going to miss her.

Once Stefanie was gone, I focused on glitzy loadout. It was going to be hard to pull off in New York. The New York stage hands were all masculine and took their jobs seriously. In New York we couldn't rush load out. The union worked at their own pace. That pace had been firmly set many years earlier at *slow*. At the end of the gig the old man, who was the head of the union, and I chatted while we rolled road cases out to the truck together. Rolling the cases was a bigger deal than it sounds. I wasn't supposed to roll cases to the truck. That was for the local stagehands, loaders, to do. The fact no one was saying anything to me about it, gave me some much-appreciated clout. When we were all done, I was in a good mood. I had had a really nice day with a girl who was pretty and whose company I genuinely enjoyed, and on top of all that, the show had been a good one.

So, the question you are dying to know. What's "glitzy loadout"? Well, glitzy loadout was where Steve, Aso, Nigel, and I would put streamers in our hair and act very, VERY effeminate, all while telling people what to do - unbolting the truss, packing the lights - you know - all that roadie stuff. No one really ever found it amusing but us. For whatever reason, the four of us morons certainly loved glitzy loadouts. I guess it brought us together in its own way.

Finished for the day, I walked out from the stage towards the buses. Cesar was sitting in a truck with his girlfriend. "Hey, Rif, come here," he said. Whenever Cesar wanted to talk to me afterhours, I was always a bit concerned. Because he was with his girlfriend, I tried to be very respectful, "Yes, sir." Cesar replied sternly and emotionless, "You got the union boss pushing road cases?" Not knowing what I could say, it was quiet for an uncomfortable moment. "I didn't ask him to Cesar. He started pushing the cases to the dock with me while we were talking. I'm sorry." There wasn't really much I could say about the situation.

Unexpectedly, he changed his demeanor, "It's OK. We got the gig in Rio. It's for Guns N' Roses. Don't fuck it up." Another quiet moment passed; I was so excited that I didn't know how to react. "Really, oh man Cesar this is so awesome," I said. "It's a job and it's only a job. Now get on the fucking bus and have a good night," he told me. I turned to rush off to the bus, which was parked close by. "Kid," Cesar called out to me. I turned back around to look at him again. "You did good today." I didn't know it at the time, but years later, Cesar told me when he saw the union boss pushing cases with me that day, it made him very proud. "It's nice to see new blood showing respect for the old guard. Ya know, Rif'?"

I walked on the bus experiencing what could best be described as pure ecstasy. That was a rare event without my dick being involved. I washed my face and hands in the sink, ate my piece of pizza, and went to sleep happier than I had ever been in my life.

Virginia... then North Carolina... The shows continued on. Scott shaved off his mohawk and was now completely bald. The tattoo artist who had been working on his arm piece flew back home. The police continued to worry about Scott stripping naked, and then wrapping himself up in the American flag each night. He had begun doing that at all the shows now. Again, and again, I'd hear Cesar speaking with the local police about how he'd make sure Scott would be a "good" boy. What I did know is that if you tell a bad boy to be a good boy, it doesn't work. We were all tired, but the tour was coming to a close. It was like the last stretch of a marathon. You don't just hang in there; you give it your all.

Chapter 65
David vs. Goliath

Once the rig was up in the air, the first thing I would do each day is roll the Marley. Once the Marley was down, the backline guys could set up their gear. A few nights earlier, my first accident had happened while on stage. At the end of the show, I would use all the stagehands to roll the Marley back onto the rolls in the Marley cart. There were four rolls of Marley and each weighed roughly four hundred pounds. It took a bunch of stagehands to roll the Marley back onto the cart and then to roll the cart itself. The stagehands were pushing the cart and didn't see me coming to the edge of the stage on the other side of the cart. As the rear casters from the cart dropped off the stage, I jumped down. The weight of the cart hit me from the distance of the bottom of the cart to the bottom of the casters. Everyone stopped and looked at me to see if I was OK. I felt fine, and I blew it off. The band called me into the dressing room to make sure I was indeed OK, and I told them I felt fine. That night when I went to sleep my knees ached. The ache never fully went away.

Because Marley is so heavy, I would use six or more stagehands to roll it out and tape it all down. I'd try to choose the biggest stagehands to help me out. At load in in North Carolina, I did just that. While we had been prepping the rig to go up in the sky, I had heard the biggest stagehand guy of the day making it very clear he wasn't happy about having to work for what he called, "a drugged-out asshole." If you can't figure it out, the drugged-out asshole this time was Scott. I ignored the guys comments. Wasting no time, once I selected him to help me with the Marley, he told me he couldn't help me because he had bad knees. It was hard not to notice the two women in their early 60's roll their eyes at his excuse.

Taking note, I told him it wasn't a problem. I asked him to sit on the front of the stage and told him I'd let him know when I needed him. I did all my work with the two women, but every time he'd ask if I needed anything, I'd smile and say "no, I'll let you know. Just sit there and supervise. You are doing a great job." Everyone on the crew loved it, especially the two women. Eventually he got up and stormed off the stage. It was funny to watch the lumbering brute whine like a little boy. Shortly thereafter, the head of the local stagehands came out onto the stage. Behind him was my big stagehand guy of the day. He felt a lot more comfortable with his boss in front of him and now had a big shit-eating grin on his face. "You have a problem here with my son?" asked the local union boss. "Oh, crap," I said to myself.

A union boss in any city is not someone to cross. I had no clue this dumbass was the union boss's son. I thought quickly about my situation and decided to plunge deep. I knew it could make the matter worse, but I was already up against a wall because I'd made his son look like the ass he was. All the stagehands stopped working and looked at us to see how this was all going to go down.

"I do, yes. He spent his morning telling everyone how he didn't want to work for a drug addict asshole. Where I come from if you don't like your boss, you keep it to yourself," I said. "Is that it, son?" he asked me. "No, sir. If that was it, we wouldn't be in our present situation, I don't believe." I paused, "When it came time to roll out the Marley here this morning, he felt it was more appropriate to let these ladies here do it. I thought it might be best for him to sit and supervise. I would certainly admit to being the one at fault for never having told him to stop supervising."

I had nothing else to say. I looked on at the union boss waiting to see what would happen next. Calmly, the boss turned to his son and then abruptly erupted. "Get the fuck out of here!" His son looked at him and turned away. "Get the fuck off my stage. You're fired," he then turned back to me. "I'm sorry about this," he said, and then turned to the stagehands. His stagehands. "This isn't how I run my crew and I apologize for my son's behavior. Everyone back to work." He then left the stage. I didn't see him or his son again for the rest of the day. The stagehands were ecstatic. I was told it had been like this for months, but no one wanted to say anything. That day, I made a new set of friends in North Carolina.

During the show that evening, a huge body builder guy jumped up on the stage. Almost without exception, when someone from the audience gets up on the stage, they freeze up and don't know what to do next. They wait for someone to grab them, or they jump back into the audience. I suppose, it is the same sort of adrenaline rush as jumping out of an airplane? I don't know. Anyhow, I walked up to the guy and both the band and I saw the look of fear in his eyes. He was at least 6'10 and bulky. All watching on, we could see his fear of what to do next, as he turned to jump back into the crowd, I quickly outstretched my hand to shake his. Hands still shaking, I walked him off the stage and gave him a pat on his back. Yes, it was his lower back, or maybe it was his ass- I'm not sure. He was fuckin' tall! After the show the band said the exchange was the single greatest stage security moment they had ever seen.

It was hard to do loadout at the end of the show that night because several girls decided to hang out on the stage naked. All the stagehands, roadies, and I worked in slow motion with our necks cranked in one direction for most of the night. Well, everyone except for my two new lady friends and the big dumbass who had evidently really been sent home.

Chapter 66
I'll take her

The next day, we had a day off in New Orleans. With Halloween coming up, New Orleans was a fun place to be. Deciding we should all make an attempt at being cultural, Aso, Nigel, and I hit up a couple of the cemeteries in the morning. It didn't take long to get that cultural stuff out of the way, and so afterwards Aso and I went on our own way to find bars to go drink all day. Nigel didn't drink, and he left us to go back to the hotel. When Aso and I got back to the hotel later that afternoon, Cesar was in the lobby. He was just getting ready to make an announcement to some of the other roadies who were lounging around. Aso and I listened up. "All you go clean up. We're all going out to dinner. Make sure you don't smell like shit," he barked at us. All of us going out to dinner? This was going to be cool. We all headed to the elevators. "Rifken, I'm serious you better smell good," said Cesar. "Yes, sir," I told him as if I was in bootcamp. "And don't write your hotel room on your hand; it makes me think you are a lab experiment," he said as I was entering the elevator. "OK," I yelled out just as the doors closed.

We all walked into NOLA's in our roadie bests. Our bests were all the same- black T-shirts nicely tucked into black jeans. A suit and tie kind of restaurant, we all certainly looked like we were in the wrong place. Imagine a group of homeless people who got one hour to clean up before a public appearance as background in a porno film. That is what we looked like. Well, except for Suzi, who of course always looked fantastic. They gave each of us dinner jackets at the door and quickly scurried us off to a more private back area of the restaurant. A food hotspot, we certainly received a few glances as we were herded off to the back. I noticed a pretty blonde girl getting ready to eat with a guy as we sat down. She smiled at us, though I thought she was smiling at just me, wondering who we all were. A waiter handed us all menus. I wasn't sure if I had ever eaten in a place this nice before. The waiter looked at the table. "Would anyone like an appetizer," he said. "We will take three of all of them. Where's your wine menu?" Cesar replied.

The whole meal went that way. Money seemed like no object. Immediately after Cesar ordered the appetizers, we had four waiters at our table for the rest of the dinner. I wondered if this was how the Queen of England felt all of the time. Mugs had got up to use the restroom and was just returning. "Hey, that hot chick over there is breaking up with her boyfriend. Who takes a girl to a place like this to break up with her?" he asked. That was all I needed to hear. I got up, with I'm sure a little too much liquid courage, and walked over to their table. I had been drinking all day and had kept drinking through the meal. Up close she was even more stunning. She had long flowing brown hair and was dressed all in black. She was perfect! Looking at her, it was hard not to notice the tears in her green eyes. The guy looked up at me. He was a preppy, college frat boy, looking kind of guy. "Bro, if you don't want her, I'll take her," I said to him. They both stared at me in astonishment. For whatever reason, when I was with Cesar, I felt invincible. A couple of the other tables looked on to see what would happen next. No one said anything. The girl's face cracked into a shy smile and the guys gaze turned into absolute hatred. I was sure I had broken a big guy rule. I wasn't sure what the rule was; I was too drunk to even think about it. But I knew what I was doing was a dick move. Who cares, I thought? When was I going to be in Louisiana again? Getting kicked out at Emeril's, NOLA's is the great chef's restaurant, would be a great story. To break up the discomfort, I looked directly into those eyes once again and said to her, "you let me know." I then went back and sat down.

Cesar thought it was great. Suzi reached out to me, "Hot Lips, what do you think you are doing?" Still watching across the restaurant, I replied, "I'm sorry, Suzi, but that girl is hot as fuck." Suzi looked at me sternly and waved her finger at me. "Bad Rifken," she said. Everyone laughed. The couple paid their bill and left. The guy never looked back, but just as the girl did, I blew her a kiss. Other tables in the restaurant looked on in shock, but I'm sure they were enjoying the show. It wasn't every day there was a bit of fun in a stuffy restaurant like this one.

We all left the restaurant with loosened belts. It was one of the most memorable dinners I'd ever had. Once we were all piled out the front door, I saw her again. "What's your name sweetie?" asked the girl. "My name is Joel," I said. "I'm Rachel, care to go get a drink?" she asked me. "Fuckin' Rifken," said Mugs aloud. He couldn't believe my luck. "Who's Rifken?" asked Rachel. That night she and I hit the town. It was great to see New Orleans through the eyes of a native.

Verso various backstage passes.

Chapter 67
The Fucker Kissed Me

The next day was the Voo Doo Fest in New Orleans. We had killer Cajun food for lunch, there was tons of female nudity, the crowd was cool, but the highlight of the event was I met a stagehand whose first, middle, and last name were all the same. His parents had over twenty children, and they said they had just run out of names. I loved the south.

Overhearing our conversation, another stagehand approached me. "You know I lived next to a Rifkin family in New York," he told me. I turned around to hear Nigel laughing. "Oh, yeah? How did that go?" Nigel said to the man. "They were good people," the man replied. "Are you related to them?" he asked me. "No sir, I'm not," I said politely. I didn't have the heart to tell the guy it wasn't my name but just a nickname after some psycho serial killer. What if he had lived next door to the psycho serial killer's family? That would have been a hell of a coincidence.

With the addition of Disturbed and Godsmack, the amount of female nudity had tripled. I was absolutely OK with that. I'm not sure if it was because of the bands, or if it was just because the seasons had changed throughout the tour. It was now hot and humid. When we had started out, it had been cold and rainy in a lot of the country. Coming from Los Angeles, I wasn't used to seasons. It really gives you a better understanding of how long a year is when you have seasonal change. When it is always warm and sunny the days just roll by.

At the end of the night when the truck was filled, I looked out onto the grass area that had been the back stage for the show. It was littered with nice wooden tables and chairs that rolled up into nice travelling rolls. "OK, everyone if you can grab all these tables and chairs and throw them in the truck, we can call it a night." Everyone started rolling the tables and chairs and putting them in our truck. We now all had nice patio furniture to hang out on outside the bus for the rest of the tour. It was excellent. I even had enough for Kid Rock's crew if we ran into them again.

Next up was Houston. Before the show Dean was drunk. He had been drinking white wine. The band went on the stage and I stood by watching him. Wasted, I wasn't sure if he would be able to play. Throughout the first song in the set, he kept waving at me to come over to him. I pretended I didn't notice. I didn't want to deal with him. Finally, after the second song and continuous waving, I walked on stage to hand him a plastic glass of wine. Instead of grabbing the wine, in front of 11,700 people he dipped, and then kissed me on the lips. I didn't spill the wine but I instead threw it at him. Still not sufficiently satisfied, I pushed him. I was furious. And the worst part was his lips were soft. Not knowing what to say, I yelled at him, "I'm going to tell your wife!" That part I should have kept to myself. The crew and band thought my retort was exponentially funnier than how angry and uncomfortable the event had made me. In hindsight I think, "fuck you Dean," would have worked out a lot better for me. For days everyone gave me a hard time about it all. I told myself that would be the last time I went on stage to help Dean with anything.

Chapter 68
I Got A Story

The 30th was a day off. Many of us cruised out to go see the Alamo. It was way smaller than I thought it would be. Later in the day Scott and I got into a discussion on whether it would be cheating to have phone sex with the hot girl in the Godsmack production office. I told him I thought it was safe. Not that I was an aficionado on such things, but though told regularly I was a bad student, I had learned something from Steve. An answer, whether right or wrong, always sounds better than an, "I don't know."

The San Antonio Halloween show fell on, of course, the 31st. The shirts Steve and I had made arrived on the 30th. They were perfect for the show. The timing couldn't have been better. Emblazoned in big white letters across what of course was a black shirt, were the words STP BITCH. We had made both a sleeveless and a long sleeve version. The long sleeve version featured flames down the arms. They were awesome. The Halloween show itself was fun. The band dressed in drag and I sported my new STP Bitch tank top. Mugs wore the leathers and assless chaps again. We all had a ball… and Mugs, it was clear, had two.

Halloween 2000 San Antonio, Texas.

After a twenty-hour bus ride we'd play in Denver, Colorado. I slept in, and then played poker in the front lounge with a few of the crew. It wasn't long until roadie stories began to circulate. On some tour, one of the guys in the band pissed in a cup and paid one of the new roadies $400 to drink it. The dude drank the cup and puked everywhere. Not done, he then offered the same guy $800 to drink a second cup. Before the guy could answer, the tour manager told the guy that if he did it, he'd fire him, and just like that, the game was over.

Nigel, Aso, and Frank, our new sound guy, had all toured with Pantera. The piss story had opened the roadie story flood gates. Once open, the Pantera stories quickly came up, as they were always just a little worse than any of the others. The first story went something like this. After the Dallas Stars won the Stanley Cup, there was a massive party, at Vinnie Paul's house. At some point during the party someone threw the cup off the balcony and into the swimming pool. That in and of itself is bad, but even worse was… they missed. The cup hit the pavement before falling into the pool. There is apparently a dent in the base of the Stanley Cup that can be attributed to Pantera.

On another Pantera tour, the roadies had begun a game where the roadie who had done the vilest thing the day before won the opportunity to do the load in the next day wearing the red robe. The red robe was a basic red bathrobe. One such victory happened when the band's bus driver did snow angels while Dimebag pissed on him. Urine is a roadie story staple if no one is picking up on that. This same driver threw back shots of Crown Royal as he drove through the night with full raves going on in the back of the bus. Average speed limit… 100 miles an hour. According to Nigel, "urine wasn't what made the usual daily winner, though." Continuing on rapidly because he was now on a roll and possibly in fear, he may forget some of these important roadie factoids: "You know, it was usually just who did the ugliest chick the day before that got to wear the red robe. The drum tech usually won. Oh, and then I almost forgot. A couple guys would always get on the bus in the mornings covered in hot wax. They'd be showing each other wax all over their bodies and would claim it wasn't gay." "What does that have to do with the red robe?" I asked. "Nothing," Nigel responded.

"I don't know where you are going with all that, but here's a story about me," Frank chimed in. "My first tour was with Soundgarden, and it was in Europe. The crew were all English and Irish. As some of you guys know, it's not easy to find showers at gigs in Europe. Well, they didn't think I could hack not having a shower every day because I was an American. I told them... 'you know some Americans are some of the dirtiest guys a guy could know.' But they wouldn't let off. They really didn't think I could handle it. So, I told them to put their money where their mouth was. I bet my per diem vs. the whole lighting department's per diem that I could go without showering for the whole six weeks we were touring in Europe. That included not taking off my shoes or socks. You know, fuck these guys! I told them that I bet I could take it longer than they could. The bet lasted two weeks until the bus driver made me stop. I had to shower because I was stinking up the bunk. You know- the mattress, pillows, sheets. I would have gone the whole six weeks, though, no problem."

Frank was a typical roadie. He had no home other than the road. He owned a storage locker in no special place, and that was where he kept his belongings. When not on the road, he'd book a hotel room, or go stay with any random girl he had met during the last tour. He was first and foremost an American. Second to that, he was he was an Italian American. Easy to talk to, he was a really great guy. If you pissed him off though he'd kick your ass. He loved his job, had been doing it a long time, and wouldn't have "changed" anything about his life. That wasn't a pun on the word change by the way. He always smelled all right to me: so, I guess you could say his hairy American Italian ass didn't mind changing his clothes when he wasn't told he had to.

Frank had replaced a sound guy whom Cesar had let go because he had published the band's tour itinerary on some website. We had started seeing fake laminates, and people began showing up at our hotels. Not knowing any better, the roadie showed someone on the crew how great his blog website looked. On the site was a tell all. Tour itinerary, scans of backstage passes, photos of us, etc. He was on a plane back to wherever he was from the next day.

STP artist pass unknown show 2000 tour.

Chapter 69
Joint to Joint

Show poster Magness Arena, 2000.

The next show was in Denver. Disturbed and Godsmack performed, set change came and went, and STP were all ready to go onstage. Well, everyone was ready except one guy. Our guitar player was nowhere to be seen. More than the other guys in the band, Robert was especially furious with his brother Dean.

Robert sent me off to see if Dean was being held up by security somewhere. He failed to believe he was the only one who had issues getting into the venues. Robert loved being known as the bass player of STP. However, for whatever reason he was the only one in the band who was often not recognized by venue security. He liked coming to the venue on his own schedule separately from the rest of the guys. When he came into the show without the band, the security would regularly mess things up and not want to let him in. It was really only amusing because of how mad Robert would get about it and that it never happened to anyone else in the band.

Roadie Ramble Moment

Speaking of the complications of getting into gigs, how do they handle the handicapped parking at the special Olympics? It must be an all-out fiasco! I googled it. I found that Seinfeld asked the question in 1993 on his show. Continuing on my search, I still can't find a good answer. My guess is shuttles. But if they use shuttle busses, how long do you think it takes to board all the busses?

While security didn't know who Robert was, I sure did, I hopped to it and started looking around for Dean. It didn't take long for me to find him. I found him outside smoking a joint with some random people. "Hey, man, we gotta go. You guys are ready to go on," I said to him. In no rush at all, Dean walked into the venue, joint still in hand. "Come on, man, throw that away. There's cops everywhere," I said to him as we walked through the concrete hallways to find the backstage area. Sure enough, moments later, we walked right into a cop. At the time smoking weed was illegal. To make the situation worse, Dean handed his joint *to* the cop. How fucking stoned was he? The cop impulsively threw the joint on the ground. Before what I imagined was clearly coming next, I grabbed Dean by his shoulder and pushed him on his way. "Sorry, man, this fucking moron has to get on the stage. There are six thousand people waiting for him to play his shitty songs," I said to the cop while physically pushing Dean along. "Hey, man, they aren't shitty," Dean said to me. The cop didn't say or do anything. I pushed Dean as fast as I could to the dressing room where the guys could better deal with him. "Come on dumbass," I mumbled to him. I was still pissed off he had kissed me. Physically, it wasn't easy for me to push him around. I was a lot smaller and a lot less tough than him. Luckily, he didn't fight back and we made it to the dressing room. I didn't stay around to hear the band yell at Dean, but I hoped they were going to beat his ass. The band went on stage a few minutes late, and the show went just fine. Scott kept taking oxygen breaks during the performance, which he always did while performing in Denver. Dean could play the songs sleeping if he wanted to. Maybe he had been a pain in the ass lately because he was just bored. I don't know.

Godsmack tour shirts, 2000.

We headed to Utah and then from there to Las Vegas to play at the Joint on November 4th. I had become accustomed to wearing mostly Godsmack shirts now. When I had enough dirty shirts, I would mail them back home. As we had less than a week left on tour, I was wearing my new Godsmack shirts and most of the crew were doing the same. While in San Antonio, a few of us walked into a bar wearing our new Godsmack gear. Once inside, all heads at the bar turned to us, and on top of the heads all cowboy hats froze in place. No one was smiling. We were clearly not welcome there. We all hurriedly left and found a different place to eat dinner. If you didn't know it, Godsmack's logo is a pentagram. Hence, the warm welcome inside the Texan bar.

The bar wasn't to be the only awkward pentagram promotion moment. When we arrived in Las Vegas, per the usual, we all grabbed our crap from the storage bays under the bus and walked into the hotel. The crew filed into the lobby to wait for the crew production assistant to check us all in and give us room keys. Once inside the busy lobby, the same uncomfortable silence fell upon us as at the San Antonio bar.

Godsmack button down shirt, 2000.

Looking around the room, I saw a large sign on an easel. Surrounding the easel was a room full of obese white women and a cheese table. I read the sign aloud to myself. It read "National Bible Association" in big colorful block letters. The looks of horror on the women's faces was awkward to most, but I found them to be priceless. The women in the lobby were preparing for national Bible week. Like the women in the rest of the room, all roadies froze. You could say it was a frozen standoff. Through all the silence the only thing that could be heard was me. Ha... ha ha... I couldn't help myself. I began to laugh louder and louder in what become a very serious room. Mugs turned to me, "Shut the fuck up Rif. Fuckin' Jew over here." He said under his breath. "You probably shouldn't swear, Mugs. I'm sure it doesn't help the situation," I said through tears of laughter. I wondered if the cheese was for everyone.

Two desk attendants had by now rushed over to us, given us room keys, and then shuttled us out of the lobby with lightning speed. Everyone went upstairs to change. The plan was to all meet back in the lobby and then go get some food. When we all met in the lobby later, the bible party was over. There were only a few churchgoers left, the sign was still up, and as expected most of the cheese was gone. While no one else did, I, of course, came back downstairs wearing yet another Godsmack shirt. Everyone else opted to wear dirty clothes. "What the hell is wrong with you?" Mugs asked me.

The Joint pass and shirt STP, 2000.

The next day we loaded into the Joint. Cesar and Nigel had decided they wanted the whole show rig up in the small venue, and we had all scrambled to get it done. The PA sound system was pieced together to provide sound for a shed tour. Sheds fit roughly 12-18k people. However, today the sound guys had set up the whole PA system in not a shed, but an enclosed room that sat 2200 people. I walked up to Cesar, who was standing at front of house. I had to ask him something. "Rif, hold on a minute. You are going to like this," he said to me. Around us, the sound guys all had protective headgear on; together, we all now faced an empty stage. Cesar, his thumbs of course pointing backwards, spoke loudly and authoritatively to the sound guys. "OK, let her rip, fellas," he said. AC/DC's song "Back in Black" started up. It was so much louder than anything I had ever heard in my life. I covered my ears, with my hands, and it was still so much louder than anything I had ever heard in my life.

White shit began to fall from the ceiling. The room shook. Roadies and stagehands rushed in from all doors to see what was going on; and at the head of it all was Cesar, with his hands on his hips, he stood smiling from ear to ear. The song finished. We didn't know it while the song played, but due to the excessive shaking, all the alarms had gone off throughout the entire building. I personally was more impressed none of the guitars had fallen from their mounts on the walls. Whoever had the job of hanging those was a much better carpenter than I. "That was fuckin' awesome," Cesar said. Which was followed with a not really controlled sinister laugh. To be honest it was, it was absolutely... fuckin' awesome.

Adrian had cruised out to Vegas with Mark McGrath for the show. That night Adrian played drums on "Plush" while Mark and I watched from the side of the stage. Dean had started wearing a beanie on stage with the word "queer" emblazoned on it. During the show at the Joint, he kept pointing at the beanie and looking at me. The last thing I wanted was to be kissed by the guy again. Every time he pointed at it, I would look at him and scowl. At some point I walked onto the stage towards him to check on a light or something, and he threw me the beanie. I guess he just wanted me to grab it from him. He didn't want to lose it. Feeling slightly foolish, I figured it was time to let my beef with the guy go.

Chapter 70
STD Playing with a Sex Pistol. Oops... I Mean STP

That night we headed to San Jose. I was feeling good about myself and was leaving Vegas $180 richer. I had won the money playing a few hands of blackjack. These last few shows were turning out all right! I was wearing my STP bitch shirt on stage and getting a lot of girls' phone numbers because of it. Steve's shirts were a hit. Steve and I both thought we should have made more. Everyone I talked to seemed to want to buy one.

Rigger Steve STP crew shirts.

From San Jose we began to head south. After playing in Bakersfield, we had the next day off in Los Angeles. As the tour was winding down, that night the band took everyone on the crew to dinner in Hollywood. They said it was to thank us for being a good crew. Both the dinner and the thank you meant a lot to me. Scott left that night in a big furry rock star jacket hand in hand with his wife. I ran after him and handed him a copy of the movie script I had been working on. I hoped that maybe he'd read it.

The next night was our second to last show. It was at the Universal Amphitheatre in Los Angeles. I had loaded up on passes to sneak all my friends in. After Los Angeles we would play one more night in Arizona, and then that was it- we were done. My parents, sisters, and lots of friends came to the Universal Amphitheatre. I loaded up both my friend's and parent's cars with all the great stuff I had gathered. A new blender, massive amounts of beer, cases of Yoo-hoo, loads of schwag, camping chairs, and of course camping tables to go with the camping chairs. Altogether, I walked ten people into the Universal show. Steve Jones from the Sex Pistols played on stage with STP as an encore. It was really an awesome evening. After Jones came off the stage, Suzi approached him. She had been excited all day he was going to be there. Years ago, she had dated him. When he walked off the stage, he didn't give her the time of day. He had no clue who she was. How could anyone forget Suzi I asked myself? We all had a good but respectful laugh, because after all, it was Suzi we were making fun of. No one messed with her. One of the other celebrities to stop by the show was a guy I had never heard of. His name was Glen Campbell. The band and the crew couldn't believe I didn't know who he was. I wasn't embarrassed about not knowing, but I bought a CD of his the next chance I got.

During the day Nigel and I took turns showing my family around the venue. While at front of house my dad met Frank. "It's nice to meet you, Mr. Rifken," Frank said. "What?" my dad asked. "I said it's a pleasure to meet you, Mr. Rifken," Frank repeated himself. Later in the bus Frank apologized as everyone laughed. "I thought Joel Rifken was your real name," he said to me. "Everyone calls you that," he said. "I didn't know he was a serial killer. I hope I didn't offend your dad. Sorry, man," he said. "I don't think he's bothered by it, Frank. It's all good. He probably has no idea what you are talking about," I told him.

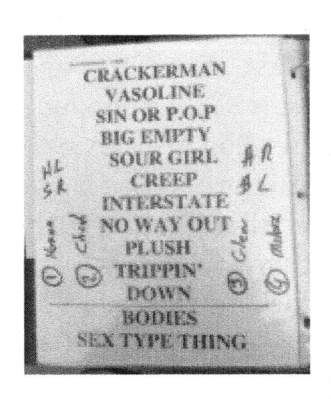

11/9/2000 STP set list and band signed drum head from Universal Amphitheatre show.

At the end of the show, I saw my father. "So, Pop, what did you think?" I said. "I like the bus," he replied. Earlier in the day I had taken him in to see the tour bus. A former race car driver, and a professional mechanic, I thought he might be impressed with the tour bus. He had walked in and sat in the driver's seat like a five-year-old getting his first Tonka truck to play with. He was mesmerized. "Yes, Dad, I know about the bus, but what about the show?" I asked. "Godsuck. They were much better than your band." I laughed a bit. "You think so, huh?" I asked. "Yes, much better," he replied again. "It's Godsmack, Dad." Though a waste of time, I corrected him. "Yes, they were much better," he repeated himself. "I know you've made that clear, Dad," I told him. "Godsuck. You should work for them." His final answer- he was certain about it.

At the end of the night my family tried to flag me down to say goodbye. I was so used to being called Rifken, I didn't pay attention as my father yelled out my name- Joel. However, I turned around immediately when I heard someone calling me Rifken. I jumped off the stage and went down into the now empty amphitheater to see my family. "Don't call me Rifken," I barked at him. I certainly didn't want my family to start calling me that. In hindsight, I think that my father was trying to join in as one of the guys. Enjoy the moment type thing. I should have laughed it off instead of making sure he knew he was separate from my new life.

Chapter 71
STP Finale

The last show was in Phoenix. I was both happy and proud I had made it through the entire tour without getting fired. I was physically exhausted but also a little concerned that the new family, I thought I had gained, would be splitting up. I wasn't sure if I'd ever see any of them again.

The last show wasn't anything real special. I wanted to sort out some last show antics, but no one really jumped on board. Throughout the tour when David, from Disturbed, came on stage in the electric chair a voice through the loud speakers listed horrible acts that he had committed. He was then executed and the show began. In-ears are little monitor speakers that fit inside your ear. I wanted to play a different track from the monitor board, one which only David could hear through his in-ears, that ran off hilarious crimes. The wind up was, he wouldn't know that he was the only one hearing it.

"You, David Draiman, have been convicted of not helping a cat out of a tree. You, David Draiman, have been convicted of stealing tampons from a CVS store. You, David Draiman, masturbate to Rainbow Brite..." We would Just continue to list lame events rather than the horrible and sadistic crimes they played nightly.

Unfortunately, it never happened. I instead gaff taped him into the electric chair so that he couldn't get up. While I did it, David didn't really care, or for that matter, make any attempt to stop me. I cut the tape off before he had to stand up. I, of course, didn't want to mess up the performance for the audience. It was all a bit anti-climactic.

Afterwards, I returned to Los Angeles. I had hoped to go visit Stefanie in New York. She had taken time off in December to see me. However, I couldn't. I was told we were to start working for Guns N' Roses in December.

At the same time, I learned Slash would not be touring with GNR. I wasn't all that excited to hear the news. I was pleased to know I was still going to be able to work though. STP had rented a house up in Malibu, and they were going to be recording a new album. This was all going well. I figured I'd be able to work for Guns N' Roses, and when that tour was over, I'd be able to hop back on tour with STP again. It looked like I had a career!

Chapter 72
Mates

I was relieved the STP tour was over. I now had my first tour under my belt: I wasn't a rookie. I was ready to tackle working for my favorite band, Guns N' Roses. All the GNR gear, was in Los Angeles so I knew we'd be setting up shop in L.A. I assumed that would get me a bit more work because they wouldn't have to fly me in or put me up in a hotel. I hung out with friends and waited for a phone call from Cesar.

On November 24th I got a call from Elise, Cesar's assistant. I had been home for two weeks and had been drunk every night. Elise asked me for my passport information so she could get my Visa prepared for Rio De Janeiro. It was really gonna happen. My second tour in and I was going to get to work for the best band in the whole damn world. I guess the stars were freaking aligned. I tried, mostly unsuccessfully, to contain my excitement because I knew excitement was a sign of weakness. After all, I was a man now. Well, at least Steve had said I was and he was pretty manly.

I kept drinking and spending time with my girlfriends until Cesar called. The call came on November 30th. Cesar had just got into town, and he wanted to see me. All the Guns N' Roses gear was stored at a place called Mates Studio. He wanted me to meet him there. When I got to Mates, I saw that things were already in motion. All the hallways were filled with GNR road cases and the big rehearsal room was crammed with both gear and backline guys. This was a whole new crew. I didn't know anyone. Cesar took me into a small office. He had already set up shop. Seeing everything, and more importantly everyone, I wondered why I hadn't been called a couple days earlier to get it all going too.

"Good to see you, Cesar. How was your break?" I asked. "Sit down, Rif," he ordered. I sat down on a chair in the room. "Close the door," he insisted. I got up and closed the door. "What's up?" I asked. Cesar looked over at me. "This is all going to be different from the last tour. There's a lot more going on. I can't watch you," he said. He started working on some paperwork. Without looking up again he said, "don't fuck up." And that was it, that was my pep talk. I got up to leave. "One other thing, Bob Dylan is here. Don't look at him. It pisses him off."

I left the office and pretended to work on stuff even though I had no clue what I was going to be doing on the tour. I knew how to look like I was busy when I was really not doing anything, so it wasn't a problem. I shuffled through road cases and wondered if I was getting paid for the day or not and if I'd see Dylan. Without much to do, I focused on walking down the halls of the studio and not looking at anybody. I didn't want to take any risks. I'd be especially careful going to the candy machine and the bathroom I told myself. Those were the places I'd most likely find Bob Dylan.

After a couple hours I headed out to meet up with the girls at my local dive bar. I had recently found I liked Bloody Mary's and so I drank a lot of them. That night I projectile vomited, all over the bathroom, at my friend Samantha's house. Afterwards, I passed out in the middle of the bathroom floor.

I woke up to a call in the morning from Nigel. I picked up the phone after what seemed like a hundred rings. "Hey, Nigel what's up?" I asked. Standing up, I saw the Bloody Mary mix all over the walls. "Cesar wants to see you. Go to Mates," he said. He then hung up the phone.

Was I supposed to go to work every day now? I washed my face and rushed back to Mates. I didn't have time to clean the bathroom. When I got to Mates, I first walked into Cesar's office. "We are going to go to Rio for two weeks," Cesar said.

I'd later find out we would be there for only one show. The time scheduled before that show was going to be for band rehearsals. "I need you to keep everything about the band to yourself. Axl has a lot of problems, okay?" Cesar waited on me for a reply. "Yes, sir," I told him.

The rest of the day I hung out at Mates trying to hide that I was hungover and ignoring calls from Samantha's boyfriend. Now, I said Samantha's house and not their house, because she and I were friends. Samantha was a cute, very petite alcoholic who always had perfect shiny hair. She was my first partner in shit-talking crime. She and I would drink beers at the bar across the street and talk shit about all our friends and then some. She was a die-hard Guns N' Roses fan, and I was a die-hard fan of the venison and sharp Pennsylvania cheese tacos that she made. We'd both giggle back and forth talking smack for hours. I wish I could say that she passed out on the toilet in the bar with her pants around her ankles only once and that I had to then carry her home. But no… no that happened a couple times. Her boyfriend was a warehouse manager, and that may have been the most interesting thing about him. His claim to fame was that he had told Samantha's parents that "she was his little cum dumpster" and they hadn't killed him. They didn't like him as much as he didn't like me. I had tried to be friends with the guy, but he just wasn't a friendly person. I'm not sure what a guy would have to do to win him over. Anyhow, their bathroom seriously looked like a murder scene, and surprisingly he wasn't happy he had been left to clean it.

Nigel told me they were going to have me run the teleprompter. I thought that would be a good gig. I could definitely learn to do that. I wondered if I'd get to hang out with Axl a lot if I was the monitor guy.

Cesar asked me to go buy a folding table, an easy enough gig. I was relieved to leave the place. Away, maybe it wouldn't be so obvious how hungover I was. When I returned with the folding table, I couldn't find the receipt. Cesar made me cover the cost of the table. I was now hungover, and I didn't have enough money in my pocket to buy gas to drive home. I had to borrow ten bucks from one of the backline guys, but I learned a lesson, and and I've never lost a receipt again.

Chapter 73
My Favorite Band in the World

On December 3rd I had my first real day working for GNR. I met with Josh in the morning. Josh had toured with GNR before as a guitar tech. More importantly he had been the roadie who had let me borrow the ten dollars for the gas. He seemed like a good guy and he was fun to be around.

Almost everyone who wasn't part of Cesar's crew had done at least one tour with them. On the 3rd my job was to go through storage to see just what was in there. No one had looked in the storage space since the mid 90's.

Josh and I opened the locked gate and began to roll cases into the parking lot to have a better look at everything. Even the lock on the gate had dust on it. The hope was to find expendables and other goods that we could use and not have to re-buy tape and stuff like that. At the very back of the storage was a Guns N' Roses pinball machine. Josh saw me looking at it. "Slash designed it," he told me. "It's really cool, man," I said to him. "Axl has fifteen more of them in storage," he told me. We pulled each case into the parking lot one by one. Having trouble rolling one of the wardrobe cases in the back, I left it be. I figured the caster was messed up and decided to leave the road case where it stood. It was already in the back of the storage unit and I wouldn't be able to use anything from wardrobe anyhow.

After the rest of the cases were in the parking lot, I came back and decided to open the wardrobe case to make sure it had just wardrobe stuff in it, as I did so I was hit by a horrible stench. Inside were leathers belonging to the whole band. Josh came back into the storage from outside. "That is stuff from the Appetite tour," he told me. "We need to air it out," I told him.

"Yeah, smells pretty bad," Josh said. "Jesus Christ," I said aloud agreeing with him.

I was totally geeking out at this point. How much could these be worth? The actual clothes the band wore for the *Appetite for Destruction* tour! My heart raced with excitement. I got on my stomach and looked under the case to see why it wouldn't roll and pulled out a piece of fabric that had been stuffed under there. Josh rolled the case outside and I had a better look at the large piece of black fabric. As I began to spread it out over the pavement inside the storage area, I realized it wasn't just a piece of fabric at all. It was the coolest piece of music memorabilia I had ever seen. I had found the Appetite for Destruction backdrop. And I found it stuffed under a road case.

My excitement built as I took it outside to air out. I couldn't wait to see what it looked like. If it had any rips, I'd make a plea that we get it repaired immediately. Maybe they'd have me personally take it to the repair place. When was the last time someone had set eyes on this grail? Spread out in the parking lot, I looked down at it in awe. It was in fantastic condition. No repairs needed. After letting it air out for a couple hours, I folded it up like a Veteran would fold up a U.S. Flag. Not to offend anyone by my analogy but this was the most precious thing I had ever laid my hands on. I was horrified these relics were being stored the way they were but pleased, because I could now properly take care of them.

Unlike a lot of roadies, Josh was a good guy. He too was enjoying himself and it was clear he still loved what he did for a living. I opened another case and pulled open one of the drawers. It was filled with odds and ends. What I noticed most were the various old passes and guitar pics. One of the picks, a tortoise shell pick, had been separated from the rest. I pulled it out of the road case to have a better look at it.

"You know what that is, man?" Josh said to me. Not knowing

he was back in the building, I surprisingly glanced back over at him. I, of course, didn't. "That right there is from the first run of guitar pics made for Slash. He didn't like them, and so not many were made. That is the first though." I ran it through my fingers. Josh smiled at me while smoking a cigarette. "It's yours man. Take a couple passes if you want too." The day had officially become my coolest day of touring yet. "Let's go get some lunch," Josh said.

Cesar had a habit of *only* telling people what they needed to know. Josh, on the other hand, had a habit of telling me *everything* I could ever want to know. I learned that we were not just doing a show in Rio, but also a show in Las Vegas on New Year's Eve. We would play in Vegas and then go to Rio a few days later. In Rio we'd have twelve Navy Seals as security, and we'd be the headliners of *Rock in Rio*. Breaking up the information overload, I asked, "*Rock in Rio* is a big deal?" Josh almost spit out his food. Roadies don't spit out food though so that didn't happen. We eat a lot and we eat fast.

"A big deal? Yeah, man we are playing for over two hundred and fifty thousand people," Josh said in disbelief. He couldn't believe I didn't already know this stuff. "Holy shit," I said to him. I had no idea. No wonder Cesar seemed a bit on edge. Yeah, this was a little bit bigger than Stone Temple Pilots for sure. We went back to storage and put everything back under lock and key. At the end of the day Josh gave me a road case.

Nigel was trying to get his lighting plot approved and if he did, he would be hiring three carpenters. I would be one of them. This road case would be a perfect place for me to put my tools. It was a big step for me, and I appreciated Josh giving it to me.

Important tools of the roadie.

Chapter 74
Welcome to the Jungle

The next day I went to jury duty. The lady next to me watched soap operas literally the entire day. I'm sure she was getting paid from her employer and was ecstatic she had no one to bother or make fun of her. If anything could slow down my excitement, it was this. I thought if Cesar wanted to keep us roadies in check, he should send us here for the day. I had a lot of long-distance minutes left on my phone, so I called Stefanie in New York and talked to her. We had a good catch up, and she questioned me on why I never got drunk with her. "Well, you intoxicate me with your beauty," I said to her. I laughed when I said it, because I knew how lame it sounded, but I honestly meant it. I told her that after the Guns N' Roses shows I'd see about going back out there to see her.

I had done a lot of rewrites for my film by this point. I had even picked a title, *An Artist's Art*. While touring I had given copies of *Part of the Machine*, about a singer/songwriter, to Scott, Dean, Cesar, and even Nigel. I was pretty sure Nigel couldn't read or write, but I gave it to him anyhow. I knew *An Artist's Art* was a good screenplay, but I had to figure out how to turn it into a feature film. As it sat it was only sixteen pages, and that was only long enough for a short film. I didn't want to make a short film.

The next day Nigel called me over to his house on an emergency. I got there to find the emergency was he needed Christmas lights hung. I had hung Christmas lights exactly ninety-seven times that year. I did not think his "emergency" was funny. I did hang the Christmas lights for him though. Nigel had himself a good laugh, and he couldn't wait to tell everyone how he had got me to come over to hang them.

On December 19th I saw GNR play for the first time. The band was Buckethead, Robin Finck from Nine Inch Nails, and Paul Tobias on guitars. Tommy Stinson from The Replacements on Bass. Brain from Primus on drums. Dizzy Reed and Chris Pitman on keys and percussion, and of course Axl Rose singing. It was a full stage. There were so many guys in the band I wasn't sure who was a roadie and who was in the band. It was like attending a rock star Karaoke event. These guys had won a contest and the grand prize was to play with Axl, and presumably get paid a bunch while doing it. Well, everyone but Paul Tobias I'm sure. He was Axl's buddy from when they were kids and had never played a show in front of a live audience. He clearly had a hard time keeping up with the rest of the band, which was understandable.

The 20th was spent cleaning up the studio in anticipation of Axl showing up the next day. I was excited to hear him sing and I didn't sleep much that night. On the 21st I met Axl Rose. To everyone's surprise he showed up at the time he said he would. He sat down on the edge of the stage and hung out for a while, looking around and chatting to people. Looking at him, I thought he seemed nervous. After a few laughs and catch ups with some of the crew guys he knew, the video guy approached him. He was going to be putting together the video show and was hoping to get some ideas for the new songs. "I mean, I'd like to know what the songs are about," he said. Axl replied to him, "they are all about hoes." I guess Axl liked farming. "They should market that to Middle America," I thought. I had met a lot of farmers in Middle America while touring with STP.

After a few minutes of sitting on the stage, Axl said to no one in particular, "It's weird being here hearing Guns N' Roses, but there is nobody here from Guns N' Roses." A few roadies popped up to tell Axl how great he was. Axl didn't respond to any of them. This first meeting wasn't going as I expected. Axl was much more human that I thought he'd be. He was honest and open.

Afterwards, he got up off the stage and sang a couple GNR songs with the band. For those, I called Samantha and left my phone on the upstairs couch. I wanted to share the awesomeness of it all. This was before you could record with your phone. I so badly wanted to share this moment with someone else who would appreciate it. Samantha and I listened on. To me, with eyes closed it sounded like GNR tearing up the stage. With eyes open, it looked like the best hired guns, no pun intended, lighting up the stage with Axl singing. It was all very different than touring with STP. STP was like a family. We all got along, pretty much, and though it was hard work, at the end of the day it was mostly fun. I realized GNR was going to be a bunch of crew tiptoeing around Axl. I didn't think that touring with bands was going to turn into a job. To everyone here that's all it was and that was clear. Guns N' Roses was my favorite band but this wasn't them. I was afraid the bubble of quick paced excitement would end abruptly. To Samantha it just sounded like noise. She couldn't make out a thing.

Now on the other side of the coin, this was the closest I would ever get to the real GNR, and I knew I needed to focus on the experience in that. I wondered what Slash and the other original lineup would think of other guys playing their songs. Are great performers impressed with other brilliant musicians playing their music?

At the end of the night Axl commented, "It's hard to act like I don't care. It's like putting on a hula hoop and doing the shaking hips thing. There, are you happy?" I had no clue what he was talking about.

I waited to see if he'd comment on the sage burning. I had been informed that Axl liked to have sage burning at all times while he was in the studio. So, I had found a shop that sold witch stuff in a city called Sunland and loaded up on sage for him. More interesting than the sage, while in the shop, I found a real Egyptian mummy. Missing it's casket it was in a regular wooden coffin. "How do you know he's Egyptian," I asked the guy? He showed me paperwork that the mummy had once been in the British Museum. "It say what he died from?" I asked. "Lack of breathing," the guy replied. So, what would any rational person do? I bought the mummy. I had to get my money together, and so I told him I'd be back. Was the mummy a dude or a chick? I had forgotten to ask.

Chapter 75
No Mummy for My Mommy

The next day while the band was practicing playing the song "Patience," I fucked up royally. I heard the phone ringing in one of the side rooms of the rehearsal studio, and trying to be helpful, I picked it up. I could only hear one of the crew guys on the other end. After a minute or so I just hung up. Unfortunately, for me, the guy calling in was Axl. After a few minutes Stu, the crew guy who had been on the phone, came out and barked at me. Axl was furious and wanted whatever "fucking idiot" who picked up the phone to be fired immediately. Axl clearly had very little patience. Cesar sent me home a bit early so I wouldn't be there when Axl got to the studio. I had spent how much time in my life on the phone, and I was going to get fired over a phone call? Would there ever be a time where I wouldn't worry about losing my job and getting kicked off the roller coaster ride too early?

I went home hoping Cesar would work it out. He told me that Axl fired people all the time. You had to hide out for a bit and then come back to work. That is how everyone handled it. I took the incident as yet another glaring example of how easy it was to get fired while on the road. What if they did fire me? Then what was I going to do? No, it wasn't time to sort out what I was going to do next just yet. I would quit drinking for a bit, keep my head down, and work hard.

When I got back to my parent's house, I sat down and talked to my mom about buying the mummy. After a bit of arguing, my mom agreed I could keep the mummy in the garage. She said she was not about to "have a dead body in the house." I figured the garage would be fine until I could figure out a better place to store my mummy.

The next day everyone got a palm pilot for Xmas. If you weren't around when palm pilots came out, let me tell you what they were. They were the first popular handheld computer. You could access the internet on them! It didn't take long for smartphones to take over, but when palm pilots came out, they were pretty darn cool. Axl bought everyone one of these bad boys for Xmas. Everyone but me that was; it wasn't because I had been fired, it was because I had left early and missed the headcount for Xmas gifts. Of all the days to have left early. Axl's assistant apologized to me, but I never did get anything. I hadn't been really doing anything for the last couple weeks, so I chalked that up as my Xmas present from Axl. It had been a couple of days now, since the phone call issue, and as anticipated it had already been forgotten about. Everyone was packing up to take a few days off for Xmas itself.

Over the next few days, I started writing a feature length animated film script about a young girl who befriends a whale. It kept me busy over the Xmas break. On Xmas day I went over to Nigel's house. Rigger Steve met us up there as well, and we had a roadie Xmas dinner. Rigger Steve had made a Viking ship out of chocolate, and at the helm of the ship sat I. He had modeled me as the ship captain eating a ham and cheese sandwich. We all had a nice night. During dinner, Nigel asked me about the mummy. "I have some bad news," I announced to them all. "Someone stole my mummy," I told them. "Someone stole the mummy?" asked Steve. "Yes, Steve someone stole my mummy," I repeated. "So, what are you going to do?" asked Nigel. "What do you want me to do?" There wasn't much else to say about the matter, and so the subject was dropped. "What would you say is the most important thing Steve has taught you, Rifken?" Nigel asked, while passing the gravy. "If you can't tie a knot, tie a lot," I said. "Hey, Rifken, do you have any sage in your truck?" Nigel's wife asked. "Sure, a shit load." At this point I always seemed to be travelling around with a garbage bag full of sage in my passenger seat. I brought in a bunch, and she lit it. The whole house soon smelled like the studio. "I told you to learn your knots," Steve mumbled.

During the Christmas holiday, Nigel scheduled a nice little one-off show. A one-off is a one-night event and that's it, the gig is over. The event was the Capitol Records Christmas party. Each department had to assemble a band and play a song that Capitol Records had released. The performances were really good. So was the lobster I might add, oh and the steak. The winner of the event pulled in a shill. They started playing an Eagles song, and Glen Frey walked out on stage to "properly" perform it. It was an easy, cool gig. I was finding myself liking working in the music industry more and more. "Rifken, you are pretty good at finding things," Nigel said to me. "Yeah, I guess so," I replied while eating more steak. "Years ago, I passed on buying a velvet painting of Jesus and Elvis," he said to me. "That shouldn't be that hard to find," I told him. "Yeah, but here was the twist. Elvis had his arm around Jesus. Not the other way around," he said. "Pretty funny, huh? Can you find me that velvet painting?" he asked. "But the arm has to be around...," he continued on. "I get it, Nigel. I don't know, man. I can find you some more lobster, though if you want." I told him. "No, I don't eat lobster," he replied. "Man, you are missing out," I told him. And I meant it too; boy, was it good.

Chapter 76
Axl Tea

On the 27th everyone was back in the rehearsal studio and hitting the pavement hard. We all had to get ready for the New Year's Eve show in Las Vegas. Everyone was nervous, including the guys in the band. Talk about a different vibe than STP. That night I heard the songs "Silkworms" and "Madagascar" for the first time. I thought "Madagascar" was an awesome song. I didn't know Axl knew how to play the guitar, but guitar in hand, while on stage, he showed the guys something he wanted to do while performing it. I was getting excited again. Realizing my ignorance, I said aloud to myself, "of course he would know how to play guitar." However, how many people ever got to see Axl with a guitar strapped over his shoulder in a rehearsal studio?

Amongst other people, I called Stefanie in New York to tell her how cool everything was. She had good news too. "I got a promotion at work. They moved me out of my cubicle, I now have my own office. And I got a better job title," she said to me. She was clearly excited to tell me the news. I waited for the grand finale, but it never came. "And you got a raise?" I asked. "No, I got a promotion but that is awesome," she said.

GNR was one of those bands that had a massive entourage. Cesar was trying to cut back expenses and get rid of as many of these hangers on as possible. For example, there was going to be a guy who flew to Rio with us to make Axl tea. His *only* job was to be the tea making guy. For whatever reason, he wasn't able to make it this night, and so I was delegated to make Axl his tea. I was fine with that; I figured it would be a good way to get to know him better and maybe I wouldn't get fired again. That night Axl and I had our first conversation. "Damn. You make a good cup of tea," he said. "Thanks, man," I replied. I asked him if he wanted anymore, and he said no. That was our conversation. It was deep and meaningful, in fact, so deep the event might have been worthy of even being a book title.

Over the next few days I was, for the most part, the only one of the crew in the studio. I was spending roughly 20 hours a day there. I'd take naps on the couch when needed. Everyone was spending time with their families for Christmas. If anything needed to be done in the meantime, I would be the guy to sort it out for them. On one of these days when it was real quiet, Axl unexpectedly strolled in with his assistant, her son, and I think his gardener. I was upstairs with Buckethead, the only other guy there at the time. I had been picking obscure songs to see if Buckethead knew how to play them. I hadn't been able to stump the guy yet. When Axl came in, I quickly ran back down the stairs just in case he needed anything. Buckethead stayed put on the upstairs couch. "Oh, hey man, how goes it?" Axl said. "Good, need anything?" I asked. "No, it's cool," he replied. It was yet another deep conversation between the two of us. Our relationship was building so fast! The tea conversation had only been days before. He sat down at the piano, and shortly thereafter began to play the song "November Rain." I didn't know why he had chosen to come to the studio or to play the song, but it was awesome. I watched on in awe, savoring the moment. When the song finished, the phone rang. I picked it up and it was Cesar on the line. "Hey, Rif, I was calling to see if you were there. Go home and get some sleep. I'm flying in and we are going to have a long night. We are pulling an all-nighter."

"Axl is here," I said quietly over the phone. "Oh, yeah? What's he doing there?" Cesar asked. "He's playing 'November Rain' for his gardener," I told Cesar.

Chapter 77
GNR Ramps Up

That night Axl was supposed to show up at 8PM for what would be the last rehearsal before the Vegas show. The crew trickled in throughout the day and night until almost everyone was there. The band rehearsed on and off for most of the night without him. At 4:30AM Axl finally did show up. For three hours the band rehearsed with him singing and they tore it up. It was the first time Axl had sang on any stage in eight years. I don't know if it was because they were all tired, and so they just fit in a pocket or they were just playing their part for the boss, Axl. Either way it was loud. A wall of "fuck you- we are Guns N' Roses." There are a bunch of us and we are loud. You can't ignore us. It had the feeling of a middle school student dumping a truck full of Brussel sprouts on their parent's bed and telling them to eat up. They are good for you. Defiance and anger… It was all a true display of power. I couldn't help but think that this was all a plan for Axl to show up the rest of the guys in the original lineup.

After the band cleared the stage, the roadies started packing everything up. My job was to hang out outside the rehearsal studio to inventory, measure, and weigh each case for our manifest. Once the cases were pushed past me, they were then packed into a big rig, which would go off to the shipping dock, and then off to Rio. The only case that didn't make it onto the truck that day was the one Josh had given me. Cesar had made me put it back in storage. It didn't belong to Josh to give me he told me. He was right of course but it would have been nice to have all the same. Case after case rolled by, and I began to wonder what we weren't taking to Rio. I had been working for twenty or so straight hours now and I was tired. STP had been physically exhausting. GNR was emotionally exhausting. The last road case came through finally. It was a large wardrobe case filled with Fiji water. Why were we shipping cases of Fiji water to Rio de Janeiro? I didn't care, but it would have made a hell of a commercial for Fiji water. I just wanted to go home and sleep for a bit.

There were a few of us from STP, Cesar had managed to get on board. Nigel, Aso, Rigger Steve, Clif, and me. I'd say we were his core crew. Get it? STP... Core...

Nigel had been giving me a hard time ever since we first got the gig. He just couldn't believe GNR was my favorite band. He had been listening to their music to piece a light show together and kept calling me to ask yet again how they I could like them so much. He thought they sucked. I drove back to my parent's house with my eyes glazed over from fatigue. I pulled in the driveway and my phone rang. It was Nigel. "Hey, Rifken, you gotta come back to the studio. Axl is going there, and someone needs to be there for him," he said.

My heart sank. I just wanted to go to sleep. No, I didn't want to; I needed to. "Why? There is nothing left in the place," I replied. "Dunno," Nigel said. When I walked in the house my parents were happy to see me. Everything was going well, and they were happy I seemed to have found a career. I pretended not to be tired, because I didn't want them to worry about me getting into a car accident on the way back. The studio was a forty-minute drive from the house. I tried to not make it obvious that I was totally burned out, but I don't think I fooled anyone in my family. I took a shower, and got back in the truck.

I made it back to the studio and it was the same as I had left it. Nothing was there. After a couple minutes Nigel called me again. All I heard on the other line was laughter. "Don't ever fuck with the old guys, Rifken," I heard Aso yelling in the background. I was too tired to be angry. To me this wind up wasn't at all funny. I sat down on the upstairs couch I had spent so much time on lately and looked down. A day ago, on the posts on either side of the stage, had been hand written lyrics. Axl had written them out and posted them up for the new lineup. One sheet had been the song "Mr. Brownstone" and on the other were the words to "Sweet Child of Mine." They were gone now like everything else in the place. Even the garbage cans had been emptied. I had hoped to take them home as souvenirs. The lyric sheets- not the garbage cans. I wondered if someone else had taken them. My eyes closed, and I fell asleep.

The next day we all flew out to Las Vegas. GNR was going to play for a lucky 1800 people at the House of Blues. Together, we would all welcome in the New Year. My excitement wasn't unjustified. It wasn't just the first show Axl was going to perform in almost a decade; I had already witnessed what was about to come, so I knew how good the night was going to actually be. Nigel sat down on the plane next to me. "How did you sleep, Rifken?" he asked. In the great words of the entire band of Everclear I looked Nigel right in the eyes and said to him, "fuck you, Nigel." I was still worn out. "I spent some time with Axl last night," he said. "I don't give a fuck Nigel," I replied. "He told me he covered 'Knockin' on Heaven's Door' not because of Dylan, but because of the Sisters of Mercy," he continued on. Nigel was a massive fan of the band the Sisters of Mercy. "So, you are now a fan?" I asked. "Well, it's a step in the right direction," he said. "Glad to hear it. Now shut the fuck up so I can go to sleep," I told him.

We got into Vegas the night of the 30th. Las Vegas was a city wide GNR fan fest. Everywhere people had GNR shirts on. When we arrived at the hotel lobby, I saw a few of my friends drinking beers and waiting for me. Not expecting them to be there, I gave them a slightly concerned glare. It was a hint for them to not talk to me while I was with the crew. It was the kind of look Superman would have no doubt given one of his parents if they had decided to drop by the Daily Planet with a pair of Superman Underoos for his birthday.

Either my friends didn't care they could get me in trouble, or they were too dumb to realize it would not be a good idea. My guess is the latter. They stood waiting for me, bags in hand. They all had nowhere to go because everyone was crashing in my room. If Cesar knew my friends were meeting up with me, I was pretty damn sure it wouldn't go over very well. I had sneaked the same group of guys into the STP show at the Universal Amphitheatre and it had come back to bite me in the ass. Even though I told them to keep a low profile, I was still contacted by security multiple times when they tried to sneak girls back stage with their STP VIP passes that I had given them. Luckily the head of security at the Universal Amphitheatre reported to me. So, no one else ever found out. At this show no one reported to me. My job was to stay quiet, work, and collect my paycheck. I was more nervous about sneaking them into the show than I actually was about working it. I was being stupid for even trying to play these silly games.

Two of them approached me as soon as we walked in. I played it as cool as I could and told them I'd meet them at the poker tables in a half hour. No one really noticed, or maybe didn't care, except Rigger Steve. He smirked at me. The smirk was a reminder that I should know better than to mess around. Would I ever complete Steve's Rifken training? I glanced back at him with my own smirk, suggesting I wasn't doing anything dumb at all. "Just random people I know in Vegas is all," I said to him.

"Do you know how many nickels and dimes they have to put in those machines over there to make it make sense. I mean what do you think each square foot is worth to the people who own this place?" I asked Steve. "Are you trying to change the subject from your friends being here to have a sleepover with you?" Steve responded. Rigger Steve wasn't dumb, but he also wasn't a snitch. He didn't say anything to anyone.

Chapter 78
Don't Befriend the Verm

The next day we headed out to the House of Blues to load in. I didn't have much to do all day. There were no backdrops for the show; instead, the entire back of the stage was a video monitor. They had hired some other guy to run the teleprompter, and Axl's tea maker had shown up. All the jobs I would have done were covered.

As the day flashed by, more and more GNR fans hoarded around the HOB in anticipation of what the evening was soon to bring. One particular guy singled me out and through a delivery gate asked to speak to me. I really had nothing to do, so I walked over to him. Normally, I would have ignored him. The guy handed me an old photograph of Axl Rose and himself. They were just kids, maybe 15-16 years old. "I'll see what I can do, dude," I told him. "I don't want anything from him. I just thought it would be cool to reconnect. We used to be good buds when we were kids," the guy told me.

I cruised back into the venue. The first guy I saw was Shaggy. Shaggy was Axl's longtime assistant when doing shows. You could call him Axl's stage handler. He would help him with wardrobe, oxygen tanks if need be, sweat towels, maybe a ball adjustment here and there- you know, whatever. Shaggy was a first-class asshole. Knowing that, I don't know why I did what I did next.

"Hey, Shaggy, some guy outside gave this to me. It's pretty cool. It's him and Axl as kids. Check it out." I handed the photo to Shaggy. "He asked if you could give it to Axl. His info. is on the back," I said. Shaggy got angry fast, his face turning bright red. It was a red that I'd say had a tomato like hue. Now it's important to note, that If he looked like a tomato, it would have been an ugly tomato. Not a nice round bulbous tomato. You know the kind you put salt on and eat as a delicacy. No, he was a ridged rotten tomato. Not the tomato you'd find at the grocery store. Anyhow, with his tomato head, Shaggy ripped the photo up in front of me and threw it away. "Are you fucking kidding me, man? You need to pull your head out of your ass. I got shit to do. Fuck off, Rifken." Shaggy put his head back into his road case and kept working. I hated the fucking guy.

I knew what was going to happen next and sure enough I was right. About an hour later Cesar called me into his office. "What the fuck are you thinking?" Cesar asked. The worst time to get on Cesar's bad side was when he was stressed out and today everyone, including him, was. Well, everyone except me. I was just concerned about getting my friends into the concert for free.

"I thought it was a cool photo," I said. There were a few people in the office, and I hated being scolded when it was in front of people. "You know, kid, I'm trying to keep as many of my guys on this gig as I can. There are a lot of crew on their side. Shit like this doesn't help me." I nodded that I understood. I left the office thinking what a little bitch Shaggy was. It took him all of thirty seconds to run off to Cesar to let him know how amateur his guys were.

Chapter 79
In Through the Out Door

All access pass for GNR New Year's show, 2000-2001.

The venue started filling up later in the evening. The Goo Goo Dolls played first. I had sneaked in four of my friends and was relieved to have the daunting task of getting them into the venue done and over with. I watched most of the set and even rang in the New Years with the band. Unfortunately, after the New Year's countdown everyone was kicked out. This was going to be a long night.... Axl wasn't even in the building yet. I heard people had paid up to five thousand dollars for tickets to see the show when the face price of the tickets had been one hundred and fifty. I wondered if he would piss everyone off and do a no show.

When the room was empty, they brought in a cleaning crew. Wandering around, because I didn't have much to do, I found a wrapped gift on the stage. It was addressed to someone named John. I figured the name John was close enough to the name

Joel and so I unwrapped the gift. Inside I found a still sealed Pez dispenser. I sat down, ate some Pez, and waited. The cleaning crew worked lightning fast and soon enough the doors re-opened again.

Next up for the evening was a full rave. All our gear was in place on stage and so the rave was held out on the floor. It didn't take long for Nigel, Aso, Rigger Steve, and I, to mix into the verm and start dancing. We were making up new dance moves and having a great time. Before long Aso and Steve had no shirts on... and shortly thereafter we were kicked out of the venue. We all knew we'd get back in easily. It's kind of hard to have a concert without anyone running the lights. We all had a good laugh at ourselves and then as a group directed one hundred percent of our laughter towards the security guys who had just kicked us out. Taking out our all access laminates, we walked right back into the venue. I don't think the security appreciated it.

Chinese Democracy gig shirt for New Year's show, 2000-2001.

At roughly 2AM they opened the doors and let everyone in. As far as I knew, none of the band was even there yet. I knew all the stories about GNR going on hours late but I figured for a New Year's show they would want to play when midnight hit. By 2:30AM the band had all finally shown up. They all cruised in individually, and none of them were in any rush at all. Crunch time was coming for me though. I knew if I was going to get my friends into the show, they had come to see, it would have to be right now. They had missed the rave to drink and gamble on the floor of the casino. So, I now met four drunk friends at the back gate. I quickly had a security guy open it up and then spoke, "Seriously, no joke. Follow me and don't lag. As soon as you hit the crowd, make your way into the middle of the floor and mix in. Then do whatever you want, but don't get me in trouble."

I walked through the venue with them behind me. When there was any security in the way, and there was lots and lots, I would tell them my friends were with me. I released them into the audience and then ran back to look like I was working on something backstage. I would know really fast if I had been busted. If busted, I sure hoped it wasn't by Shaggy.

It had worked. All my friends were now in the venue, and no one had said a word to me about it. Now, like everyone else, I waited in anticipation for the show to start. 3AM came and still no one in the band was even getting ready. I absolutely wasn't used to this. I'm a very punctual person, so while I didn't care, or rather shouldn't care because I was getting paid, I did wonder when they were ever going to get around to actually performing. I heard rumors amongst the crew that Slash had shown up and Axl refused to enter the building with him on site. My mind raced as I thought of possible reunions. Maybe Slash had jumped into Axl's limo and they'd hug it out. Man, that would be awesome, I thought. Finally, a few minutes before 3:30AM, the band got on stage.

Shortly thereafter, a video short Axl had made played for the audience. The video was really Axl just poking fun at himself for being absent from the music scene for so many years. After the video a couple minutes passed, and all any of us could hear were musicians testing their instruments, while music that sounded like the beginning of the GNR song "Oh My God" played over the PA. That was shortly all interrupted by some dialogue, probably from some movie or something, and then... finally the guitar lick we had all been waiting for, the beginning of "Welcome to the Jungle." The crowd erupted and I smiled from ear to ear. This was going to be so awesome. The show lasted for 2 hours. I loved every minute of it. I was the smallest part of the GNR machine and very proud of it.

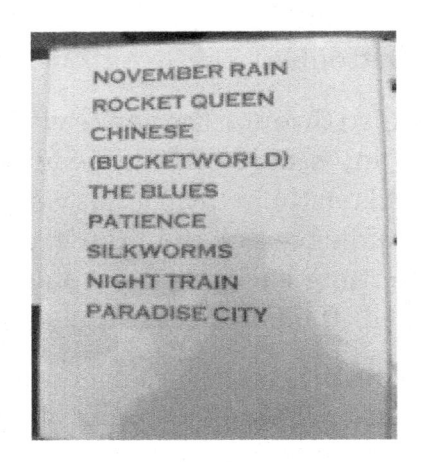

```
JUNGLE                      NOVEMBER RAIN
EASY                        ROCKET QUEEN
BROWNSTONE                  CHINESE
LIVE & LET DIE              (BUCKETWORLD)
OH MY GOD                   THE BLUES
MY MICHELLE                 PATIENCE
THINK ABOUT                 SILKWORMS
YOU COULD BE MINE           NIGHT TRAIN
SWEET CHILD                 PARADISE CITY
KNOCKIN' ON HEAVENS DOOR
OUT TO GET ME
RHIAD
```

GNR set list New Year's show, 2000-2001.

Throughout the show, Axl was pretty chill. I was waiting for him to break out into one of his tirades, but he never did. I think if there were any shit talkers there, they didn't have much room to talk shit that night. The band was great.

The big joke amongst the crew had become whether Paul's guitar would even be plugged in during the show. The guy was clearly nervous, but I think any nervousness stood out considerably more as no one else in the band was nervous at all. I quickly decided if you hated the show, you weren't a GNR fan. During the set I still didn't have anything to do. So, I waited on standby, ready to help if anything came up. During the song "Rocket Queen" we had a pair of go-go dancers on stage. My job was to help one of them up on a pedestal and then hold the pedestal steady while she danced on it. From where I knelt, the only thing I could really see was a view up her skirt. It wasn't a bad job for a 22-year-old guy. I thought if I could sum up my entire roadie experience by one image, I would want this moment to be it.

Chapter 80
Happy New Year!

When the show ended, instead of loading out, all the roadies drank. The band and most of Axl's side of the crew immediately began to drink champagne. Axl himself drank a beer called St. Pauli Girl when he felt like having a beer. Someone had stocked some in the fridge backstage, probably Shaggy, and I was tempted to grab one but I knew if Cesar saw me, he'd fire me for sure. I certainly thought about downing one real quick. It would be pretty cool to finish out the show drinking one of Axl's personal beers. After all it was New Year's Eve, right? Reluctantly, I didn't do it. I had to remind myself that during work hours it was a no-no to party at all. Cesar, I think really felt he had groomed the most elite crew of roadies possible. To be honest I think he had. I couldn't jeopardize that for him.

Josh ran up to me, bear hugged me, and wished me a happy New Years. He had a bottle of champagne in each hand. "Here, bro, take one," he said. "I can't, man. I appreciate it, though," I said. Someone had let a load of girls backstage and I could tell this post show party was going to go on for a while. I decided to walk out to the loading dock to wait out the partying. When it all quieted down, I could then finish working. I walked out to the loading dock and found the rest of Cesar's crew.

Not hanging out would further separate me from the Guns N' Roses crew but partying would end my roadie career with Cesar. I wondered if any of the other guys on the dock had weighed their options too. Most of the guys on the dock had been through rehab. Aso and I were the only ones that drank at all. Everyone sat quietly as we watched the sun rise. The only slight movement among any of us was from Aso. Smoking his cigar, we all heard his occasional puff.

There was still a lot of work left to do. Cesar greeted us out on the dock. "Good job, guys," he said to us. He knew his elite crew wouldn't be partying but I think was pleased to see I had the sense to not indulge. This moment certainly won me some brownie points with the big guy. However, with all my heart, I wished I was inside motor boating tits and drinking champagne by the bottle.

Aso pulled a cigar out of his pocket. "Cigar?" he asked as he handed it out to Cesar. Cesar put the unlit cigar in his mouth. To break up the serenity, Josh ran out onto the dock. His pants were unbuttoned, he had a bra around his neck, and lipstick was all over his face. He now had a bottle of Jaeger Meister in his hand instead of champagne. Jaeger was Dizzy's drink. I had learned that while I had made the road cases ready a couple days earlier to go down to Rio. Dizzy had packed more bottles of Jaeger for the trip than T-shirts.

Josh moseyed over to Cesar and awkwardly tried to hug him. A big guy himself, he came up to Cesar's armpit. However, when putting his arm around Cesar, he wasn't close to being able to embrace him. I had only ever seen one other person try to hug Cesar. That guy was Matt Roberts, the guitar player from the band 3 Doors Down. Matt was always fucked up. He would walk up to Cesar, hug him, and want to give him continuous high fives. Cesar was always cool about it, partly because the guy was trashed and it was just easier to deal with him, but also because 3 Doors Down may be a band that would hire him one day. You never know where your next gig is going to come from, Cesar always told me. I liked the rest of the guys in 3 Doors Down, but I stayed away from Matt.

Cesar was neither friendly nor unfriendly to Josh. "Zip up your pants," he said. Josh zipped his pants back up, burped, and stood there uncomfortably. It took him a moment to realize he wasn't going to win over this crowd. The party would have to continue on without any of us. I watched on as something clicked in his head. Being inside was way more fun than this loading dock. Click, click… he left us. As he pranced back down the hallway, we all heard him yell over and over again, "Happy New Years!" "Guy wants to give me a hug with his pants down," Cesar said to no one in particular.

Saying nothing, we continued to watch the sun rise over Las Vegas. Aso handed Cesar his lighter. "Hey Nigel," said Aso. Nigel turned to him, "Yeah?" he asked. "Happy fucking New Year's, you limey prick." Clif the stage manager smiled. Nigel and Clif still hated one another.

I got back to my hotel room at roughly 4PM. I had left the same room a little over thirty hours earlier. I'd been running off of pure adrenaline for I don't know how many hours now. Finally falling asleep, my eyes closed. It was the best New Year's I had ever had.

Chapter 81
Stage Right Goners

On January 4th, at around noon, we all arrived at the hotel in Rio De Janeiro, Brazil. It was not just hot, but really hot. The hotel was surrounded by fans- no, not the circular kind- and reporters. There is a saying, "seeing is believing." It's true, arriving in Rio I understood just how huge Guns N' Roses really were. As we walked into the hotel lobby, I saw a young guy with a tattoo covering his entire back. The entire tattoo was just Axl's face. "What the hell is that about?" I rhetorically asked Aso. "Don't give a shit. Where's the pool?" Aso replied with the now usual cigar hanging out of his mouth. "You sure they are going to let your fat ass in the pool?" I asked him. "Fuck off," he replied with a grunt.

It didn't take too long to get our rooms. I used my credit card at the desk, to cover any incidentals, and I got my room key. I rushed up to my room walking by the hotel maid with a courteous smile. I wondered what my room would look like. It was a resort hotel and I hoped the room was as luxurious as the rest of the hotel. I opened my hotel room, and to my surprise walked in on a couple having sex in the bed. You might think it was awkward for all of us, but upon hearing me, they didn't even glance over. I walked back out of the room, past the maid, and back down to the lobby. The guy at the desk apologized and gave me a new room key. The new room was on the same floor as the sex den I just had walked out of. I rushed back upstairs, past the maid, and got into my room as fast as I could. I hoped all the while I didn't find a naked guy in the hallway brandishing a gun. Arriving safely in my room I threw on my swimsuit, wrote my room number on my hand, and rushed back downstairs to have some fun.

Within an hour everyone was at the hotel pool. The pool was

an assortment of rock star's, roadies, hookers, and of course the hotel staff. It looked like a convention celebrating unemployment at a hotel swimming pool. But it wasn't. It was the best the music industry had to offer. Rio was not going to suck. An hour later the GNR camp was as drunk as everyone else at the pool. On a level of 1 to 10, I would conservatively have marked all of us at a level of... fucking drunk. The rest of the day was a blur of Caipirinha's and tits. What's a Caipirinha? The Caipirinha is Brazil's national cocktail. It is made from cachaça, sugar, and lime. Cachaca is a Brazilian white rum made from sugarcane. Caipirinha's are delicious but pack a serious punch.

Stage Right Goner's crew shirt from Rio De Janeiro, 2001.

Josh, being a nice guy, offered to buy a round of drinks for all of us hanging out. That quickly turned into everyone indulging in drink after drink on Josh's tab. Later in the day Josh showed up with orange Hawaiian shirts to be worn by everyone who stood on stage right during the show. He dubbed us the *stage right goners* and wanted us to wear the shirts with pride. I liked my shirt but wondered if he realized there was no way in hell we could wear them on stage. Was he so drunk he didn't realize they were orange and not black? I think I was the only one who refused to partake in bankrupting Josh that day, but I did keep the shirt.

At around 4PM I headed back to my hotel room. I rode the elevator with Dave Grohl. "This place ain't that bad, huh?" he said to me. "I've been in worse, brother," I replied. I got back to my room, puked, and passed out for a few hours. That night a group of us headed to Ipanema. Hungover, I hurriedly ate a spaghetti dinner in an effort to suck up some of the alcohol. After dinner we headed to Copacabana and partied all night. Rio was going to be tough on my liver.

Chapter 82
... And Then the Cop Cupped Aso's Balls

The next day I followed Aso and Nigel out of the hotel. They wanted to go "explore." We started at the mall which was just across the street from the hotel. It was a high-end mall complete with shops full of stuff that roadies would never buy. After walking through the mall, Nigel decided he wanted to check out a favela. "Why?" I asked.

Favela is the Portuguese word for slum. I knew it was a bad idea to follow them, but I did it anyhow. The farther we got from the hotel, the less I wanted to walk back to the hotel by myself. To make matters worse, I had a few thousand dollars in my pocket. I hadn't wanted to leave the money in the room for fear of it getting stolen. I tried talking them out of it, but they both ignored me and kept walking. "What is it you expect to see?" I asked. Nigel replied, "No one is making you go, Rifken. If you don't like it, go back to the hotel."

Perhaps anti-climactic, we walked through the favela without incidence. The three of us got both inquisitive and dirty looks from various locals as we walked down the streets. Looking back at those, looking upon us, I was witnessing extreme poverty first hand. Dog carcasses in the street, rows of cardboard boxes that people were sleeping in, visibly hanging rotten chickens people intended to eat, and filth everywhere. We had walked around enough to understand just how bad a Rio De Janeiro favela was and had now found ourselves back out on the main streets of Rio. None of us said anything to one another, but the three of us were relieved to get out of the favela unscathed.

Moments later while crossing a main street, two Brazilian police officers stopped us. This was now going to become a bad situation. I told myself if they tried to take my money, I would just run. A very busy street, there were hundreds of cars passing by. I was hoping all these passing viewers would keep the cops from doing anything too bad to us. In good English one of the police officers told us to empty our pockets. I held my money and hotel key in my hand high. I tried to make it look like the bundle of money was no big deal.

"OK, take off your pants," he said. Standing on a center divider the cars began to honk at us as they drove by. Listening to orders, we all dropped our pants. Nigel was so white he glowed green and it hurt my eyes. Aso, of course, had on no underwear. The second cop patted us all down and we stood silent. "Pull your pants back up," he said. We all pulled our pants up, and relieved, I quickly put my money back in my pocket. "Why you go in there?" he asked us. "We were just wandering around," Nigel replied. "Go back to the tourist area. This is not smart," he said. We all nodded and walked off towards the hotel quickly. "Good job, assholes," I said to them. "Are you kidding? That was great," Nigel replied with an extra stride to his step.

When we got back to the hotel I went straight to the pool and ordered a Brahma beer. After that first day's hangover, I was not drinking Caipirinha's anymore. The pool itself was much the same. The Foo Fighter and Papa Roach guys were still there. The only thing that might have been a bit different than the day before were the girls. I didn't' recognize any of them. I told Dizzy, Josh, and a few of the other guys what had happened on our favela walk. Not long after, Cesar came downstairs and joined us poolside. Josh immediately clued Cesar in on what we were talking about. Cesar had come downstairs with his fiancé. She knew as well as I that this was not going to go well for me. Cesar's mood changed to a very serious one as he listened to Josh. Neither friendly nor rude, he spoke with absolutely no emotion. "Come here, Rifken," he said to me. Together we walked back into the hotel. It wasn't till we got to the hotel lobby that his mood changed. He open palmed smacked me in the back of the head. "What the fuck are you thinking? You know what could have happened to you? You know what should have happened to you? Those favela's are some of the most dangerous places in the world. You are not allowed to leave the hotel again." Cesar pointed his finger in my face. "I'm serious." Very angry, he walked back to his room. I felt bad. He had come down with his fiancé, his swim trunks, and his towel. Now he was heading straight back to his room, mad, to no doubt work more.

Later that day Nigel and Aso approached me. "What the hell you tell Cesar for?" Nigel asked. "I didn't. I told the guys at the pool and they told him," I said. "You need to learn when to shut the fuck up," Nigel barked at me. I guessed they had got yelled at as well. I went back to the pool, got a Brahma, and wondered if the chlorine killed all the STD's in the water.

Chapter 83
That Sure is A Big Jesus You Got There

That night rehearsals started. The rehearsal room itself was a decent spot. The only real issue with it was it was hot. As stated before, not just kind of hot but very, very hot. Luckily, there were a few fans, the circular kind, there. I wasn't sure if it was my punishment to be there every night, or if it was something I would have been made to do anyhow, but my job was now to be the band's babysitter. Everyone else from the crew went out and partied every night. However, I was to be the liaison at the studio if the band had any problems.

It made sense that I'd be the one stuck there. Nigel ran the lights, and Aso fixed the lights, but when rehearsing, there were no lights. The gear hadn't even arrived yet, so there were no lights for them to set up, even if they had wanted to.

So, it was a few backline guys and I there with the band every night. My job had become keeping the whores out and making sure the band practiced. Robin and Paul took the rehearsals seriously and non-coincidentally ran the show.

Being the guy who kept the whores away wasn't much fun. But it was a job, and someone had to do it. I hadn't been told anything about keeping the drugs out, so cocaine was rampant. I'll note Buckethead never indulged. I learned he had never done any drugs in his life. I don't think the dude had even drunk a beer. The guy continued to baffle me.

At the end of the rehearsals everyone would head out to Copacabana and go party for the rest of the night. Well, everyone but me that was. I couldn't go because I wasn't allowed to leave the hotel unless I was physically with Cesar or going to the rehearsal studio to babysit. It didn't make any sense to me. Aso and Nigel could do what they wanted and both of them had been just as guilty as me. I rationalized it all by figuring if I was murdered, people would care, but if anything happened to either of them, no one would give a shit.

During the days I really didn't have anything to do, and Cesar couldn't give me too much crap about getting drunk at the pool with the Foo Fighter and Papa Roach guys. While the roadies went on stupid explorations, the rock star guys seemed to just hang out at the pool all day. I guess they didn't want to deal with the press outside the hotel. So, day in and day out it was rock stars, cocaine, booze, whores, and me. I know what you are thinking, poor me. And you're right it was awful...

My one real issue was the damn hotel maid. I kept putting the little card on the doorknob to sleep in and she kept ignoring it. I was working through the night, and there wasn't a day that went by where she wasn't waking me up. Finally, I'd had enough. I opened the door stark naked. "What the fuck do you want?" I not so politely asked her. It was rude, aggressive, but most importantly, it worked. She finally stopped bugging me. I was able to catch up on some sleep over the next few days.

After several days of rehearsal studio monotony and pool partying, Cesar grabbed me and together we went to go see Christ the Redeemer. Christ the Redeemer is a massive Jesus statue on a hill. It's just the thing a young roadie would want to spend his time seeing. A fan of the movie *Dogma*, the highlight of the day was throwing the buddy Jesus salute to the statue. I got lots of dirty looks and loved them all. The same day we took a trip through the jungles, and I got to see some of the monkeys of Brazil. That night Cesar took us to an upscale restaurant that was an all you can eat place. The steak was the best I'd ever had in my life. They walked around the restaurant with meat on huge skewers, and you could take as much as you pleased. The band and crew took up most of the restaurant. It was awesome. At the end of the feast, I was dropped off with the band at the rehearsal studio. Very full, I dozed off listening to GNR practice again, and then again, and then again. It was my roadie lullaby.

Chapter 84
Well Look at the Big Brain on Brain

On the 8th I saw the best drum solo I've still ever seen in my life. We started rehearsals at 8PM and at around midnight, out of nowhere, Brain busted out with this incredible attack on the drums. It was defiant, it was angry, but most of all it was genius. When he was done, some of the best musicians in the world and Paul looked on at him. "I'm fuckin' out of here," he said to no one in particular. He threw his sticks across the room, and they flip flopped across the floor like dead fish. We all watched on as they rolled to a stop. A now quiet room, Brain stood up and left.

Robin went outside to talk to him, and I followed. By the time Robin and I got outside, Brain had four or five girls hanging on him. It wasn't much of a surprise to me, but he didn't come back into the rehearsal studio that night. I understood where the guy was coming from. He could play these songs in his sleep. Why did they really need to practice them every day? The answer was simple, because that is what Axl wanted. I went back inside and continued to sweep up the cocaine that had fallen on the concrete floor. These rock stars take so much for granted I thought to myself. They live in this built up, pampered world that has no structure. There is no foundation to it set in any reality. I threw the swept-up floor cocaine in the garbage and sat back down on the couch.

The next day, per the usual, I reported back to Cesar. That was my job. I was the band narc. My mantra had become... keep the rock stars in and the whores out. I recited it in my sleep. Meeting with Cesar early, a few of us were heading to Sao Paulo, where all of our road cases had reportedly arrived.

The two GNR wardrobe girls had decided to take a ride with

us. They were eager to get into their cases to start working on something or another. These two talked so much, and so fast, that I don't think anyone had paid attention to anything they had said in many years. I had come to the conclusion that was why they always worked together. Everyone needs at least one person to pay attention to them and these two had found one another. When looking at the relationship that way, it was a beautiful bond.

Though it was certainly beautiful, it wasn't long before I wanted to waterboard the two of them with Axl's Fiji water. As they rambled on, I learned how rock stars didn't like to shower. I knew most roadies didn't, and so that made sense. Maybe we were all forming a music fashion trend to just appear like we didn't shower. Or it was quite possible this phobia of water had been spreading under my unsuspecting nose the whole time. I wondered if I was going to join the music fashion statement. If so, I'd have to fill my house with knights in armor and pretend to live in the Medieval age. The people back then must have smelled terrible, but they sure looked cool. The girls continued on, and I watched as their interest level continued to rise throughout the day. Their hands became more animated and their smiles and laughter more regular. I'm quite certain it was because they thought they had found a new audience. However, what they talked about the rest of the day was honestly a blur to me. After thinking about being a Medieval knight, I had begun picturing them naked in the shower together and really hadn't strayed away from that train of thought all afternoon.

After Sao Paulo I was dropped back off at the studio. That night Brain came in and "practiced" quietly. I'm not sure if it was because Cesar had talked to him or if Axl had spoken to him directly. Either way, someone clearly had. In fact, he wasn't just quiet that night. He was quiet for the rest of the time we were in Brazil. Though Brain had quieted down, I think the point had been made, and things chilled out a bit as far as the work regimen while in the rehearsal studio. They still played the same songs every night, but the vibe in the studio was getting friendlier and less like a work routine. That's not to say Robin and Paul didn't still take the rehearsals very seriously, they most certainly did.

They weren't the only ones to take them seriously either. Tommy piped up and made comments more and more, as he was increasingly trying to impress this girl. She was one of the women who was a local hire for the band. Tommy and the woman had found a connection. The joke would be that she was after job security, but I think they actually did like one another. I think he liked showing her his obvious importance to the group.

The other runner was a girl named Adriana. Cesar took a liking to her because she worked her ass off. She would end up working for Cesar and later toured with Parker, the tech from STP, whose job I saved. Parker took a liking to her too. They got married and had a family together.

Buckethead hadn't hung out much. Anytime he was in public he'd wear the bucket and mask. Who wants to wear a KFC bucket everywhere they go? So, I don't think he did too much tourist stuff. He had been spending most of his days with a runner buying porn films for his collection. I'm sure it was a way more exciting hobby before the internet became porn central.

I'm not a geography guy, but Rio is surrounded by Rainforests. I'm also not a weather guy, but rainforests rain a lot. If you spend the time to break it down, Rio has on average 46 inches of rainfall a year. I live in Los Angeles. We have an average of almost 15 inches a year. On the 10th a storm came in and it rained, and rained, and then after that it rained some more. While on my first tour with STP, I had for the first time in my life been exposed to the four seasons. I had only seen rain, like

Rio rain, a couple times in my life. It was hot, incredibly hot, and yet it rained hard and kept coming.

The pool wasn't as interesting in the rain. I think it is because when it rains that hard, it becomes a bit hard to see titties bounce or play ball in the pool. You can still drink though… and everyone was still ordering drinks on Josh's tab. Albeit not as much, a few of us in the group had a little more class than that. Actually, that's not true- we didn't… but either way less people were mooching off of Josh.

Chapter 85
It's True the English Don't Love Their Mothers

On the 11th I was allowed to leave the hotel again: my grounding was over. No one loves shopping malls more than Junior high school students and roadies. And so, I celebrated my freedom by heading across the street and down a block to the shopping mall with a bunch of the other crew guys.

While in the mall, we were followed around by packs of young girls who had followed us from the front of the hotel. A group of these girls were convinced I was in the band. I told them that I wasn't, but they wouldn't believe me. After a while I figured it would be easier to take a photo with all of them and be done with it. That's what I did, and the girls were ecstatic about it. The problem was when one group sees another group making a big deal out of someone, the second group naturally assumes that person is someone special too. Before I knew it, I was a runway model. I was taking lots of photos with cute young Rio locals. It was all fun... until it got irritating. Once that happened, I headed back to the safety of the hotel swimming pool.

That day Del James, the band's road manager, and Hank, another roadie, arrived. I wondered if Hank was the new tea guy. Cesar successfully got rid of quite a few hangers on but the tea guy hadn't been one of them. However, the tea guy became one of the people never seen again when he missed his plane to Rio.

Hank was a grouchy roadie but he must have been a good guitar tech because I had seen him around with various bands when I had toured with STP. I don't know if Hank was his real name or his roadie name. I would have asked him, but I don't think he would have answered me. He had lost a few pieces of his gear at a gig. I had found them and got them back to him safely and had made a friend. The roadie community really is small. With Del in town, that meant Axl would be arriving soon. In other words, shit was getting real.

That night Aso and Nigel showed up at the studio. They acted as if they'd been there working for weeks, and like me, were really tired of looking at the studio walls. Walls I don't think they had ever seen before now. The two of them set up a few lights on the stage. It was a good attempt at validating why they were on the payroll. During the night, Shaggy showed up with a few different girls and brought them into the studio. As discussed, that was a no, no. I didn't have to recite my mantra about whores this time. Luckily for me, Cesar was there. If it had just been me, I know I would have had issues with Shaggy. He would have been happy to reiterate to me that he had worked for GNR since the 1980's and he could do as he fucking wanted. It wouldn't have helped me that he had also come into the studio drunk as hell. It didn't take long; Cesar kicked the girls out of the studio and a pissed off Shaggy left with them. I was glad I didn't have to deal with the asshole.

That night I learned from Nigel that I had pissed off Axl again. This time because I had been telling all the press I was his little brother. "I didn't tell anybody that," I said to Nigel. I now wondered who on the crew was out to get me fired. I told Nigel I didn't believe him, but the truth was he was quite convincing.

Rehearsals were a bit different with Del in town. Everyone knew it was time to be serious. Most of the crew were going to the Copacabana, but I knew I wouldn't be able to go. I didn't even ask. I'd be at the studio all night. The band rehearsed 'till 4:30AM. I think Del was pleased. They sounded good and everyone knew it.

The next day I slept in and hung out at the pool in the morning. The band had booked an additional hotel room and were using that as a production office. I decided to go to the production office so I could call my parents and say "hi." I talked to each of them briefly and then hung up the phone.

"What are you doing?" Cesar asked. "What?" I replied. "You don't tell your mother you love her when you talk to her?" he asked me. "I mean not really, no. I'm English we don't do that. She'd probably freak out and wonder what was wrong." I started to walk out of the hotel room. "Come back here," Cesar said. "Aw, come on, Cesar," I whined back at him. "Call your mother back and tell her you love her." His look was stern. He meant it. "That's not a good idea man," I said. "You want to keep working for me? Call your mom back and tell her you love her." I reluctantly reached out to grab the phone. I sat down and redialed the number. "Hey, Mom, sorry I just wanted to let you know I love you," I said into the phone. "Is everything all right?" There was clear concern in her voice.

I brought my film script to the rehearsal studio that afternoon and worked on it all night. The band rehearsed hour after hour. When Axl showed up he played one song, "The Blues," and then left. I wondered if he headed into Copacabana or not. Either way, he didn't say a word to me about being mad at all. The whole brother thing was bullshit. I stopped writing and began to think about how I could get back at Nigel and Aso. That night we left at 4:30AM again.

When I got back to the hotel, I practiced sounding like Axl. Once I thought I had it down pretty good. I called Nigel and Aso in their hotel rooms and pretended to be him. I fired them both and told them to meet in the lobby in the morning. Pretending to be Axl, I told them I was flying their "dumb asses home." Half asleep, they both believed me. I would have loved to have seen their faces in the morning, their crap in tow, looking like bitter idiots in the lobby, but I missed it. I was sleeping.

The next day was a relaxing one. I went to the beach with Nigel and Aso in the morning. During the day all the people from the favelas spend the day on the beach. The beaches were full and everyone was having a good time. It was nice to get out after the storm and walk around. This was the last excursion any of us would get in Rio. The Foo Fighters were playing that night, and so they were already at the venue. Never fear, the pool wasn't boring though; the Papa Roach guys kept the party going. I waved goodbye to them as I headed out to the venue with Nigel and Aso.

Chapter 86
A Riot Today Will Shoo the Helicopters Away

GNR Rock in Rio pass, 2001.

Because the roads were congested going towards the festival, the GNR crew left throughout the day and into the night to make their way into the venue itself. On the afternoon of the 13th, I arrived at Rock in Rio with Cesar. Cesar had shipped hundreds upon hundreds of pounds of duvetyn. It was my job to cover all our gear with the plastic material because the rains were still coming and going. He had brought more than we would ever need with the intention to sell it to other bands. Sure enough, he was right- we soon found out none of the other bands had brought rain cover for their gear.

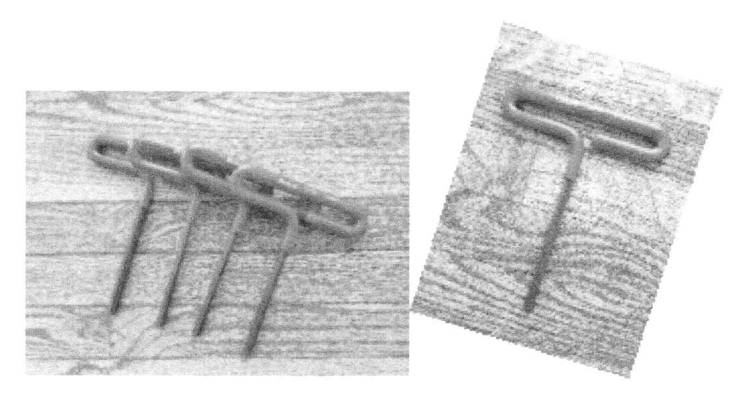

Drum riser keys.

Thinking like Cesar, I had brought multiples of everything I needed. My job was to assemble the drum riser, and so I had a dozen or so drum riser keys. A drum riser key is a 5/16th T handle hex key. You use the key to lock all the pieces of the drum riser together, and then when done, the drums and rock star go up on top. The guys from the band REM had forgotten their key and needed one to assemble their riser for the evening's performance. It was my time to shine, and I was happy I could make a few bucks by selling them one of my keys. Unfortunately, Cesar wouldn't let me and I had to give them a key. "Don't be an asshole, Rif," Cesar said. It was confusing. These guys had spent so much time molding me into being a real prick and then would tell me not to be an asshole when it seemed like it was a perfect time to be just that... an asshole.

That night REM and the Foo Fighters played. I watched the shows and the massive crowd. This was an event like I had never been to before. It was just all so big. I slept on the floor in the production office on and off that night. It was a plywood floor and so it wasn't the most comfortable. Oh, and did I mention it was *still hot... REALLY hot*?

Nigel and Clif had made a bet. To win the bet, Nigel would have to keep his sweater on the entire time we were at the gig. The winner would get... you know, I never did find out what the winner actually got. Anyhow, the next day we started setting up the lights and getting the stage ready for the performance. Surprisingly to me, Nigel had kept his sweater on all morning. Cesar kept telling him how dumb he was. Nigel didn't help us with load in. Not that he had to, because he was the lighting designer and not one of the grunts, but he usually lent a hand.

The venue was a full house, two hundred and fifty thousand documented people. That meant there were upwards of two hundred and seventy thousand people there, I was being told. The fans created an ocean of people. As midday approached Nigel couldn't handle it anymore. Though he hadn't done the load in, he still had to stand on stage to do the focus of the lights. He took his sweater off, and Clif won the bet. Clif wasn't polite about it. I had no problem watching Nigel lose either.

Night came quickly, and though tired, I was excited. My back hurt from trying to sleep on the wood floor, and I hadn't showered. I wondered if this was what Rock 'n' Roll really was about. Was it all about being primal? Smelling like shit, working exhausted, and jumping up and down on command till the show was over? Local bands played all day, and the hours ticked by quickly. I tried to cat nap knowing that the night was going to be a very long one.

Papa Roach hit the stage and the singer, Jacoby, was clearly drunk. While the roadies had all been driven into the venue earlier, the band members were flown in and out by helicopter. I wondered if they had been at the pool all day drinking again. Watching him, it was a pretty safe bet he had. In the middle of the performance, he puked on stage. I heard later that the record label was furious about it.

I had a different take on Jacoby puking. How a guy that drunk, in that heat, could still perform at all was impressive. Fans always hope the concert they attend will not just be memorable but a stand out performance. Well, this dude puking onstage and still finishing the gig was absolutely that.

After Papa Roach got off the stage, the audience's chanting got louder. They had begun chanting Guns N' Roses earlier in the day and hadn't stopped. Soon after Papa Roach, Oasis hit the stage. I watched on as the audience chanted "Guns N' Roses!" without break throughout Oasis's entire performance. To a GNR fan it was killer. To the singer of Oasis, it wasn't all that cool.

Oasis got off the stage, and the crowd got *even* louder. They knew who was coming next and they had been waiting for almost a decade to hear it. The last time Axl had played in Rio, there had been a full-scale riot. Someone had thrown a water bottle at him, and, angry, he had left the gig. The stage was stocked with security, and there were helicopters backstage to get us all out of there if something went down. We were instructed by security, if there was a riot, not to grab anything and just run to the helicopters. I put on my best Arnold Schwarzenegger accent and said aloud, "get to the chopper," but no one laughed.

As it got later and later, I waited for the chanting to lull but it never did. I looked out at a mass of more people than I had ever seen in my life and then looked way back to where the helicopters were waiting. I was trying to figure out how, if there was a riot, I wasn't fucked. There would be no way I would make it to the helicopter before the crowd made it to me on the stage. Maybe if I threw my walkie talkie and laminate away, I could just blend into the crowd I thought? That's what I would do. And then once I was blended into the crowd, I would find the twenty thousand people who had sneaked into the show. They would probably be more chill during the riot. They didn't pay to get in, and were just there for the ride. One thing I was certain of was I couldn't rely on the security. They hadn't even got my Arnold Schwarzenegger reference, and that was funny! I wasn't going to trust those guys, and that was for sure.

Chapter 87
OK, Never Mind

The night came, and though it was still stifling hot when I looked out over the crowd, it felt like mother nature had spread a warm blanket over all of us. I felt as if we were all one. All two hundred and seventy thousand Brazilians and me. Maybe it was the chanting? I kept it to myself, but in my head I was chanting, too. Not long after, the guitar lick we had all been waiting for -"Welcome to the Jungle"- burst through the loud speakers and the crowd erupted. The show had begun.

The vibe of the show was way different than the Vegas show. Axl was like a different person. He seemed to have a chip on his shoulder for some reason. Maybe he was nervous? He sang the songs, but he seemed angry. Early in the performance he yelled at security to kick this guy out of the concert who was holding up a shirt that said, "Slash is GNR." I began to seriously wonder if Axl was going to start another riot. I was ready to throw my walkie talkie at Cesar and run into the audience with my new found chanting Brazilian brothers and sisters, but nothing happened. The show went on, and I have no idea what happened to the guy. My guess is security grabbed him and then released him back into the crowd.

I learned that before the show, Doug Goldstein, GNR's manager, told the security that if they saw any banners that said, "what about Slash" or anything along those lines, to take the banners. I guess Axl was just taking the security's job into his own hands.

```
* JUNGLE Run + Ayo         MADAGASCAR
  EASY                     BUCKET CHUCKS
  BROWNSTONE             * NOVEMBER RAIN Ryo
* LIVE & LET DIE Run+Ryo   ROCKET QUEEN
  OH MY GOD              * CHINESE  Flare
  THINK ABOUT              CHICKEN BINGE
  YOU COULD BE MINE        THE BLUES
  ROBIN PORTUGEEZ          PATIENCE
  SWEET CHILD              SILKWORMS
  KNOCKIN' ON HEAVENS DOOR MY MICHELLE
  OUT TO GET ME            NIGHT TRAIN
  RHIAD                  * PARADISE CITY Run+Ryo
```

GNR Rock in Rio set list, 2001.

The show was plagued with sound issues. During the song "The Blues," later called "Street of Dreams" on the *Chinese Democracy* album, Axl yelled the words "Ok, nevermind" at the sound guys. After the show, fans were able to watch the Rock in Rio performance online. Through the years I've listened to the live version of the song "The Blues" hundreds of times. When the *Chinese Democracy* album finally came out in 2008 it was odd not to hear Axl say the words "Ok, nevermind" in the middle of the track. Most of us fans felt the same way. Truth be told, the Rio version of the song is better than the track on the actual 2008 album.

,
The security for the gig was crazy; there were swarms of them everywhere. I wondered if they were instructed to get in the helicopters before us or after us. I asked a couple of the security guys, but they didn't answer. What that meant to me was before us, definitely before.

Rock stars and a very handsome roadie on the far right.

It was at this gig that I realized my hearing was now getting to be really bad. I always kept the walkie talkie close to my ear but even still, I had trouble hearing it. I had spent too much time in front of large speaker cabinets. Nigel would yell at me, "there is something wrong with the light on stage right," and I'd answer back through the walkie. "No sir. No monkeys in sight." We were in Rio and I had seen quite a few monkeys, so I figured maybe a monkey had got trapped up in the truss. "No, Rifken, the light on stage right," Nigel would repeat himself. "Monkeys will come out tonight?" I asked. I thought how cool that would be. My dad had raced cars with his pet monkey. Now I was going to get to hang out in Rio with GNR and monkeys. The band played for roughly two and a half hours. I don't know what happened to either the light or the monkey's, but I'd safely say it all worked out.

The end of the gig wasn't quite the celebratory event New Years was. We were all wiped out. I hadn't had any real sleep in almost two days and the hard work hadn't even began.

Hours and hours later, the road cases were filled and pushed aside. They were all ready to be shipped back to Los Angeles. I was exhausted. The last thing to do was to help Aso pull in the snake from front of house. The snake is the cable that goes from the front of house, the lighting and sound boards in the audience, to the stage. By the end of the show it is covered with piss, shit, puke, blood, and other wonderful bodily excrements.

Roadie Ramble Moment

Since we are talking about piss and other gross shit, I figure this is an opportune time to discuss ball hair in urinals. Every time I use a urinal, there is hair in it. I don't think my balls drop hairs when I take a leak? Guys, do your ball hairs fall out when you cup your junk? Have you noticed that the ball hair always seems to be black? Do people with black hair lose more ball hair? Either way, dudes hear me out: when using urinals, piss that hair down the urinal drain like a goddamn gentleman.

That's my piss problem. Now let's discuss my shit problem? Yeah of course I have one. Like me, I'm sure you have always wanted to know why corn seems to be the only food that doesn't break down when you take a crap. What makes corn invincible to my colon? I looked it up and I'll fill you in. The answer is the hull of a corn cornel is made of cellulose. The human body's digestive system is unable to break down cellulose. So, I ask you this. If we put chocolate bars inside of cellulose, would it still taste good but we'd be able to shit out most of it and not get fat?

Aso and I stood on top of the stage and a slew of local stagehands pulled the snake through the mud and sludge under us. Aso and I together coiled it into the road case. The work was hard and there was absolutely nothing enjoyable about any of it. It didn't take long for Aso and I to start talking shit to each other. By the end he was making Holocaust Jew jokes that I didn't think were very funny. "The one time your parents don't have anal sex, you pop out," I said to him. I could tell he wanted to punch me, but he didn't have the energy.

It took a while to coil the couple hundred-foot-long cable back into the box. We put the lid on the box, and we were finally done. Aso and I went our own ways, and I found myself talking to Cesar while looking out on now what was an empty field of garbage and mud. "How you doing?" Cesar asked me. "I'm tired of being surrounded by these fucking idiots," I told him. I could have phrased it a bit better, but I was ready to pass out from exhaustion. I was at the point of delirium. I looked him in the eye. "I don't know if I'm meant to do this, Cesar." He didn't say anything to me. I don't think I remember him ever being speechless other than that one time.

Chapter 88
When Security Takes an Eternity, Josh Gets Sneaky Sneaky

There were quite a few roadies waiting to get on a passenger van to go back to the hotel and get some sleep. It took time for the vans to make it out to us even though the show had ended hours and hours earlier. Aso and I walked up to wait in line and the crew guys offered us a free pass to the front of the line. Both taking the opportunity, we hopped in the van. We looked and smelled awful. Everyone, of course, wanted to get back to the hotel, but I guess we were being given a little bit of roadie compassion.

The van took off with a few other backline guys in it as well. Aso and I sat on the back seat together. Even though we were still not happy with each other, no one else was going to sit next to us and we knew it. Even with the windows of the van open, the smell of the two of us was intense. Everyone in the van covered their noses for as long as they could until each person separately gave up and dealt with it. The van drove off and no one said a word for a solid forty-five minutes. One of the backline guys, Curtis, broke the silence. "I miss my dogs," he said. No one replied. We all kept staring out the windows with glazed over eyes. A solid five minutes later Curtis spoke again to deaf ears. "I miss my wife, too," he said. I waited a minute or so and decided to open up the conversation. "So, you miss your dogs more than your wife?" I asked. He had mentioned missing his dogs before saying he missed his wife, so it made sense to me that was what was going through his head. "Had them longer," Curtis answered me. No one responded or said anything for the rest of the drive.

When we got back to the hotel, I walked up to my hotel room

and I had a tough decision to make. I had been awake for over two days now. Should I take off my clothes and go to sleep? It didn't matter how bad I smelled; I wouldn't be sleeping in that bed again. Exhausted, being covered in disgusting muck made no difference...

No, that wasn't the answer. I convinced myself, I should take a shower. I took off my shoes and stepped in, under the water, with all my clothes on. I washed my clothes off and then left them on the balcony to dry. I then slept for fourteen straight hours. I woke up in time to go downstairs, check out, and head to the airport. Checking out of the hotel, I paid for my incidentals, and headed to the front of the lobby for the last time. I was leaving Rio. I left Josh arguing to the front desk attendants about his room bill. "How can you charge me if I didn't order any of these drinks? If I drank this much, I'd be dead," he was yelling to them.

I learned Axl and some of the other guys in the band had hung out at the pool all day. I really needed to get a job where I too could hang out at the pool all day rather than work like a slave. The job was cool to talk about but when it was time to work, man, was it hard. I didn't think about the previous week and a half, or whatever it was, that I had been at the pool getting paid to hang out.

When it came time to board the plane to leave Rio, each one of us had to open our luggage and let security look through everything. None of us were too excited about it because we all just wanted to board the plane and get some sleep. While on STP, Nigel had spent his time collecting collectibles but while in Brazil he had been buying what I'd guess were chicken bone sculptures. None of us quite having gone through veterinary or possibly doctoral school, we weren't sure what the bones were actually from. We watched on as Nigel brought out his new chicken serial killer art collection. The crowning piece was a 3-foot-tall T-Rex. I think Nigel himself was surprised when security pushed him through.

The guitar techs all walked through unscathed. Having been in charge of loading all the road cases, I knew that a couple of the guitar tech cases were going to come home on the cargo plane a little heavier than how they had left. It wasn't drugs one of the techs was after; it was Brazilian rosewood. Brazilian rosewood is the holy grail of instrument woods. However, it's illegal to bring out of Brazil. If the tech was able to bring nice pieces into the States, he could have guitars made from them. He had struck a deal with a major guitar manufacturer in the States to do just that. I watched on to see if any of them had brought any wood in their personal luggage; none had. Conclusion: tech guys are certainly smarter than lighting guys.

A lot of us on a small plane, the GNR crew filled most of the aircraft. "Why didn't you put all that shit in one of the road cases Nigel?" I asked. "They are sculptures Rifken and mind your own bloody business," he responded. "Walking around with half a fuckin' cows worth of creepy bone art like you are Ed Gein or something," I continued on. Needing more space, Nigel pulled my backpack out of the luggage compartment above our seats and threw it at me. "No, fuck you, Nigel. You are acting like you are bringing home the crown jewels of Brazil..." I would have continued on but I was interrupted by Josh boarding the plane. "That was awesome. Dude, I sneaked by security and was able to get on the plane just using my ticket like normal bro," he told us. He had skipped the pat down and suitcase search that we had all undergone and was now pretty proud of himself for having been successfully so underhanded. Hearing Josh boast was the last thing I remember before finally falling asleep. I'm not sure how long I was sleeping, but I was awakened soon after nodding off. Hearing the loud speaker click on, I listened. "Pardon me passengers but I've been informed that one person boarded the plane today without going through security. We are sorry for the inconvenience but due to security reasons I must ask that everyone please remove all their belongings to once again go through security in the terminal. We hope you understand as it is for safety purposes." If she spoke more, I do not know. The "are you fucking kidding me?" comments within the plane were definitely loud after that. I for one was ready to shove a bone T-Rex sculpture up his ass. I looked at Josh. No, we ALL looked at Josh. If he had done this on purpose, as payback for everyone drinking on his bar tab for the last couple weeks, I would have appreciated the depth of the wind up. However, Josh wasn't smart enough to have orchestrated anything like this. He was lucky we didn't leave him in Rio. Unbuckling my seat, I looked on at Nigel's collection of donkey bones and shook my head. This was going to be a long trip.

Chapter 89
The Roadie Rules

Cesar clearly wasn't happy with me. I had told him I wasn't sure if I wanted to be a lifer, a roadie forever, but as I figured it, at least I had been honest with him. I had broken one of the roadie rules. The rules were simple. Don't be a pussy, shut the fuck up and do your work, and don't be too fucked up to do your job. I had been a bit of a pussy by whining about Aso and saying I didn't want to deal with this kind of crap anymore. I hoped I hadn't burned the bridge I had built with Cesar. He was the one who hired me for gigs. He was the only boss I knew.... He was my road dad.

On the 17th the road cases were set to come back to Los Angeles. For me that meant one more day of paid work. However, when the 17th came, no one called. I wasn't sure if I was being blown off, but it sure seemed that way. When my check came in the mail it was made out to Joel Rifkin. The crew guys thought that was hilarious. I didn't. I couldn't deposit a check made out to someone else. I had to wait another week to get paid, while the Gun N' Roses accounting people fixed their books.

Sobriety photo #1, 2001.

Not sure what was going on with work, I went up to Mammoth for the weekend with a group of friends. My plan was to get trashed while I was up there. The first night in Mammoth we stumbled into a local dive bar. At the bar sat a truly massive man. The guy may have even been bigger than Cesar. To compliment his bulk, he was wearing animal furs from head to toe. Though both my friends and the bartender told me to leave the man alone multiple times, I couldn't stop trying to strike up conversation with the mountain man by offering to buy him a beer. Eventually he conceded. The bartender gave me two bottles of Coors Light and looked at me sternly. "You are playing with fire. Take it easy before I kick you out of here," she said. I wondered if it was a good time to hit on her or not. I handed one of the beer bottles to my new furry friend. As he stood up off of his bar stool, he was even bigger than I had realized. The entire bar watched on to see what would happen next.

We gave each other a "cheers" by clinking glasses- you know, like civilized drinkers fucking do; and then something that had never happened to me before happened. The entire glass bottom of my full beer fell out onto the floor. My beer spilled all over both of our shoes. There I was holding what was left of an empty bottle. I gave the guy a look of disgust. Grabbing the beer I had just bought him out of his hand, I downed it. My friends, the patrons at the bar, and the bartender all looked on speechless. I was too drunk to notice the awkward moment. The big man broke out into laughter, grabbed me, and bought us both shots. For the next hour we drank at the bar together. When it was my turn to buy him another drink the bartender handed it to me and made sure to tell me, "you are an idiot." I still think she secretly liked me.

Sobriety photo #2, 2001.

The next day I ate mushrooms, drank a bottle of Jack Daniels, then shots of Jaeger Meister, and chased them all down with beers. Wanting to cool off, I jumped off the second story balcony into the snow. Luckily, I survived unscathed but most certainly a few more brain cells short. It was a crazy weekend.

Over the next couple weeks, I tried calling Cesar here and there but he never returned any of my calls. I thought maybe I'd have to go back and work on the phones. On the 28th of January I drove home after a heavy night of drinking, to find a police car parked in my driveway. My parent's house alarm had gone off and the cops had come to see if everything was OK. I parked my car in the driveway, kept my head down, and beelined to the front door. I opened the door and hurriedly went upstairs, leaving the front door wide open. I figured if I made it into my house, my parents could deal with the cops, and I would save myself from getting get a DUI. The cops must have known I was drunk but didn't say anything to me.

The next day Cesar called me back and we chatted a bit. Everything was OK; I was relieved. I went out and celebrated by getting drunk again. When I left the bar, I pulled out directly in front of a police car with my lights off. The police officer told me to roll down my window and so I did. "Turn your headlights on," she said. "How about if you let me see your headlights," I replied. She showed me her boobs and we drove off. I had got lucky yet again! No- it didn't happen that way, but I did turn my lights on and she didn't give me a ticket. It is a better story the other way, though. Regardless of what really happened, my partying was getting out of control. I needed to get back to work.

My mom, noticing I had some time off, thought it would be a good idea for me to go to the hospital and have my hearing checked. When I got there, I realized she was totally right. It was absolutely a good idea. The hearing doctor lady was stunning. She looked like Halle Berry. She walked me into a sound booth and handed me a little box with a button on top of it. I put headphones on and sat with the little button in my hand.

"OK, when you hear a noise, if you can please push the button," she said to me. I sat in the booth and did what I was told. "Sir, are you just pushing the button," she asked me. "Am I allowed to do this with my eyes closed. I mean, should I concentrate?" I asked her. "Just push the button when you hear a noise." Figuring it was about time she made a noise, I pushed the button a few times. What I learned when I left was that my hearing was awful.

January ended, and February began. I worked a couple days for STP moving things around in their storage, but there was no real work in sight. I had been happy to get home to get some rest, but now I was absolutely ready to start working again. I spent my off time working on my film script, and I'm sure, not surprisingly, at this point continuing to drink heavily. STP had started recording their new album *Shangri-La Dee Da* in a huge house up in Malibu. I was now in the habit of going up there with Nigel and raiding their pantry. The house was stocked with awesome food.

One day, while hanging out at the house, I got a call from

my credit card company. Someone in Brazil had been using my credit card. They had purchased $500 in food. That was enough money to feed an entire village down there. I told them I had only used the card once. It was at the hotel when I checked out. The credit card representative didn't seem to care. I guess they don't extradite people from Brazil for petty credit fraud theft. I asked the credit card lady if I could tell people I was a humanitarian even if my charitable accomplishments weren't intentional. She hung up on me.

Chapter 90
Back to Throwing Shit at a Wall

I was pleased to find out STP was going to play a show in Cleveland. But though they booked me to work it, the show was cancelled. When we found out the show wasn't going to happen, Cesar told me he wanted me to go work for a company called LSD. They were a big lighting company that supplied the lights on many tours. He wanted me to learn how to fix stage lights. I knew I didn't want to be a lighting guy, and so I dragged my feet on showing up there to work.

Sobriety photo #3, 2001.

At home I had been arguing with both Megan and Stefanie. Stefanie must have started dating someone because she wasn't returning my calls. When I did get a chance to speak to her, I didn't want to ask. I didn't want to know. My life was all just getting dull. Who was the next band I'd work for?

My father, seeing I wasn't doing much of anything, asked me to help him with some work. He was looking at buying a couple vintage cars to resell. Some old guy in Pasadena had a warehouse of cars and wanted to get rid of a Rolls Royce from the 1920's. The issue with the car was that it had been converted into a camper long ago. "You know, Dad, you can sleep in your car, but you can't drive your house," I told him. Nigel had told me that. "I don't know. If you were a gypsy, you could live in and drive this," he replied. It was true. Why the hell was I quoting Nigel? "The issue is, it has the wrong engine in it, and is really just a "botched up" car," he told me. I was listening to him talking himself out of it. "How many people would know that other than you?" I asked him. "People know," he said. "It does look cool," I said. "It is cool." It sounded funny to hear him say the word "cool." After much deliberation my father decided not to buy it. "It's just as well, Dad. It wouldn't fit in the garage anyhow," I told him as we got back into his VW pickup truck to drive home. "That's true- it wouldn't have." My father had this rule that if a car couldn't sensibly fit in a garage, we couldn't buy it.

On the 23rd of February I had what had become a normal night of getting drunk with my friend Tracy. We would drink beers and play drinking games. Her boyfriend was an old friend of mine. She was good on the eyes, and like me, an alcoholic, so hanging out with her wasn't that bad. She had dark brown hair but light blue eyes. Whether you believe in a higher power, or you would be more prone to blame her mother; she had the perfect number of freckles on each cheek. She laughed a lot, and for some reason the uneasiness that came across in that laugh drove me crazy. I'd say she held strong like a Siberian Husky but had the finesse of a Pomeranian. Across the street from their apartment was a liquor store, so it all worked out.

We got drunk, built up a bit of sexual tension, and when

Michael, her boyfriend got home, they went into their bedroom together. I kept drinking beer by myself. Not long after they left the room, I heard them having sex. Tracy and I had been drinking an Italian beer called Peroni. On the front of the bottle was a man wearing a fedora. I started writing a poem called "God's Reasons" on a napkin. I was writing it loosely to the man on the bottle. The poem started with the words "drunk in a stupor all alone, drank too much and I just can't drive home," and it went on from there. I drank by myself until I passed out. Years later the lyrics were used for a song performed by none other than Darius Rucker. Hey, everyone needs five minutes of fame!

At the end of March, I went out with a few buddies of mine to Hermosa Beach. We went to a place called Sharkeez where they give you two for the price of one drinks. The whole bar was watching this gorgeous girl. I made a bet with all the guys at my table that I could get her phone number. It was so ridiculous, the table next to me all got in on the bet too. No one thought I could do it. The bet was for a round of drinks. If I won, I got a free drink. If they won, I'd have to buy everyone a drink. I walked up to the girl and told her I was a casting director. If she wanted to give me her number, I'd call her in for an audition. She gave me her phone number, on a napkin, and I walked back to the table a success. I ordered the same thing my friend was drinking, a Belvedere vodka on the rocks. Because we were at Sharkeez, I was brought over two. The first sip was a bit stiff. "What the fuck are you drinking?" I asked him. My buddy laughed. "You will get used to it, bro," he told me. He was right. For years my signature drink was a Belvedere on the rocks with a lime. A bit hungover I spent the next day at the STP house in Malibu, eating food and hanging out at the pool.

Scott played tennis and swam a lot at the house. They were paying 10k a month to rent the place, so I'm sure they wanted to make the most of it. While hanging out at the pool, we got to chatting. "What's Axl like?" he asked me. "Well, he's not nearly as talented as you," I told him. Scott tipped his glasses down. "Just kidding. The guy is temperamental but fucking talented as hell. I don't know, man, I'm a really big GNR fan," I honestly told him.

"He lives next door. I haven't seen him around yet," Scott replied. "He's a hell of a tennis player," I said. "Seriously?" Scott asked. "No, I don't know." I was having fun giving Scott a hard time. I wonder now if Scott knew he'd one day be the singer of the band Velvet Revolver. I think Scott was a GNR fan. He seemed eager to meet Axl when we talked about him. It sure would have been cool if they had done a duet together.

The days continued to tick by. I was told I was going to go on Ozzfest, but then that changed to working for Jennifer Lopez. More and more I didn't care who I was going to tour with. I just wanted to work again. With nothing else going on, I conceded to Cesar's wishes and went to go work at LSD.

Chapter 91
LSD

The letters LSD stood for the now defunct Light and Sound Design. One of the owners of the company, Marvin- the guy who stood by the console from the introduction of the book, was a family friend, and then I knew most of the guys working there from gearing up for both the STP and GNR tours. Maybe working in a warehouse for a while wouldn't be that bad?

My first day there Raul, the guy who ran all the worker bees, wanted me loading and unloading trucks in the back. Loading trucks was something I had done a lot of times. I did the work, but I wasn't happy about it. I was there to learn about lighting. Not to help pack fucking trucks.

That night I met with all the girls and we went to BJ's Restaurant. We sat down, and a pretty blonde waitress with just the right number of inspirational buttons on her vest got us our drinks. After a usual amount of time the same waitress came back to take our food order. I got myself a big, greasy, burger with French fries. Megan was the last of our group to order. The waitress turned to her and asked, "and what would you like to order, ho?" My eyebrows raised to the top of my forehead. This was going to get good. Something told me that Megan had been called a ho before. She knew exactly how to react. She wasted no time. "Excuse me, you fucking bitch," she responded. Things were getting heated. I thought I was just going to get a hamburger, but no- this night was going to be so much more. "Go get your manager," Megan barked at the girl. "I'll take another beer please," I said to the waitress as she left the table. Megan gave me the death stare. "You two must know one another. Maybe you can introduce me?" I asked. "Shut up, Joel," she said. "Ever wonder if Mick Jagger or Steven Tyler's teachers told them to shut up when they were kids? 'Mick Jagger, you shut your big mouth.' The teacher would say. Mick and Steven showed those teachers, huh?" My tangent story didn't help the matter. "OK, seriously, she's pretty cute. Think she'll remember my beer?" I asked no one in particular, and in return no one in particular responded. "What if the manager is another hot chick and you fucked her boyfriend too, Megan?" Tracy asked, jumping in on all the fun.

I'm not sure what happened to the waitress, but we got a new one, and the manager apologized to Megan. After eating we all went line dancing. I had a great time. There were maybe eight girls and me, and we all got really drunk. A young man couldn't have asked for more.

The next day I showed up to work and was told they wanted me to pack trucks again. Dave, the dock supervisor, looked at me and said, "I don't care what Raul says. This is dumb. Go talk to Glenn inside and see if he can put you to work." Glenn was a Harley Davidson type guy who only showed up to work for his check. He couldn't give a shit about the place. I walked in and told him what Dave had told me. "I don't give a fuck what you do," he replied back to me and then went back to pretending to work. I was much better suited to work for Glenn. I walked over to the work desk of one of the guys I had talked to a couple times before. I stood by and watched him take some strobe lights apart and put them back together again. Glenn's department would be great for me. No one cared what I did there. I figured I could just hang out, and Cesar would never know that I wasn't actually learning or doing anything. I did not want to be a lighting guy. Later, when back on tour, I'd just pretend I didn't have the knack for it.

The next morning Raul called me to his office. While waiting for him, I chatted up his secretary. I could hear Raul in his office on the phone. He was laughing and joking away. I wondered what could be so funny about lighting equipment. After a few minutes I heard him ask the guy on the phone to "hold on a minute." He yelled out of his office, "Rifken, come in here and sit down." I walked into his office and took a seat. He then walked out to his secretary's desk. "What the hell are you thinking telling this guy about your college daughter? Are you fucking kidding me?" he barked away at her. It was true that it probably wasn't that smart for her to be telling the roadie staff about her hot daughter. Raul came back into the office and sat down again. "How about you, Raul? Have any good-looking daughters?" I asked him with a smirk. "Shut the fuck up," he said and picked up the phone again. After a conversation that was clearly full of humdingers because he was again laughing away, he hung up the phone to tend to me.

"I thought you were told to load trucks. What are you doing working in electronics?" he asked. That was interesting; I had now learned that Glenn's department was called "electronics." I didn't know that the day before. "I got a promotion," I told him. Raul liked to be the man in charge. He didn't like that I was working there and there was nothing he could do about it. I worked for a guy who was one of LSD's biggest clients, and as aforementioned one of Raul's direct bosses was a good family friend. I'm sure it didn't help that I was usually a prick to him too. "If you are going to work here, under me, you are going to do what I say. I don't give a shit about Nigel or Cesar." His eyes stared into my very soul.

"Any of the guys in the warehouse know the story where you got hammered on Michael Bolton and made out with a chick all night who turned out to be a transvestite?" I asked him. "You know, sometimes it's better to figure out in the afternoon who you are going to go home with at night." I continued on. "Get the fuck out of my office, you little fucker." He said to me under his breath. Today nobody cares about trannies, but back then… well, nobody cared either, but I was a young man, and it was still fun being a smartass. The contempt in his voice was quite clear. "Any interest in doing lunch later?" I asked him sincerely. He sat their looking at me coldly. "Aw, come on, Raul. I'm just winding you up a bit man," I said.

I walked out of his office and made a point to lag a bit at the secretary's desk. "It really was a pleasure speaking with you," I said to her. Raul was already on the next call. He put the phone on mute and came to the door. "Get your fucking ass back to work," he yelled at me. I worried about lasting in this stressful and hostile environment.

Chapter 92
Nigel's Dick Extension

Nigel was a car collector. Remember, I initially met him through my father who was fixing his Jaguar. Nigel had decided it was time to sell his 1969 Corvette. He had been putting a lot of money into a couple other cars and decided to sell this one. The car was pretty tough. It was black, had black interior, and the exhaust pipes ran down the sides of the car. It was damn cool. He wanted me to buy it he said, "to keep it in the family." Nigel had history with the car. Years earlier, before he was a bald asshole, he had been a long-haired asshole. Long hair sweeping past his ankles and filled with various pieces of metal, he looked very goth. I say goth, but he would have said "goff." While working for Rob Zombie, he looked more like he should be in the band than be their LD. Living off Sunset, in Steve McQueen's old house- pretty darn cool- he drove the Vette down to fill it up with petrol one day. Getting out of the car and closing the door behind him, his hair got caught in the door, and he was pulled down to the ground with his head rocking back, hitting the pavement. Standing back up and people looking on, he removed his hair from the door that had once been attached to his now bleeding head. Still trying to look "goffy cool," he walked into the gas station to pay for the gas. "You looked like an idiot though - right?" I interjected. "I did, Rifken. Thanks for making sure to point that out." he said. Nigel loved this car.

I didn't know how sincere that was, but either way, I agreed to take the car on a test drive. That's what you do when you are looking at buying a car. I took the car out of the driveway and onto the street slowly. I wanted to get a feel for it. "Jesus Christ, Riffy, give it some gas," Nigel said. We pulled down a side street and I put the gas pedal down a bit. The car was fast, silly fast! We pulled around the block and I started to head back to Nigel's house. I had got the idea of what driving the car was like now, and I don't like playing with other people's toys.

"What the fuck was that?" Nigel asked. "What?" I said. I honestly had no idea what he was talking about. "You crossed over your hands," he told me. "Huh?" I wondered what the hell he was talking about. "When you took the bend, you crossed your hands. You never cross your hands on the steering wheel," he told me. Nigel seemed amazed, but I had no idea what he was talking about. We got a bite to eat at a local place, and Nigel drove the Vette back to his house. He drove like a maniac. I almost shit both my burger and my French fries. My beat-up Toyota truck was way easier on my intestines.

When back at Nigel's house, he called my dad. "He crossed his hands," was all I heard. "It was like driving with my grandmother," he reported. My dad didn't care. "What, you are telling on me now?" I said to him. "So how about it, Riffy- you going to buy my Vette or keep driving like a little sissy girl?" he said. "You know you really need to brush up on your sales skills, Nigel," I told him.

Chapter 93
The Air Conditioning People

The air conditioning people, the nickname of the guys working in the offices upstairs, had hired some guy to run quality control for the place. His job was to walk around and figure out where money was being lost. As you can imagine I was a perfect target for this guy. I sat in a chair by a window all day and talked on the phone. If anyone came around who seemed to matter, I would go stand by one of the work tables and talk to whomever was working there. Me getting paid anything at all, really did not make any sense, even to me. I was counting days to get out of there and didn't care what anybody thought of me.

The last thing any of the guys in the warehouse needed was a ball buster and that was this dude. Because he was spineless, everyone blew him off. It was really quite amusing. There was one guy in our whole department who loved what he did and would love to talk to the QC guy. His name was Jason. No one had ever asked Jason about his job, which was to fix and clean the color changers. The color changers were lights that had a colored piece of plastic in front of them. They would change at the flick of a button to the color you chose. On the weekends he'd fix TV sets and VCR's for extra money. He loved showing off what he could do to anyone who would pay attention. Everyone else in the place answered with the same response to basically anything the QC guy asked. That answer was, "fuck off." I had been waiting for him to approach me. We had actually *all* been waiting for him to approach me.

"So, I've been asking about you," he said to me. "Hear anything I should know about?" I asked him. "Well, I'm trying to figure out what exactly it is you do," he said. "I'm glad you asked. Well, when one of these guys gets a bit tired you see, I get on my knees and give them a good old-fashioned cock sucking.

You know to keep them working. Gotta get all those lights out you know. Now lucky for me, I love cock. I just fucking love it, and these guys here, I mean in this department, the men that surround us right now, are all hung like horses. So, as I'm sure you'd understand, I hang out here the most." I knew the guys around me were enjoying this. Not being done quite yet, I continued on… "I mean Glenn's wife probably has trouble walking a lot of the time. I'm talking huge. I got into the whole cock sucking thing because I was touring in Thailand and a roadie told me that the little boys were a little more expensive than the little girls, but they were totally worth it. So, I figured, fuck it. And boy, was he right. Now a good cock sucking makes my day." Waiting for him to say something back to me, my cell phone rang. "Oh, I have to pick this up. It's my mom." Anger welled up deep down in his belly. He turned around and walked away. The part about the little Thai boys was a joke Nigel told all the time. He had told me it was a common roadie joke, but I had never heard anyone else tell it. The rest I had come up with on the spur of the moment. I was proud of myself.

While it was fun to be a smartass, I was actually becoming more and more depressed. I was bored and I didn't want to be working for a lighting company. I decided to take a break from drinking to clear my head. It didn't help that when sober all my friends would tell me how dull I was.

Raymond was a friend of Nigel's and another Lighting Designer. Amongst a slew of other acts, he had toured with Bauhaus and Kanye West. I had helped him out by working for free as a runner for a music video done by Dolf Moncreif. Dolf's big claim to fame was he did the lights for Pink Floyd. Pink Floyd being arguably my favorite band, other than Guns N' Roses, I of course thought Dolf was cool. However, when Raymond and Dolf called me to be a runner on their next music video,

I turned the gig down. I don't like driving and didn't want to run around doing errands all day. I had already been beat up by both the film and music industry, and I figured it was time to push myself into a position where I wouldn't take entry level gigs anymore.

Around this time, I was informed that Scott Weiland was back in detox. That was upsetting to hear. I liked the guy; I was hoping he would conquer his demons. Then the big blow came. I had been waiting for Cesar to start Ozzfest. The problem was he did start Ozzfest, but he didn't hire me. Dolf Moncreif had told Cesar I walked off their music video.

I started to think of what else I could do with my life. Maybe build some sort of company from the ground up? Maybe make a movie? I had been working on scripts for a while now. Maybe it was time to take the plunge into filmmaking.

Chapter 94
I Don't Wear Undies on Sundays
(It's Laundry Day)

I gave the script I had been working on to a guy named John Dozier. John was a major prop. master in Hollywood. My mom, a realtor, had sold him a house. At the same time, I started calling around looking for work from someone other than Cesar. I figured I may be a better tour manager than a stage manager. Even though Cesar had laughed at me when I said it, I really did work better with my wits than with my hands. I called the Kottonmouth Kings but they had just hired someone. If I had called a couple months earlier, I would have had the gig for sure, they told me. So now what? My hiatus hadn't been long; I started drinking a lot again. I was now going to LSD during the day and drinking every night.

While on the road we used to pack the road cases with underwear. I've never been sure why women throw their underwear at the stage. Maybe there was a Victoria's Secret ad campaign I missed? I also wondered why I collected so many panties but never saw women in the audience taking off their panties. Anyhow, we would take all the collected underwear and stuff it into the road cases to "help protect the lighting equipment." We really did it to make the guys in the warehouse jealous. The guys in the warehouse all hoped to be roadies one day; it ate them up inside having to wait for the chance. Now here I was unloading all the underwear out of the cases too; it sucked.

After a week or so, I finally struck a lead. One of the opening bands from STP, Palo Alto, said they would hire me as their tour manager. They were a small band and they would be touring in a van. A gig was a gig, and I was bored out of my mind. I told the guys I would take the job. It would be good for me. I could learn how to be a tour manager and then maybe work as one for a bigger band. Around the same time, I booked Fishbone to play a "Men against Rape" rally at UCSB. I was going to make $400 for booking the show.

Nigel had three dogs. XK, Shelby, and Cuddly Muffin. No, I'm kidding the last one's name was Aston. If you are not a car person, the dogs were named after masculine cars. Shelby was a huge Akita, Aston a big Doberman, and XK was possibly the largest German Shepard you'd ever seen. During this time Nigel and his wife went out of town for a week. I was to stay at Nigel's house and take care of his dogs. He had spent years toughening them up. I was determined to spend the week I had with them helping them each discover their sensitive sides.

I had trouble bonding with the Akita. She would sit and stare at me or go to the side of the house and wait for Nigel and his wife to get home. The German Shepard had separation anxiety. The dog had been abandoned and Nigel got him through a rescue. XK would continuously push up against you, but because he was so big, you'd find yourself leaning against the wall a lot. He would just keep inching his way closer until you had nowhere else left to go. XK and Shelby would get into fights over dominance. Both the dogs and Nigel had had to get stitches several times. The Doberman didn't try to fight for dominance. She could certainly hold her own though.

When feeding these beasts, you'd have to be sure to feed all three of them in separate rooms. When girls would come over, I was trying to keep a constant flow, I'd lock the dogs up behind the metal gates Nigel had separating the living room from the rest of the house. Nigel's house was cool. He had a life size pirate at the dinner table, numerous RIAA records from Marilyn Manson, Rob Zombie, STP, and Pantera hanging on the walls, and original H.R. Giger props all over the house. Even though I'd tell each and every girl to ignore the dogs, it amazed me how many didn't listen to me. I'd tell them sternly, "I'm not kidding, the dogs will attack you." Yet almost every woman who entered the house would try and win the dogs over.

When feeding the hounds one day, Nigel called in to check on the place. I had got into the habit of feeding the Akita last because she was my least favorite of the three animals. When Nigel called, I was in the middle of yelling at Shelby. "If you are going to act like an asshole all the time you are going to keep being fed last. Get it?" I said to the dog. Shelby growled at me. "Is my dog looking at you like she's going to eat you alive, Rifken?" asked Nigel. "Yeah, we are trying to work some things out," I said back through the phone. "Don't think she won't attack you," he replied. "Yeah, well if she does, she isn't going to get fed for the rest of the fucking week. How does that sound, tough guy?" I told the dog.

The Akita never really conceded. She didn't hang out with me and the other two dogs, who had become inseparable from me. When Nigel came home, I was watching TV with the Doberman in my lap and the German Shepard lying next to me on the couch. "What the hell did you do to my dogs, Rifken?" Nigel asked. The Doberman got up off of my lap and moved to the other side of the room. She sat down and tried to assess the situation. "She's not a fuckin' lapdog?" he said. The Doberman raised her lip, growled, and showed her teeth to me. "Oh, don't be silly cuddly muffin. Now you come over here and give your uncle Joel a big hug." The dog leapt back over to the couch and sat back down on my lap again. "Oh, Jesus Christ! What the bloody hell? Cuddly muffin?" Nigel asked. Shortly thereafter Nigel's wife walked into the room. The Doberman didn't move. "Aren't you happy to see your momma?" she asked. I laughed and made the dog get up. My work here was done.

Chapter 95
POP

I started calling in sick to LSD; bored of it all now, I hated going in there. It didn't help I had also lost favor with many of the guys working there. The guys in the warehouse didn't like one of the female roadies. Many of the roadie's personal road cases were stored in the warehouse in between tours, and hers was one of them. Knowing she would be going back on the road in a couple days, a couple of the guys had bought a big fish and left it in her road case. I knew the girl was a friend of Aso's, so I decided to call him and clue him in. By narcing out the guys, I had set myself even farther apart from them. Now going to work there was just awkward. I didn't care, doing a solid for one of the working roadies was a smarter move than being a bud to the dumbasses at the warehouse.

Something had to switch up soon, though. Both Nigel and Raymond had made it clear that by not showing up at LSD I was totally fucking myself. I did care that I was losing face with my higher ups, but I just couldn't keep going there every day. It sucked. I was also putting much more time into the Fishbone gig than I had expected. I was learning it was a lot of work putting a show together. I was certainly going to earn my $400.

Homemade ~~STP~~ mix tape – I mean Bush....

Raymond called me. He was prepping to go on tour with the band Bush. He had been hired to be their lighting designer. It was an easy gig for me; I was to set up their stage in a warehouse for rehearsals. It was a couple days work and Raymond appreciated the help. I was happy to be working again on something cool.

A few days later, on May 12th, Raymond called me to work another gig. It was a good paying gig too. He hired me on as one of the high-tech lighting coordinators for NSYNC's music video *POP*. The lighting crew was Raymond, Nigel, and me. The pay was $375 for a ten-hour day and then double time after that. I had never received overtime before. On May 13th we started to load in. We brought in the lights and spent the morning hanging them. After that, the set guys started to move the set pieces in. The set itself was over 2 million dollars and by far the most expensive location I had ever worked on. Once in place, I realized something. If there were any problems with the lights, we wouldn't be able to fix them. Was I the only one who realized the set itself was in the way? A union set: we weren't allowed to step out of the catwalk to fix anything from above either. So, I kept quiet and didn't let anyone see that I had nothing to do. This gig was Raymond's way of thanking me for working for him previously for free. Sunday, Monday, and Tuesday came and went before anyone realized I hadn't actually left the studio. No one ever told me to leave, and so I stayed quiet and slept in one of the lighting cases. I was making a ton of money in overtime, and I was beginning to love the film industry. When they finally did tell me to go home, I didn't spend much time there. I rushed back to the set to get paid again with a new clean shirt on, and this time, I left a couple spares in the car.

I spent time talking to Joey Fatone, who was in the band. The dude was on crutches and didn't have much to do either. While eating M&M's one day, JC jumped in and the three of us got into a music conversation. JC told us that he felt a punk band became a pop band once they made a music video. It was an interesting conversation topic to me; it gave the three of us something to talk about for a while.

Nigel had managed to stay on the payroll but had actually gone home after the first day. If anyone needed him, and no one ever did because none of us had anything to do, I would cover for him. Eating M&M's and chatting about music all day was a job I could handle.

Working for NSYNC wasn't all dull. Part of the fun had become Lou Ferrigno. He had been hanging out so much that it had become an issue. He too was shooting something on the Sony lot but clearly preferred to hang out with the band. While we all thought it was cool to meet him it became problematic when he wouldn't leave. They ended up hiring security guys whose main job was to keep the incredible hulk from bothering NSYNC.

Because I basically never left the set, I heard the song about a million times. At one point in the song Justin Timberlake says, "man I'm tired of singing." The irony of hearing him say that over and over and over again began to drive me nuts. The Chinese have water torture. To me this was pop music torture.

With all that being said, it was interesting to watch a completely different type of show. Scott Weiland really was a gifted front man. He could absolutely control his audience. He wasn't a bad dancer and I understood his sex appeal. Axl did that snake type dance and fans loved it. I got that too. However, to date I hadn't seen a properly choreographed performance. These guys were really good dancers. As good as the group was, Justin stood out as being even better. I wouldn't tell my friends it, but I was impressed.

I worked straight through May 17th. My birthday had been the day earlier and I hadn't left the set. The 17th was of course quiet. I think the day after someone's birthday is the loneliest day of the year. Everyone called you yesterday. So, no one calls you the day after your birthday. However, I wasn't thinking about my birthday; all I could think about was how NSYNC was fast becoming my favorite band of all time. I didn't know how much I had earned but it was more than any other band had ever paid me.

As Thursday came, I was a bit nervous. On Friday evening we were supposed to be doing the Fishbone concert. What would I do if NSYNC wasn't wrapped yet? Things have a funny way of working out sometimes and luckily, we finished loading out Friday morning. I'm not sure if anyone noticed how many hours I worked or if my paycheck was inconsequential. Either way they cut me a check. I had worked something like one hundred hours in five days. Including the overtime, my check was huge. I was over the moon with the money and happy to be busy again.

From the NSYNC gig I drove home, took a shower, and met with the Fishbone guys to drive up to Santa Barbara for the show that night. I met up with everybody at Angelo's dad's house, which was across the street from my parent's house, and where I was still living. There were over twenty people cruising up. Angelo had shorts on that were too big for him and no shirt. His shorts ran low and it looked like his willie could pop out over the top at any moment. "Perfect attire for a 'Men against Rape' concert Ange," I told him. "I got a shirt in the van," he responded to me. We all loaded into cars and headed up to Santa Barbara.

Chapter 96
Back to School

The Fishbone gig was important to me. I had always hoped I could help Angelo out when I was a kid. I wanted to make him money as a musician. I knew this little gig was the closest I would ever get to accomplishing that.

At the UCSB campus, we had put together an outside show that was free to students. There was a good turnout. As soon as we got there, my friend who had called me to organize the show handed me the money. I gave some of it to Angelo to give to the band. I figured getting some of the money up front would make everyone happy. Seb, my friend, introduced the band. The guys played a song and then Angelo decided to talk up the crowd. "I love the beauty. The absolute beauty of a big booty black woman. I really do," he said. A few of the guys and I laughed a bit. Angelo looked over at me with a big shit-eating grin, and I in turn twisted my face to give him a dirty look. I think he knew it wasn't sincere and so he decided to continue on. Seb and his girlfriend urgently ran up to me. "What is he doing?" Seb asked. "Being an asshole," I told Seb. "Well, he needs to stop. You need to stop him right now," Seb angrily told me. "If I tell him to quit it, he will just get worse," I told Seb. Seb looked at his girlfriend frustrated. I laughed. "OK, OK. Seb let me go handle it," I told him.

I waved for Angelo to come over to me. He came over, walking tall and proud of himself. "What's up, Joel?" he asked. "They haven't paid me the second half of the money. Quit with the bullshit," I told him. "Oh, OK. No problem." As the old adage goes… money talks. I walked back over to Seb and his girlfriend. "We should be cool now," I told them. Angelo continued on, "You know the most important women in a man's life are his mother and his grandmother. We are really happy to be here." Angelo said while looking at me. I waved my hand at him, clearly suggesting he start playing another song and quit with the talking. The band played the rest of their set and the crowd, Seb, and his girlfriend were now all copesetic.

My momentum had changed shortly thereafter, On May 22nd to be exact; I landed in Amarillo, Texas. Nigel had brought me on as a carpenter to tour with the band Poison on the *2001 Glam Slam Metal Jam*. It paid $500 a week plus per diem. If you worked out my pay on an hourly basis, it was the worst paying job I had ever had in my life. I think I made more money washing cars as a kid. I had been a roadie for a calendar year now. Better than hoping to get paid by Palo Alto, I happily turned down the tour manager job with them, and took the Poison gig.

Chapter 97
Poison

Poison tour itinerary & all access pass, 2001.

Touring with Poison brought it all back home for me. I had worked for them as a runner at the recording studio years earlier. Seeing these guys again, I felt like I was developing into an industry veteran. I had been depressed and bored while working at STD, or LSD, or whatever they called it, but things were now back in gear, and though I pretended I was tired of touring, I was really, really glad to be back out on the road.

Poison was a lot different than both Guns N' Roses and Stone Temple Pilots. The biggest difference was the budget. The band stayed on the tour buses with the crew. The band stayed in the same hotels as us. The band ate with us. We were all with each other all of the time. Anything I would need to buy for work would need to be approved by the band. When working for Cesar I could, and would, buy whatever I needed to keep the stage looking good. On Poison a bag of 3-dollar nuts and bolts would need approval.

Our boss, Dean Tarish was a reasonable, laid back, guy whose deepest love was Indy car racing. Speed TV was not just the only thing on both televisions always, but the main topic of most conversations on the bus. Our bus was also fitted with a genuine C.C. Deville. He was always in the front lounge hanging out.

When I first met both Rikki, the drummer, and Bobby, the bass player they were very nice. Both made a point to shake my hand and introduce themselves. Rikki liked being an activist and would spend time working on various animal rights issues. Bobby had a girlfriend who was a good 20 years younger than him that he was enamored by. He spent all his time with her. When I met Bret, he was also very polite. He cruised up with two gorgeous women and seemed to enjoy talking to everyone. I never saw Bret and C.C. in the same space other than on stage ever. This was the dynamic of the entire band.

Dean Tarish seemed to be intrigued with me. I knew I had been labeled as Cesar's new guy. I was being groomed to be one of his stage managers and then inevitably a production manager. That meant I would one day become a big production manager in the industry. It all made for general interest in how I both behaved and how good I was at what I did. I kept it quiet that I thought Cesar was mad at me.

On Poison I worked strictly as a lighting guy under Nigel. I didn't know much about lighting, and I'm sure to absolutely no surprise to you, I hadn't learned anything at LSD, so I wasn't all that good. But I could focus the lights very quickly, I was very good with a crew, and I knew how to set up both the truss and motors safely and efficiently. One of Rigger Steve's lessons had been if you don't know what you are doing, tell people as if you do. At least you are being assertive enough to make a decision, he'd say. Oh, that and never drop a carabiner. I assertively told everyone on stage to never drop a carabiner - not that I knew why it mattered.

Because of the poor pay, we had the C list of lighting guys. We were the D in the window at your favorite restaurant. James, we called him Hacksaw, was my immediate boss and one of the biggest assholes I have ever met in my life. His wife had recently left him. I don't know if his impending divorce made him a bad-tempered prick, but I bet she was glad to be away from him. Like a toddler, he'd throw anything in his immediate reach. He was a dirty, unshaven, bitter man. Oh, and did I mention he was an asshole?

The other lighting guy was Jack. Jack was a good dude but certifiably bat shit crazy. I would think he would have leant himself to being the easiest roadie to give a nickname to, but we all just called him Jack. I was told Jack had been caught bringing LSD, not the lighting company, into Japan while on tour with Pink Floyd. He was arrested and kept in solitary confinement there. I don't know how long he had been kept in solitary, but it absolutely cooked his noodle. He was a super nice guy and for me that goes a long way. He knew how to fix the lights, but he was really slow at doing it. I think that had a lot to do to him talking to the lights while fixing them. There was no question Nigel was disappointed in his crew. The crappier his crew was... the more he'd have to do the work himself. All he wanted to do was to hang out in the tour bus talking cars with Tarish.

I heard Nigel several times call Raul at LSD to try and get some better crew, but each time he got nowhere. The other issue was Nigel liked to "double dip." Double dipping meant that he would get paid for doing two jobs at the same time. He often paid himself as a lighting guy but didn't really help at all. It could easily be argued that was the luxury of being the boss that hired the crew, but it also meant the crew would have to work that much harder because we were down a worker.

Chapter 98
Being Poisoned

Poison tour band and crew food pass, 2001.

A few days into the tour, Nigel and I went out to dinner with Hacksaw and Jack. We both later agreed never to do that again. While at the table, Jack had several conversations with his meal. Overly excited about the bread rolls, he ate roughly 15 of them, as we all watched on. Hacksaw, per the usual, was angry about everything, and I thought he was going to stab the waiter for bringing the French fries out cold.

Now, I must say cold fries are pretty not cool and if it hit the news that a roadie working for a band called Poison had killed a waiter over being served cold fries, maybe, just maybe, it would start a nationwide movement where restaurants would be more careful about such things. I, for one, was willing to sacrifice a waiter to see what would happen. The other upside to the scenario would be Hacksaw would be arrested for the killing of a fry waiter and would be jailed. Meaning, I would not have to see him again. I'm sure it wouldn't be a loss to anyone else either.

On a more positive note, the hamburger I ate was very good. I unfortunately never had the opportunity to try the rolls, though I heard about their splendor for most of the next day.

Glam Slam Metal Jam 2001 tour laminate.

On May 23rd we started the tour in Amarillo, Texas. The line-up was Enuff Z' Nuff, Quiet Riot, Warrant, and Poison. The tour was called the *Glam Slam Metal Jam*. I had gone from working for two of the best bands in Rock 'n' Roll, STP and GNR, to working for a boyband, NSYNC, and now I was on the *Glam Slam Summer Jam*. Or *Glam Slam Metal Jam*, whatever they called it. I felt like the bands willing to hire me were degrading rapidly. To keep my cool and still be able to hold my head high, I vowed to shave my head on stage every day. It was a personal pact I kept.

If you were a music snob, like me, you were going to the wrong show. If you liked girls, you were absolutely in the right place. There were more women who flashed their tits, or just got straight naked, at the first gig than all the STP shows I had worked at combined. Because both the pay and the music sucked, I figured the nudity was what I was getting out of this tour.

The tour schedule was grueling. Three days on, one day off, two days on, one day off. Keep in mind all those days on are 16 to 20-hour workdays. That's a lot of tits but also a lot of sweat. When you do have to work, it is hard work.

Making an effort to get to know the guys on the tour, struck up a conversation with Kevin Dubrow over lunch. He seemed like a pretty decent dude. He told me that Randy Rhoads had started the band. I thought that was very cool.

When Quiet Riot went on that night, I was standing at front of house. Kevin played the first song and then started talking to the audience. "You know what blows me away, man? This dude who works for us. Yeah, for us… didn't even know Randy Rhoads started this band. I mean what the fuck, man."

Wait, was this asshole talking about me? Maybe his long hair had been blocking his ears while we had what I thought was a pleasant chat. The fact was, I didn't work for him. I worked for Poison. The second fact was… fuck that guy. After they performed, during their set change, I had the stagehands take a break. The drummer, Frankie, approached me and the four other stagehands hanging out with me. "Mind helping us out, guys?" he asked me. "Yeah, we are kind of busy right now. Maybe Kevin can give you a hand. There seems to be a misunderstanding about A. who is paying me and B. how not to be an asshole." Frankie remained calm, "Oh, is that what this is about. Ok, dude listen. I know the guy can be a dick but the rest of us aren't. We could totally use your help." That made sense to me. We helped them do their set change, and I learned the rest of the band were good guys. It was a glaring example of the old music industry adage: one bad singer can ruin the bunch. I never did talk to Kevin again, and neither he nor I gave a shit that we didn't.

We played Texas show after Texas show: Amarillo, El Paso, San Antonio, Houston, and Dallas. Between San Antonio and Houston, I slept three hours. The other night's maybe a couple more. The only one who didn't mind the lack of sleep was Jack. I'm not sure if he was aware when he was sleeping or awake, so he cruised along as usual either way. By the time we got to Dallas, I felt like we had been on the tour for a month already. It had only been six days. I was running strictly on adolescent admiration. I wasn't admiring the bands, I assure you. I was admiring the women. I felt like I was on a tour showcasing the boobs of America. While in Dallas, a large group of gorgeous girls in pink cowboy hats found themselves on our tour bus. Within minutes all they had on were their hats. It was a wakeup call to accept bad music into my life! How could this many hot women love Poison? While in San Antonio, I got on the bus and a pair of identical twin sisters were hanging out in the front lounge. I think they had been playboy playmates. Back then being a Playboy playmate was a good thing. Now that the magazine is defunct, it just means the girl is old. They were wearing the same clothes, tight black skirts, high heels, and cut off Poison T-shirts. In short, they were stunning.

Roadie Ramble Moment

Why do identical twins wear the same clothes? Like we can't tell they are identical twins? We need to be helped out to identify the situation?

"I got a question for you two?" I said to the girls. "Yes," replied both girls at the same time. I wondered if they were going to do that the whole time. "OK, I saw a woman pushing triplets in a stroller recently and an odd thing struck me... she had no tits. I mean she was totally flat. How the hell can you breast feed three kids with no boobs? It seems to me like a natural selection flaw," I said. "I don't know. That is a weird question," one of the girls said. "Does your mom have big tits?" asked one of the pyro guys. "Normal size, I guess," replied the other girl. "Is Bret on this bus, by the way?" piped up one of the twins. "Nope," replied Tarish looking up from his computer. Within a couple minutes the girls shimmied off the bus and were gone. "That was great!" I said. "That was awesome!" said Tarish. "You know what would have been better, if they got naked!" I said. "Yeah, a lot better!" said Tarish. Having fun being over the top, we both fake laughed for a while. "What would you faggots have done with them if they were naked?" interrupted Davey. I would have let them squish my bagpipe, Davey." I said to him. Dean got quiet. "What does that even mean?" he asked me. "I actually have no idea," I replied.

Continuing on, "OK, serious question. If a baby has down syndrome and when complimenting the mother, you do what any normal guy does- not pay any attention to the baby's looks and still say the usual adage, 'Oh, what a gorgeous baby. He has your smile. What a cutie pie.' You know, that sort of stuff- are you offending the mother? I mean you would be saying the mother looks like she has down syndrome too. Assuming she doesn't, of course. Then I guess it would be a moot point." No one said a word. "What the fuck is wrong with you, Rifken," Davey finally said to me.

"It all dates back to when I was born, Davey. I was born in the old workhouse building in Cambridge, England. In the morning my father dropped my mother off and then went to work. My mother, God bless her soul, Davey, walked the corridors all day until she was ready to give birth. When the time came, the doctors were all busy, and so I was birthed by the custodial staff. That's what my mother called them at least. Now, when I was born, my mom said I had a skin thing, or again as she would say because it is her story, an 'appendage' hanging from my head and then a big birth mark. By now I'm guessing there must have been a nurse in the room because my mom says she asked her, 'what's wrong with him.' The nurse replied, 'it's amazing how much isn't wrong with them, don't you think?' So, in summation, it's rather amazing how much isn't wrong with me Davey." Dean Tarish stood up and clapped. "That is a beautiful story, Rifken. Seriously, epic," he said. Unable to control myself, I bowed.

Chapter 99
A Perfect Mississippi Bust in An Alabaman Tour Bus

Every day I had to climb up in the rig and adjust hundreds of par cans. It took over an hour, and every minute of it sucked. Waiting on the stage for Nigel to come from the bus to redo a few of the lights for the focus, I had nothing to do. I stood still and looked around the stage. While doing so, I noticed something I had never realized on stage before... every roadie secretly wanted an office. The one commonality of any office space are photos of family. The bus driver had photos of his family all around his driver's seat and on stage all the road cases had photos of family members in them. My colleagues who were always proud to tell anyone they had found a career outside of an office, were actually subconsciously fighting to make an office out of their non-office existence. I was walking back to the bus to share my new profound insight when I saw two girls making out in the crowd. I scrapped the psychology lesson and headed out towards the girls.

During the show there were key truss movements. Nigel had designed the rig to move in different directions throughout the performance. Their movements were controlled by motors and operated by Jack on a remote. Jack took this job very seriously. He would chain smoke and move the truss up and down with the precision of a surgeon. I'd often stand next to him as he did it, because from where he sat, there was a good view of the audience, and I could get my fill of nudity to keep me going through loadout.

"So, Rifken, I've been meaning to ask. Are you related to Joel Goldsmith?" After a brief moment I replied, "Well, no Jack. Usually, people are related because they have their last names in common. Not their first names." "Oh, yeah," he replied. I looked over and saw that Jack had put a couple of photos of his parents up in one of the road cases. I was surprised they looked pretty normal. Who the fuck is Joel Goldsmith I thought?

That night at the beginning of the show I met Pantera. I learned that when they had first formed as a band, they too were a hair band. They had all been friends with the Poison guys for many years. I had not expected that. The Pantera guys all hung out for the show and partied a bit with us afterwards. If my memory serves me correctly, they actually left with all the pink cowboy hat girls.

From Texas we made our way to Birmingham, Alabama. We arrived in the early afternoon. Everyone shit, showered, and shaved and headed back down to the lobby to hit up the local strip club. I wasn't a fan of strip clubs, but it was fun to get out and have some drinks with everyone. When I was seventeen, I would regularly put on a suit, so I'd look older, and go to the strip club with a couple friends. One of those friends would later become the DJ and the other the security at the front door of the club. Regulars, we had all become very friendly with most of the girls. The girls would give us money before going up on stage. We would then sit down at the stage and throw their own money back at them. We'd build money houses and then knock them over on to the stage. We'd throw credit cards on the stage. We made it fun. Now, if you haven't picked up on the scam there was, of course, one. The other guys in the bar would try and compete with us, and the girls would of course then make more money. Much more money. After the girls got off work, we'd usually all hang out.

However, I wasn't seventeen anymore, and the allure of a girl having to get naked for you because that is her job has never interested me very much. As such I would often be selected as the guy to hold the money. Strippers are gifted pickpockets. Selecting a guy in a group to hold everyone's money, and then forbidding the strippers to touch that lucky guy, is an important function in the healthy lifestyle of frequent strip club attendees. So important, there is an entire chapter dedicated to its very necessity in the unprinted strip club handbook.

In between performers they played the jukebox, and someone kept picking Poison songs. When the girls stripped many of them chose to perform to Poison too. It was nice to have a day off, but it would have been nicer to get a day off from hearing the same damn songs.

The next day, Wednesday the 30th of May, Poison and company performed at the Oak Mountain Amphitheatre in Birmingham. The morning started off well. I had asked the tour PA, Cindy, AKA Knuckles, to get Yoohoo. I had become quite the fan of them while touring with STP. I also asked for small bags of Funyuns. It was on this morning I got my fix. I was given a case of Yoohoo's, and a big bag of Funyuns, to put on the bus. I was happy, of course, about the case of Yoohoo, but I had asked for small bags of Funyuns. I found Knuckles and brought it up.

"You are kidding me, right?" she asked. "Well, no I don't want to share a bag with all these dirty fucks. That is why you get the small bags," I said to her. "Yeah. Well, you are just going to have to deal with it," she replied. "What a pile of shit," I said under my breath. I helped Knuckles put all the rest of the stuff on the buses. She was cute, I already lived with her, and I figured it wouldn't hurt giving her a hand.

Afterwards, I headed to front of house. The house music was on, and that meant people were now flocking into the venue. To clarify, the house music is the venue music that plays before the bands begin to perform when the doors open. I'm talking to this good-looking girl, when an obscenely hot chick walks up to Nigel and says to him, "I'll do anything to get back stage." Nigel was married, and didn't cheat on his wife, so he looked at me and smiled. This chick was the ultimate babe. It was my time to shine. Hand in hand, I walked by the band, and most of the crew, with my great catch. The girl, Susan, and I sat down in the back of the tour bus, and wasted no time. Just as things were getting heavy, the tour manager, Stefan, threw the back-lounge door open. "You are supposed to be on stage. Warrant is on right now," he said. I replied, "okay, sure, sounds good," and hurriedly closed the door again. Wasting no time, I jumped back on Susan, and now completely naked we started going at it again. Uncomfortable, she stopped me. "Should we maybe go?" she asked. It didn't take long for me to make a decision. It was to get back to work…. Yeah right! I figured they could fire me; Susan was so gorgeous I would, and should, brag to my great grandkids about this moment. So, I told her that I was that guy's boss and I actually ran the show. I tried to comfort her by letting her know we truly had nothing to worry about. Unfortunately, the uncomfortable break slowed things down, and we started chatting instead of having what would of course been great sex. Roadies are never guilty of having bad sex.

Once in conversation, Susan let me know she had been a runner-up in the Miss Mississippi beauty pageant. At my request I asked her to spell out Miss-iss-ippi for me. I found that sexy. It wasn't long before we were right back where we had left off, when my real boss threw the back-lounge door open.

Now, I know what you're thinking. Dude, why didn't you lock the door? The answer was that, trust me I would have, but there was no lock. "What did you say to Stefan to piss him off so much?" asked Dean Tarish.

I literally begged Tarish to give me ten more minutes. He smiled and left, but by this point the girl was over it. She put her clothes back on and walked out of the back lounge pissed off. I followed her out of the tour bus like a beaten dog trying to figure out how to get any kind of leftover bone.

Outside, we found the whole crew and band hanging out at the rear of the bus, laughing their asses off. Stefan had left a taped-up walkie-talkie in the back lounge. They had all listened to me telling the girl that I was the boss, they heard her do the Mississ-ippi stuff, the weird mule sounds... I mean everything. The girl looked over at me partly embarrassed, partly angry, and partly amused and asked me point blank, "What the hell is this?"

I told her the truth. "It is called a wind-up. The guys are fucking with me," I said to her. Her response was to slap me hard. I mean HARD, and then bail. Everyone was crying with laughter as we watched her strut back into the verm. Well, everyone but me that was.

During the show I went back into the audience and found her again. I managed to talk her into coming backstage a second time, but this time round Hacksaw was in the back lounge typing on his computer and refused to leave. Now more interested in the show itself, I reluctantly walked Susan back into the audience. The guys later told me they pulled the "wind up" because they were all jealous.

I was mad about the situation. I was working hard, getting paid nothing, and I was cool to everyone. So why pull this shit on me? The girls were the only good part of this tour. The answer was simple; people who work in the music industry are assholes. Everyone on the crew thought the incident was hilarious. Everyone but Jack that was. Jack made a point to tell me that he found nothing funny about the situation. I appreciated my buddy Jack. I wished I had a dinner roll to give him.

Chapter 100
Bret's Cousin Brett

So now that we have an in depth and thorough understanding of what goes on in the back lounge of a tour bus, let's talk about what went on in the front lounge of the bus. The front lounge was home to the sound and pyro guys. They were a permanent fixture there. They all chain smoked and ate Vicodin out of a large jar like it was candy. One of the sound guys had brought his wife on the bus, and I wasn't sure if she was going to stay for the whole tour or not. Usually, wives could stay on the bus for a couple shows max, and then they'd have to go on their way. I didn't see her going anywhere. She could chain smoke cigarettes and had an unlimited supply of prescription drugs. Why leave? The extreme amount of cigarette smoke in the bus was hard to handle. Walking to the back lounge, I had led Susan through all this shit.

The next show was in Atlanta. I was back at the venue with the stagehands who had had my back during the Green Day debacle. Today was a different scenario though. Word was spreading like wildfire about the Miss Mississippi wind up. Stagehand and roadie alike loved the story. I'm not sure if it was because I was tired of hearing about it, or I just was being careless, but that day I slid off the front of the stage and scraped up my calf badly. Complemented with my wrists aching, I was feeling the war wounds of hard physical labor. All in all, I was ready for a day off. I wanted to get drunk and forget about my woes, aka Susan. Luckily the next day off, was the next day.

Our day off was in West Palm Beach Florida. Bret Michael's cousin, his name is also Brett, and one of his friends Rob, had been following the tour buses and hanging out with us at the shows. I had become accustomed to seeing both Brett's car and another car following theirs behind our bus. I felt a bit spoiled in our nice bus watching them follow us in their cars daily. The second car was a group of girls who were part of the band's fan club. Every year they all met up and travelled to a bunch of Poison shows together.

I told Brett if both he and Rob wanted to save money, they were of course on a budget, they could crash in my hotel room. They jumped at the opportunity. I think they had been slumming it. In West Palm Beach we cleaned up and headed down to the pool. Bret Michaels was already down there sunbathing with a couple of hot chicks. Bret didn't hang out at the venue's much, and so I hadn't really talked to him. We started chatting and the conversation quickly turned to film. He is a big movie fan. After rapping back and forth a bit, he told me he'd put me in touch with a friend of his who makes low budget movies. He told me that no matter how much writing meant to me, to them it always just meant money. At the time I blew off the remark, but it was actually great advice. We then talked about music, and he told me he wrote the song "Something to Believe In" about a friend of his who passed away. I quickly liked Bret. He was a good dude. The only problem that day was he was wearing a Speedo. I've never met another American who wore one. It's difficult to have a serious conversation with a dude wearing a Speedo. Maybe if I sunbathed more, I'd realize they are more common than I think. Then again, hopefully not.

Roadie Ramble Moment

What's in a name? The purpose of a name is so that when you want to get someone's attention, not everyone in the room turns around. So, what's with giving everyone the same names? Especially, when you are in the same family. Isn't getting people's attention difficult enough already? Is that why we give people nicknames? If someone's nickname is snowfucker for example. I bet only one guy would turn around if I yelled out, "hey snowfucker, wait up for me!" Whoever first named their own kid with the same name they had been given at birth, really jacked things up even more. A further case in point, what if your name is Mario and you work in construction. Why would you write your name on your tools? Half the people on the worksite are named Mario!

Chapter 101
NASCAR

For lunch we met up with Rikki. He talked about how when the movie *Almost Famous* was released, he got a lot of shit. His girlfriend wanted to know if the road was really like that. He said it was hard to tell her with a straight face that it wasn't like that anymore, that it only used to be. He went on to tell us that he was afraid of marriage because of money. I told him I was afraid of marriage because of women.

Rob, Bret's cousin, and I cruised out and we hit West Palm Beach that night. We got drunk and checked out a shit load of bars. The Miss Mississippi wind up had really sunk in now. It wasn't cool. I decided that night if Poison fired me, I didn't care. I'd still do my job to the best of my ability, but I was going to start partying my ass off. Cesar wasn't watching me, and a bit of fun would not only compensate for the lack of pay, but also for having to be surrounded by a bunch of pricks. My focus on what I wanted to do with my life was also changing. I was thinking more and more of making my film in the next year and not touring anymore. So, I continued on and worried about very little.

Poison set list, 2001.

BLACK UNTIL HOUSE LTS OUT
POISON'S SETDROP / PYRO SET 2001

- New Drop With Flames - **INTRO**
- **CAT DRAGGED IN** – Flames Beginning
- **I WANT ACTION** – Gerbs Beginning
- Pull Flame Drop - **RIDE THE WIND** – Flames Beginning
- **CRY TOUGH**
- Black Backdrop - **SOMETHING TO BELIEVE IN**
- PTTP Drop - **MAMA DON'T DANCE** – Flash Pots Beginning
- **CC SOLO** – Fireballs Beginning
- **FALLEN ANGEL** – Flames Beginning
- **ROCK STAR** – Flash Pots Beginning
- **RIKKI SOLO** – Gerbs & Flames End
- Black Back Drop - **EVERY ROSE** – Waterfall Beginning
- Brown - **UNSKINNY BOP** - **RUN AWAY!** Flames Throughout
- **NOTHING BUT A GOOD TIME** - Fireballs Beginning, Gerbs Middle, Confetti & Flash Pots End
- **TALK DIRTY TO ME** – Flames Beginning, Spinners, Air Burst, Flash Pots End
- New Drop w/Flames **ROCK & ROLL** – Confetti & Gerbs Beginning, Flash Pots End

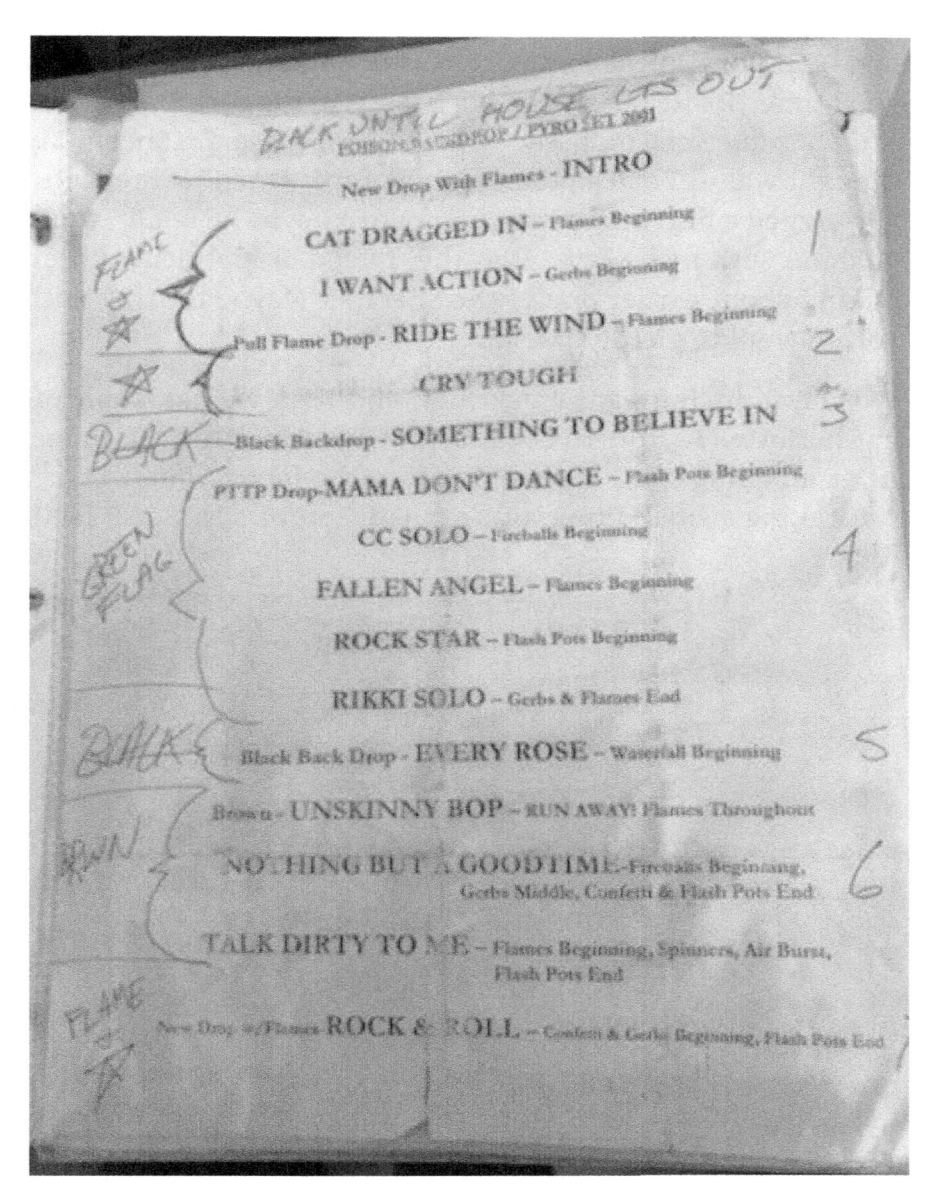

Poison set list, 2001.

On the 2nd we played in West Palm Beach. I was hungover. I focused the entire rig myself, per the usual. It was a hell of a workout and it always kicked my ass. When the show started, I knew it was going to be killer. The audience were all there to party. I had never seen so much nudity at any concert in my life. Everyone in the audience was drunk and it was a damn good time. Dean Tarish, the big boss, told me that Bret owned a film production company with Charlie and Martin Sheen. My thought was, if I had a plot now it just thickened. If Bret actually owned a film production company, maybe he really would help me with my movie. Was the "friend of his" he had been talking about earlier one of the Sheen's? Maybe touring with Poison wouldn't be all that bad.

We played in Tampa the next day, and then we had a day off in Charlotte. I wrote to Susan hoping she'd write back to me. After emailing her I rushed down to the lobby. Dean Tarish was taking a small group of us to Jeff Gordon's NASCAR facilities.

Jeff Gordon Nascar facility, 2001.

It seemed like money was no object in NASCAR. We were informed that they needed 87 million a year to just operate their team. Not open to the public, we were not well received by anybody working there. We were not allowed to take photos of anything under the hood of the car, even though I didn't know what I was looking at. To me, the coolest thing they had was an oversized floor scale. They would drive the car on it, and it would x-ray the entire car from top to bottom. How cool is that? After seeing the place, we went to lunch with a few of the guys from the team. Outside of the facility everyone was way nicer. After the day trip I went back to my hotel room. It was one of the biggest hotel rooms I'd ever had, so I wanted to spend some time lounging around in it like a rich person. It had a kitchen, living room, den, and a massive bedroom. I know what you are thinking. What about the bathroom? But it had one of those too!

From Charlotte we headed to Raleigh. While in Raleigh, Jason Alexander from *Seinfeld* joined the tour and hung out. A super nice guy, he emceed the shows in both Raleigh and Virginia Beach the next days. The next celebrity up was Gwyneth Paltrow, who joined us in Virginia Beach. Bret was clearly friends with a lot of different famous people. I had met a lot of celebrities with STP. Edward Norton, Salma Hayek, Jewel, Chris Rock & Sylvester Stallone had all watched the guys play. I enjoyed not knowing who the next celebrity stopping by would be. Cooler than any of the celebrities, the nice thing about Poison was, like STP, it was as if I was touring with a family again.

Chapter 102
Running the Light Show at Chuck E. Cheese's

Something in the air at Virginia Beach made Hacksaw even harder to work with. The day started with him telling me he didn't want me to touch any of his equipment. I didn't know what made the equipment his, but either way he was quite clear. I wasn't to be touching any lighting equipment period. I told Nigel the dilemma, and he told me to ignore the guy and go work. Throughout the day I tried to work, but every time I started, Hacksaw told me to get away from his equipment. At lunch time I brought a plate of food up to the stage and rested it up on the edge. Hacksaw flipped the bottom of the plate up and threw it. Food went all over the place. "You having a rough day bro?" I asked him. "I told you to get the fuck away from my stage," he yelled at me. I left the stage and went back to the bus, after I got a new plate of food of course. My options were to piss in his bunk or talk to Nigel and Dean Tarish about this now worsening situation.

I don't think Nigel was happy about being interrupted while talking about cars and watching Speed Vision. He reluctantly got up and walked with me to the stage. "When you gonna man up and handle things yourself Rifken?" Nigel asked me. "Manning up scares me, Nigel. I'd have to then work harder."

When we got to the stage, all the truss was in position, meaning the rig was in the air. "All right - let's do the focus," Nigel said to me. I went to the workbox and pulled out the harness. As I pulled it out, Hacksaw snarled at me. "They are either going to fire you or me, Rifken, and I assure you it ain't gonna be me," he said to me through clenched teeth. I told myself if he tried to punch me, I was going to beat the ever-living shit out of the guy. I decided not to say anything to him and just nodded my head in agreement. He was digging his own grave, and I was enjoying watching it happen.

I got on the stage, standing next to the ladder, I began to put the harness on. First leg in… second leg in and… as I expected Hacksaw was now up on the stage standing next to me. "What do you think you are doing?" he asked me. I glanced over at Nigel. "OK, Hacksaw take it easy," Nigel said to him. "He's not going up in my rig," Hacksaw barked while not breaking eye contact with me. Nigel now got more serious about the whole situation. He was starting to tire of it all. He wanted to go back and watch car racing. "Hacksaw, why don't you go eat your lunch and cool off," he said. Hacksaw now turned to Nigel, "I don't work for you, Nigel. You work for me. I run this operation, buddy." He turned back to me. "Take that fucking harness off."

That was it. Nigel had had enough. Without saying anything more he walked back to the bus. I walked back stage and finished putting my harness on. I was pleased. That should have done the trick I thought. I waited about fifteen minutes, and I, too, walked back to the bus. Neither Nigel nor Dean were in it. I sat down with Davey Kirkwood, our sound engineer, instead. Davey was an old Scotsman. He had run sound for The Rolling Stones for a long time. He was a true veteran. He drank all day and was fond of telling everyone how stupid they were. "What you got your harness on in here for?" he asked. "Helps keep my pants up Davey," I replied. "Want a drink?" He always drank scotch straight. "Nope, but give me an hour and I'll be happy to have one with you bud," I told him. "I'm not your blinking bud," he drunkenly snapped at me.

He then leaned back, suddenly chilled out, and completely changed his entire demeanor. Quietly he asked me, "all right Rifken what's going on?" I too was in anticipation. "Oh, you'll see" I replied with a big smile. Davey got loud again. "I will see what?!" he yelled at me. A few moments later the band bus door opened, and Bret Michael's security walked in the bus with Hacksaw in front of them. We all knew what this meant. He was getting escorted out of here. Roadies don't travel with much, so the escort doesn't take long.

"You fucking American's with your constitutional laws," Davey spouted out at no one in particular. "What the hell are you talking about Davey?" I asked. "Fucking stupid American's," he mumbled away. "I'm not American, Davey; I was born in England," I said to him. Davey leaned back once again and intently looked on at me. "Oh, yeah?" he asked. The security walked back down the bus. "You better hope you don't see me again," Hacksaw told me as he walked by. "Not sure where I'd see him," I told Davey. Not like I go to Chuck E. Cheese often." "Chuck E. Cheese's?" Davey asked. "Yeah, his next job," I replied.

"All right - pour a drink, Davey," I told him. "What document was the constitution modeled after you stupid git?" He inquired. "We have to answer riddles to get a fuckin' drink now?" I asked him. I waited a moment before answering his question. Davey sat still. "Several documents Davey but you are wanting me to tell you the Magna Carta. Give me my drink before Nigel gets back." I pulled up on my harness straps as if they were suspenders.

Davey laughed aloud while rocking back and forth. "I knew you weren't like the rest of these idiots," he said. He poured me a drink and put it down on the table, all just in time for Nigel to walk into the bus. Nigel was, of course, agitated. "All right, come on, Rifken, let's do the focus," he said to me. I put the drink back down as quickly as I had picked it up and got up from the table. "He's no fucking idiot," Davey said aloud. "Could have fooled me," Nigel replied. "Lots of things fool him Davey," I said. I stood up and walked towards the stage with Nigel. "You better not be drunk already if you are climbing up in the rig," he said to me. "I was hoping to look like a swashbuckler up there," I responded back.

Chapter 103
The Scoop

This is what had gone down after Nigel had left the stage. Walking into the production office, where Dean Tarish was working, he told Dean what had happened, and together they conference called Raul at LSD. Raul had already been getting shit from Nigel for sending both Jack and Hacksaw in the first place. When Raul found out how Hacksaw was behaving, he was furious.

The normal protocol when leaving a tour is you get either a one-way plane ticket back home or a plane ticket to meet up with a different tour. The flight is usually the next day, and so you are taken to a local hotel to wait for the next plane. LSD pays both the hotel fee and for your plane ticket home or wherever. In Hacksaws case, he was driven outside the venue and dropped off. Raul told him to get a bus ticket and submit *that* to LSD.

That night, when the tour bus pulled out of the venue, I wondered if I'd see Hacksaw waiting still on the side of the road. I was pleased to see he wasn't there. The bus went on, and I felt a blanket of peaceful tranquility. I smiled, and inner reflection brought me to finality of the situation. Yeah, fuck that guy.

While I was in this wonderful state of peace and harmony, Dean Tarish struck up a conversation with me. He was a nice guy, and I wondered how he handled having to can a roadie. Not uncommon like most of us, he, too, was getting pretty liquored up. Scotch poured on the bus like water.

"I was looking over your shoulder the other night when you were writing, Rifken," Dean said to me. I still sat next to the driver regularly and watched the road while writing poetry. I sent Stefanie most of the poetry I wrote. I tried to email her a poem a day. Most of them were awful, but it gave me something to do. "I'm really impressed with you. I can see Cesar's training for sure watching how you run a crew," he said to me. Dean's conversation was all over the place. Davey filled my tumbler of whiskey back up.

I knew I was good at running a crew. It was really the only thing about being a roadie I was any good at. The conversation attempt pleased me, because I quickly realized he wasn't mad at me for all the issues with Hacksaw. "You should really be a writer. You are too smart for this business," he said as he got up to call it a night. "That's nice of you to say Dean," I replied. "Glad to have you around, man," Dean said with an extended hand. "Glad to be around, sir." I shook his outstretched hand. I guessed I had a bit more job security. The situation had ended well. I, too, called it a night.

Chapter 104
Throw Momma Off The... Stage

The next day was a day off. Nigel was busy, because he was gearing up to do some STP shows. I wasn't going to be able to work them, because I was out with Poison. It's hard to not be able to do a gig, because you are already working on one that is paying a lot less.

I had talked to C.C. about going to a museum earlier in the week, but he wasn't up for it. So instead, I went to lunch again with Rikki. We spent lunch talking about going off-roading in his Hummer when we got back to Los Angeles. "That would be fun, man," I said. "Dude, we should also cruise around the next show in a go cart and pick up chicks," he said. "All about it, brother," I replied. Rikki and I had deep meaningful chats.

Since we are on the topic of driving around Hummers, the year earlier my dad had a customer who had driven his new Hummer over to my parent's house. In addition to the Hummer and lots of other cars, the guy had a fancy Jaguar my dad had been working on. "Joel, why don't you take the car for a spin around the block," my father said to me. He said car, but he really meant the Hummer. I didn't really want to drive the guy's Hummer, but the man gave me the keys, and I drove the beast around the block. I went the shortest route possible, as I didn't care at all about driving the thing. Glad to be back at the house, I parked it curbside. What I didn't realize was how wide of a vehicle the Hummer is. I hit my parent's brick mailbox and scratched the side mirror on the passenger's side. No one had seen it happen, so I kept the accident to myself.

Later that day the man called my dad. "Does Joel have the keys to the glove compartment?" he asked. He didn't ask about the scratches, which was good, but I didn't have the glovebox keys.

This was a new unexpected issue. "This is why I don't like driving people's toys, Dad," I told my father with a bit of attitude. "Yes, but did you have a fun spin?" he replied back.

Next, we played in Bristow, Virginia and then Hershey, PA. After the show in Hershey, we got two days off in a row. That was a rare event. In fact, it was the only time on the whole tour we'd have multiple days off in a row. On June 11th, the first day of the two-day vacation, our new crew chief flew into town. I spent the day at Hersheypark and rode the rides all day with Bully. Afterwards, we went to the bar and met up with Nigel and our new crew chief. Nigel had brought these two women into the bar, and within minutes they were showing off their G-strings. The new crew chief approved. Grabbing a beer, I played partner pool with Jerry Dixon from Warrant. C.C. played against us with whomever he could get to play for most of the night. I sucked at pool, but Jerry didn't complain much about having me as a partner. I learned from Jerry that the guys in Warrant could only be in the venue a half hour before they played and a half hour after. They also couldn't sell CD's at the show. I had wondered why I never saw anyone from the band hanging out at the venue. I'd also learn why Nigel wasn't allowed to run the lights for Warrant.

It was all because years earlier, Jani Layne had kicked Bret's mom off the stage. There was still bad blood in the waters. C.C. didn't get involved in the conversation. Now, towards the end of the night, I was getting drunk. So drunk, that I even stopped throwing tantrums every time someone at the bar played Poison on the jukebox. I couldn't understand why the crew and band didn't get as mad as me. Who wanted to hear this crap on their day off?

C.C., the new crew chief, and I went back to the hotel with a few of the girls we had been hanging out with and raided the tour bus. I can't remember much about what happened after that. I do remember, though, the new crew chief being very excited to learn we were playing lots and lots of festivals. "You know what that means?" I interrupted him from answering himself. "Lots of dirt," I said. "That, and we can eat fried cheese curds every day, Rifken. Man, this is going to be great!" he was so enthusiastic about it. Whatever a fried cheese curd was, it must be fantastic. I would soon make a point to find out.

I woke up hours later in the front lounge. When I awoke, I found food everywhere and porn playing on both TV's. No one else was in sight, and the front door of the bus had been left open. That was a big no, no. I looked out the door, and there was our new crew chief, my new boss and Hacksaw's replacement, lying face down arms outstretched on the grass. He looked like an overweight roadie Jesus. I jumped to his side, but I didn't yet know his name. I had just met this roadie Jesus yesterday. I gently kicked his side. "Boss, Boss you gotta wake up," I urged him. He didn't move. "Man, this guy is a deep sleeper," I said to myself. I kept shaking him until he started growling. I stood up and there was Dean Tarish looking over both of us. The bus door was still open, porn was still on the TV's, and food wrappers were everywhere.

"Hey, good morning sir," I said to Tarish. I left the boss on the grass and jumped into the bus to do my best to quickly clean it all up. Tarish didn't say a word. He just smiled and drank his coffee while watching me scurry around. I ran back into the hotel to get my stuff. The internet was still in its infancy. I'd got into the habit of leaving my computer on all night to download porn. So, with the computer already on, I did a quick check to see if I had any emails. Sure enough, Susan had written to me.

> Sorry its taken a while to get back to you, I've been busy and out of town. I have an old head shot from about 3 or 4 years ago, it was from a pageant shoot. You're right my back stage experince wasn't quite what I expected but I didn't know what to expect. I'm sure you

here that line alot, however I had never used it and was surprised it worked. I've never tried to do that before but I was drunk and my friends all had dates or husbands so I was trying to entertain myself. Well, have fun on the road.

Talk to you later,

Susan

I guess it pays to be in the right place at the right time, I thought. I closed the computer and rushed downstairs to get on the bus and get to the gig. As I hurried through the lobby, Knuckles gave me a lot of dirty glances. I don't know why the girl didn't like me, but she didn't, and that was for certain. Over the next week we played Delaware, Connecticut, New York, and New Hampshire. During this time, my new boss, I learned his name was Milton, sorted out how to get all the lights working much more efficiently. The lighting department was now Milton, me, and crazy Jack. If it wasn't clear to anyone why we didn't have desk jobs, but were roadies, I assure you they didn't have a desk job either.

Chapter 105
Anybody Need a Carpenter?

After New Hampshire we played at the Coors Light Amphitheatre in Scranton, Pennsylvania. I'm pretty sure all the stagehands at the amphitheater were drunk. Loading in, I found out quite quickly the stagehands were useless. In the mornings I would set up the front truss on the stage, and then as it was taken up into the sky, it would swing out to its intended position. That position was in front of the stage. I was crouched down and making sure all the bolts were tight on the truss when the truss began to move. The truss would easily have pushed me right off the front of the stage, but thinking quickly, I jumped up on it and held on. No harm was done, but I was pissed off. I crawled on top of the truss and jumped back onto the front of the stage. "Who the fuck told you to run the motors man?" I yelled at the stagehand with the remote, also known as a pickle, in his hands. "I always run the motors here," he replied. "Oh, yeah? Well, not fucking today, you don't. Put the pickle down and don't touch it again," I yelled firmly at him. I was hungover and really didn't want to deal with crap like this.

I lined up all the stagehands, and we pulled the truss back onto the stage and dropped it so we could finish our work. Our work was to check the bolts to make sure they were tight before raising the truss in the air. The dumbest mistakes could really hurt someone. It's a scary thought when you are dealing with morons most of the time.

Realizing I had been a bit aggressive right out of the gates, I decided to lighten the mood a bit. I pulled all the stagehands together. "OK, everyone while we load in today, we're gonna sing the song "They Long to be Close to You" by the Carpenters. It was better known to Milton and me as the song "Why Do

Birds." Milton looked at me aghast. Was I really going to sing our song! Anytime anyone asked for a carpenter on the stage, I would begin to sing it. But thus far it hadn't been a public event. Pretending to be oblivious to the looks, I began to sing in my most sultry of voices... "Why do birds, suddenly appear, every time, you are near? Just like me, they long to be, close to you..." It didn't take long before a couple of the women and Milton began singing along with me. From that day on, while doing most load ins Milton and I would sing the song "Why Do Birds." It was great fun.

In the mornings JR, the stage manager, would separate the stagehands up. Giving a certain number of heads to each department. I would then split the guys that JR gave to the lighting department between Milton, Jack, and myself. Every day, after about fifteen minutes, Milton or I would take the stagehands from Jack and start using them ourselves.

Practically, Jack was unable to use the services of a stage hand. The stagehands would stand around and watch him work. He didn't have the ability to direct people. More entertainingly, when we took the stagehands from Jack, he'd freak out and get mad. That was of course great fun. If neither Milton nor I needed the stagehands, we'd leave them watching Jack until they would inevitably come up to one of us. On occasion, someone from one of the other departments would steal Jack's stagehands as well, but that we couldn't let happen. So, we'd grab them back for us to again use in the lighting department.

The following conversation happened almost every workday. "Hey, you are Rifken - right?" a stagehand would ask me. "Yep. That's me. What's up?" I'd ask back. They'd reply, "Well, the guy you gave us to just stands there talking to himself. We've been watching him for over an hour now." I'd look at them as if I was taking every word they said into heavy consideration every day. "Did he answer himself back?" I'd probe. "Well no," the guy would say. "That is good. Means we are having a good day." I'd reassure them. "If you notice he's probably talking to the lights and not to himself," I'd clarify. "There is a difference?" they would almost always ask. "Oh, yeah. A big difference," I'd say with a smile. Without further explanation I'd then send them off to do some work for me, or over to help Milton. Not long after, Jack would come over to me flustered asking, "Where are my stagehands, Rifken?" I'd always reply with the same answer. "It's hard to find good help these days, Jack."

During the day I met Rikki's parents. His dad had set up shop in the VIP area of the venue and was selling buck knives out of the back of his SUV. This isn't a setup for me to make fun of anyone btw. I, like a few of the other people on the crew, bought one.

Throughout the Quiet Riot set a pretty blonde lady in the front row kept flashing her boobs. After maybe twenty times she completely removed her top. Jack couldn't take his eyes off of her. He was in love. Because I liked picking on him, I figured it was about time I'd throw him a bone. After all, he was the only one who had stuck up for me over the Miss Mississippi incident. I walked down to the barricade and directly to the woman. "Any interest in taking naked pictures with that guy up there?" I asked her while pointing to Jack. "I'll do more than that. You bring me backstage, I'll suck his fucking dick," she yelled at me. Though the music was loud, I couldn't help but hear myself laugh a bit. "I guess you will do then," I told her. She was clearly one of the finest women in Scranton. She immediately took her shorts off and handed them to the man standing next to her. He had her shirt over his shoulder already and was left holding her shorts and purse in hand. The guys face was frozen with frustration. The poor dude must have been bummed. Security helped her over the barricade, and in no time at all she was on the stage. She jumped up and down in excitement. As if she was just introduced as a new contestant on the "Price is Right," we walked down the side of the stage and then up the steps.

"Boyfriend took you to see Poison, huh?" I asked her. "Na, that's my fucking fiancé, man," she informed me. "Doesn't look like he's so happy," I replied. "He'll get over it. This is a once in a fucking lifetime opportunity." I thought about it and it was true. Not too many people were as crazy as Jack.

I introduced her to my friend Jack and he smiled ear to ear. His expression was as the old adage goes like a deer in headlights. The headlights were, you guessed it, her beautiful eyes. Jack was excited, but also very shy about the situation. We had quite a few eyes on us, one of them being a security guy. I signaled for him to come over. With the security guy by my side, I got some great photographs of Jack and the girl. Jack proposing to her. Jack giving her a piggyback ride. The girl on Jack's shoulders. The prize, though, was the one with Jack behind her, resting his chin on one of her shoulders. His long hair fell in front of her, covering her boobs. If they had been a hippy couple it would have been on the mantle over the fireplace for sure. I smiled to the security guy. "OK, brother that's a wrap," I told him. Jack didn't miss a beat. He stepped away from her. "It was a great pleasure to have met you, fair lady," he said as he cupped her hand and bowed towards her. "What the fuck is this? I want to meet the band?" she yelled back. I signaled for the security guy to wisp her back to the verm.

He walked her back down the stairs and the other security guys helped her back over the barricade. Angrily she grabbed her shorts and put them back on. Her guy hadn't moved, still standing there he didn't say a word. He was happy to see her back though, which I frankly didn't understand. I guess love can be blind.

Speaking of being blind, I had ensured she never left his sight. I did that intentionally, I wanted to make sure that he and the rest of the verm would know things didn't get too shady. I don't like upsetting people. I went to the edge of the stage and yelled down to the guy. "Saved you years of shit hopefully bro. Find a new girl." Everyone around the two of them clapped in agreeance with me. "You know what? Fuck all you mother fuckers!" she yelled directly into their faces. Pleased, I got back to work. My efforts making friends with the good people of Scranton were done for the day.

Towards the end of the night, the band would play the song "Rock and Roll All Nite" by KISS and invite the audience up on the stage. It was mostly women who would rush up, and most of them would pull their tops off once up there. It wasn't the worst way to end the evening. I'd worked a lot of shows now, and when the audience was let up with the band, it always made me a little nervous.

That night the security stopped more people from coming up, but the stage was already full. Bret always hated when the security stopped people coming up. A super smart guy, I wondered what he was thinking. The stage was small and the audience was huge. People were being pushed off, and C.C. was trying to get enough space to still play guitar. To get away from the crowd, Bobby had run up to the top of the stage, but the verm had followed him. It was absolute mayhem. Bret told the security to let everyone in the audience up after that. The crew all watched on, waiting for the encore to end, and everyone to get off our stage. The show ended and no one got hurt. It was a kickass show and probably the best of the tour.

That night Nigel packed up to go do the couple STP shows. While I was having a lot of fun, I wished I was going with him. I had grown tired of every other band I had worked for, and I dreamed I could watch STP perform again.

Chapter 106
C.C. For Sale

The next day was a day off was in Green Bay, Wisconsin. Waking up, I decided I'd walk across the street to Target and buy some DVD's to watch. I'd spend the day relaxing. While shopping, I started talking to a young lady who worked there. She agreed to meet me in the hotel after her shift was over. It wasn't too often I had a date.

That night I went out with Bobby and Rikki, and I got a surf and turf dinner. I paid $150 for the meal, which was a heck of a lot of money for a guy earning $500 a week, but the meal was awesome. After eating, we went to the casino and I lost five whole dollars at the table. It was time for me to leave! The casino was attached to the hotel, and so I walked back through the lobby to call it a night. When I walked by the hotel bar, I saw the Target girl drinking a martini by herself. I had completely forgotten; I was supposed to be meeting up with her. I sat down next to her and ordered myself a drink.

I learned she was a new mother; this was her first date in a while, and here I was now showing up late. I apologized profusely, but being gracious, she blew it off. The night was a rarity for her, and she was determined to make the most out of it. Lying, I told her being late was out of my character and rude. I don't think she cared. She was happier to be on an actual date than being concerned with whom the date was with. That was good for me, because I was beginning to realize I was a jackass. We talked for hours, and I was pleased when I realized I was enjoying her company. I found myself hoping that she was also enjoying mine. Throughout the evening, the young lady was becoming a steadfast dose of reality for me. Motherhood had been a struggle for her. As one can imagine, it didn't help that the father was out of the picture. As the night evolved, I was trying to understand why he had left her. She was stunning. And I don't mean attractive. Attractive has one meaning, and stunning has another. She was definitely stunning. She explained, meeting up with me had been a big deal for her. She had to plan for it. First, she had to find a baby sitter, then make dinner, and then, and only then could she make the time to look good. The time it had taken to make herself look good, she confessed she had thoroughly enjoyed. Further confiding in me, she told me that it had been nice for her to dress up. It had been a while since she had. It was sinking in that what was a lot of work for her, was just another night on the road for me. I was lucky to be living the life I was leading and fortunate I had been in her city that day. Seeing Bobby and Rikki walk back through the hotel lobby, I flagged them down and they too had a drink with us. Having them pop by hopefully made her date that much more special. "Do you want to come to the show tomorrow? I can put you on the guest list to get in for free," I said to her before calling it a night. "I wish I could, but I have to work," she replied. She didn't seem to be upset about it, though, and left with a big gorgeous smile. I'd like to say I saw her again, or even that we stayed in touch, but that didn't happen. I never saw or spoke to her again.

While I'd like to think I've always respected women, my age mixed with my touring experiences had made my testosterone run rampant. I loved all the craziness I was experiencing and couldn't get enough of the opposite sex. While I think that it was healthy for a young man, meeting the Target girl had forced me to take a few minutes to think about other things. A lot of what I was experiencing, was what I'd like to think was the insanity behind the concert experience. People go to a show to leave their baggage at home, kick off their shoes, and have a great time. I was lucky to be part of that great time. This young lady's adulthood had seemingly been forced upon her. While I was searching out what it meant to become a man, a young mother, was being forced to become a woman.

My exploration, or my training, depending on how you chose to look at what was happening to me, wasn't including something very important: respect. Being a man wasn't only about toughening up, finding a career, and leading a responsible life.

If she had made such a profound influence on me, by reminding me how important respect was, you may ask why the only name I give her is the Target girl. The answer is simple- I didn't want to degrade her by giving her a fake name. Why don't I remember her real name? Well, because even though I certainly respected her, I still must be an asshole, because I can't remember it.

Taking in a night of a lot of self-reflection, the next day while still in Green Bay, I watched C.C. make a clapboard. It read, "$2 dollars for a handshake, photo, or autograph. $5 dollars for all three." "Say cheese," he'd say and collect the verm's money.

Roadie Ramble Moment
Why do we say cheese when taking a photograph? While no one knows who came up with the saying, or why, if you watch yourself say the word cheese in a mirror you will see your lips move in a smile like fashion as you enunciate the word. It's thought that is the reason.

Before the show C.C. relentlessly combed the crowd and even the parking lot. After the show he cruised the parking lot a second time. At the end of the night, he added up all his money on the table in the front lounge. He had pulled in $250. He had clearly enjoyed himself and this became C.C.'s new thing. He started doing it at all the shows.

I don't know whose idea it was, but at the same event we started the puppy dog project. The project... we rented a different puppy dog for every show and walked it around the venue to meet women. Who wouldn't want to hang out with a different puppy every day knowing they were giving it back that night to get a new one the very next day?

The band signed schwag at each show. Because C.C. was cruising around collecting money our tour manager began signing the schwag for C.C. Stefan was amazing at forging signatures. On a piece of paper, he began signing famous rock star signatures for me. I don't know if he had worked for all of them, but his talent blew me away. I loved watching him sign all the photos for the band.

Knuckles liked the dog project but didn't like me walking around with the dog. She did not like me. It's always good to work at being on good terms with the PA on a tour, because they can make your life miserable. So, I kept trying to win her over. Each time was more unsuccessful than the last.

We played North Dakota, Minnesota, and then had our next day off in Kansas. On that day off Milton, C.C., and I, met up in the hotel lobby to go out. We walked into the hotel bar, but it was filled with Poison fans, so the three of us hailed a cab and asked the driver to take us to the worst dive bar in town.

Chapter 107
Tank Girl

The three of us hung out playing pool in what was a pretty shitty bar. Within fifteen minutes Rikki Rockett showed up and joined us. A coincidence we all liked dive bars? I doubt it. Anyhow, some fucker had put Poison on the jukebox and Rikki literally walked in to Poison music playing. Per the norm, I was on a mission to get overly drunk. It wasn't a hard mission for me to accomplish.

While C.C. and I hung out at the bar a lot, he didn't actually drink. He would chill, and if there was a pool table, he'd play pool. An interesting and fun conversationalist, we had become steadfast friends. I spent my night both talking to C.C. and hitting on this pretty young lady named Desiree. Desiree and I seemed to be kicking it off. I bought her drinks, and we talked throughout the evening. For some reason C.C. was particularly down on himself that night. I juggled between trying to cheer him up and hitting on Desiree. He complained that he couldn't break out of the genre his songs fit in. Furthermore, he was tired of the label C.C. "Come on, bro, you have songs that have sold millions of records. That's fucking awesome," I told him. "Talk Dirty to Me' is my claim to fame, and I find it unfulfilling," he told me. He seemed to be so down on himself. "Well, I'm glad you are the only one who thinks so. How many thousands of people a night are you meeting right now who would disagree?" Before C.C. could say anything further, I continued on, "Oh, and certain people, like me, really appreciate your music. I have a job because of what you've done man."

"Hey, guys. Do you want to go with us to a different bar? It's getting loud here," Desiree interrupted us. Before I could reply, Rikki jumped into the conversation. "Yeah, sure we're down," he said to her. Desiree beamed with pleasure, and we all left the bar together. I smuggled my beer out of the bar, and stood on the curb next to C.C., Milton, and Rikki. "OK, you guys just follow us and we will take you to a cool spot," she said. We watched as she jumped into the back of a full-size Chevy truck. We had all taken taxis, and so we stood there with our hands in our pockets. "How about we jump in the back with you?" Rikki suggested. Her smile widened, and her eyebrows raised a full inch. "Yeah, sure no problem," she told Rikki as her heart jumped out of her chest. The four of us jumped into the back of the truck. Rikki was successfully stealing my chick away. Clear to anyone, she had found enlightenment now that she had climbed the ladder from roadie to actual Rock Star.

Rikki sat right next to Desiree and a few of her friends. C.C. and I leaned up against the tailgate. I pulled the glass of beer I'd been hiding out of my jacket and started drinking again. "What about 'Every Rose...' man? Everyone loves that song." I continued on with the conversation I'd been having with C.C. Having lost Desiree to Rikki, there was no real point trying anymore on that one. My new plan of attack was to make Rikki buy me beers to replace the ones I had bought Desiree. "That song is a piece of shit," depressed C.C. chimed in. "Yeah, so bad that they played it at the bar twice tonight," making my point. C.C. hung his head low. "The roadies play Poison songs in the bar because they know it pisses you off," he replied back to me. "Those mother fuckers," I barked back as we pulled up to the next bar. Seeing the bigger picture, I had to find out if that was true. "They really play Poison songs at the bar, because it pisses me off, Rikki?" I asked, interrupting the lovebirds. "Yep," he responded. "Fuckin' bullshit," I said to no one in particular. We jumped out of the truck and headed into the next bar. Before we walked in, I handed C.C. some poetry I had written. I know that sounds kind of odd, but I hoped he'd make a song out of it. He was clearly in a self-reflective kind of mood and that's how songs get written.

The next morning, during load in, C.C. came up on the stage and hung out. A loud guy, he has a built in PA system; I heard him, we all heard him. "Joel here is a really good writer. I mean really good. He's a great poet," he was misinforming the stagehands. "So, the guy who wrote 'Talk Dirty to Me' thinks I'm a good writer?" I asked. C.C. gave me a smug smile. "Is that a compliment or not? 'Cause I'm taking it as one," I said to him. I guessed he was in a better mood today. I walked back out to where most of the people on the stage could hear me. "Which one of you useless pieces of shit thinks it's funny to put Poison on at the bar?" I announced loudly. A few of the stagehands raised their hands. They didn't know the wind up though. "Aww, who told you?" Nigel asked me. I stared on at Nigel's bald shiny head, I should have guessed this asshole sure knew.

I was having a good time and chalking up experience, but I wasn't making any money. I figured I'd play hardball, and tell the boss that I needed a raise on the next leg. I was friendly enough with the band now and had proven I was doing a good job. I deserved a bit more than what I was getting in pay. I didn't think anyone would argue. I asked Nigel to have a word with Tarish. Nigel reported back to me that Tarish was going to see if he could get it approved. Neither Nigel nor I thought it was going to be an issue.

That night Desiree showed up in the audience. From the front row she yelled up to me on to the stage, "Hey, Rifken, can you tell Rikki I'm here with a couple friends?" My adolescent jealousy kicked in. "No clue where he is," I told her. "Can you go look for him?" she asked. "Nope- sure can't." I kept on with my work.

Later that night Rikki found me to let me know Desiree, known as "Tank Girl," had come to the show. "Why do you call her 'Tank Girl'?" I asked him. Rikki didn't answer me. Not getting any answer made me wonder what the big secret was. The next night in Bonner Springs, Kansas she came back again. I nodded "hi" at her, and she scowled at me. That made me feel good; I figure if you can't win them over make them hate you.

Chapter 108
Rifken Swatting

Poison Rockin' The Hills all access pass, 2001.

The next day was a show in Bottineau, North Dakota. Bottineau is just about ten miles from the Canadian border. The city is very proud of being the owners of the world's largest turtle.

"Tommy the Turtle" is made out of fiberglass and is thirty feet tall. As we drove by the turtle, on the way to the gig in the morning, I watched on out the window and said aloud, "Behold the wonders of America, Davey." His eyes widened as he looked on at the turtle in all its splendor. "Fuckin' brilliant," he said enthusiastically. Davey didn't have much good to say about anything. "You like it?" I asked surprised. "Well fuck, who wouldn't like a 30-foot turtle?" It was a point hard to argue with.

I turned around and was smacked by a fly swatter. Written across the swatter it read "Rifken Swatter." Nigel had smacked me with it. "You think that's fucking funny?" I asked him. "I do - yeah," Nigel replied. I punched him in the arm. "I'm gonna shove that thing up your ass," I told him. "We will just buy ten more," Tarish barked out from a table while drinking his morning coffee. "I know you guys are too cheap for that," I replied. "You wanna try me?" Tarish said. "Confrontation" seemed to be the bus word of the day. I pushed Nigel out of my way.

The gig in Bottineau was a good one. The acts weren't all hair bands, and it was a nice change. Amongst the bands performing were Herman's Hermits, Edgar Winter, The Turtles, and the Violent Femmes. The surprise of the event was The Turtles. Their act was a musical history lesson of each reincarnation of the band. They played their songs in a sectionalized format which followed their careers. It was great fun. C.C. and I watched the show together from the side of the stage. He left towards the end of the show, but I watched their entire set. I hadn't watched a whole set for any band, other than the band paying me, in a very, very, long time. At the end of the show, Flo addressed the audience. "For all of you who came here to fuck C.C. Deville, we fucked your mothers. You are second generation groupies." I loved it. Firstly, the women that came to the shows to "fuck," came to fuck Bret, not C.C., I assure you. Secondly, I thought it was hilarious. They made me an instant fan.

Chapter 109
Show Me the Money

I had begun to look forward to New York, which was in a week. We had a day off there, and I had organized hanging out with Stefanie.

The days were passing quickly, and the first leg was going to finish soon. I was hearing things about my pay increase, but nothing had yet been confirmed. Tarish was still working on getting me more money, and Nigel had told me he had heard they were going to offer me a bit more to stay on. I hoped Tarish would succeed and Nigel was right. I was realizing that I was enjoying myself.

We played in Wisconsin, Michigan, Chicago and then went back to Michigan for another gig. However, as the shows continued to count down, there was no firm commitment about me getting a raise. I was beginning to have a change of heart. I was now getting annoyed; if they didn't hire me for the next leg, I told myself I didn't care. I laughed thinking about how bad their next $500 a week guy would be.

Separately, while in Michigan, Jack finally made his stand. "Rifken, I want to split up the stagehands in the morning," he said. I think Jack was surprised when I didn't argue. I figured it would be entertaining, and it would show the guys above me I was absolutely worth a few more bucks a week.

Jack took the stagehands in the morning and sure enough things took a lot longer to get done. Eventually, we finished up everything, and the rig hung in the air. Later in the afternoon I put my harness on and climbed up the ladder and into the rig to do the focus.

I adjusted the par cans in the first truss fast. I shimmied over to the second piece of truss, but as I did so, the piece of truss suddenly dropped. I grabbed on tight to the piece of metal. It probably only dropped a couple inches, but it felt like we had fallen a yard.

"What's going on up there, Rifken?" asked Nigel. "Come on, get on with it," he continued on. I didn't answer. I was pretty sure I had just shit myself. I slowly latched my harness onto the truss. I really only locked into the truss when I was in a big unionized city. Otherwise, the harness just got in my way. I'd have it on, but I wouldn't use it. Once locked in, I looked around. I could see one of the pieces of truss in front of me was missing one of the four bolts, but I couldn't tell if the others were loose. "Fucking rig dropped," I finally said aloud.

"You all right?" Nigel asked. He actually sounded a bit concerned. "Get out of the way in case this thing falls," I said to anyone who may be standing under me. A couple roadies wasted no time and moved out of the way. I very slowly inched my way to the end of the truss to where the bolt was missing. What I found was, only one of the bolts was actually tight. Able to tighten the other two bolts using my fingers, I knew this wasn't a good thing. It was straight scary. I dropped a rope down.

"Hey, Nigel, send me up a bolt set and a couple spanners." Nigel tied the tools to the rope I had dropped, and I pulled them up. I soon learned that it wasn't fun tightening bolts from up in the sky. As I shimmied along each truss focusing the par cans, I tightened each and every nut and bolt that day. I had no problem letting Jack run the crew, but I sure as hell was going to check all the bolts myself from then on.

That night happened to be the 4th of July. At the end of each performance, every night, the pyro guys would blow off fireworks. That night they kept the fireworks going a little longer. The verm loved it and we all had fun.

However, hours after the show was when we really had our fun. There might have been a few stragglers in the parking lot looking for autographs and some others trying to figure out what happened to their ride, but the place was pretty much empty. The pyro guys and the local fire department had set up a post-show fireworks extravaganza display for band, crew, and fire department folk. It started with a couple of fireworks, but kept going. We all watched our personal fireworks show for the better part of an hour and drank beers a plenty. I wondered if they would have any fireworks left for the next show. I wouldn't have been surprised if they had had to ship some in.

Chapter 110
Women... Geez

Davey had begun to scream in his sleep. It's a difficult thing on a bus if someone sleepwalks, snores, or causes any other issues while they are sleeping. There are too many other people in the bus who need to sleep too. Yelling amongst the crew seemed to be fairly constant over the next couple days because of it.

As the days counted down, I had hoped C.C. would play a song he wrote out of my poem or Bret would come talk to me about making a movie, but neither happened. As it became apparent, they weren't going to hire me for the next leg. I began thinking about how I would start making my movie myself. I felt confident that should be my next hurdle to tackle. It could, and should, be my next step. One-night Bobby told me he had never wanted to be a musician but a rock star. I liked the idea of that. I would be a rock star amongst film director guys, I thought. "That's what I should do," I said aloud, but no one was there to listen.

Knuckles had become accustomed to me helping her stock the buses now. I figured that could be another thing I should take off my additional work routine. While in Chicago I didn't help her with the buses. Instead, I took a nap. Waking up, I jumped down from my bunk. Tarish had just got on the bus and was going through some stuff. "Hey, Knuckles's pissed with you for not helping her today," he said to me. "I don't give a shit. I help her with her job almost every day and she is a total bitch to me. She can do her own fucking job. Fuck that chick." I buttoned up my shirt. Tarish stood there smiling underneath his oversized mustache. "She's on the bus, isn't she?" I asked him. His smile got even bigger. "She sure is, bud. I'll let you handle this one." Dean walked back into the front lounge and sat down at the table. I walked into the front lounge as Knuckles was leaving.

"Aw, fuck," I said to no one in particular. "Good job, Rifken - you fucking idiot," Davey said. Nigel hit me with the Rifken swatter. I grabbed him and wrestled the fly swatter out of his hand. Blocking the entrance to the bus, Nigel ran towards the bunks. I chased him and smacked him repeatedly as hard as I could with the swatter. Once in the back lounge, he had nowhere else to go. I wrestled him to the ground and smacked him real good in the head with the swatter once. "Hit him one more time Rifken and I'm buying everyone on the crew a Rifken swatter," Dean told me. I got up off of Nigel laughing. I'd like to say Nigel was mad, but he was laughing as hard as I was.

I stayed away from Knuckles for the rest of the day. I had made a new enemy. That wasn't good. Knuckles heard all because she worked in the production office. She could, and I figured would, put her input in if she overheard anything about me.

The next day we were in Clarkston, Michigan. Clarkston's population in 2010 was 882 people. We probably had more road cases on the Guns N' Roses tour than they had residents. In the morning JR, the stage manager, came up to me in a bit of a huff. "Hey, man, why aren't you handling the stagehands?" he asked. "Jack wants to do it," I told him. "Well, that ain't gonna fuckin' work - the guy talks to himself," JR said to me. "No, he talks to the lights," I corrected him. Not happy, JR walked off. I shrugged it off, it wasn't my problem.

After load in I took my usual nap and then went to the production office to order some supplies. I wasn't looking forward to it. To get them, it was Knuckles I'd have to talk to. I walked into the office while hoping to not make the situation any worse.

"Hey, Rifken, how are you doing?" Knuckles asked before I could say anything. She had never really addressed me before. It threw me off guard, and I didn't quite know what to think of it. "I'm good. How are you?" I replied. "I got you something," she said. Knuckles threw me a large plastic bag filled with small individual bags of Funyuns. I couldn't help but grin like a five-year-old. "Thanks, Knuckles," I said awkwardly. I opened the plastic bag and offered her one of the small treasures that laid within. "Would you like one? They are very good," I said to her. "No, I'm good, but thank you," she replied with a cute laugh. I gave her a list of the supplies I needed and headed back to the bus. That had not gone at all like I thought our next encounter was going to go. Relieved, I was certain women were crazy but glad she seemed to now like me for whatever reason.

When I got back to the bus, Tarish was at the table in the front lounge with Davey. "So, you staying on board Rifken?" He asked. "You guys paying me more?" I replied. "I'm afraid not." That wasn't the answer I was hoping to hear. "Pile of shit, pay the boy more money, Tarish," Davey spit out. "It's not my call Davey," Dean said. It was nice that they all wanted to keep me around. I just questioned who wouldn't approve a couple hundred bucks more a week. "Bunch of fucking wankers. I toured with Mötley Crüe back when they were at the top of their game. These guys are a joke. Those guys knew a fucking party," Davey mumbled. Tarish found that especially funny. We liked our drunk Scotsman. Once again, I had no idea what the tangent had to do with the conversation though.

That night Nigel got on the bus pissed off. "All good, man?" I asked him. "They won't pay you more. I tried. It's bullshit," he said. "Sorry, man. I want to stay around, but I'm literally working for $5 an hour, and it's hard work," I said to him. "Oh, I'm not mad at you Rifken. It's OK," he said and climbed into his bunk.

Chapter 111
It's Raining Wrenches AKA
Bad Roadie Rain

The last few shows went by quickly. Jones Beach, the Tweeter center in Massachusetts, and lastly the PNC Arts Center in New Jersey.

While at the Tweeter center I had another scare up in the sky. When you climb up into the rig, the truss moves around a bit. They are hanging on chains, so it only makes sense. I was doing the focus during sound check, which was the norm. However, today during this sound check Bret Michaels was actually on the stage.

I saw it fall. A big crescent wrench descended off of the truss and hit the deck. I looked over at Bret; he hadn't seen it happen. It would have been loud, too… but with the sound coming through the speakers, no one had heard a thing. I was the only one who had noticed. Curtis Mayfield was paralyzed from the neck down, when a crescent wrench fell from the truss and hit him while on stage. It angered me someone could be so haphazard. Through my walkie talkie I told Nigel to go pick up the wrench, and he did. I didn't need to tell him what had happened. I did make sure he knew it wasn't me who had dropped it.

I felt comfortable with leaving Poison. I wasn't one to jump ship, but I was glad I had made a stand whether right or wrong. Maybe that was what being a man was about, and the roadies had finally taught me how to be one. Knuckles and I talked more over the last few days. I learned she had changed her attitude towards me because C.C. had talked to her. He had told her he thought I was very talented. While she listened to C.C., she said that when I was mad, I never really said anything bad about her. I had just said that she was mean to me, and she knew that she was. During one of these conversations I gave her the now famous Rifken swatter. "Just in case I act out of line again," I said to her and handed it over. She gave me a big hug. I was pleased I had made a friend.

On July 8th we played at the PNC Arts Center. Our last show, I met up with Stefanie and her friend. At the end of the gig, the three of us partied in my hotel room. We set up candles throughout the room, turned the music on, and cracked open the mini bar. The sound of a mini bar opening and closing was a sound that could be heard throughout any hotel by all roadies. Some of the crew came over and we all partied late into the night. At around four in the morning, C.C. knocked on my door in his underwear. When I opened the door, Tracy Chapman was playing on my sound system. I know - kind of lame, but to be candid the party was mellowing out. "Turn that cunt off!" C.C. barked at me. "Aw, come on, C.C. It's good shit. She's got a great voice. Come on in and hang out. Well, go put some pants on first, then come hang out," I said to him. "I'm serious, Rifken, turn that shit off," he yelled back at me as I imagined him goose stepping back down the hallway.

We ignored C.C. and kept partying. When I checked out in the morning Stefanie, her friend, and I hadn't slept at all. We had all been hooking up all night. It was great. It was a perfect way to end the tour.

I walked up to the front desk to check out. I was tired but had a big shit-eating grin that I wasn't trying to hide. "Hey, my name is Joel…" I was interrupted. "We know who you are, sir. We are just glad you are leaving," the woman at the desk told me. I walked out of the hotel feeling like the Roadie King.

Chapter 112
$100 Bucks for One Real Beat Up Truck

Over the next week I hung out with Stefanie in New Jersey, where she was from, and New York, where she lived, instead of flying back home. I met her family for the first time, and the two of us tackled the town. I had a great time. For the first time in my life, I was head over heels in love.

When I got back home, I had new found energy and I began working on my movie. I met with John again and my friend Jason. We each agreed to put 100k into the film. John wanted to direct the film and said he could get Tobey Maguire and Drew Barrymore to play the leads if he did. My head spun at the idea. I didn't know how I would get my cut of the money, but If they were going to put in their 100k, I would have to figure out how to raise mine. Maybe I could sell copies of the script outside of bookstores?

There was one thing I told them we needed to be sure about. In the movie *Snow White and the Seven Dwarfs* the wicked witch is by far the best-looking woman in the movie. If my movie was to have a wicked witch, I wanted her to be just as good looking as any evil Disney witch.

The second thing I was sure about was I needed a massage. My back had tightened up from all the climbing every day. My best friend growing up was a massage therapist. A big guy, 6'8 and 200 pounds he beat the crap out of my back. The relief was amazing, and I had a new found respect for my friend's career.

While figuring out how to save money, I was wasting lots of it at the bar on drinks. Lots and lots of drinks. A month or so passed and the Poison tour was cancelled because Bobby hurt his neck. The crew had been getting paid to hang out and play volleyball on a beach somewhere for a week. If I'd only had a crystal ball - maybe I would have known to stick around. I knew it didn't sit well with Nigel or Cesar that I hadn't signed on for the next leg. Even though Nigel said it was OK, I knew it wasn't. Furthermore, my film wasn't moving along. My buddy Jason wasn't answering my calls, and John wasn't prepared to do anything until he saw the money from both Jason and me.

I had become a fixture at my local dive bar, Casey's Tavern. I'd sold my fancy Porsche, just before going on tour with Guns N' Roses, and was now driving a beat up 1986 Toyota pickup truck. I had bought the truck for $100 from a scrapyard and rebuilt the damaged front end myself with the help of my dad's friend, Chalong. Chalong did some autobody, sort of, and so gave me a hand. Together we wrapped a chain to a light pole in the street in front of his shop, and with a winch were able to pull the front end back into place, again sort of. It looked good enough. The truck had been in an accident but was mechanically sound. Once the body looked OK-ish, I replaced the front panels and the hood. I didn't paint the front end but left it primer. The cab, the doors, and the bed were blue. Both sides of the truck were heavily scratched up; I called the scratches my racing stripes. Lastly, I threw away the dented tailgate and put in an off-brand gator net called the "Turbo Net." It was the final touch to my masterpiece. I loved my new beat-up truck. The best part was because the truck was such a mess, being mostly primer, my father couldn't give me a hard time about not waxing my car. Big on cleaning vehicles, he would regularly clean, and then wax, all our cars. I'd finally found a car where I didn't have to worry about him driving me nuts about it.

I had found a photograph of a really cute blonde girl in the Casey's parking lot, and I kept it on the dashboard. For weeks I drove around with the photo, waiting for someone to ask me who the girl was. I couldn't wait to tell the person who asked that I had no idea. I had my answer locked and loaded, "I just found the photo and thought she was cute," would be what

I'd say. It was both creepy and funny. At least I thought so. The radio in my truck didn't work, and I only owned one tape cassette. The tape cassette was the Def Leppard album *Hysteria*. I had listened to it a million times now. At least it sure seemed that way, but It was probably more like a few hundred thousand.

To paint a full portrait of how I now drove around, because I'm sure you are on the edge of your seat, I'll make one more mention. Some guy had left me a voice mail in the middle of the night. It was a Persian dude singing in Farsi. He was super drunk, and the message went on and on until the phone eventually cut him off. He knew some of the words to whatever he was singing, and the rest he filled in with humming. He was clearly too drunk to know he was leaving a message for someone he didn't know, but he sang and hummed with great passion. My outgoing message was a girl I had been dating singing. Her message made no sense as well. The whole thing was an art piece to me. I listened to his message while driving home every night from the bar until eventually my phone company automatically deleted it. Ashes to ashes and dust to dust, I guess.

If the photo and the messages didn't make it clear, a month after I had left Poison, I had accomplished nothing. C.C. gave me a call on the 12th of August to tell me that he was afraid I'd never be happy. However, he loved and believed in me as an artist. It was nice to hear from him, albeit an odd call. But then again, he's kind of an odd guy. He told me I have to be creative or I'm going to commit suicide. Knowing he liked my poetry, or at least pretended to. I read him a poem I wrote for Stefanie. "You are in trouble from the waist down. Love is cool man, but you're always wondering how much they love you, ya know," he replied. I agreed, and then we agreed to chat more later. It was a good feeling to know we'd stay in touch even though I no longer worked for him.

I like being friends with people who strive to do amazing things. Outlandish, hard to accomplish, achievements are cool. Success is hard to come by, and I'm whole heartedly impressed by it. It's nice to surround yourself with the successful when you can. While C.C. sometimes had self-doubt as to his personal accomplishments, I certainly never did. When I hung up the phone, I smiled knowing we'd be staying in touch.

Chapter 113
Sunset Strip

The next day I flew out to New York and hung out for another week with Stefanie. It was fun to hang out in New York again. At the end of the week, we rented a car and went camping up in the Adirondack mountains. I wasn't working, but things were good!

The Go-Go's all access pass, 2001.

When back in L.A., On the 24th of August to be exact, I went to a Go Go's concert to see most of the Poison crew. Almost everyone from Poison was working the gig under Tarish. It was good to see everyone. Rikki Rockett was there and had brought Bianca from the Humble Gods with him. She was better known as the lead singer of a band called Betty Blowtorch. I didn't know they knew each other, and I hadn't seen her since I was seventeen years old. I was super excited to catch up with her. A few months later she hopped in a car with a drunk driver and was killed in a car accident. It was sad, but I was glad I had the opportunity to see her before the accident happened.

Humble Gods T-shirt, late 1990's.

After the show I went to the Sunset Strip with Jerry and Mike from Warrant. Jerry and I met these two women and hung out most of the night with them. Jerry's girl was of course gorgeous. Mine was a bit overweight and talked A LOT. When someone talks a lot, you are stuck listening a lot. I listened to the woman go on and on. Jerry was clicking with his girl and I was drinking on the Warrant tab, so I dealt with it. After a while my girl must have gone hoarse, because she finally stopped talking. Not long after, it was time for her to go home. She asked me to walk her back to her car and I somewhat reluctantly did. Though I wanted to drink more and maybe meet another chick, it was the gentlemanly thing to do. When I got back, Jerry, his girl, and Mike the drummer of Warrant, asked me what I thought of her girlfriend. I assured them I didn't think much. All three of them were laughing at me, and I didn't understand why. I assumed Jerry was just trying to be cool in front of his new girl, who he was clearly going to spend the night with.

Now, if Mike seemed to be missing for most of this story it

was because he was. He was off doing his own thing all night. However, at the end of the night he couldn't miss out on a laugh at my expense. After a while, with the three of them laughing at me, the girl must have felt sorry for me. I used to hang out at a place called the Cat Club a lot on the Sunset Strip. It was owned by Slim Jim, the drummer from the Stray Cats, and we were there all the time. Holding my hand, she walked me into the Cat Club's bathroom. When I looked in the mirror with her standing next to me, I saw I had lipstick all over my face. I was busted! I didn't wash any of it off at all; I figured I'd embrace the shame. I walked back into the bar and bought another drink on the Warrant credit card. The girl Jerry met that night would later become his wife. Life can be crazy. Mike's nickname was The Sack. I told him I now knew why. It was because he was a sack of shit. I didn't mean it though.

Hanging out all the time now, I got letters of intent from Jerry and Mike. I hoped if I got enough letters of intent from people in the industry, a financier would help me make my film.

Chapter 114
9/11

Things were picking up. Stefanie was now calling me all the time. I was getting lots of letters of intent I could use towards making my movie, and I had come up with an idea to get by until I raised enough money to make the movie. I was going to start a chamber of commerce. The Pacific Rim Chamber of Commerce is what I'd call it.

The idea was this. I'd basically start a boy's club with a fancy name. I would get company executives to join my chamber of commerce for a fee. Once they were members, I would then charge them to come to events. After that I'd charge people to speak at those events.

This was a perfect gig for me, and I hit the phones hard. I first started with the ad agencies in New York and then the airlines. I hoped this would give me the ability to fly for free and a reason to be in New York more often. I quickly got a few ad agencies, media conglomerates, and airlines to join the chamber.

Our first member was one of the largest media conglomerates in Japan. We will call them MJMC, standing for Massive Japanese Media Conglomerate. I took the GM of MJMC, Haruto Watanabe, to a Stone Temple Pilots concert. They were touring with Marilyn Manson, and Haruto was extremely excited to meet Manson. Having his driver pick me up at my house in a limo, we started off our evening going to Jerry's Famous Deli. He ordered a Guinness beer and a bowl of matzo ball soup. An odd combination- I thought I might like this guy. "You know, man, it's going to be pretty cool to go into the show with our own private security," I said to him. "Security?" he asked. "Yeah, the driver guy. He's not security too? He's a pretty big fella,"

I said. Haruto thought this was very funny. "I am samurai. I do not need security. You are very funny," he told me. "You are a samurai, dude? I think you mean you're like a blackbelt," I said to him. I wasn't laughing when I said it, but I did kind of chuckle. Very seriously Haruto replied, "No, I mean samurai. A samurai means ready to die." Ready to die. Well, that's pretty serious, I thought. "Well fuck, that sounds way scarier than saying you're a blackbelt," I said. "Can we drink any of the alcohol in here, Haruto," I asked. "Yes, help yourself," he told me. I poured a glass of vodka and sat back in the comfy seat. "Ready to die... Jesus," I said to myself. Haruto smiled at me. I smiled back and in midair toasted my vodka.

When we got to the show, I told Cesar the guy was a bit eccentric, but quite the character. "Oh, and don't bring up black belts and karate and stuff," I made sure to tell him. Cesar could care less about my new friend. While Manson played, I spent the time catching up with Cesar in the production office. During the show one of the roadies ran into the office. "Hey, Rifken, your Japanese important guy... You gotta see this, bro," he said. "Dude, what the fuck did you do to him? He's an executive of a big fucking company. The guy is a big deal," I said. I ran out to the stage. Bored of watching the show on the side of the stage, he had jumped into the mosh pit in his suit and tie. Actually, let me correct myself. He didn't jump into it. He started it. Even cooler, the guy was out there rampaging shit! Clearly a crowd favorite, I watched on dumbfounded. Cesar, now behind me, spoke up, "Look at this guy. What a fucking trip, Rif," he said laughing. "Haruto is fucking badass," I said aloud. Watching this Japanese executive party his balls off was certainly something neither of us had ever seen. Cesar patted me on the back and went back to the production office. I watched on, not to see Manson but to fucking see Haruto, man! Back in the limo at the end of the night, in a ripped-up shirt and no tie, Haruto put on his glasses, that were amazingly not broken, and wrote me a check. It paid the Pacific Rim Chamber of Commerce's first phone bill.

With Haruto's check I was able to keep grilling the phones. My partner, Holmes Stoner III, and I offered free memberships to companies that would let us use their business space for events. Food and refreshments were either provided by the hosting party or were bartered out for memberships. It all came easy. Like anything else, when a few people are on board, it isn't hard to get more people to jump on. MJMC, a well-respected conservative company's membership, certainly helped a lot. Within a few weeks we had moved our office from Holmes's apartment living room in Marina Del Rey to a corner office in Beverly Hills. Rent paid by, you guessed it, another free membership to the Pacific Rim Chamber of Commerce.

The lady who ran the PR firm and gave us the office to use, wanted me to try and get this Korean guy's piano music into movies. I had no idea how I could do that, but I began to listen to his music all the time. When I played it for my mom, she said, "he sounds like the piano player at Nordstrom Rack." "You mean Nordstrom mom. Nordstrom Rack's don't have piano players." I corrected her. "No, I mean Nordstrom Rack. The players at Nordstrom are a little more interesting." I stopped working on trying to figure out how to get his music into film after that.

We set our first event for the night of September 11th. By the 10th I had a couple hundred RSVP'S. Each person was paying $10 at the door. It would be enough money to keep us going until our next event. September 11th came and went. It would be one of the most memorable days in 20th century history and not because of my chamber of commerce event. Watching the news repeatedly play the world trade center falling was devastating. There had never been a world event I genuinely felt impacted by. Stefanie worked right down the street from the World Trade Center. I was relieved to hear she was OK but wanted to get to New York as soon as possible to be by her side. I booked a ticket to be on one of the first planes out of Los Angeles. Realistically, it was probably one of the safest days in flight history but when the plane took off with me on it, it was empty. While on tour, when you were the only one in a row on an airplane, we'd call that a sky couch. When there was no assigned seating on a plane, we'd sit in the middle seat. No one would want to sit next to a stinky roadie, and we'd all hope to get our sky couch so that we could sleep a bit lying down. That day the whole plane was a sky couch.

When I landed in New York the pain throughout the city was clear. The subway walls were filled with missing persons flyers. It wasn't an art installation. I wished it was. I tried to look at each flier, but there were just too many. I was witnessing the repercussions of a heart wrenching catastrophe. The next day Stefanie and I took the trains down to ground zero. She wanted to see what it looked like. As we got closer to the site the subway emptied. When we got to the site itself, there were very few people there. A stench still in the air, workers were removing large metal beams in hopes of recovering yet more bodies. Being together during this time brought us closer together. I began to feel like we were a couple.

When I flew home a few days later, it soon sunk in how hard a long-distance relationship was. The romance of living far apart was wearing thin. We began to discuss Stefanie moving to Los Angeles. I told her I would focus on the chamber and stop touring if she did.

Chapter 115
Love is Fleeting

On December 16th I randomly saw Angelo outside of his parent's house. Happy to see one another, we decided to go to a local dive bar and catch up. We hadn't hung out in a long time. It was karaoke night and after some cajoling from locals who recognized him, Angelo got up on the stage and sang Karaoke. He picked a Johnny Cash song. We watched, as I'd say he did a shitty job singing it, but we are friends, so I'll just say he did a poor job. However, everyone else there would have said he did a shitty job. Drunk, he sang it poorly intentionally.

We drank all night, and at the end of the night some guy in a cowboy hat invited us up to his house. He was a rancher/inventor of some sort and lived in a big house in Malibu. He had had a party the night before and the pool house was still filled with food. Angelo and I gorged and smoked weed till the sun rose. In the morning we got the guy to give us a ride back to the dive bar.

Once we got back to the dive bar, I hopped in my car and told Angelo I'd follow him home. We got to the first red light, but when the light turned green, Angelo's car sat still. His head up against the driver's side window, I could see that he had passed out in the car. I got out of my truck and started banging on his window. His door was locked. "Move the fuck over," I yelled at him through the closed window. Finally, after a few tries he acknowledged I was there and opened the car door. I parked his car and drove him back to his parent's house. When we got to Angelo's parent's house his uncle, who lived there, opened the door. Angelo beelined into the house and passed out face first on the sofa. "Angelo, ain't you a little old for this? And you Joel, you should know better." His uncle scolded us both. I went back across the street to my parent's house and went to sleep.

When I woke up hours later, my dad had washed and waxed the primer on my truck. As manipulative as I tried to be, there was no changing him...

Stefanie planned to fly into Los Angeles on New Year's to see me. I was of course very excited. We had been talking every day. If anything, I'd get a New Year's kiss from a lovely young lady and who wouldn't want that? On the 31st Stefanie missed her plane. She called me crying. It was hard not to feel horrible.

Our conversations over the next few days were about how she wasn't going to move to Los Angeles; she couldn't leave New York. She couldn't "turn her back" on her city she told me. The events of 9/11 made her realize she had a true connection to NYC. She asked me to fly out to see her again and so I did.

When I got to NYC, what I didn't realize was she wasn't just questioning her true connection to the great city, but also her true connection to me. Getting to NYC was a tough feat. I'd take a taxi to the airport. Then I'd fly into Islip, Long Island. Once on Long Island, I'd take a taxi to the train. The train would then drop me off at Penn Station, and from there I'd walk a few blocks to Stef's work. Often, she'd still be working, so I'd hang out across the street at a cool little dive bar until she was off. Pitchers being cheap, I'd regularly buy a dozen of them and hand them out to the locals. I'd made quite a few friends by this point. They all thought I was nuts. They'd come to the bar to bitch about their wives, and here I was flying across the country to try and get one.

On this particular trip the rain was coming down hard. By the time I got to Stef's work, I was both soaking wet and exhausted. I waited outside for her for twenty minutes before she came downstairs with an umbrella. By the time she handed me the umbrella I felt foolish holding it. Hand in hand we made our way back to her house.

Various people on the subway looked on at us, trying to piece together what our connection was. Why was this soaking wet bum looking guy with this attractive woman in a business suit? I sat emotionless. I wasn't going to make their ride boring. If they couldn't figure out that I'd crossed the US for this lady to stand outside in the rain for a half hour, I wasn't going to tell them.

Stefanie interrupted my train of thought. "I didn't think you'd be so quiet. Aren't you happy to see me?" I didn't quite know how to answer that. "Oh, I don't know; I'm fucking tired" would have been the fitting thing to say, but instead I said, "it's been a long day." When we got back to her house, I took a quick shower and changed into some dry clothes. Done for the day, I just wanted to go to sleep. We sat together on her small bed. I laid down and closed my eyes. "I don't know how to say this but we should talk," she told me. I didn't say anything. "I love you, but I'm not in love with you," she continued on. This wasn't what I was expected to hear. "You couldn't have told me this on the phone?" I asked her. "It's not the kind of thing you talk about on the phone. I thought you deserved for me to tell you in person. I owe that to you." I sat back up. "I mean there is a lot I still want to do in New York. You are a serious relationship kind of guy. I want to have sex with a girl before I get into a serious relationship. I want to make love to a black man. I still have life experiences I want to have. I also kind of met someone else," she told me.

What the fuck was going on here? I didn't know what to say to her. I began to put my clothes back on. "I'm sorry. I just wanted to be honest with you. I don't know if the guy I met is anything serious either, by the way. We've just gone out a couple times," she told me. "He's a black guy?" I asked her. "He is, how did you know?" She looked inquisitively at me like I had been stalking her or something. "I think your subconscious is screaming out," I told her. "I don't know what that means," she said. "You told me you want to make love to a black man. I think there is a pretty good chance the black man is the guy you just met." She giggled a bit. "You think?" she asked. I put on my jacket. "That's not necessarily true, ya know. Where are you going?" she asked me. "I don't know, but I'm not going to stay here," I told her and began walking towards the door. "I didn't want you to be upset," she said to me. What the hell was I supposed to say? "I'll be all right." I left.

I did know where I was going to go. STP was renting a rehearsal studio in NYC, and I knew I could go there. I walked into the studio and found Scott and Dean still hanging out. "Hey Rif," said Dean. Then it was Scott's turn: "Hi Joel." He was still the only person in the whole music industry who called me by my actual name. I waited for either of them to ask me what I was doing in New York, but neither did. I pulled up a road case and put my jacket up on it. To clarify, when I say "I pulled up" a road case, I didn't actually pull on anything. Pulling up a road case had become my personal terminology for putting a jacket on a road case, to use as a pillow, and going to sleep.

The next morning, I called the airlines to see how much it would be for me to fly home that day. It wasn't cheap. Stefanie had left me a couple messages. I didn't really want to talk to her. It was all just awkward, and the truth was, though I was absolutely going to hide it, I was hurt. I really did like her. I was about to give her a call when she sent me another text. *Do you want to meet at the bar across the street from my work at 5 today? I'd say earlier but I have to work.*

Looking at the airplane prices, I thought maybe it would be smarter for me to meet up with her. I weighed my options. I would either maybe get laid and sleep in a bed or beat off in the rehearsal studio bathroom and sleep on a road case. I had done both before. I spent my day walking from where the rehearsal studio was located to the dive bar across from her work. I stopped at any place that looked interesting. When I got to the bar, my local friends were glad to see me. They were pleased to hear that I was prepared to chime in on complaining about women. I had become one of them, and they accepted me with open arms. Well, with as extended open arms as a New Yorker can have. "Hey, get this fuckin' guy a drink already," one of them said. We all toasted our beers and began to drink heavily. We drank pitchers of beer and bitched about not just our problems, but all the issues in the world. No one would accuse us alcoholics of being self-absorbed.

The good thing about the bar that day was that Jägermeister had a young lady there marketing Jäger and giving us free shots. She and I hit it off. It didn't take long until she was sitting in my lap, feeding me shots of Jäger. I was drinking the nectar of the Gods and had a great set of knockers in my face. Life was back to being awesome.

Interrupting my fun, one of my friends at the bar spoke up. "Hey, Joel - your girlfriend is here," he said. "I don't have a girlfriend, man," I drunkenly replied. The Jäger girl got up out of my lap, and there stood Stefanie. The mood of the place became awkward fast.

Back on the subway again, I got looks from the people sitting across from us. This time I think it's safe to say they were wondering why this attractive woman in a suit was mad at this really drunk guy with lipstick all over his face.

Chapter 116
Who the Hell is Katie?

For the next four months I worked at expanding the database of the Pacific Rim Chamber of Commerce. When my mom asked, "What exactly is it you are doing? How is this a career?" I told her the truth. "I have no idea. I set up parties and try and get free stuff." The events we set up were kickass parties with the executives all tipping well. Megan, Samantha, and Tracy would all dress up and work as the waitresses, and my other friends would all come and drink for free. I had several alcohol companies on board. For food I even got the California Sushi Academy to join. They catered all our events. The next thing I was working on was arranging party trips with Aero México throughout Mexico. When not working, I mulled around dating lots and lots of girls and drinking lots and lots of vodka now paid for by the chamber.

By now a few people had asked about the photograph of the girl on the dashboard of my truck. Most of them being girls I was dating. You would think it would be awkward when girls asked me about the photo, but it wasn't. I loved when someone asked who she was. She had become this fictitious princess. I thought it was all rather poetic.

On one particular evening I was giving Aaron, a guy I knew, a ride home from the bar. Aaron was a bit of a prick, but I liked him because he would do this whole dance routine with his hands while singing the song, "Desperado's Waiting for a Train." I really don't know what it was that I found so compelling about the performance, but I loved it.

Anyhow, I was giving Aaron a ride home when he nonchalantly asked me, "So, how do you know Katie?" I had no clue who he was talking about, "Who's Katie?" I asked. "She's the girl in the photo, dude. She's my cousin," he said. Aw shit, she wasn't so perfect now. Now the girl had a name. The blend of creepy and funny had just strongly slanted towards being only creepy. My explanation made it all even worse. "I found it in the parking lot. I don't know her. But Here you go. Give it to her," I said handing him the photo. He got out of the car with the photo in hand. He either lied and now had my pretty girl photo or had a good story to tell over the next Thanksgiving dinner. Either way, Katie was gone forever. Things were just not going well for me.

I came up with other ideas I thought might be money makers, but I couldn't get any of them off the ground. I wanted to make rolling papers used for cigarettes or weed and put band's logos on them. I knew they would sell like crazy at concerts. I couldn't find any bands that would endorse it though. Even Phish turned me down. Tom Petty almost jumped on board, but then decided against it. I wanted to start an online survey company. I wanted to make double sided bras. I was full of ideas, but none of them were getting me anywhere.

During this time my parents took a trip to China. Unfortunately, my father was ill most of the trip. When he came back, he was having issues with one of his fingers. Turning black, it was quickly becoming gangrenous. None of us had ever had health insurance. My father paid money to a doctor to cut the top of his finger off, but the next day he got himself health insurance. It was the first time I had ever seen my dad hurt in any way. He was tough as nails. Stefanie had constantly told me I needed to grow up. Seeing my father struggling, I was beginning to feel that maybe that was what was happening. I felt my youth fading away as all this life stuff was beginning to pop up.

Chapter 117
The Cranberries

The Cranberries tour itinerary & all access pass, 2002.

On May 11th 2002 I got a call to go on tour with the Cranberries. I had to give them an answer quickly, my plane ticket would be for the next day. There was an emergency, and the carpenter had to leave the tour. It meant I wouldn't move in with my friend Chrerilyn, which I had been planning to do. The Chamber of Commerce I had been working hard to build would fall flat. And the numerous relationships I had with new women would come to an end. That part didn't matter so much; I knew I'd meet more. On the upside, I'd be bringing back seven thousand dollars in a few months. It was a quick decision; I even already had a packed suitcase ready to go. There was no need to call them back, "Yeah, I'll go, I said into the phone." I wasn't sure if taking the job was the grown-up thing to do, with my dad being sick, but I figured I would worry about that when I returned. Nothing much would change in a few months and I wanted to have a bit more fun.

I had only missed three shows with the Cranberries, so it was easy to catch up. The carpenter on the tour was doubling up. That meant he wasn't just the tour carpenter- he was also one of the tour drivers. I learned that he was being forced to leave because of his mother's failing health. I now felt comfortable with the duties of a carpenter, so I wasn't worried about what the job entailed. The nice thing about the tour was the schedule was friendly. We took a lot of days off, and the tour paid way more than Poison had. I was glad to be on the road again, but my first few days on the Cranberries was rough. I was sick as a dog.

Roadie Ramble Moment
Where did the saying sick as a dog originate from? It is a phrase that dates back to at least the 17th century. Being sick in Britain means to vomit. Dogs vomit a lot. Hence the saying, sick as a dog. Why do cats love fish but hate water? I'll let you stew on that one. I don't have a clue.

The stage consisted of several square boxes made of metal rods that connected together. Those square boxes were then covered with black cloth, which was tied to all sides. When done, they looked like big black squares. Or if you have ever seen a changing booth, that is exactly what each were. Each box was a place where the backline could set up shop and work for the day, and one of them actually did serve as a changing booth for Delores. The setup couldn't be much easier for a carpenter.

The guy's name I was replacing was Mike. He was a big guy, and a total truck driver looking dude. Mike had numbered every piece of metal for every square and none of that made any sense to me. "Hey, Mike, if all the pieces are the same size, and all the squares look the same, why are we building them using numbers?" I asked. The fury built deep down inside of Mike. "If you can't do the job the way I tell you to, I'm not leaving. This is an important job, and it needs to be done right," he told me. All I heard was no explanation to the question I had just asked. "OK, man no problem," I replied. I wondered if he'd let his mom die without him being there, in order to make sure the Cranberries stage looked good. Maybe he believed in one of Nigel's prized adages, "a little death never hurt anyone." Nigel was such an asshole, and yet I found myself now quoting him all the time.

The only roadie I knew on the tour was Aso from STP, and though he had got me the job, for whatever reason he wasn't being overly friendly. So, I figured I'd keep to myself and do my job and maybe he'd come around, but if he didn't, I would live. I had to finish the tour with no issues so that I could get back into Cesar's good graces and get work from him again. Keeping that in mind, I didn't talk to anyone but was always friendly.

Now knowing a bit about being a Rock 'n' Roll carpenter, the first thing I did was to replace Mike's ties with strips of Velcro. The second thing I did was a bit trickier.

Let's say Train A and Train B began traveling towards each other from opposite ends of a 500-mile long track at 1:00 PM. If Train A traveled at 35 miles per hour and Train B traveled at 25 miles per hour, at what time did the trains meet?

The answer is, drum roll please... the answer is, I don't give a fuck. Nor did I give a fuck about Mike's number system. The change I made wasn't trickier at all; In fact, I made it a lot simpler. Sober, I could set the stage up in just under 15 minutes with one stage hand. Hungover, it took about 40 minutes. Hungover and sick, in about an hour. Mike had taken two to three hours a day to set the stage up. That was because he was slow, had implemented an unnecessary number system, and he chose to tie the soft goods to the metal poles around each cube. I now slammed the cubes together fast without paying attention to any numbers and, I didn't tie off shit.

The genuine hardest part of the tour was to try and make sure the ping pong table the band had taken on tour with them didn't get too damaged in the truck. This job really was trickier; with the mileage we did, it wasn't that easy of a task. However, I devised a system of pillows, towels, and wood that seemed to work quite well. There was no question I spent more time sorting out the ping pong table than setting up the stage at any of our shows.

The show itself was very different from the other tours I had done. I was used to high testosterone, and the Cranberries shows were a lack there of. Large amounts of the audience were lesbian couples. The change was nice. Poison had been a big topless event. The Cranberries shows were different, they featured more lighters than naked women in the air. The gigs were calm, other than maybe Delores, who always looked a bit hostile as she paced back and forth on the stage. To me, she looked like she was psyching herself up for a fight when performing.

Roadie Ramble Moment
This is perhaps a touchy subject, so I'm going to approach it head on. Does a butch lesbian consider herself a butch failure if she catches a guy staring at her tits? I mean, if you are working at making yourself look male, it must be seriously disappointing. I'm not trying to be mean either. As a straight male when I see a butch lesbian, my eyes go straight to the tits. I want to see what's happening there. Luckily, all butch lesbians I've met are smarter than to want to hang out with a dumbass like me.

Chapter 118
Tumbleweed

We had been spending a fair amount of time driving on this tour. We were covering, and would be covering, a lot of U.S. miles. During that time Aso had created a new identity he lovingly labeled Tumbleweed. Tumbleweed was the biggest, dumbest hick in New England. Tumbleweed was a mixture of a few characters from the movie *Raising Arizona* and, of course, a compliment of Aso himself.

On our way to Boston from Philadelphia, we pulled into a truck stop. The entire front window of the truck stop was a nicely arranged display of window washing fluid. There were probably a couple hundred, gallon sized bottles stacked up. Tumbleweed pulled off his shirt, letting his huge belly flop over his belt, and put his fake teeth in. This truck stop was to be a first public appearance. With cigar in mouth, he sauntered into the truck stop and we all followed. Tumbleweed had quickly become a roadie favorite, and we all looked forward to seeing how the outside world would react to his genius.

"Got any window washing fluid for sale?" Tumbleweed seriously asked the clerk. He fixed his gaze directly on the man, waiting for an answer. It was the funniest thing I think I had ever seen. Tumbleweed did not laugh. "Um, yes, sir," said the store clerk. "Mind if I clean the windows of the bus out there with it?" he asked. "No sir," replied the store clerk. The man pulled a bottle out from under the counter. That made Aso, not Tumbleweed, laugh; but not ruining the moment, he pulled back into character quickly. How much window washing fluid did they have? There were hundreds on display, and yet they still had more under the counter?

"I'm glad you had some left," Tumbleweed said. He paid for the fluid in all change and walked out to the bus with the bottle. The bus was parked just outside the window and the rest of us mulled around the store looking for snacks, porno magazines, and any other crap to buy. I heard Deckie, one of the most Irish of the crew, laugh aloud and I looked up to see what he was laughing at. Deckie was a skinny fellow with hair down to his shoulders. He loved to smile but had rotted out teeth. What Deckie was laughing at was Tumbleweed, outside now, washing the windows of the bus completely naked. His balls kept slapping against the window as we watched him reach higher and higher to clean. The bus driver, who was still in the driver's seat, was a pretty serious sort of fellow. He looked on at Tumbleweed absolutely mortified. I hoped he'd be able to drive us out of there. When Tumbleweed was done cleaning the front window, he came back into the store naked and put the rest of the gallon of fluid back onto the counter. "I didn't need the whole bottle. Just in case you run out- ya know, fella," he said to the clerk, clicking his teeth without waiting for an answer and walked out of the truck stop and back onto the bus.

Chapter 119
McDonald's is a Restaurant

My 25th birthday was quiet. It was a driving day and so I didn't have much to do. On this tour we had had a lot of days off. I had done five shows with the Cranberries and had five days off in between. All the down time was unheard of for me. The tour was turning out to be a breeze. It was nice to have an easy, well-paying gig. I had never had one before. Earlier in the day we had driven from Boston to Wallingford, Connecticut. Wallingford was the place of the last witchcraft trial in New England in 1697. A small town, there are roughly 50,000 residents there. It's a nice little town. I think Aso may be the first man banned from there since that last witch trial.

A leisurely drive, the driver pulled into another truck stop as we got into Wallingford. This time, in honor of my birthday, Tumbleweed came out of the bus wearing nothing but his birthday suit and his fake teeth. A massive truck stop, he walked through the whole place looking at stuff in the buff. At this point I had seen Aso naked so many times I was as used to seeing his balls as he was. I went about my shopping and didn't pay much attention to him. Not that many other roadies on the tour bus would want to pay much attention to a fat naked guy. After I had bought a couple snacks, I got back onto the bus. Shortly thereafter, Tumbleweed was escorted out of the truck stop by an armed security guard, who had made it his job to ensure Aso got back onto our tour bus and left. I watched on while eating a bag of Funyuns. I delightfully washed each one down with a swig out of my personal bottle of vodka. I was drinking a bottle a day now. What a loser Tumbleweed was, I thought.

While back on the bus Aso showed me that he had actually taken the time to buy something while in the truck stop. He put two birthday cards down on the table. One had a cartoon caricature on the front and was clearly a funny card, while the other was a romantic card and so of course had a rose on the cover. "Here you go, Rifken," he said. Aso pushed both cards towards me, "I usually write the romantic shit down in the funny card and then throw away the romantic card when I give this to my wife, but you know she gives me a blowjob afterwards. So, I'm just gonna give you the cards and we will call it a day. You can write the romantic shit in the funny card yourself if you want to, though," he said. "Well, how thoughtful of you," I replied. And it was, it was very thoughtful.

Our next drive was to New York City. On the way we stopped at a McDonald's. Tumbleweed felt compelled to make yet another appearance. "McDonald's is ma favorite fine dining establishment," he told us while still on the bus. A large sign in the window for all to see stated, "No shirts No shoes No service." Tumbleweed took his shirt and shoes off in the front lounge of the bus. He left his socks on, which were full of holes. An upscale area, I wondered how many people walked in there with no shirts and shoes? Did they really need a sign? A few of us, including Tumbleweed, sat down at a table by the window. A lot of time off, complimented with easy workloads, meant that the crew could all be massive drinkers if we wanted to be. And we all wanted to be. The fact that most of the crew was Irish didn't make for less drinking, either. I had become accustomed to drinking a bottle of vodka a day. However, the drink of choice was Irish whiskey, and the bus went through a case of it a day. I kept to myself, but massive fights over football and European politics were daily occurrences that often led to fist fights.

Roadie Ramble Moment
Who is responsible for this global naming confusion of the most popular sport in the world? American football vs. football vs. soccer. For an American it's a mess. Let's begin

with soccer. The word soccer is believed to have originated in Britain roughly 200 years ago and it derives from the official name of the sport, "association football." As other games developed like Rugby Football, the British made different colloquialisms for each sport. American football is called as such because of its similarity to Rugby football. So now you know.

So, a bunch of very drunk roadies, with black eyes from fist fights over football, walk into a McDonalds in New York State. We all sat down, and within a few minutes the manager walked over to the table. "I cannot serve you without a shirt on," said the manager. "It's OK. I just came in to take a shit," replied Tumbleweed. It wasn't that funny, but we were all so drunk we were still impressed with the quick retort. The manager blew his lid. "This is a restaurant!" he yelled back in this odd, squeaky, angry little man voice. Tumbleweed took his cigar out of his mouth, removed his teeth, and fell completely out of character. "It's a fucking Mcdonald's, man," Aso said. Barrel laughing, Aso definitely thought the situation was much funnier than it actually was.

Out of nowhere Deckie yelled at me, "Rifken, you know I hear that Nanci Griffith slags off the crew." Anger built up within me. "You fucking plastic Irishman son of a bitch," I yelled back at him. Sensing Deckie was going to hit me, I abandoned my mission to get two cheeseburgers and a 6-piece chicken Mcnugget and rushed him. I slapped him once in the face, and then attacking sly like a fox, I took out his legs. He hit the floor like a broke' necked rabbit. None of this was hard to do- he was a bottle of whiskey deep. The sheer savagery of the event caused the other roadies to pull me off of him. While this is how I saw it all go down it is quite possible what really happened is I tried to walk over to him and knocked him over when I fell. The world may never know, as all the other roadies were just as drunk as we were.

"Jesus Christ, Rifken! That was brilliant," said Conor, another one of the roadies. "What you get so mad for?" asked Deckie. "Don't talk shit about Nanci," I barked at him.

Let's take a step back here for a moment. The randomness of the situation won't help with the understanding of it all, but let me explain the background behind the event anyway. I'm a big fan of the folk singer Nanci Griffith. This had been the only tour I had done where anyone had even heard of who she was, and that didn't surprise me. She had worked with the Chieftains at some point and had toured through Ireland. Knowing I liked her, Deckie had pushed my buttons a couple times. Using her as a carrot, he would entice me, and we'd start fighting. I wasn't going to let him talk shit about her.

Conor was enjoying the moment. He took a swig of whiskey and put the bottle back in his vest pocket. The Mcdonald's manager watched on in horror as he did so. "You know what slagged off means?" he asked me. I remained real serious. "Don't fuckin' start with me Conor," I said. "It just means talks shit to 'em a bit. What the hell you think it means?" he said to me. I had thought it meant sucked off the crew or something like that, but I didn't want to tell them that. "And you call him a plastic Irishman. That is pretty rude," Conor continued on. To explain, a plastic paddy is a person who doesn't act very Irish. It's rude, and to Deckie it was a touchy subject. Deckie hated to discuss it, but he had been born in England and raised in Ireland.

"Hey, I just gave him a little slap," I said. I'm going to go get a cheeseburger. "No, no you are not. You must leave," the manager said to me. I had totally forgotten about the manager being a problem. "Who's this asshole?" I asked. Deckie stepped next to me. "Yeah, who the fuck are you? We came in for some cheeseburgers?" None of us noticing, including the manager, Tumbleweed had made his way to the front of the MacDonald's line and was trying to order food himself.

We were all kicked out of the McDonald's after being told the police had been called. Since we had no food, we drank more. As the bus rolled on down the highway, I found myself slagging off most of the Irish crew. Bunch of fuckin' wankers.

Chapter 120
"With Arms Wide Open"

New York was bittersweet for me. While a great city, the last time I had been there I was head over heels for a girl. On top of being alone, it was my birthday and I had nothing to do. I had planned to go out with a few of the guys from the crew but they never called me. Making my way into Times Square, I looked for a lively bar to sit down and drink a few beers at. Fortunately, I found one; there was one seat left at a busy bar. I sat down on it. Looking around, there was a lot going on. It's not like a bar on Times Square is going to be quiet. The guy sitting next to me was wearing a full suit. I figured he had come from work. Most of the people in the bar were dressed nice, and so it was an easy assumption that most of them had come from work. The bartender was a younger guy who must have been on a coke bender. He was serving up drinks at a mile a minute while orchestrating the personnel in the place like a fine-tuned instrument. A song from the band Creed came on the jukebox, and I saw the bartender break his well-structured routine. His head cocked to the right and he stopped making a martini. "I hate this fucking song," he told the bar back. "I know," she said to him. He rushed over and skipped the song on the jukebox by pushing a button behind the bar. "I fucking hate that band," he mumbled to himself as he went back to work. My head jumped back to when STP played with Creed. I remembered that Creed had come on after Black Sabbath each night and the audience had all left each time.

The wheels in my head began to turn. It was time for a wind up. After all it was my birthday; If I had to, I'd create my own fun. I looked over at the man in the suit sitting next to me. "Watch this," I said to him. I walked over to the jukebox and played the Creed song "With Arms Wide Open" ten times in a row. Afterwards, I sat back down and waited.

I didn't think about it, when I put the money in, but I soon realized it could take hours for the music to play. "You in a rush, bud?" I asked the guy. "No, not really," he replied. "That's good." I bought him a beer and we started chatting. A little over an hour later Creed played on the jukebox. The bartender cocked his head to the right and stopped making a Manhattan. "Are you fucking kidding me?" he barked out to the same bar back. He walked over to where the little button hid that enabled him to skip the song. He pushed the button and went back to making the Manhattan. I nudged the man in the suit. "Yeah, he hates Creed," the guy said. I smiled widely and put my finger up. "With Arms Wide Open" started playing again. "What the fuck man!" yelled the bartender. He walked over and pushed the button and went back to his station. Again, the song played. And then it played again. The guy in the suit and the bar back were laughing hard now. "Yeah, fucking hilarious. I find out who did this, you're fucking cut off not for tonight, but forever." He said to the entire bar. "With Arms Wide Open," played again.

"Fuck. He may actually kick me out of here. I think there are still three more times it's going to play," I said while laughing. "Don't worry it will be hard for him to kick you out. I kind of own the place," said the man in the suit. My eyes opened wide. I couldn't even begin to guess what this bar must be worth. "With Arms Wide Open" came on again. "All right - fuck it. You guys can listen to this shitty song too. I'm fucking over it." The song played almost all the way through, but he couldn't handle it and skipped it once again. Luckily, that was the last play. It's nice when a wind up works like it is supposed to. I told my new friend it was my birthday, and he covered my tab for the night. In all I was having a good birthday.

Chapter 121
When Life Gets in the Way

When I got back to my room, I called this girl in Florida I had been speaking to a lot lately. Her name was Sam. While on the phone with her, my friend Matt called. He was the first of the friends I grew up with to deal with the untimely death of a loved one. His father had cancer and was dying. I didn't pick up his call, because I was talking to the girl. It was of course more important at the time. I talked to her for an hour or so. I'd be hanging out with her in a couple weeks when the Cranberries made their way down to Florida. When off the phone, I called Matt back. He was sobbing and told me he wasn't ready for his father to die. There wasn't much I could say. I went to sleep. It was kind of a somber way to end a birthday. The next morning we'd play at the Hammerstein Ballroom. I thought it would be a fun show.

After New York, we flew home for just short of a week. While there, it was obvious there was clearly something wrong bigger than a messed-up finger. In China my father had had some blood circulation problems, and my mom said he could hardly walk. Now that they had health insurance, they were going to the doctor to see what precisely was really going on.

We learned that the top of his finger needed some more work. While I was at the hospital, they drugged him to clean it up, and he started hitting on the nurses. To stop that, they drugged him up more. The problem with those drugs is that when you come down, you crash hard. He slept the whole day. I'd never seen him do that before.

I tried to spend time with both my friend Matt and my family, but truthfully, I was anxiously waiting to go back on the next leg of the tour. It was an easy gig and I was having fun getting plastered every day. A close second to the fun of screwing off on tour was the thrill of seeing Puerto Rico and Mexico. A big fan of Mexican art, I was very excited about seeing Mexico City and all the murals firsthand.

On May 24th I flew out to meet the rest of the crew in Detroit. I always liked Detroit. Squirrel, one of the lighting guys, set up a double date with a pair of professional ice skaters. We had a good time with the girls. We would have invited them to the show the next day, but we were informed Delores didn't like girls hanging out unless they were "legitimate girlfriends or wives." Squirrel and I were pretty certain that no girl would want to be legitimate girlfriends, and absolutely certain not wives, to either of us, so we decided to drink more rather than deal in women woes.

That night I found out that Holmes had continued the chamber of commerce without letting me know. At first, I was mad that he was going to keep running the machine I had created, but then thought about it and was glad that it had legs without me. Maybe Holmes could make a career out of it without me?

We played a couple nights more and then cancelled a show. Dolores had laryngitis. We were heading to Florida where I was going to hang out with Sam. Word amongst the camp began to spread that we may cancel the show in Florida as well. Hearing the news, I started stock piling alcohol. If we cancelled the shows, that would give me lots of time with nothing to do. Sam and I would party our asses off! While I did party for four days with Sam in Florida, Delores and the Cranberries did do the show. It was the best of both worlds. They had put me up in a suite that overlooked the ocean; I had lots and lots of alcohol, and now a pretty decent looking chick to hang out with. Life was good.

Unfortunately, while having fun in Florida my friend Matt lost his dad. I was sorry I was away and I wasn't able to be there for my friend. I thought about my own father at home sick with pneumonia. It's tough to not be around sometimes.

Leaving Florida, we headed to Puerto Rico. Landing just outside the city of San Juan, we drove into the city. The band had put us up at a resort that had a full casino in it. A quick glance over, the place felt like a mini Rio De Janeiro to me. I walked through the lobby grinning. This place was going to be fun. Upon arrival, we found a bunch of good blow. So now we had booze, blow, gambling, and a bunch of hot chicks patrolling the hotel lobby. It was like a mini Rio! I was starting to like the Cranberries more and more. That night we stayed in the hotel and partied. The more blow I did, I felt like I was surrounded by leprechauns. The remedy to me was to drink more vodka. At some point during the night, I took a couple of the girls down to the casino. I lost $150 within 10 minutes and walked them back up to the room. The night soon turned into day and then back into night again. At the end of it all, I had an extra $350 from the casino and a bad hangover. On the 9th the Cranberries played at Roberto Clemente Coliseum in San Juan. The show was pieced together by a bunch of very hungover leprechauns dressed up as roadies.

The Cranberries tour rain slicker, 2002.

After the San Juan show, we headed to Atlanta. I was looking forward to getting there; I was going to take a much-needed rest. Puerto Rico had been a lot of fun, but I needed to recover.

I cruised up to my suite and ran a bath. I had grabbed a bottle of Irish whiskey from the bus. It was June 10th, 2002 and things had been going well but, then real life decided to step in the way.

I called home now that I was back in the United States, and my mom picked up. Her voice seemed distant, and I immediately knew something was wrong. "Something has happened," she told me. The conversation was a quick one. I found out that my father, the toughest guy I had ever met, was in the hospital and was in a bad way. He had been complaining all day that he wasn't feeling well. Towards the evening he asked my mom to take him to the hospital. On the way, my mom said he was cursing and thrashing around in the car. He then called out my name and went quiet. My mom thought he had fallen asleep, but he had actually stopped breathing. Upon arriving, she ran out of the car and into the emergency room. Quickly, they had him on a gurney and rushed him in. Far away in a hotel room I was picturing all of this happening in my head. My mother was strong, but I couldn't get the visual out of my head of her running into the hospital while my dead father was in the car.

The staff told my mom that it was good she had driven to the hospital and that she made it just in time. They were able to resuscitate my father. Calling 911 would have taken longer, and he wouldn't have lived. She told me that they had him heavily sedated. When he started to wake up, not understanding where he was and what was going on, he'd start punching people. He had already hurt a couple nurses. Her words were few, and her sentences were short. I could hear how tired she was. She was emotionally wrecked and I was far, far away.

I knew how difficult and strong my dad could be, and I didn't envy those nurses. The image of my father chained up in a hospital bed further upset me. I drank most of the bottle of whiskey in the bath and thought about how my life, and the life of my family, was now destined for change.

On June 13th I waited in the airport ready to fly home. I had decided not to tell anyone at work what was going on. I wanted to make sure I would keep my job. If my father wasn't going to be able to make any money, someone would have to. If I let anyone know what was going on, they would have let me go. They would replace me with someone else, just like they had done with the guy I replaced. I wasn't just thinking about having fun on the road anymore. I was thinking about making some money to help my family if they needed it. It had been three days now and my father was still constantly fighting. He kept trying to break through the chains. I wish I could say they were metaphoric chains, but they weren't. I was informed all four of his limbs were chained to the bed. To make matters worse, my mom had recently had a mammogram and the results of that hadn't come back good either. She had cancer. I was eager to get home to support my family the best I could, but also fearful for the next chapter of my life.

Chapter 122
If you Really Want to, Dad

In the airport waiting, I decided to call the girl whose phone number I had got the night before. It would be a good distraction. When I called, I got her answering machine. "Hey, guys. This is Jessica. Leave a message. Tee hee." I didn't leave a message but wondered how many guys had. The word *guys* had stood out enough on the machine message that I really felt it was directed to an amphitheater of men. I wondered if women ever left messages for this Jessica. Did she not want them to? Did she have a separate number for her girlfriends? While boarding the plane and heading back to Los Angeles, my mom informed me they had stopped sedating my dad. I wondered if he'd know who I was when I got there.

The next day I got home and went to the hospital to see what was going on. I was told by the nurse on duty that he had been physically fighting to get out of bed for four days now. He hadn't recognized anyone yet but kept using all of his energy to try and break free from the bed restraints. I could see his hands and legs had marks on them from the chains. Not much I could do; I held his hand and sat with him. He just looked so tired.

I was informed they had unchained him at one point and he had removed the catheter and breathing tube from himself. They had left the breathing tube out but put the catheter back. The nurse told me pulling that out must have been extremely painful, but he did it. After that they hadn't removed the chains again. I cringed thinking about the pain of putting the catheter in a second time.

The nurse left the room, and immediately my dad opened his glossed over eyes. Hearing the faint whisper, "Joel," I leaned in to hear him. "Yeah," I quietly replied back. "Volkswagens are the greatest car ever made," he said. No, that is not what he said but he did look at me sternly. "Get me out of here," was what he said. Though quiet, he spoke with the fury of a caged lion. I smiled. I knew they weren't going to keep him down! He was way more alert than anyone thought. He took his hand away from mine and picked up the arm restraint. "Dad, I'll loosen them but you got to be good, okay?" My dad glared at me; his eyes filled with frustration. "Dad, I really mean it." I loosened one of the restraints and my dad seemed to smile a faint smile. I had left the lion's cage ajar. He pulled his hand out of the cuff and began to get out of bed. "Dad! Dad! you have to take it easy. You are going to hurt yourself," I yelled at him. He still had the catheter in. He was going to rip his dick apart. I tried to push him back into the bed, but though I had started this myself, I knew I wouldn't be able to fix it myself. I had totally messed up, and I knew it. I ran to the door and called for help. The nurse ran in and, she called for help. It took three nurses and me to push him back down to chain him up again. What had I done? Throughout the experience my father's eyes remained focused on me. I took a step back, and the nurses stepped in front of me to tighten his restraints again. I watched on as he clenched his teeth in anger. Reminding me of the Incredible Hulk, his hands then balled in tight fists of fury and his legs bulged as he flexed them, unable to move. Heavily sedated, he again fell asleep.

I was devastated. This was not easy. The nurses and I left the room. I apologized to them, but I wasn't surprised when no one replied. My apology held no water. No one was happy with me. Perhaps the consolation prize of replies, I was informed by one of the nurses, "Your father needs to conserve his energy," and then she left me alone to sit in a chair outside the room in a state of confusion. Within a few minutes, some doctor came up to speak with me. "Can we chat for a few minutes?" he asked. If I had hoped for good news, he wasn't the one to give it to me. "Your father is really sick." I didn't need him to tell me; I didn't respond. "Are you going to be able to be around?" he asked me. "I'll be here for the next week or so and then I have to leave again," I told him. The doctor took off his glasses and looked at me. "I'd be surprised if your father lives for more than a few weeks. I really think you should change your plans and stay local. If you could try and be around during shift changes it would be better. Usually, we ask for family and friends to leave, but he hasn't been easy to deal with. We have to change the sheets, and it might be easier if you were here to help." He replied, picking up his notepad and leaving.

This was all a lot to take in. I walked back by the room and saw the lion now sleeping. I left. As I walked out of the hospital, I felt like I was turning my back on my father. He had asked me for help, and instead I had locked him back up. He had never asked me for anything in my life. He didn't like anyone helping him. It would have been easier if he had asked me to move car parts around all those years. Underlying all of this though, in the deep part of my belly, I was proud. It seemed my father thought that I was the only one who could help him in his time of need. There was clearly a lot going on in my head.

I went home to see my family. My grandmother, on my father's side, had flown in and was staying with us. A horrible person, none of us were happy she was there. Talking to her was tough. I tried my best to be nice to her because she was my grandmother. My sisters and my mom most certainly didn't make any effort at all. They were smarter than me. I thought maybe one day I could win her graces and she'd be nicer to talk to, but that never happened. Nothing my sisters or I ever did was good enough. She was just flat out mean. My father's father had passed away when I was very little. I don't remember much about him, but I do remember him calling me Jammy. My middle name is Adam and so my initials are JAM. I suppose he thought it was a cute nickname. However, at six years old I didn't understand why he called me Jammy. The look on his face of him thinking I wasn't very bright is emblazoned in my head. It's my only real memory of the man. Well, that and him on a gurney being carried off to the hospital. Ahh, the memories.

Over the next two days my dad began to make some progress. I spent Father's Day with him, helping him walk to the bathroom and change his diaper. He had remembered everything. He pulled the catheter out because he was trying to make it to the bathroom without relieving himself in the bed. When explained that he was supposed to relieve himself in the bed, his response was, "How ridiculous."

Though it was horrible to see my father in this state, I had never spent as much time with him, and I was appreciating that. Within no time at all he was trying to get the nurses to date me and was back to being a smartass. While I did my best to explain to him this was all serious, I don't think he could help himself. He was happy to be alive and ready to get back to his old self. Several times he openly cried, shocked by modern medicine. "I was dead, and they brought me back, Joel," he kept repeating to me. "Can I call you Rifken?" he asked me. It was hard not to laugh a bit. Was that really what he was worried about? "Yeah, if you really want to, Dad."

For a day they brought him to a new shared room and removed his permanent sitter. I had known that would be a bad idea. He had been in his own room and had the permanent sitter because of both how hard he was for the nurses to deal with, and how he kept pulling things out of himself to try and get out of bed. The guy he was now in the room with kept shouting out racial slurs. "This is America," my father would scream at the guy after the asshole would yell out the word "N-gger." "Do you think your father may really get up and do something to him?" one of the nurses asked me quietly. "If you are asking me, you already know the answer," I told her. I think she was questioning whether my father would hurt a man who was only semiconscious. I looked at my father with tears of rage and then back at the nurse. He was moved back to his own room not long after that.

I'd sit with my father and try to have conversations, but some things don't change. He wasn't easy to talk to. When one of the big male nurses would come in, he'd half joke with them. "If you hadn't have had me chained into this bed, I would have hurt you, you know," he said. The nurse smiled. "That's why we had you chained up, sir," was the nurses reply. My father was the king of awkward conversation. Truth is, he would have hurt him. They must have been very aware of that though, considering the shiner and concussion the absentee nurse now had. He had been sent home on paid leave.

My grandmother interacting with my father was very strange. Watching the two of them, it was clear they didn't know one another very well. She had never really been a mother to him. She had sent him away at five years old to a boarding school and kicked him out of the house when he came home at sixteen. And yet she flew out immediately when he was ill? For her, motherly love worked in strange ways. I don't know what they talked about while visiting with one another.

The days crunched on, and various tests came back. They found my dad had a tumor in his colon. This greatly upset him because it was how his father had died. He was tired of the tests and wanted to go home. To pick up my dad's spirits, I figured I'd call Jay Leno and ask him to call into the hospital to see how he was doing. Jay had no problem doing it. I didn't tell my father, and asked Jay to call in to the nurse's station. The staff was super excited that a celebrity was on the phone, and Jay joked around with them a bit on a speaker phone. They then patched the phone call into my dad's room. I walked into the room pretending not to know a thing. Pleased, I could hear Jay talking to my father.

"What the hell is wrong with you? I'm in the hospital and you want me to fix your car? Are you kidding me?" My dad abruptly hung up the phone. Well, that didn't go well, I thought. I rushed back out to the nurse's station and asked to use the telephone. I called Jay back, and when he picked up, all I heard was laughter. Luckily, he thought the situation was hilarious. "I hope your dad gets better, Joel. I'd really miss him."

The next day the full diagnosis came back, and it wasn't good. A cancerous mass had spread throughout his body. It wasn't just in his colon. They had found some in his liver, his spine, and his rectum. If they looked on, I was told they'd probably find more. He had water around his lungs and heart, and his blood pressure was still very high. On top of it all, his kidneys were no longer functioning. That night my uncle, a cancer doctor, came over to visit my mother. He told her that things were not good and my dad wasn't going to get through this.

I was supposed to be leaving to go back on the road in three days. I still didn't know if I was going to get on that plane. I had been putting together a business plan to try and make teddy bears to sell to the Cranberries. I figured if I could make Cranberries teddy bears, I would sell a lot at the shows. However, with everything going on, I hadn't had the time to finish the presentation.

As things were coming down the pipeline, I learned they were going to let my dad come home for a few hours, and my mom was going to go in for breast cancer surgery the day after I was scheduled to leave. I knew I should be there for those things. I hoped my father got through all of this and defied medical odds. If he did, I was certain he would enjoy his life a bit more. He would undoubtedly be a bit more appreciative of what he had and maybe even have a bit of fun rather than just work all the time.

The following day my little sister graduated high school. My father came home for a short while to see her walk across the stage. I don't remember ever seeing him happier. He was ecstatic to be home. I worried if we would be able to get him to go back to the hospital. He didn't argue when the time came though. Rushing to get as much done as he could in the last few minutes, when we did take him back, he was worn out. I rolled him in a wheelchair back into the hospital room. A nurse took over from there. He sat in the chair with his head hung low. He looked like a little school boy. He was beaten and he knew it. He wasn't going to win this fight. The hope was that he could do chemotherapy from home, but the doctors didn't think he'd live long enough to make that a reality. I gave him a hug and a kiss on the head. One of the few times I had ever shown either of my parents any affection.

Chapter 123
Tequila

That same night I left to go to Mexico. Not knowing where money was going to be coming in from, it was something I needed to do. It was perhaps the first multi-layered decision of my life. I left, not knowing if I'd see my father again, and I hoped the last image of him wasn't to be a broken boy in a wheelchair. I wondered if this was the same look he had when he was five years old and his parents sent him off to that boarding school. Was I leaving him like they had?

From the airport I called Stefanie in New York. I hadn't talked to her for a while, and I was looking for comfort from someone. She probably wasn't the right person to call, but I couldn't think of anyone else. I explained to her what was happening. "Well, you know, Joel, sometimes people need heavy things to happen to get their butt in gear," she told me. It wasn't what I had hoped to hear. I got off the phone and waited for the plane. I'd be gone for two weeks.

The Cranberries artist pass Mexico City, 2002

I landed in Mexico City on the 23rd of June. This was the part of the tour I had been most excited about. I was going to be able to spend a full four days in Mexico City. I would be able to see many of the murals I had learned about in college. While the ticket sales in the United States hadn't been that great, Mexico City was different. The Cranberries were hugely popular there. There were hundreds of people outside the stadium, and at the hotel, hoping to get a glimpse of the band members. I knew Mexico was going to be a memorable experience.

That night, Aso and I went out and hit the town. I told him what was going on at home but asked him not to tell anyone. It felt good to confide in someone. That night he was a good friend, and we had a muy bueno time. The band were all hanging out at the last bar we hit up. They had all already been drinking and were overly happy to see the two of us. Delores made a point to have me sit down next to her. I still hadn't talked to her the entire tour. When she spoke to me, I'd nod. When on stage, I'd point. However, I'd never speak. I had figured early on that if I didn't say much, I wouldn't have any problems with her.

"Now, Fergal says you speak and I want to hear it," she said to me. I smiled back at her. It was hard not to. "I'm buying you a tequila." She seemed to be excited at the thought of drinking the stuff. "I actually don't drink tequila," I replied. "You will when I'm buying it." Not the time to argue, I nodded approval. "What's your name?" she asked. "Rifken," I responded. "No, what's your real name?" That night we had shot after shot of truly amazing tequila. In due course, it didn't take long for me to become a big tequila fan, but though polite, I still kept my words few.

When I got back to the hotel room, the ceiling in the bathroom had caved in. Was this symbolic of my life? No, I was just drunk and tired in Mexico. I moved some of the debris out of the way, used the toilet, and went to sleep anyhow.

The next day was a day off, and I was going to go see kickass murals and the Museum of Anthropology. I first changed my hotel room, and then on my way out ran into Aso in the lobby. We decided to have brunch at the bar across the street from the hotel where we had drunk most of the night before. We walked out of the hotel to find a girl waiting out front. "I'll give you $20 bucks to kiss her feet Riffy," Aso told me. "That American money?" I asked. Before I could get a reply, I walked over to her, got down on my knees, and tried to kiss her feet. She backed away, very embarrassed, and hurried off. The hotel staff and Aso loved it.

When we got to the little bar across the street, we were glad to find that the staff working there were as hungover as we were. Having a good chat with the workers, we informed them that we intended to be cultural that day but would probably be back a little later. They, in turn, informed us that the museums were all closed on Mondays. "Well, I guess we'll just start drinking then. Huh, Aso?" We walked around most of the day and drank at various bars. I got back to the hotel in the afternoon and passed out until 11PM. We loaded in at midnight for the show. Other than drinking, I spent most of the day thinking about what I could do with my life next. I thought more about being a singer of a band. I couldn't sing but I understood stage presence, which I clearly saw had a lot to do with success. I thought about writing a script about two elderly people who were terminally ill but fall in love, but that was a bit somber. Through the midst of all the life thoughts and tequila, I called home to see how things were going. The call was a good one. The doctors now didn't think my father's cancer had spread as much. They were sending my father home and my mom would be taking him to UCLA for more testing. My mom's cancer was also not going to be life threatening. All was better than when I had left. I hung up the phone beaming. Life was good!

Chapter 124
Guadalajara

The Cranberries all access pass Guadalajara, 2002.

We all worked most of the night, but the next day we again had off. I was finally going to be able to get to go see Mexico City. Knowing things were getting a bit better at home, I was able to relax slightly and see the city I had only dreamt of visiting. I hired a driver for the day and got to see most of the murals and sights. I am quite certain I never broke my smile the entire day. The only damper on the situation was I didn't feel very well. Both my head and stomach ached all day. I didn't let it get to me, though, and savored my day. That night the Cranberries played the first of a two-night gig at the Auditorio Nacional. I still felt sick; I should have been drinking more tequila and less water. I had somehow got Montezuma's revenge and it was kicking my ass. I spent as much time as possible sleeping ("aka pulling up road cases") behind the stage.

The next morning, I again called home to see how things were going. My mom hadn't gone in for surgery but instead had some more tests done. What they found was she had a small growth of cancer in her breast. The situation was still not life threatening.

On the 27th we flew to Guadalajara. I was still fighting off being ill and spent most of my time in the hotel. I figured out quickly that the room service in Guadalajara sucked. Wanting to get a feel for the place, I watched the streets while on the trips from the airport to the hotel and from the hotel to the venue. The first thing I noticed was a billboard that was advertising a man who was both a lawyer and a dentist. Talk about being a jack of all trades. I wondered what his office looked like. Had he become a lawyer or a dentist first? The next thing that struck me was a beat up 1970's Toyota on axle stands in front of a mechanic shop. It was spray painted "completo" on the side of it. Did the humor bring in business? It didn't look very completo to me. Just before we got to the venue on the other side of the road, a cop car rushed by us. It was a 1980's Toyota, and smoke was coming out of the exhaust pipe like John Candy's car in *Uncle Buck*. It sped down the road at top speed, maybe 40 miles an hour. When we got to the venue there was a Virgin Mary altar. Above it was a no smoking sign and all around that were lit candles. I wondered if fifty lit candles were safer than one lit cigarette. Rushing off to the bathroom for the 100th time in two days, I'd have more time to think more about all I had just taken in. During the show that night, I found out that all Mexican girls had one thing in common. They weren't interested in me.

During the performance one of the local security guys kept standing in my way. I asked him to move the first time and didn't think anything of it. By the third time I was wondering what the hell was wrong with the guy. I wasn't used to this. Usually, at gigs the security people are easy to deal with. This guy was just dumb. "Hey compadre, get the fuck out my way," I said. The guy turned around to look at me. "How many times do I have to fucking ask you to get the fuck out of my way," I said again. He turned back around and didn't move. The issue I had was he was standing right in the path where the band would soon be exiting the stage. I walked over to another security person. "Tell your director of security to fucking come up here." Shortly thereafter, the director of security came up to the stage. "Tell this asshole to get out of the fucking way. Better yet, just tell him to get the fuck off my stage." The director of security looked down at me. "You are in Mexico, not in the United States." That was all he said, and he walked away. I didn't know what to say to that. I couldn't help but laugh. When the band came off at the end of the show, they ran around the security guard. I guess we all have to make statements in life. This guy's statement was to not only stand tall, but to be in the way, both whenever and wherever. The next day we flew to Las Vegas. We'd be there for four days.

Chapter 125
A Hotel Room Fit for A Princess

The Cranberries tour T-shirt, 2002.

I was glad to be back in the United States. If I did need to fly home, it wouldn't be a big deal now. I was also starting to feel better. I wouldn't wish Montezuma's revenge on my worst enemy. It is rough stuff.

The night we arrived in Vegas, we all went out and hit the town. I think most of us arrived drunk, so the natural thing to do was to keep the party going. That night the band and crew hit the casinos and strip clubs hard. We started off at the Hard Rock and quickly found ourselves mobbed by a large bachelorette party. The girls had a list of things they had to try and do before the end of the night. One of the things on the list was to take a photo with a rock star. The girl handed her camera off to Fergal, the drummer of the Cranberries, to take a photo with Deckie. The irony was remarkable, of all the people in the casino to hand her camera off to. I really wanted to tell her how funny what she had done was. The band, and especially Fergal, didn't want me to though, and so I reluctantly kept it to myself and she never knew.

Roadie Ramble Moment

Who created the bachelor/bachelorette party? Who was the superstar who talked his soon to be wife into throwing one last hurrah? If marriage is supposed to be so exciting, why would you need a big party before entering into it?

This is how I envision it having happened. "Hey, honey pooky bear," said the guy to his fiancée. "Yes, love of my life," replied the woman. "Can I go out with Stan and Jim for a quick little send off before we tie the knot?" he'd ask. She'd giggle and say, "Oh, like you aren't going to hang out with your friends once we are married?"

"Well, sure I am honey. We are just going out for a bit of fun is all," he'd say. "Oh, OK, well I hope the three of you have a bit of fun then," she'd tell him through a gorgeous smile. She'd have to be pretty right? This guy was a super stud to pull this one off.

That night the guy, we will call him Joel, went out and got lots of hookers and did cocaine all night. He came back a total mess. But the important part was he came back. He still got married, but once married, Joel couldn't hang out with Stan and Jim much. Now when Stan and Jim were ready to get married, Joel's wife told their fiancées they better have bachelorette parties. That must be how the traditions began.

The night continued on, becoming mostly a blur. Having partied all night, in the morning I found myself playing the card game War at a table with a really gorgeous card dealer. "Honey, you are really sweet. Do you know you are betting 100 to 500 dollars a hand and you are playing the game 'war'?" I didn't know that. Nor did I really even know where I was. However, her words snapped me out of my haze. I put the chips in my pocket and smiled at her. "Thank you so much! I want to give you a hug," I said. Immediately, two big casino security guys flanked her. "I want to, but I'm not gonna," I said through what I thought was a coy smile and headed off to find my room. I slept all day, and when I woke up, I found $1100 bucks in casino chips in my pocket. I knew I hadn't started with much, so it was a pleasant surprise. For the next couple days, I hid out in my hotel room. I left once and lost a quick $150 at the blackjack table before scurrying back to my suite to hide. I was determined to leave Vegas up a few bucks. The hotel in Vegas was nice. I got chocolates every day, and it had a big heart shaped bathtub in the bathroom.

On July 2nd we played our show in Vegas. I had been there for two and a half days already. Other than the first night I hadn't hung out with anyone and instead happily ate the new chocolates they left in my room every day.

I spent most of my time on the phone with my parents making sure they were doing well. My mom was nervous about her own health and my father was very down on himself. He kept saying, "everything was so perfect." You could feel the cogs in his head crank slowly as he was trying to digest his own mortality. "I'm going to die," he'd tell me. It seemed that no matter how he ran through the shuffle of cards in his head the outcome was always the same. He had lost. "We are all going to die, Dad," I told him, doing my best to make sense of the situation. I had begun lecturing my two sisters about life goals and direction. It wasn't appreciated. My little sister shut me up quickly. "What do you want me to do? Sleep with a bunch of women, do a lot of drugs, and drink every day?" she yelled at me over the phone. I didn't quite know how to answer that one. But I didn't have to, she hung up on me. She had never been confrontational towards me. I had never lectured her on life, though. "I do not do drugs," I replied to no one. It was true. I didn't do that many drugs.

My sister took no shit. I liked that. That day, I spent the rest of my time in my hotel room going through my little black book and throwing away phone numbers from girls I either didn't remember or wasn't interested in seeing again. A little roadie housekeeping.

Before the show in Vegas, Delores made a point to find me. "Hey, Joel, what do you think of your hotel room?" she asked. "Very nice. Thank you," I responded. "Like the heart shaped bathtub?" she asked. "Oh, you had one too?" I asked back. "We put you in the honeymoon suite. It was a joke," she said to me. "Oh, I wondered why I got chocolate every day," I replied. "No flowers?" she asked. "Oh, no. I had flowers too," I said laughing. She winked back at me and walked out on stage.

Chapter 126
The Warfield

From Las Vegas we flew to San Francisco. We were playing the Warfield. The venue is suitably named. The Warfield was originally built in 1922 as a Vaudeville theater. It is a cool venue in a really bad area of San Francisco called the Tenderloin. While hanging outside and waiting for the show to start, I watched a car accident where a guy got out of his car and punched the other driver in the face. I saw a bum take a shit on the street, though I tried not to. I witnessed a whole bunch of different drug deals go down, and all this happened while hookers, cops, and I watched on. We were all eyeballing one another. It was business as usual at the Tenderloin. Most of the band's road cases were lined up outside the venue and for whatever reason nobody on the street paid any attention to them. I wondered if that was the one rule of the Tenderloin: don't mess with the Warfield's stuff. Eating my lunch, I wondered who would go see the Cranberries when they could watch the street. It was a much better show.

After San Francisco we headed down to Los Angeles. We were playing the Greek. It was our second to last show of the leg. The next leg was going to be in Asia. The band put us up in the hotel I had become all too familiar with. It was the same hotel where I had knocked my head on the doorknob, where my girlfriends had partied all night only to then embarrass me at the bus in the morning, and where I had stayed while working for Guns N' Roses when I was too tired to drive back to my parents' house.

Across the street from the hotel was where one of my ex's lived. I usually reached out to her when I stayed there. When I called her this time, she informed me she couldn't meet up because she had to clean her closet. I loved the excuse. I found it incredibly cute that it annoyed her that I found it so funny. The fact someone would rather clean their closet than hang out with me was too good to make up. I went downstairs to the hotel bar and found Aso. I told him what had happened. "I think you should go over there and see if she's really cleaning her closet," he told me. "I totally should, shouldn't I?" I replied. "She have a restraining order against you?" he further pried. "She sure doesn't," I said. "Well, then what are you waiting for?"

I got up and walked towards the front door of the hotel. "Oh, and Riffy one last thing," Aso cried out. "Yeah?" I turned back around. "You should totally be naked," he said. "Of course, I should," I quickly replied, not missing a beat.

When I got to her apartment, I knocked on her door, and she opened it abruptly. She looked great. No woman looks sexier than when wearing a Rock 'n' Roll shirt and jeans. The first thing I noticed was, I hadn't remembered her tits being so big. "What do you want," she said to me. I wanted to say tits but I knew she'd slam the door in my face. "To help you clean your closet. I know it's a big undertaking," I told her. She shook her head and let me in the door. "Years ago, you used to get excited when I came over," I said. "Yeah, well, times have changed," she replied. She had piles of clothes out on the floor. "Holy shit, you really are cleaning your closet." She laughed a super cute laugh. "Yeah, I told you I was. If you piss me off or try and touch me, I'm kicking you out of here." Across the carpet were various photos of a man. Seeing the photos, I quickly pieced together what was going on. "Going through a break-up?" I asked her. "I don't want to talk to you about it," she replied. "I tell you what. Why don't we put these photos in a shoebox together, and you agree not to open the box up for a while." After a moment she agreed, "You know what, that is actually a good idea." Together, we put all the photos into a box and when done, I taped the top shut. We found our eyes awkwardly locking. "Why are you staring at me?" she asked, breaking up the moment. "Your tits are way bigger than I remember," I blurted out. "Ok, I warned you," she said and directed me to the door. Through laughter I told her, "OK, OK, I'll be good." She gently pushed me into the hallway. "I warned you." Laughing, she closed the door in my face. It was a nice day, and I had a good stroll back to the hotel where I found Aso still at the bar. "How did it go?" he said. Most of the crew were with him now. "She call the cops?" one of the crew guys asked. "I made a comment about her boobs and she kicked me out," I said to no one in particular. The whole bar laughed and I witnessed money and drinks exchange hands. "She definitely has a restraining order now Riffy, so I'd watch yourself," Aso said, not wanting to miss an opportune moment. Since no one else did with their new found riches, I bought myself a beer. I didn't know why I was proud of myself. I couldn't think of a single reason I should be, but I smiled from ear to ear.

The show at the Greek was nice. My mom and two sisters came and had a good time. My father was still in the hospital and so didn't make it. We hung out as a family, and no one discussed health problems. I knew the tour would end in a few days and I'd be back home anyhow, but it was still good to see them. I introduced everyone to the band and we all had a relaxing evening. Pleased that LA had been a break of fun for my family, I went off to do the last show of the leg in San Diego.

Chapter 127
The End of the Road

The Cranberries VIP access pass & Viejas Concerts sweatshirt, 2002.

The highlight of the last show actually happened before the show began. A truck driver who was backing up into the loading dock hit a fire hydrant. The promotor's liaison had just introduced herself to Aso and me by informing us what a big fan of the Cranberries she was. This was a clear indication she was new. Anyone who had been doing her job for any period of time knew better than to talk to the road crew. We weren't polite, and we didn't care. In fact, if you were any kind of corporate person, you could rest assured, we would ramp up the attitude. Most of the time what the suits didn't realize was they were in our way, boring, and not helpful at all. In summation, they just pissed us off.

So back to the story, this woman is talking to Aso and me while thumbing through some crap on her clipboard. While pretending to listen to her, Aso and I were really paying attention to this big rig truck as it was backing into the loading dock.

The guy seemed to have it under control, but then all of a sudden, he started cutting the wheel towards the fire hydrant. He smacked the hydrant good and proper, and water spouted everywhere. The driver pulled the truck forward, and we watched on at the now twenty-foot geyser. It looked like a mini "Old Faithful." Not that the driver could hear him, but Aso yelled out a necessary, "What the fuck, dumbass? Is this your first day driving a truck, you fucking idiot?" The truck driver jumped out of the truck and put his head into his hands. He threw his cowboy hat at the floor and started cussing. He knew this was going to be a nightmare for him. "Little late to get out of the truck now, dumbshit. What the hell you expecting to see? It not being a big deal?" Aso continued to yell to the guy.

The lady escalated the situation by panicking. "We need to close off the area and call the fire department immediately," she told me. I looked on at her and smiled. I said nothing. Neither one of those things were my job. I knew better than to get involved in anything that had nothing to do with me. More and more people headed over to see what the commotion was all about. The lady kept droning on in a panic driven frenzy. She began to grab safety cones and put them around the lake that was now forming in the parking lot.

In a moment of roadie genius Aso and I looked at each other knowing what had to be done. He took the cigar out of his mouth and smiled at me. He put on the southern drawl. "Boy, Tumbleweed hates getting hot," he said. Aso took off his shirt, put in his fake teeth, and started jumping around in the man-made lake. I took off my shirt and ran after him. The lady went berserk. She was furious. Aso took off the rest of his clothes, leaving just his shoes and socks on, and rolled around in the water like an elephant seal. I jumped around and wondered how long it would take for her to lose her voice. I laughed and was about to tell the lady to calm down, when Aso tackled me. As I stood back up, I saw the fire department pulling up. Very calmly, Aso looked at me and brushed his bare chest off. "Well, that was quick wasn't it?" he said. "Excellent public services in this city, Aso. Where are we again?" I rhetorically asked him. Aso grabbed his clothes and we both ran back into the venue, his willie flapping in the wind. That night I worked the last concert I would ever work.

Chapter 666
But Wait There's More! J/K this is it

Signed on to the do the next leg in Asia, it never happened. I had filled out the paperwork, and in doing so, the tour manager saw my British passport. I'm not sure if that is why I wasn't hired on, but that's what I think happened. Regardless, the Cranberries never did the Asian leg of the tour. It was cancelled due to poor ticket sales.

So, what happened to everyone? Well, life isn't a book. The pages continued to turn on. The roadies that aren't dead are still on tour. The women I cared about are mostly married with children. My father did pass away. We wanted to bury him in his Volkswagen Beetle but the Jewish cemetery wouldn't let us. Oh, and Heather in Portland, Oregon. I'm not sure if I flat out said I did or just alluded to it, but I never did fuck, fondle, noodle, canoodle, or even cuddle with her. I wouldn't want to finish the book without coming clean on that one. I didn't want to... well, yeah, I did. Here I am lying to you again while trying to come clean. You never should trust a roadie.

So that leaves us with me? I'm still breathing. Every day I'm turning a new page and trying to keep the content interesting. After being a roadie, the next step for me was to jump into movie making. I'd of course end up broke after that, because that's how the movie industry works. Tired of being broke and searching for something, I'd plunge into the blooming (the pun is intentional) California marijuana industry. It would turn out to be profitable but tumultuous for me. No business is easy and running an illegal one is even more complicated. My marijuana career climaxed in, you guessed it, me getting my first felony. My arrest didn't slow me down, but maybe it should have. If you can stomach another book, the next one will feature fewer rock stars and more drugs. Unquestionably, a literary first.

Dedication Page

I'd like to take this opportunity to dedicate this book to my mother. Without her guidance this memorable piece of literature would have never come to fruition.

Just kidding! Can you imagine having read a book about a roadie's journey that was penned that boring. If you think the book was a decent piece of literature, I'd like to instead dedicate it to my friend Michael Grais. Years ago, he told me to write a book about my experiences on the road. It took me over a decade to listen to him, but I'm glad I finally did. I can't say the world is a better place because of it, but Michael told me it wouldn't be. Thanks to him, I wouldn't be able to say any part of the process has been a letdown.

Now, if you think the book sucks, and you wished I never listened to Michael Grais in the first place, then please ignore the part about him telling me to write the damn thing. Instead, please focus on the dedication to my mother. A mother's love knows no bounds.

All kidding aside, I love you momma!

Made in the USA
Monee, IL
09 September 2021